W9-CSK-919

The MXF Book

The MXF Book

Editor
Nick Wells

Principal Authors
Bruce Devlin
Jim Wilkinson

Contributing Authors
Matt Beard
Phil Tudor

ELSEVIER

AMSTERDAM • BOSTON • HEIDELBERG • LONDON
NEW YORK • OXFORD • PARIS • SAN DIEGO
SAN FRANCISCO • SINGAPORE • SYDNEY • TOKYO
Focal Press Is an Imprint of Elsevier

Focal Press

Acquisitions Editor: Angelina Ward
Project Manager: George Morrison
Assistant Editor: Rachel Epstein
Marketing Manager: Christine Degon Veroulis
Cover Design: Cate Richard Barr
Interior Design: Isabella Piestrzynska, Umbrella Graphics

Focal Press is an imprint of Elsevier
30 Corporate Drive, Suite 400, Burlington, MA 01803, USA
Linacre House, Jordan Hill, Oxford OX2 8DP, UK

Library of Congress Cataloging-in-Publication Data

British Library Cataloguing-in-Publication Data
A catalogue record for this book is available from the British Library.

ISBN 13: 9780240806938
ISBN 10: 0-240-80693-x

For information on all Focal Press publications
visit our website at www.books.elsevier.com

Printed and bound in the United Kingdom
Transferred to Digital Printing, 2011

Table of Contents

Acknowledgements   vii

Author Biographies   ix

Preface   *Nick Wells*   1

1   Introduction and Scene Setting   *Jim Wilkinson*   6

2   What Is an MXF File?   *Bruce Devlin*   24

3   Physical and Logical Structures within an MXF File   *Bruce Devlin*   44

4   Operational Patterns and Constraining MXF   *Bruce Devlin*   96

5   How to Put Essence into an MXF File   *Jim Wilkinson*   112

6   Audio in MXF   *Bruce Devlin*   147

7   DV, DVC Pro, and DVCam in MXF   *Bruce Devlin*   166

8   D-10 and D-11 in MXF   *Jim Wilkinson*   173

9   MPEG, MXF, and SMPTE 381M   *Bruce Devlin*   201

10   Generic Data Streams, VBI, and ANC   *Bruce Devlin*   220

11   DMS-1 Metadata Scheme   *Jim Wilkinson*   239

12   Index Tables   *Bruce Devlin*   264

13   The MXF Data Model in Context   *Phil Tudor*   280

14   The MXFLib Open Source Library   *Matt Beard*   301

15   Practical Examples and Approcaches to Using MXF   342

16   JPEG 2000 Essence Container and Its Application   *Jim Wilkinson*   375

     Index   391

Acknowledgements

The MXF specification took five years to get from concept to standard. All the authors would like to thank the vast array of people at Focal Press who have helped get this book finished in less time than the standard took. Particularly, we would like to thank Joanne Tracy and Angelina Ward for their continual encouragement to finish the book; and Isabella Piestrzynska for the enormous amount of effort it took to bring the different chapters together and make them look consistent.

Many thanks to Oliver Morgan, without whom there would be no MXF, and no MXF book. Work commitments prevented him from authoring chapters for the book, but his overall contribution to the contents has been immense.

Special thanks must also go to Bob Edge for his words of wisdom, which kept some crazy ideas out of the MXF specification, and to Mike Cox and the SMPTE W25 committee who had to read all the standards documents more times than any living person should have to.

Also, special thanks go to the authors who contributed or put together sections for the chapter, Practical Examples and Approaches to using MXF. These authors are: Henk den Bok, Peter Brightwell, Bob Edge, Philip Livingston, Paul Cameron, Mike Manlove, and Todd Brunhoff,

Thanks go also to our reviewers: Jim Defillipis, Brad Gilmer, Oliver Morgan, Clyde Smith, Hans Hoffmann, Thomas Edwards, Chris Golsen, John Varney, Gavin Schutz.

Bruce Devlin would like to thank Gary Duncanson and the team from NoMagic whose magic-draw software was used to make most of his UML diagrams in the book. The master UML file for Chapter 4 can be downloaded from *http://www.themxfbook.com* and there you will find a link to the NoMagic website where you can download evaluation copies of their software, or a free viewer. His thanks also go to David Schweinsberg for his tireless implementation efforts in creating S&W's MXF Express and to Kaaren May for picking up his baton as one of the MXF SMPTE editors. Last but not least, Bruce's biggest thanks go to his wife, Jane, for putting up with him living nocturnally in his study for about a year while the book was taking place.

Jim Wilkinson would like to give thanks to the following who had specific contributions, either directly or indirectly in this book: a) to Mike Cox and Gareth Sylvester Bradley for their considerable contributions to the development of DMS-1; b) to Hiroshi Nakano for his support, initially of SDTI-CP, and latterly for his work on MPEG long-GOP Constraints; c) to Katsumi Tahara for his continuous and patient support of standards development. And a special thanks go to his wife, Maggie, for her patience throughout the production of this book.

Finally, Nick Wells as editor would like to thank the principal authors, Bruce Devlin and Jim Wilkinson, and the contributing authors, Phil Tudor and Matt Beard for all their hard work and dedication in the lengthy process of producing this book.

Don't forget that there are links, bios, and downloads at *http://www.themxfbook.com*.

Author Biographies

Nick Wells

BA, D.Phil
Research Leader, BBC Research & Development

Nick studied physics at Cambridge University and then obtained a D.Phil from Sussex University for studies of radio wave propagation in conducting gases. In 1977 he started working at BBC Research and Development and has worked in many areas related to broadcasting, in particular image compression and the use of compression in production. Nick played an active part in the standardization of MPEG2 and he has led large European collaborative projects related to the use of MPEG2 in the professional production environment. More recently, he has helped lead work strands related to radio cameras and new modulation schemes for radio. He is chairman of Professional MPEG Forum, which played a major role in the creation and promotion of MXF.

Bruce Devlin

MA C.Eng MIEE
Vice President, Technology, Snell & Wilcox

Bruce graduated from Queens' College Cambridge in 1986 and has been working in the broadcast industry ever since. He joined the BBC Research Department working on Radio-Camera systems before moving to France where he worked on sub-band and MPEG coding for Thomson. He joined Snell & Wilcox in 1993 where he started the company's work on compression coding. Bruce holds several patents in the field of compression, has written international standards and contributed to books on MPEG and File Formats. He is co-author of the MXF File Format Specification and an active contributor to the work of SMPTE and the AAF association. Bruce is a fellow SMPTE (Society of Motion Picture and Television Engineers).

Jim Wilkinson

C.Eng, FIEE
Chief Research Scientist, Sony BPRL

Jim first worked in the area of broadcasting joining the IBA's Engineering Headquarters in1974. During his time with the IBA, he worked on DICE, video compression using DPCM at 34Mbps and other video projects. In 1979 he joined the newly created Advanced Development Laboratories of Sony Broadcast as one of the founder members and where he continues to work. Over the years, he has been awarded over 80 patents; both UK and international. He has participated in many standards activities in the AES, SMPTE, and EBU. He was an active and prolific member of the EBU/SMPTE Task Force and is now equally active within the SMPTE engineering committees on the follow-up work now being undertaken, with particular emphasis on metadata and file/stream formats. In 1995 he was awarded the Alexander M Poniatoff Gold Medal for Technical Excellence by the SMPTE. Jim is a Chartered Engineer and a fellow of the IEE, SMPTE, and the RTS.

Contributors

Matt Beard

M.Eng, MIEE
Broadcast Technology Consultant, freeMXF.org

After spending eight years as a software engineer, Matt studied Electronic Engineering at the University of Portsmouth. During this course he was awarded the IEE Prize for Academic Achievement for his work on a digital video decoder. In 1996, he joined Snell & Wilcox, where he worked on a number of video processing products. In 2000, he joined BBC Research and Development, where he spent the majority of his time working on the standardization of MXF. In 2002, he left the BBC and set up freeMXF.org, concentrating on the development of the MXFLib Open Source library.

Phil Tudor

Phil Tudor is a Senior Engineer at the BBC's Research & Development Department at Kingswood Warren, Surrey, UK. He studied Electrical and Information Sciences at Cambridge University, graduating in 1990. Over the last five years, Phil has been active in industry efforts to develop standard file formats for use in program making, in particular MXF and AAF. He represents the BBC on the board of the AAF Association, and leads the engineering work of the AAF Association. Phil's technical background includes MPEG-2 video standardization, video coding optimization, and MPEG bitstream manipulation. His current work areas include file-format standardization, metadata interoperability, and technical architectures for program making. Phil is a Chartered Engineer and member of SMPTE W25 technology committee.

Co-Contributors

Henk den Bok, *NOB Cross Media Facilities*

Peter Brightwell, *BBC*

Bob Edge, *Grass Valley*

Philip Livingston, *Panasonic Broadcast & Television Systems Co.* (Including: **Hideaki Mita, Haruo Ohta, Hideki Ohtaka, Tatsushi Bannai, Tsutomu Tanaka**—*Panasonic AVC Networks Company, Matsushita Electric Industrial Co. Ltd.*)

Paul Cameron, *Sony*

Mike Manlove, *Pinnacle Systems*

Todd Brunhoff, *Omneon Video Networks*

Preface

Introduction

Problems with interoperability within the professional production environment have always been with us. Traditionally, there are the differences between 525-line and 625-line NTSC and PAL systems, and we have used expensive standards converters to move between the different scanning formats. With the move to digital, Recommendation 601, with its common "4:2:2" sampling structure and a common sampling frequency of 13.5 MHz, has been an immensely important foundation for the production industry. Today, compression is being applied in production to both the audio and video components because of the huge reductions this can bring in storage and networking costs. Unfortunately, this makes the interoperability situation worse because of the many different types and flavors of compression. If these compressed signals are stored as files on servers, then traditionally each manufacturer has their own proprietary format, making interchange of files between manufacturers nearly impossible. To add to this, program makers and broadcasters now want to exchange program metadata along with the video and audio, and this brings with it a whole new range of interoperability problems. It is very difficult to get different organizations to agree on a common metadata model and syntax, making exchange of metadata between databases very difficult without expensive, multiple translations between systems.

However, many organizations have worked together pre-competitively to define and agree upon a standard, file-interchange format called the Material eXchange Format (MXF). This format is compression-format independent and contains a standard data model for metadata. Within the Professional-MPEG Forum and the AAF Association, many organizations and individuals have put in a huge amount of work for several years to specify and document MXF, and the documents produced have been taken to SMPTE for standardization. This work has had enormous support from the EBU and SMPTE.

Future TV production architectures will be based around networked file servers with disc-based storage rather than tape-based storage. The majority of future program material exchange between organizations and systems will be accomplished by file-to-file transfer rather than by exchange of tapes. A widely accepted standard for file interchange will therefore be essential for efficient and cost-effective TV production. Since MXF has the support of all the major manufacturers and end users, it is likely that MXF will become the most widely used and accepted format for program exchange.

History of MXF in the Pro-MPEG Forum and the AAF Association

The Professional-MPEG Forum started initially testing the interoperability of "streaming" formats for MPEG in the professional environment. However, the end-user organizations within Pro-MPEG started to request the ability to do non-real-time file transfer between systems from different manufacturers. It appeared unrealistic to expect manufacturers to agree on a common native *file format*, but there was a glimmer of hope that it might be possible to get them to agree on a common format for the *interchange* of files (with the assumption that each manufacturer would translate to and from their own native formats). In 1999, Pro-MPEG started work to define the "Material Exchange Format" (MXF). Existing (proprietary) formats were reviewed to see if these might be suitable to build upon, but there did not appear to be one that met all the necessary requirements, in particular for the carriage of metadata with program material.

Fundamental initial requirements for this *file interchange format* were as follows:

1. It should be able to carry program-related metadata components as well as the video and audio components.

2. It should be possible to start working on the file before the file transfer is complete. This is particularly important when sending large files over slow networks.

3. It should provide mechanisms for being able to decode useful information from the file even if parts of the file are missing. This might happen, for example, if a file transfer (e.g., over satellite) is picked up half-way through the transfer.

4. The format should be open, standardized, and compression-format independent.

5. The format should be aimed at exchange of completed programs or program segments.

6. Above all, the format should be simple enough to allow real-time implementations.

Around the time that Pro-MPEG started to work on MXF, representatives from AVID started to attend the meetings and they stressed that, in their experience, what Pro-MPEG was attempting to do was much harder than they realized—especially if it were important to achieve all the desired functionality. In addition, AVID were in the process of launching an association to support the Advanced Authoring Format (AAF), which is a file format for use in the post-production environment. AAF had the support of several manufacturers and end users.

AAF did not meet all the requirements intended for MXF, in particular the requirements a) to be able to start using a file before transfer is complete and b) to be able to form up and read files simply in real time. However, there was clear end-user pull for MXF to be easily interoperable with AAF, with the particular desire that it should be possible to carry metadata transparently from post-production through to the distribution/exchange of the completed program. Consequently, Pro-MPEG and the AAF Association decided to work closely together on the project to define MXF.

In order for AAF and MXF to be easily interoperable, their underlying data structures and data models should be the same. There is a lot of complexity in defining how the components in a file are related to each other and to a timeline running through a file. AAF was already defined in the form of open source software known as an "SDK" (Software Developers Kit) maintained by the AAF Association. However, this SDK was fairly opaque to the predominantly video engineers coming from Pro-MPEG. Also, video engineers traditionally look toward SMPTE as the place where their standards are documented and these standards are traditionally described in words not in software. In the early days of MXF, there was a real culture clash between the different perspectives of the engineers coming from a background of video engineering and the engineers coming from predominantly a software background.

The Relationship between MXF and AAF

MXF is simpler than AAF in that it does not support all the rich functionality provided for in AAF; for example, MXF does not provide the capability to describe complex transitions between two clips in a file. Also, it has been a fundamental requirement within the MXF development work to keep the structure as simple as possible while meeting the requirements placed upon the format.

Different users have requirements differing in complexity, and therefore MXF defines separate *operational patterns* that support different levels of complexity. For example, the simplest operational pattern, "OP1a," carries a single program or program segment within a file. A more complex operational pattern can contain several program segments with the ability to do cut edits between them (useful, for example, when distributing one copy of a program to different countries that may require some scenes to be removed). Also, more complex patterns may contain more than one version of the same program—for example full-quality and browse-quality versions.

Whatever the complexity of MXF, there has been a fundamental requirement running through all MXF developments that it should be as simple as possible to transfer metadata between the two file formats. In order to achieve this, it is important that the data models of the two formats should be as closely aligned as possible. Therefore, Pro-MPEG and the AAF Association agreed between themselves a Zero Divergence Doctrine (ZDD) that enshrined the principle that all MXF developments should be aligned with the AAF data model. Also, if new requirements emerged during the development of MXF, then the AAF data model would be extended in ways that were compatible with MXF. This ZDD continues to exist today, even though some of the later developments in MXF have been done within SMPTE.

In summary, AAF is intended for use during program production and post-production and MXF is intended for the exchange of completed programs or program segments.

MXF and SMPTE

Pro-MPEG was the main organization responsible for the early development and promotion of MXF in collaboration with the AAF Association. Pro-MPEG also organized early interoperability demonstrations of MXF developments at the relevant trade shows in Europe and the US.

As neither Pro-MPEG nor the AAF Association was a due-process standardization organization, the MXF specification was taken to SMPTE for standardization. MXF is now described by a suite of more than 20 separate SMPTE documents—most of which are covered in this book.

Following a period when document revisions were discussed by Pro-MPEG and then again by SMPTE, it was decided that further development and maintenance of the MXF standard would be taken over completely by SMPTE.

Benefits Brought by MXF

The major benefit of MXF is that it provides a standard format for transferring completed program files between systems and companies. Also, it provides for a standard method of exchanging meta-data within these files, independent of the compression format used for the video or audio. It is difficult to see how server/network/file-interchange architectures of the future could possibly work without such an interoperable standard.

In addition, MXF will be an ideal format for archiving material where it is desirable to store all the metadata associated with the program along with program itself.

Another advantage of MXF is that, as a quasi-streaming format, it is a very convenient bridge between areas that uses conventional streaming formats (such as SDI/SDTI for ingest and playout) and editing/production areas that are based on file transfers and AAF.

A further advantage of MXF is that it is based on *KLV coding* in which the value of each item contained within the linear file is preceded by an identifying key followed by a length in bytes of the item concerned. This makes it very easy for a hardware or software system to parse the file and skip items in which it has no interest.

MXF will also provide a mechanism for defining cuts between video clips in the file and cross fades between audio clips. This can be used to generate different versions of a program from a single file. For example, it may be required to remove certain scenes when played in certain countries.

However, MXF is not a panacea for interoperability. It cannot solve the many problems associated with incompatible compression formats nor with incompatible user metadata schemes. What it does do, however, is to stop the interoperability problems getting worse when there is a requirement for combining and exchanging program material with metadata. MXF is only one very necessary link in the chain of production technology.

Purpose of this Book

It is the purpose of this book a) to introduce and explain the MXF standard; b) to help engineers write MXF applications; and c) to help explain the reasons behind many of the details of the specification documents.

The authors involved in writing individual chapters within the book have all been major players in the design and specification of MXF. Bruce Devlin and Jim Wilkinson have been actively involved from the beginning of MXF, in both Pro-MPEG and SMPTE. They have written the majority of the chapters explaining the background and the details of the standard. Phil Tudor, who is Head of the Engineering Group of the AAF Association, has written a chapter explaining the MXF data model from the perspective of the AAF data model from which it derives. In addition, Matt Beard has written a chapter describing the open source MXF software that is publicly available and which has been mainly written and maintained by him. This software was first supported by BBC Research & Development in order to promote and assist the adoption of MXF by developers and manufacturers. Oliver Morgan, who has also been actively involved in the specification of MXF from the beginning, has also played a significant role in planning and scoping this book.

Also, a final chapter has been included that gives examples of the different approaches taken by end users and by manufacturers when adopting MXF for their production systems and equipment. It is hoped that through these different perspectives, the reader can get a flavor of the real-world applications of MXF.

It would not be possible to get a more authoritative and informative perspective on MXF than from the authors of this book.

In summary, the goal of this book is to explain the MXF standard that at times can seem complex, arbitrary, and difficult to understand. The different chapters explain a lot of the background and the philosophy behind the design, as well as delving into details that are necessary for a full understanding of the file structure. In their respective chapters, the different authors have taken different approaches to explaining various aspects of MXF, and it is hoped that these slightly different perspectives manage to illuminate the standard more fully. Some particularly dense bits of detail have been included as appendices to a couple of the chapters and these appendices could perhaps be skipped on a first reading. In the end, this book should be seen as a companion to the MXF standards documents and not as a replacement for them.

I hope that the efforts made by the authors in this book to explain MXF, and the reasons behind the design choices, help you to appreciate and understand the structure and potential of MXF.

Nick Wells
Editor, *The MXF Book*
Chairman of the Professional-MPEG Forum
BBC Research & Development

1 Introduction and Scene Setting

Jim Wilkinson

This chapter will start with the ground-breaking work of the EBU/SMPTE Task Force that originally recognized the need for a standardized file format for TV program production and program exchange, since there was nothing suitable at the time (around 1996). Most file formats in use at the start of the Task Force work were either raw essence streams or proprietary formats.

Where Did It All Begin?

The EBU/SMPTE Task Force (with the full title of "EBU/SMPTE Task Force for Harmonized Standards for the Exchange of Programme Material as Bitstreams") started as an informal meeting of EBU and SMPTE members at IBC in Amsterdam in September, 1996. The first formal meeting took place in November, 1996, at the EBU headquarters in Geneva. Meetings were then held at regular and frequent intervals until the summer of 1998.

The Task Force produced a first report of User Requirements in April, 1997, then a Final Report in September, 1998. These reports are available via the SMPTE web site on the page: *http://www.smpte.org/engineering committees.*

The work of the Task Force was used to rearrange the SMPTE committee structure, and much of the work in SMPTE is now geared toward implementing the ideas described in the Task Force Final Report. In particular, SMPTE developed the *Content Package* and the *Unique Material Identifier* (UMID), both of which are cornerstones of the MXF specification.

The Mission

The mission of the Task Force was to study the new technologies relating to networking and storage that promised to yield significantly enhanced creativity, improved efficiency, and economies of scale in the origination and dissemination of program content. It was seen that the potential of these technologies was such that they could practically dominate all television production and distribution facilities worldwide during the first decade of the new millennium. Since it was expected that a major migration and a huge investment in technology would take place within the next few years, it was therefore critical that the right decisions were made about the technological choices and the management of the transition to the new forms of production and distribution architectures.

It was foreseen that significant efficiencies would have to be made in the process of program production because of an expected proliferation of distribution channels. With this proliferation would come a fragmentation of audiences, which in turn would mean smaller budgets available for specific productions. Therefore, more efficient ways to produce content had to be found literally through remodeling the industry with new workflows, system designs, and reduced cost structures.

The Assignments

The Task Force was charged with two assignments:

1. To produce a blueprint for the implementation of the new technologies, looking forward a decade or more.

2. To make a series of fundamental decisions leading to standards that will support the vision of future systems embodied in the blueprint.

These assignments led to the creation of the first and final reports that are available at the link already noted above. These reports are summarized next.

User Requirements, April 1997

The first User Requirements report was produced by a group of some 80 experts from Europe, Japan, and North America who met formally five times over a period of less than six months. It represented the first attempt by the several industries involved to look into the future of the audiovisual content industries together and to set the future direction for all to follow. It took, as its premise, the need to identify requirements that users will have as they adopt the new methods. It includes the views of users and manufacturers, both of which were needed in order to get a picture of what will be implemented and how it could be done.

Compression technology was one of the core topics. But there would be no one particular compression technology of choice. It was seen that the greatest benefit would come from providing mechanisms that would permit systems to easily handle various different compression schemes while maintaining the maximum quality of the audiovisual elements.

One of the most important findings of this effort was a new class of program-related data called *metadata*. Metadata refers to all the descriptive and structural data related and connected to programs or program elements. Although metadata has been used for decades (think *timecode*), the scope of metadata was extended to include all the information that could be used directly in the creation and use of content and to support the retrieval of content during the post-production process. Metadata should be in the form of electronic data and not in the traditional form of handwritten or typed paper records.

Final Report, August 1998

The Final Report, the production of which was the Task Force's second assignment, was produced by a group of over 200 experts from Europe, Japan, Australia, and North America who met some 17 times over a period of 18 months. It was intended as a guide, and represented the culmination of a unique effort by several industries to look into the future jointly and to agree their course together due to a recognition that they stood at a crossroads in their collective histories. It took as its premise the need to identify requirements for the development of standards that would enable the exchange of program material in the new forms and that would support the construction of complete systems based upon the new techniques.

In particular, the report included a section on the importance of the use of object-modeling techniques to describe the structure and interrelation of the information within the metadata. Object modeling has become a hotbed of activity and an essential tool with which to achieve interoperability of metadata between different systems with the aim of minimizing the amount of metadata re-keying required.

What Happened Next?

SMPTE reorganized its committee structure around the findings of the Final Report and many of the members of the Task Force actively continued their work under the SMPTE banner with the EBU continuing to strongly represent their users' interests. The new engineering committees were (and are) Systems, Compression, Networks, and Wrappers and Metadata. In conjunction, there are the more traditional engineering committees such as Audio, Video, Interfaces, and Recorders.

Since that time, a further engineering committee (Registries) has been established to manage the new data-centric dictionaries created by (mostly) the Wrappers and Metadata Committee.

By the time of this new structure, SMPTE had already entered the world of data through the standard SMPTE 298M[1] that defined an SMPTE Universal Label as a publicly registered, 16-byte, universally unique number providing the foundations for all future work in the Wrappers and Metadata Committee.

Where Does MXF Come In?

MXF is a specification that builds on the foundations created by the SMPTE engineering

---

[1] SMPTE 298M-1997, Television – Universal Labels for Unique Identification of Digital Data

committees, mainly in the Wrappers and Metadata Committee. From the time of the Task Force closure, several projects were started that had a major impact on the design of MXF.

The first of these was a form of coding called *KLV* (Key-Length-Value), which is enshrined in SMPTE 336M[2] and is the cornerstone of the coding of MXF files. Everything in an MXF file is KLV coded. It is possible in a few limited cases that a *run-in* precedes the first KLV packet of an MXF file, but this is not typical for most MXF files.

The second development was of the *UMID* (or Unique Material Identifier). This is one of several identifiers used in MXF files, but the UMID is reserved for identifying the *packages* of audiovisual content.

The third development came out of the Task Force requirements for a *content package*. This was first enshrined in a form to be used on SDTI (Serial Data Transport Interface—a development of the video-based SDI coaxial serial digital interface that allowed data to be carried instead of video). This development is called SDTI-CP, and it was originally designed by the Wrappers and Metadata Committee members to provide a general method of synchronously transporting compressed video content over SDI. Sony and Gennum produced chips to support SDTI-CP, which was implemented initially as an interface to the Sony Type D-10 (Sony IMX) digital video recorder.

The final important development was that of the Metadata Dictionary as a central public repository for all SMPTE metadata definitions. This is enshrined in RP210.[3] A later, though similar, development was RP224,[4] which defines SMPTE Universal Labels as self-defining values.

Each of these key foundations will be discussed in detail later in this chapter.

Requirements for File Interchange

The MXF specification is designed for an environment where content is exchanged as a file. This allows users to take advantage of non-real-time transfers and designers to package together essence and metadata for effective interchange between servers and between businesses. MXF is not a panacea, but is an aid to automation and machine-machine communication. It allows essence and metadata transfer without the metadata elements having to be manually reentered.

Contrast this with much current practice where there is effective interchange of audiovisual content but with limited metadata support. In most cases, transfers are linear and in "real time," so that the receiver can continually display the signal as it arrives. There are cases currently where faster or slower than "real time" can be used, but this is usually a customized operation.

---

[2] SMPTE 336M–2001, Television – Data Encoding Protocol Using KLV

[3] SMPTE RP 210, Metadata Dictionary Registry of Metadata Element Descriptions

[4] SMPTE RP 224, SMPTE Labels Registry

What Is a File and What Is a Stream?

In order to appreciate the differences between stream and file transfers, we can summarize the major characteristics of each as follows:

File transfers—

1. Can be made using removable file media;

2. Use a packet-based, reliable network interconnect and are usually acknowledged;

3. Are usually transferred as a single unit (or as a known set of segments) with a predetermined start and end;

4. Are not normally synchronized to an external clock (during the transfer);

5. Are often point-to-point or point-to-multipoint with limited multipoint size; and

6. File formats are often structured to allow access to essence data at random or widely distributed byte positions.

Stream transfers—

1. Use a data-streaming interconnect and are usually unacknowledged;

2. Are open ended, with no predetermined start or end;

3. Streams are normally synchronized to a clock or are asynchronous, with a specified minimum/maximum transfer rate;

4. Are often point to multipoint or broadcast; and

5. Streaming formats are usually structured to allow access to essence data at sequential byte positions. Streaming decoders are always sequential.

Why Develop MXF?

MXF was designed to allow the interchange of captured/ingested material together with finished or "almost finished" material. It was designed to allow for the interchange of content in both conventional real-time streaming modes (as found on SDI/SDTI connections) and as a non-real-time (i.e., "conventional") file transfer. How can it serve both uses? The answer lies in the design of the MXF *generic container* described in Chapter 5. Even before the start of the Task Force work, there were individual custom products that used file transfers—mostly for JPEG files and for MPEG-2 Program Streams. There were also several early file formats, such as Apple QuickTime (which became the MPEG-4 file format) and OMF (Open Media Framework). Supporters of all were invited to the SMPTE Task Force meetings, but none of the early file formats solved all the problems posed by the varied requirements for audiovisual file transfers. However, the promoters of OMF were more interested in pursuing this new goal and were proactive in the Task Force and later in the SMPTE engineering committees. In the late 1990s, the OMF was transformed into the Advanced Authoring Format (AAF).

AAF was designed as an "authoring" format (as was OMF) and intended to be used during program editing and creation. By comparison, MXF was meant to be a simpler "interchange" format intended for the exchange of completed programs or program segments. The two formats were seen as complementary, and MXF has been developed with the explicit intention of maximizing the interoperability between AAF and MXF.

This close mix of two environments (authoring and program exchange) has resulted in the capability of AAF authoring tools to directly open and use an MXF file efficiently without having to do lengthy file conversions. A goal has been to ensure that not just the audiovisual content is preserved in any exchange between the two formats, but the metadata as well. The nirvana is to achieve a conversion chain MXF->AAF->MXF->AAF full-round tripping with no loss of information.

Is MXF the Perfect Solution?

The MXF specification was carefully crafted to ensure that it could be efficiently stored on a variety of media, as well as streamed over communications links. Also, the MXF format has not forgotten about linear recorders based on tape. There are structures and mechanisms within the file that make MXF appropriate for data-tape storage and archiving of content.

The MXF specification is intended to be expandable. Considerable effort was put into making MXF both compression-format independent and resolution independent, and it can be constrained to suit a large number of application environments.

So do we have the perfect solution? The balance to be achieved is one of flexibility versus simplicity. Users like the equipment to "just work" yet also want a wide range of features, including the use of the latest and best quality audio and video coding. Having a system in which everything is set to four audio channels and one video bitstream at 30Mbps intra-frame coding makes for a simple life. But this approach does not provide for future developments. Indeed, video compression has moved on in a non-backwards compatible way. So flexibility is also of key importance.

MXF is only one part of the equation. It defines a format for audiovisual content and metadata that can be created, edited, and delivered in real time or at any speed that the interconnection allows. It does not solve the problems related to file access, file storage structures, network connection issues, or remote file browsing; these are solved within the system layer that provides for networking and storage.

However, MXF has been designed to allow the file to be used in operations where the file can a) be subject to deliberate fragmentation (e.g., for reasons of rapid random access) or b) be recovered after unintentional connection breaks.

Does MXF Solve the Requirements?

One of the early tasks for the MXF design was to create a list of user requirements. (These requirements are encapsulated in Table 1 in SMPTE EG41.[5] This document contains a lot of helpful information and guidelines about the MXF standard.)

---

[5] SMPTE EG41—MXF Engineering Guideline

Examples of some of the requirements are as below.

"Pull" (e.g., over network) and "push" (e.g., over satellite) capability: While not strictly a file-format issue, the use of a file with metadata both inclusive within the file and exclusive at the file-storage level allows network tools to provide intelligent file operations. In a network environment, a user should be able to browse the metadata within the file and, in some cases, browse a proxy (low-resolution) version to decide on a file operation such as copy, move, or even delete. In specialized networks such as satellite links, the user should be able to move or copy the file over the link with the optional feature of providing real-time playout at the receiver in order to monitor content during the transfer.

Compression-format independence: The members of the Professional MPEG Forum, which was the organization responsible for all the early development of MXF, decided at an early stage that, although they saw MPEG compressed video as their primary format for video content, the file format must be independent of the compression format. This was a significant move away from most existing file formats such as MPEG, JPEG, and TIFF that provided just for one kind of content payload. This independence was close to the aims of both the Task Force and more sophisticated file formats such as AAF.

Quick and easy identification of file contents: As audiovisual files can easily reach sizes of several gigabytes, there is a critical need to know up front what is in the file and what is the complexity of the file structure. It was clear that there needed to be some simple ways to identify these key points within the first few bytes of the file. Although the file system might provide a file extension, this could not provide for all the possible future combinations within an MXF file. As an example, an .mxf extension would not indicate that the file contained DV video rather than MPEG video.

Monitoring of content during file transfer: With the huge file sizes that result from typical high-quality, audiovisual content, it was important that MXF readers should be able to decode and play out the content while the file contents were being written or transferred. As well as being useful for many typical production operations, it would be frustrating for users to find that the 20-minute file transfer was of the wrong file!

Use of early parts of transferred material before file transfer is complete: In many live operations, working with files before the transfer is complete is common practice and MXF files were designed to support this requirement.

Elements that are closely related in time should be close together within the file: This is related to the requirement for monitoring of content during file transfer where there is a general need to play out and view the audiovisual content with perfect lip sync. If files are to be used with linear devices, such as tape, then this requires that the co-timed components within the file can be easily accessed together. This constraint is less of a problem for non-linear-access devices where random access allows the audio and video content to be physically separated on the storage device.

Partial file restore: The increasingly popular operations such as partial file restore (e.g., picking out a small piece of content from the middle of a large file) from stored/archived MXF files must be supported. This is supported in MXF by the use of *index tables*. A related operation is file recovery from a damaged file or from an intermittent network connection.

Storage device independence: The MXF file format specification defines only the file structure and not how the file is stored. This storage independence allows MXF to be used on many kinds of storage devices.

File Concepts

The design requirements led to a number of key concepts such as:

- The file is constructed as a sequence of primary modular components consisting of *header metadata*, *essence container*, and *index table*.

- The file can be split into *partitions* that provide rapid access to key parts of the file and permit special operations such as partial file restore.

- The header metadata comprises required structural metadata (describing the structure of the MXF file), together with optional descriptive metadata (giving information about the program content contained within the file).

- Metadata can be carried not only within the header metadata, but also within the essence container or as part of the essence data.

- The structural metadata in the header defines the contents of the file through the concept of *packages*. A package is a construct that groups together components, together with tracks and timelines, to enable synchronization of the essence components. Packages can be *nested* such that one package may be contained within another package to provide historical information about a file's origins.

- The header metadata is designed around a consistent data model that is compatible with the AAF data model.

- The topmost package represents the material as it is to be played out and not the essence container itself (which may contain more material than required for final playout). This is an extended abstraction of a simple machine playout where the output is simply the recorded essence. This abstraction comes from AAF and provides a powerful tool that allows the file to contain multiple essence containers/packages that are assembled for playout under the control of the topmost package.

- The essence data may be either interleaved within the essence container (much like SDI with embedded digital audio) or it may be multiplexed (in a manner like an MPEG Program Stream).

Use Cases

To illustrate how MXF might be used, a number of typical use cases will be introduced. These will be reused later when the technology used within each use case is explained in more detail.

VTR Replacement

Since VTRs have formed the backbone of most television operations, it is essential that MXF can be used in tape-based infrastructures. This determines the simplest form of an MXF file that has a simple start/stop timing and a predetermined mix of audio and video essence data that is frame interleaved. The essential requirements for an MXF-based VTR are:[6]

1. To be able to create an MXF file easily from a conventional video-tape source. This means that the header metadata must be recreated first (e.g., from the digital audio tracks in the e-VTR). Then the audiovisual data from the conventionally recorded tape is converted "on-the-fly" to create the body of the MXF file. A simple file footer is created as needed when the file is completed.

2. Where existing tapes are analog, provide the appropriate conversion to digital audio and video essence data.

3. Be able to accept a pre-existing MXF file (of the right kind) for recording on the VTR and be able to store the header metadata for replay without change.

4. Provide network ports and appropriate file management software, typically based on FTP.

Assemble Edit Operation

In this use case, an MXF file might contain several essence containers containing a sequence of video clips, several sequences of audio clips, and some subtitles text. On playout, the required output is "assembled" as required along the output timeline (this is analogous to a non-linear edit session), though the difference is that the source clips and sequences are kept in their original form within the file.

When this *assemble edit* operation is supported using a shared storage, disc-based server system, the video and audio are likely to be sourced from separate (MXF) files stored on the server and not from sequences embedded in the MXF file. The *output* MXF file in this case will be quite small in size, containing only the metadata and effectively providing the functionality of an assemble edit list.

Note that if the compiled (or output) file is destined for delivery to a stand-alone playout station, then the MXF file will need to embed all the video, audio, and text clips to make a self-contained file that can assemble the desired output directly from its own internal essence containers.

MXF provides the mechanism for describing how sequences or clips should be assembled together (as in an *assemble* or *butt* edit) during playout of a file. But it should be noted that it does not provide the mechanism for describing transitions between clips or sequences as this is more the domain of the Advanced Authoring Format.

Multiple Versioning

This use case is similar to a multiple language DVD where the DVD first presents a choice of playout options for different languages.

---

[6] The main physical issue is where to store the header metadata. This has been resolved in the Sony eVTR where the header metadata is stored in the digital audio tracks for two seconds preceding the start point.

MXF can provide this feature by having more than one topmost package, each topmost package having a different arrangement of tracks and timelines for playout. When presented with such a file, the user will be offered a choice of topmost package and hence the choice of the playout desired.

As in the case for assemble editing, the essence might be stored separately on a local file server when the MXF file looks like a selection of edit lists. Where the file is destined for delivery, essence should again be embedded in the file.

Satellite Transmission

In any transmission system, the operation must support possible breaks in reception caused by transmission problems. It is also desirable that it should be possible to access the stream at some arbitrary time after the transmission has started and still be able to make sense of the stream from that time.

Typically, an MXF file prepared for transmission will be simple in construction and must use either a single interleaved essence container or a rapidly multiplexed sequence of essence containers (so that video and audio, etc., can be reasonably decoded together on reception). In both cases, it is necessary that important header metadata is repeated regularly throughout the transmission and therefore the file will be separated into frequent file partitions, for example, with a new partition starting every second or so. Each partition will include a copy of the header metadata so that important features relating to the whole file are regularly described. In certain in-line operations, some header metadata values may not be known or may be changing as time progresses. MXF provides for such cases where metadata values may change over time.

At the receiver, any breaks in the reception can be handled in a manner not unlike that used for traditional audio-video streams and recovered data can be reassembled into a valid (though maybe incomplete) MXF file.

MXF Foundations

This section sets out to explain the underlying SMPTE technologies used by MXF: UMIDs, ULs, KLV, dictionaries, and registries.

SMPTE ULs

A UL (Universal Label) is defined as an object identifier by ISO/IEC 8824; it is a sequence of bytes that may vary in length from 4 bytes to 64 bytes in 4-byte steps. Each byte has one or more values that have semantic meaning and the coding syntax of the bytes uses ASN.1 (Abstract Syntax Notation 1).

An SMPTE-administered UL has a fixed length of 16 bytes and all SMPTE ULs start with the following first 4-byte values:

06.0E.2B.34

where the "06" is a fixed value for all ISO identifiers, "0E" is the length (of the remaining 14 bytes) and "2B.34" is assigned to SMPTE by ISO.

Thus SMPTE ULs have 12 remaining bytes that are available for SMPTE use and MXF uses these ULs throughout.

The first 4 bytes were shown simply as bytes because the MSB of each byte is zero. In all cases where the byte value is less than 7F (hex), then the ASN.1 syntax defines that the value is kept simply as is. In most cases, this is true for all SMPTE ULs; however, there are instances where this may not be appropriate. So what happens when the MSB of any byte is "1"? The coding then follows what is known as *primitive coding* and is described as follows:

Any byte that has the MSB set to "1" indicates that the value requires more than one byte to represent it. The value is divided into groups of 7 bits and these are used to fill contiguous UL bytes as needed. The first and subsequent bytes have their MSB set to "1" except the last which has its MSB set to "0." This last byte uses the MSB to signal that the multi-byte value is complete.

At the time of writing, MXF does not use multi-byte values (although an example of this technique is illustrated in Section 3.5.3 of the MXF document, SMPTE EG41). The specification for SMPTE ULs is defined in SMPTE 298M. In this standard, it is stated that ULs are a universal labeling mechanism to be used in identifying the type and encoding of data within a general-purpose data stream. This leads us on to KLV coding.

KLV Coding

KLV coding stands for **K**ey - **L**ength - **V**alue. This is one of a class of coding syntaxes that are numerically based and language independent. It contrasts with the other class of syntax coding that is language based—of which SGML and XML are examples.

KLV coding is enshrined in SMPTE 336M.

The Key

The *key* field describes the type of data that is contained within the following *value* field. The key field uses the same hierarchical structure as an SMPTE UL with the first 4-byte values defining the key as an SMPTE UL.

SMPTE 336M defines the following values for byte 5 of the SMPTE UL:

01 = Keys for SMPTE Dictionary Items

02 = Keys for SMPTE Groups (as sets or packs of metadata)

03 = Keys for SMPTE Containers and Wrappers

04 = Labels

Other values may be defined as new uses arise.

The values of 1, 2, and 3 for byte 5 define that the UL is a key where a key is a UL identifier that can be used for KLV coding in the context of a data-coding mechanism. The same key value also performs the function of identification of the value within the KLV triplet. The use of a value of 4 for byte 5 means that the UL is not a key but simply a 16-byte identifier (in the form of an SMPTE UL). It can be used as a unique identifier in any coding application and may occur as part of the data *value* within a KLV data construct.

SMPTE also defines the purpose of bytes 6 to 8 as follows:

- Byte 6 is dependent on byte 5 and is used to define the kind of dictionary, group, container, wrapper, or label.

- Byte 7 defines the registry that is used to catalogue the kind of dictionary, group, container, wrapper, or label. A new value identifies a new and non-backwards-compatible registry.

- Byte 8 defines the version of the registry. A new value identifies a new entry within a backwards-compatible registry.

The remaining 8 bytes of the SMPTE UL are then defined by the appropriate SMPTE registry.

The Length

The *length* field defines the length of the following *value* field. The length field is coded in ASN.1 BER notation. Lengths requiring use of multiple bytes use *big-endian* notation, meaning that the last byte is the least significant (otherwise called *network byte order*).

If the length value requires a single byte with the MSB equal to zero, then the length field can use that single byte directly. This means that length values in the range 0 to 7F(hex) can be a single byte.

If the length value is greater than 7F(hex), then the first byte is set to 8x(hex) where "x" defines the number of bytes to follow. MXF typically uses length fields of 4 or 8 bytes leading, respectively, to hexadecimal values of 83.xx.xx.xx and 87.xx.xx.xx.xx.xx.xx.xx .

The Value

The *value* field is the data of length as defined by the *length* field. This is coded simply as a sequence of bytes. In many cases, zero represents a default value and should not be interpreted as the end of the data; that is determined using the length value.

In some cases, the data length may not be known in advance so a default length value can be used to indicate an indeterminate length. For example, an incoming MPEG bitstream may have an unknown length, so to save delay (in having to wait until the end of the bitstream before forming a file), the bitstream can be packed into the data area and transmitted on with an undefined length. However, the data structure must provide another mechanism for indicating data termination; otherwise, the decoding of the file will fail (or may report an error) at the end of the data stream.

Coding of Groups

The use of a 16-byte universal label key to preface each and every data item is an excessive overhead for items that may themselves be only a few bytes in length, particularly for metadata items.

It is also very attractive to gather metadata items into sets of related metadata components.

The K-L-V data coding protocol defines five basic types of data groupings as *sets* or *packs*:

- Universal sets
- Global sets
- Local sets
- Variable-length packs
- Fixed-length packs.

Each of these five types will now be briefly described.

Universal Sets

Universal sets are a logical grouping of data items in which all key values are full 16-byte universal labels.

An instance of a universal set starts with a 16-byte set key which identifies it as a universal set followed by the set length and then all the individual KLV data items that make up the universal set. Universal sets are used a) for interchange of data groups between different systems and b) where set size is not an issue.

All the remaining four groups are capable of conversion to a universal set for interchange with other systems.

Global Sets

Global sets are used for coding logical sets of data items with a common root node. Global sets are not used in MXF and are mentioned only for completeness.

Local Sets

The most popular grouping in MXF is the *local set* where each data item has, as an identifier, a short local *tag* defined within the context of the local set. The local tag is typically only 1 or 2 bytes long and is used as an alias for the full 16-byte universal label value.

An instance of a local set starts with a 16-byte key identifying it as an SMPTE-registered local set. Via an appropriate specification (e.g., MXF), the set key identifies all the data items and their local tags that can be used in this local set, together with the size of each local tag word and the associated size of each local length word.

The local set key is followed by a length value for the total length of all the data items in the set.

The local tag and length values may be set to either BER coding, or to fixed binary values of 1-, 2-, or 4-byte length fields. MXF files typically use 2-byte local tags and 2-byte local lengths.

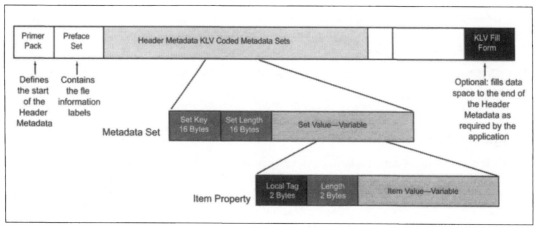

Figure 1.1 Local Set Coding

Within the specification, each local tag is defined as a value that is local to the local set. The specification also defines a mapping from the local tag to the full 16-byte key value for each data item in the set.

The format for an individual data item then comprises typically the 2-byte local tag, followed by a 2-byte length field, followed by the corresponding data value.

Variable-Length Packs

Variable-length packs are similar in principle to the local set, but each data item comprises only a length and a value. No tags are required because these packs contain a standardized set of data items in a defined order. However, variable length packs do allow the length of each data item to be specified only by the length field of the item.

An instance of a variable-length pack has a 16-byte key that identifies the variable-length pack, followed by a BER-coded length for the subsequent pack of data items. The value comprises a standard set of data items in the predefined sequence (but each item consists of only length and data). The length field of each data item uses BER coding by default, with (standardized) options for fixed-length fields of 1, 2, or 4 bytes.

The appropriate specification is required to define the full 16-byte UL for each data item.

Fixed-Length Packs

Fixed-length packs contain data items that are coded simply as values with no key or length. This is possible because the length and order of the data items within the pack are predefined in the fixed length pack standard. The name may become "defined-length packs" because it is possible for this pack to permit the last item in the pack to have a variable length, the end of the pack being defined by the pack length.

An instance of a fixed-length pack starts with a 16-byte SMPTE key identifying the fixed-length pack, followed by a BER-coded length for the data pack value. The value comprises the data items in a predefined sequence and each with a predefined length.

The fixed-length pack specification also defines the full (16-byte) dictionary UL value for each data item.

Set and Pack Issues

The order of individual data items is, by default, unordered in a set but, by definition, ordered in a pack. When converting a pack to a set, there needs to be a recognition that a pack requires all individual data items in a specified order. A universal set that is representing a fixed-length pack needs to include the attribute that the set originates as a pack and has to be treated accordingly.

Sets can define individual data items that are themselves sets or packs. Thus an item can itself be a set or a pack and multiple levels of recursion are possible. It is not uncommon for a local set to include either variable- or fixed-length packs. The standard makes no reference to set recursion and provides no limits or structures. However, individual applications are free to make such constraints where needed. Note that set recursion means that any change or addition of an item within a set will require the length values of that set and any higher order sets to be changed accordingly.

SMPTE Registries

SMPTE registries are lists of values of data items. The primary registries are those that are defined for use with KLV coding. The SMPTE Metadata Dictionary (RP210) is actually a registry, the name "dictionary" referring to its historical pedigree.

MXF uses the following registries:

Title of Registry	Relevant SMPTE Numbers	Comments
Groups Registry	-	Work in progress at time of writing.
Elements Registry	RP210	The sole registry in this category (at the time of writing) is the SMPTE Metadata Registry (called "dictionary" at this time).
Data Types Registry	-	Work in progress at time of writing.
Enumerations Registries	RP224	The sole registry in this category (at the time of writing) is this SMPTE Labels Registry.

A *Groups Registry* provides a list of data groups that can be coded as sets or packs. These registries provide a UL as an identifier of the group (and one that can be used as a key) and list the elements within that group as well as a group name, a description of the groups and other group attributes.

An *Elements Registry* provides a list of individual data elements that can be coded as items—perhaps for use in a data group. This registry gives each element a name, a UL, and description for each element, as well as other attributes.

A *Data Types Registry* provides a list of element types as a text string, 16-byte integer, etc., for each element in the Elements Registry.

Enumeration Registries provide a list of values that can be used for certain data elements where the value has some semantic meaning. For this, we preclude data types that have a few values that are easily defined in the data type definition and those where the enumerated values are private.

SMPTE labels are a special case of an enumeration of a data type (SMPTE labels) and have been registered in RP224. But there are other data types that can be enumerated and these remain to be fully registered. This is a lengthy task, particularly for those elements and data types that are text based and subject to a specific language.

Unique Identifiers in MXF

MXF uses several types of unique identifiers: SMPTE universal labels, local tags, UUIDs, UMIDs, and other miscellaneous identifiers such as track IDs.

SMPTE ULs have been explained above and these are registered, unique identifiers that are static in value.

Local tags are also static unique identifiers, but the scope of the uniqueness must be constrained because of the small number of unique tag values. Local tags are generally defined for use within particular sets. Local tags can also be defined at the time of creation of an individual MXF file and these local tags must then be consistent for that file; i.e., within MXF, where header metadata can be repeated at intervals within a file, a given local tag is unique within any one instance of the header metadata.

MXF also uses globally unique IDs (e.g., UUID) that are generated during the course of file creation. This type of identifier is widely used in the computer industry to identify specific instances of objects. In MXF, although UUIDs are globally unique values, the header metadata can be duplicated within a file, and this means that the same UUID values may be present in several places in an MXF file. Because of this, the scope of resolving a UUID value is limited to one instance of header metadata. Note that a file copy will also result in duplicate UUID values across identical files, so care must be adopted in their interpretation within MXF files.

MXF uses identifiers to identify such things as a TrackID and a Track Number. These have the scope of the instance of the header metadata in which they are found.

MXF uses the basic Universal Material Identifier (UMID) to identify packages within an MXF file. UMIDs are defined in SMPTE 330M. Basic UMIDs are 32-byte numbers that identify a piece of material such as a film, TV program, or episode, etc. Again, these are globally unique, but identical copies of the same piece of material (with no editorial changes) will result in duplicate values, including their use in MXF files.

The extended UMID (64-bytes) may be found in the essence container and can be used to identify each material unit in a content package.[7]

---

[7] At the time of writing, SMPTE RP205 is being updated to address the management of UMID values, both basic and extended.

MXF Document Structure

The MXF specification is split into a number of separate parts in order to create a document structure that allows new applications to be covered in the future. These parts are:

Part 1: Engineering Guideline—an introduction to MXF.

Part 2: MXF File Format Specification—the basic standard on which all else depends.

Part 3: Operational Patterns—these define limits to the file complexity.

Part 4: MXF Descriptive Metadata Schemes—about adding user-oriented metadata.

Part 5: Essence Containers—defines the generic container used for all essence types.

Part 5a: Mapping Essence and Metadata into the Essence Container—individual mappings of essence and metadata into the generic essence container.

Part 1 provides the MXF engineering guidelines that offer an introduction and overall description of MXF. These documents introduce many of the necessary concepts and explain what problems MXF is intended to solve. Part 1 currently comprises EG41, which provides the guide to MXF and EG42, and gives guidance for the design and use of M schemes in MXF.

Part 2 is the fundamental MXF file specification (SMPTE 377M). This is the complete toolbox from which different file interchange tools are chosen to fulfill the requirements of different applications. This MXF file format document defines the syntax and semantics of MXF files.

Part 3 describes the operational patterns of the MXF format (of which there are currently 10). In order to create an application to solve a particular interchange problem, some constraints and structural metadata definitions are required before SMPTE 377M can be applied. An operational pattern defines those restrictions on the format that allow interoperability between applications of defined levels of complexity.

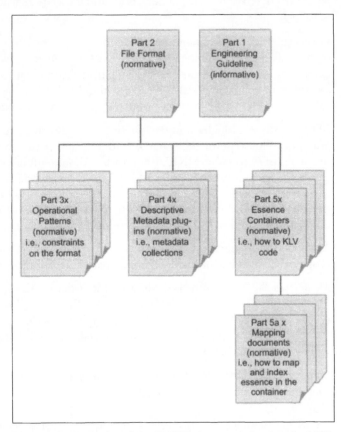

Figure 1.2 Illustration of the SMPTE document structure for MXF

Part 4 defines MXF descriptive metadata schemes that may be optionally plugged in to an MXF file. Different application environments will require different metadata schemes to be carried by MXF. These descriptive metadata schemes are described in the Part 4 document(s).

Part 5 defines the MXF essence containers that contain picture and sound (and other) essence. The generic container provides the sole standardized method for providing an encapsulation mechanism that allows many existing and future formats to be mapped into MXF.

Part 5a comprises a number of documents for mapping many of the essence and metadata formats used in the content creation industry into an MXF essence container via the generic container.

The MXF document suite makes reference to other documents containing information required for the implementation of an MXF system. One such document is the SMPTE Dictionary (SMPTE RP 210) that contains definitions of parameters, their data types, and their keys when used in a KLV representation. Another is the SMPTE Labels Registry, RP 224, containing a list of normalized labels that can be used in MXF sets.

2 What Is an MXF File?

Bruce Devlin

In this chapter we will go through the basic structure of an MXF file. We will illustrate the various structures and components of the MXF file with diagrams and descriptive text. Many of the diagrams will be oriented toward the structure of an MXF file that contains a short movie with long-GOP MPEG video and BWF (Broadcast Wave Format) stereo audio. The MXF file is intended to be played out in a software application and consists of some color bars, slate, the movie, and finally some black/silence. We will look at the two different aspects of an MXF file, the way the file's bytes are physically stored on the disc or tape, and also how the structural metadata describes what the MXF file is intended to represent.

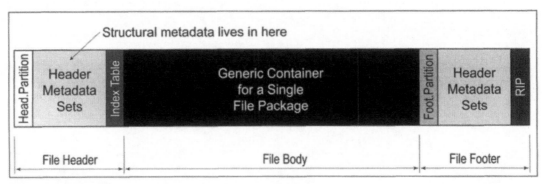

Figure 2.1 Basic structure of an MXF file

This chapter is intended to be a quick run through the concepts and structures in MXF. All of the topics are covered in more detail elsewhere in the book.

In Figure 2.1, a very simple MXF file is represented. At the beginning of the file, there is the *file header*; in the middle is the *file body*; and at the end, the *file footer*. We will expand on the fine detail of the *physical structure* of an MXF file later in this chapter. For now, we will look at the *structural metadata* stored in the header to describe the structure of the MXF file and the multimedia content contained within it.

Structural Metadata

The header metadata of an MXF file is a comparatively small amount of data at the beginning of the file. It may be repeated at points throughout the file. It contains a complete description of what the file is intended to represent. The structural metadata does not contain any of the video, audio, or data *essence*; it merely describes the synchronization and timing of that essence.

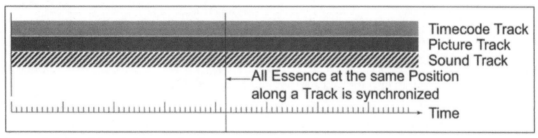

Figure 2.2 Header metadata synchronizes essence using tracks

Everything that is to be synchronized within an MXF file is represented by a *track*. An MXF track is merely a representation of time that allows different essence components to be synchronized relative to each other. In Figure 2.2 above, you can see a representation of a timecode track, a picture track, and a sound track. The metadata that describes these tracks can be found in the header metadata area of the MXF file. The structural metadata is very compact and allows the picture, sound, and timecode to be synchronized during playback or during capture. In our example, the picture track would describe the duration of the long-GOP MPEG video; and the duration of the Broadcast Wave audio would be described by the sound track and a timecode track would describe any timecode that was present in the original content (e.g., that was generated when that content was captured).

MXF is intended to be used for more than just the simple playback of stored essence. The intention has been to provide a mechanism for simple editing or selection of material from content stored within the file. Therefore, it is necessary to provide tracks that describe the required output timeline as well as tracks that describe the material as it is stored. Figure 2.3 shows an example of two collections of tracks within an MXF file. The upper collection of tracks is called the *material package* and this represents the required output timeline for the material as it is intended to be played. The lower collection of tracks is known as the *file package* and this describes the content as it is stored within the MXF file.

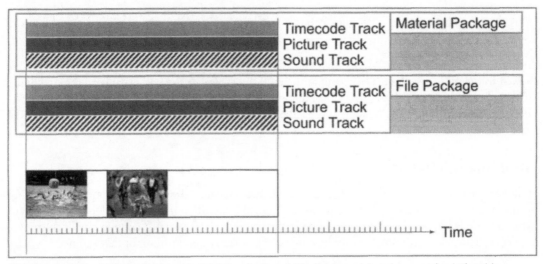

Timecode Track | Material Package
Picture Track
Sound Track

Timecode Track | File Package
Picture Track
Sound Track

Time

Figure 2.3 OP1a Material Package (output timeline) and File Package (stored essence) relationship

The MXF Specification places constraints on the possible relationships between an MXF material package and an MXF file package. These constraints are known as *operational patterns*. A file with the simplest standardized operational pattern is known as an "OP1a" file.

So what exactly is the structural metadata? The underlying *class model* is described in detail in Chapter 13, and many of the specifics of the classes and properties are dealt with in Chapter 3. For now, we will look only at a few of the properties that allow the synchronization of essence along the timeline. Figure 2.2 shows a conceptual model of several tracks being synchronized for a given *position* along the timeline, and Figure 2.4 shows the actual MXF data sets that make this possible.

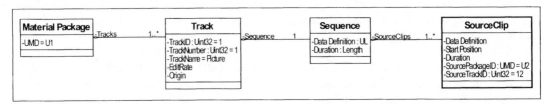

Figure 2.4 MXF metadata sets controlling synchronization

The material package has one or more tracks, each of which has a *TrackID*, an *EditRate*, and an *Origin* property. The Track has a sequence of one or more *SourceClips*, each of which has a *StartPosition*, a *Duration*, and the *PackageID* and TrackID of the file package track where the actual essence can be found. Using the SourceClips on the material package, we can convert any position on a material package track into a position on a file package track. Then we can use *index tables* to convert these time-oriented positions into byte offsets within the stored picture and stored sound essence to play back synchronized material.

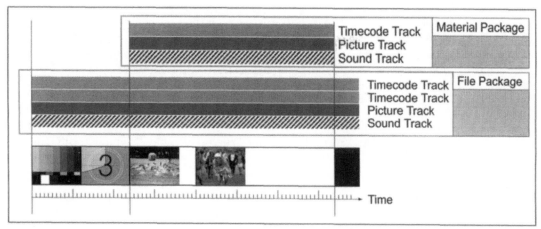

Figure 2.5 Material Package (output timeline) and file package (stored essence) relationship

Figure 2.3 shows an OP1a representation of our example file where the material package *start* and *duration* are identical to the file package *start* and *duration*. In other words, the output timeline is equal to the timeline of the entire stored content; i.e., what is played is equal precisely to what is stored.

In some applications, it may be desirable to play out only the central contribution portion of our example file. In this case a material package is used that describes only this central portion of the file, and not the color bars, slate, or black portion of the stored content. The operational pattern that describes this functionality is OP3a. In order to playback this file, random access functionality is required in a decoder to skip over the unplayed portions of the file. In this way, operational patterns are used to describe the complexity required in coder and decoder functionality. We will return to other representations of the file and more operational complexity later in the chapter.

Tracks

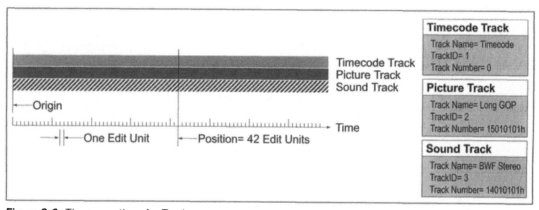

Figure 2.6 The properties of a Track

A *track* is the basic structural metadata component allowing the representation of time in MXF. The *duration* property of a track describes the duration, in terms of *edit units*, of the corresponding essence. The position along a track is used to describe the expected playout time of the start of a given sequence and, in this way, synchronization between two different tracks is obtained.

The origin of a track is a property describing the start point of the content (for example, the sound track may start at a different time from the video track). The tick marks shown along the track in Figure 2.6 correspond to the edit units that have been chosen for that track. Typically, edit units will correspond to the video frame rate of the combined audio/video file. An edit unit will typically have a duration of $^1/_{25}$ or $^1/_{30}$ of a second.

A collection of tracks is known as a *package*. As previously explained, the material package describes the output timeline of the file, and the top-level file package describes fully the stored content of the file. Lower-level file packages may be present, but these are only used to carry historical metadata about the "genealogy" of the stored content.

For each component of the output timeline, there will be a track. Typically, there will be a single picture track and a there will be an audio track for each of the audio channels. Stereo audio may be described by a single sound track.

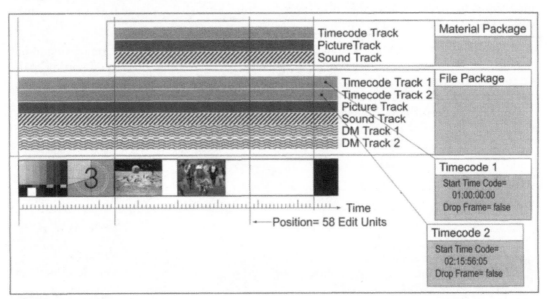

Figure 2.7 The Timecode Track

Timecode is also represented by a track. A *timecode track* is actually stored metadata that describes timecode as a piecewise linear representation of the actual timecode value. The timecode is calculated by an MXF playout device when the file is played, and the timecode would normally be reinserted into the output of the player. For example, Figure 2.7 shows a file package with several tracks, two of which are timecode tracks. This file was created as an ingest process from tape where there was a requirement to keep track of the timecode originally found in the VITC of the tape. A second timecode track that corresponded to the LTC of the tape was added at ingest. MXF allows as many timecode tracks to be stored in the file as are needed. The only hard requirement is that a material package must contain at least one timecode track that is linear and monotonic.

Why is timecode stored this way? In some applications, timecode can become discontinuous. This, in turn, can lead to synchronization errors between the various elements of a stream. MXF uses the position along a track as its internal synchronization mechanism, not the timecode value. This means that synchronization within a file is always preserved, even when an MXF file must recreate a discontinuous timecode at its output. The goal of MXF is to faithfully describe content while preserving synchronization between the tracks.

Timecode is defined by the SMPTE specification SMPTE 12M. There is a counting mode defined in that document called *drop frame* mode that is provided for use in countries with TV signals that work at the 29.97 fields per-second rate. The important point about drop frame is that it is a *counting mode* and does not actually change the number of frames of video that are stored. To quote from SMPTE 12M:

Because the vertical field rate of an NTSC television signal is 60/1.001 fields per second (» 59.94 Hz), straightforward counting at 30 frames per second will yield an error of approximately +108 frames (+3.6secREAL) in one hour of running time.

To minimize the NTSC time error, the first two frame numbers (00 and 01) shall be omitted from the count at the start of each minute except minutes 00, 10, 20, 30, 40, and 50.

When drop-frame compensation is applied to an NTSC television time code, the total error accumulated after one hour is reduced to –3.6 ms. The total error accumulated over a 24-hour period is –86 ms.

Drop frame will be revisited in the Timecode section of Chapter 3.

Descriptive Metadata

Up until now, this chapter has considered structural metadata. This is metadata that binds the file together, controls synchronization, and identifies the various tracks and packages. In general the structural metadata is machine-created metadata intended for another machine, such as an MXF player. The two lower tracks in Figure 2.7 are labeled descriptive metadata (DM) tracks. *Descriptive metadata* is usually created by humans for human consumption.

Like all "things" in MXF, descriptive metadata is represented by a track. In the design of MXF, it was realized that creating a single vocabulary for the description of broadcast and film content was neither achievable, nor really desirable. However, without a standardized structure for the interchange of descriptive information, the power of MXF could not be realized; so an attempt had to be made at the start to create a structure that was good enough for a large number of applications.

The result was SMPTE 380M—Descriptive Metadata Scheme 1. This scheme divided metadata descriptions into three broad categories:

- **Production Framework**—descriptions that relate to an entire production.

- **Scene Framework**—descriptions oriented toward a scene/script or what the content is intended to show (e.g., nightfall over Moscow).

- **Clip Framework**—descriptions oriented toward how the clip was shot (e.g., shot in a back lot in Hollywood).

Descriptive metadata may not be continuous along a track in the way that video and audio essence tends to be. A description may last only for the portion of a timeline where the information is valid. For this reason, there are different types of track defined within MXF.

1. **Timeline Track:** This track is not allowed to have any gaps or overlaps. This is the sort of track used to describe the video and audio essence.

2. **Event Track:** This track can have components on it that overlap or are instantaneous—i.e., have zero duration.

3. **Static Track:** This track is independent of time and is used to describe static content. Note that this is not the same as an event with zero duration that occurs at a specific time. A static track contains metadata that is always valid for the whole length of a sequence.

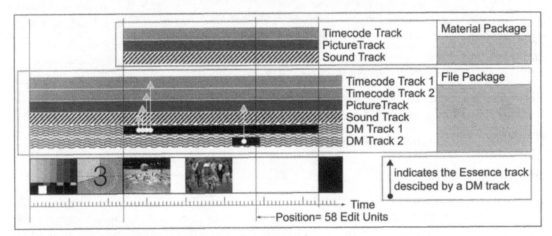

Figure 2.8 Descriptive metadata tracks describe other tracks

In Figure 2.8, the validity of the metadata has been shown on the metadata tracks. The track labeled DM1 is valid from the end of the slate until the start of the black content at the end of the example. This might be a production framework with a producer's name and contact details.

The track labeled DM2 has a framework lasting for a small portion of the middle of the clip. This might be used to indicate a shot list on a scene framework highlighting some significant event in the clip, such as the cyclists cresting a mountain.

Finally, descriptive metadata tracks are able to describe one or more essence tracks in a package. For example, the DM1 Track describes the Picture, Sound, and Timecode Essence Tracks. This is shown in Figure 2.8 by the arrows between tracks. DM2, however, is an annotation of only the picture track. This is shown by the single arrow in this figure.

The Source Reference Chain

This is a grand title for a simple concept. One of the goals of MXF was to fully describe the content and where it came from or, in other words, the *derivation* or the *genealogy* of the content. This means that the MXF file should be able to store the relationship between the output timeline and the stored content, as well as information about what source file and source tapes were used to make the content in the first place. The designers recognized that a full, in-depth history of every frame was not needed for every application, but there were some applications for which it was vital. This area of functionality is extremely well designed within the AAF data model and is one of the reasons why MXF designers put the AAF model at its core.

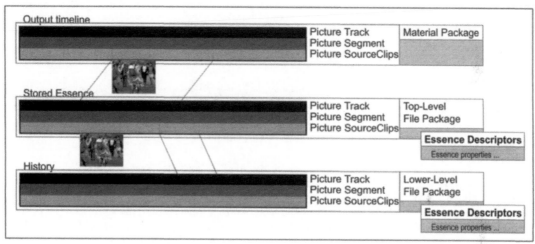

Figure 2.9 The source reference chain

The *source reference chain* is the title of the linking mechanism between different packages. When there are several packages linked together, the links form a chain from the top-level material package down to the lowest level file package. In an MXF file, the material package is responsible for synchronizing the stored content during playout. The top-level file packages describe the stored content within the MXF file, and each of the lower-level source packages describes what happened to the content in a previous generation. This metadata allows an audit trail to be built up of the processes the content has undergone. Each package is identified by a UMID—a *Unique Material ID* (SMPTE 330M). Each of the UMIDs associated with the previous generations is preserved, along with a description of the essence that was contained at that time.

Each of the essence tracks in a top-level file package has associated with it an *essence descriptor* describing the parameters of the stored essence. Lower-level source packages may also contain essence descriptors that describe the physical parameters of previous generations of the material. These essence descriptors allow an MXF application to determine if it is able to handle the stored content. They also allow the source reference chain to be "mined" for information relating to the current pictures and sound. For example, a file containing a lower-level Source Package that describes the content as DV, 720 x 576 x 50i and also containing a top-level file package that describes the content as long-GOP MPEG, 720 x 480 x 59.94i, must have undergone a frame-rate standards conversion and a DV to MPEG transcode at some stage.

Generic Sound Essence Descriptor

Name	Type	Meaning
Instance UID	UUID	Unique ID of this instance
Generation UID	UUID	Generation Identifier
Linked Track ID	UInt32	Value of the Track ID of the Track in this Package to which the Descriptor applies.
SampleRate	Rational	The field or frame rate of Essence Container (not the audio sampling clock rate)
Container Duration	Length	Duration of Essence Container (measured in Edit Units)
Essence Container	UL	The UL identifying the Essence Container described by this descriptor. Listed in SMPTE RP 224
Codec	UL	UL to identify a codec compatible with this Essence Container. Listed in SMPTE RP 224
Locators	StrongRefArray (Locators)	Ordered array of strong references to Locator sets
Audio sampling rate	Rational	Sampling rate of the audio essence
Locked/Unlocked	Boolean	Boolean indicating that the number of samples per frame is locked or unlocked.
Audio Ref Level	Int8	Audio reference level which gives the number of dBm for 0VU.
Electro-Spatial Formulation	Uint8 (Enum)	E.g. mono, dual mono, stereo, A,B etc
ChannelCount	Uint32	Number of Sound Channels
Quantization bits	UInt32	Number of quantization bits
Dial Norm	Int8	Gain to be applied to normalize perceived loudness of the clip, defined by normative ref 0 (1dB per step)
Sound Essence Compression	UL	UL identifying the Sound Compression Scheme

Figure 2.10 Properties of the Generic Sound Essence Descriptor

---

Essence descriptors fall into two broad categories: *file descriptors* and *physical descriptors*. A file descriptor is basically a description (e.g., resolution, sample rate, compression format, etc.) of the stored content of an MXF file. It may be attached to a top-level file package, in which case it describes the content that is actually in the file. It may be in a lower-level source package, in which case it describes the content as it was stored in some previous generation of the file.

File descriptors are intended to provide enough information to be able to select an appropriate codec to decode/display/reproduce the content. They are also intended to provide enough information to allow an application to make decisions on how essence might be efficiently processed. An example of typical parameters is given in Figure 2.10.

A physical descriptor is basically a description of *how* the content entered an MXF-AAF environment. This may have been as the result of a tape digitization, in which case you might find a tape descriptor in the file; or it may have been a result of an audio file conversion operation, in which case you might find an AES audio physical descriptor in a file.

Physical descriptors are intended to give enough information about the original source of a file so that the content may be appropriately processed. When the physical descriptor defines another file format, the physical descriptor is often the place where extra metadata is placed to allow transparent round tripping to and from the MXF environment—e.g., MXF → BWF → MXF (BWF is Broadcast Wave Format).

Operational Patterns

Controlling the complexity of the source reference chain also controls the complexity of the MXF encoder and MXF decoder required to generate or play an MXF file. In the design of MXF, there were several attempts to categorize applications in order to simplify the vast flexibility of the MXF format. In the end, the approach chosen was to control the relationship between the material package(s) and the file package(s) in an MXF file.

During the design of MXF, the words "templates," "profiles," "levels," and others were used to describe the constraints on the file. Most of these words already had various meanings coming from the video and IT industries. The phrase "Operational Pattern" was chosen as this was reasonably descriptive and did not carry any historical baggage.

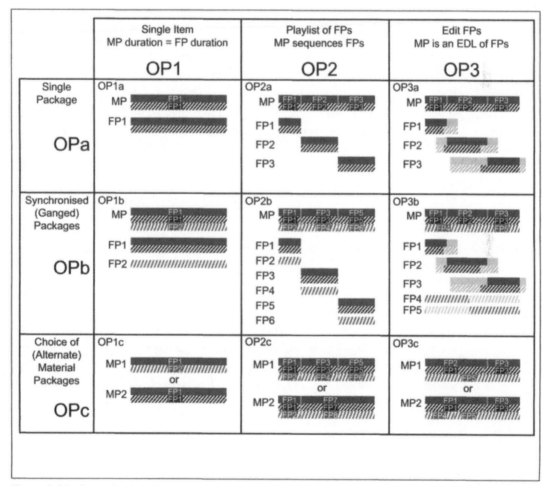

Figure 2.11 Operational patterns

Figure 2.11 shows the 3x3 matrix of standardized, "generalized operational patterns." The different constraints on MXF functionality can be described by looking at the columns and rows independently. There are also operational pattern qualifiers within the file (not shown in the diagram) that carry extra information about the operational pattern, such as whether the bytes are physically arranged to make the file "streamable."

The operational pattern columns differentiate the time axis complexity of an MXF file. The first column constrains a material package to play out the entire timeline of the file package(s). This means everything that is stored is played out. The second column constrains a material package to play out the file packages one after the other according to a playlist. Each of the file packages is played out in its entirety. The third column requires some kind of random access in an MXF player. Here, small portions of essence within an MXF file can be played out one after the other. This functionality allows cut-edits to be expressed using the source reference chain.

The operational pattern rows differentiate the package complexity of an MXF file. The first row constrains a material package to have only a single file package active at any one time along the output timeline. The second row allows two or more file packages to be synchronized using the material package to define the synchronization. The third row allows there to be more than one material package in a file. This allows the selection of different output timelines in a file to cover versioning and multi-language capabilities.

Heading upwards or leftwards in the diagram of Figure 2.11 indicates decreasing MXF encoder or MXF decoder complexity. Any encoder or decoder must support the functionality of operational patterns that are above or to the left of its stated operational pattern capabilities. The MXF rules state that a file must be labeled with the simplest operational pattern required to describe it. This is to ensure maximum interoperability between all applications.

Physical Storage

So far in this chapter, we have concentrated on the logical view of an MXF file—i.e., what the file is intended to represent. We will now look at how MXF arranges the bytes on a storage device. One of the goals in the design of MXF was to create an extensible format. This means that a device built with revision 1.0 of the specification must be able to parse and decode a file that is version 1.2 or 2.0 without modifying the device. A device must be able to ignore elements of the file that are unknown to it and yet still be able to decode known elements.

The low-level mechanism for achieving this is Key Length Value (KLV) encoding described in the previous chapter. Every property, set, and chunk of essence in an MXF file is wrapped in a KLV triplet as shown again in Figure 2.12. The key of the KLV triplet is a 16-byte number that uniquely identifies the contents of the triplet. If an MXF parser does not recognize the key, then the length property can be used to skip the value bytes. If the MXF parser does recognize the key, then it is able to route the KLV payload (the value field) to the appropriate handler.

Comparing 16-byte keys can consume time and storage space when there are a large number of small values that need to be KLV wrapped. In addition, it is useful for the KLV structure to be able to group together a number of different KLV properties together as a single set. For this reason, KLV

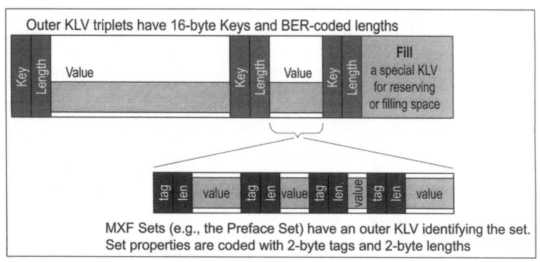

Figure 2.12 KLV coding and sets

allows local set coding—a mechanism where 2-byte *tags* are substituted for the 16-byte keys as shown in Figure 2.12. To ensure that a decoder is able to associate all the 2-byte tags with the 16-byte keys, a lookup table to convert tags to ULs (called the Primer Pack) is included in every file.

The Generic Container

Essence is placed in an MXF file using KLV encoding. The generic container, which is described in detail in Chapter 5, was created to provide a mechanism for encapsulating essence in a way that was fast, could be frame oriented, and provided easy implementation for streaming/file-bridging devices. Inside the file, *essence in a generic container* is often referred to as the *essence container*, and MXF allows several essence containers to be stored in a single file. Each essence container in a file is associated with a single top-level file package that holds the metadata description of the stored essence.

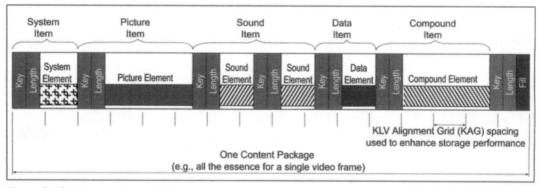

Figure 2.13 The generic container

Figure 2.13 on the previous page shows the basic structure of the generic container. It divides the essence up into *content packages* (CP) of approximately equal duration. Many (in fact probably most) MXF files are divided up into content packages that are one video frame in duration. These files are called *frame-wrapped files*. When the duration of the content package is the same as the duration of the files, these are called *clip-wrapped files* (because the entire clip is wrapped as an indivisible lump).

Each content package is categorized into five different essence categories called *items*. Within each item, there may be a number of individual *essence elements*. For example, the content package in Figure 2.13 has five items of which the sound item contains two sound elements. Each content package may only have a single essence item from each category, and the order of the items in the file should be the same in each and every content package. This makes it easier for parsers to work out where one content package starts and another ends. As well as keeping the order of the items constant in the file, it is also important to keep the order of the elements within the item constant. Each essence element is linked to a unique track in the top-level file package using the KLV key of that essence element. It is therefore important to ensure that the order of the elements remains constant, *and* that the Element in any given place within the content package has a constant KLV key because this is the binding that ties the logical description to the physical stored content.

- **System item:** Used for physical-layer-oriented metadata. System elements are used to provide low-level functionality such as pointing to the previous content package for simple reverse play. There is no system element in our example mentioned in the opening paragraph.

- **Picture item:** The picture item contains picture elements that, in turn, contain essence data that is predominantly picture oriented—e.g., the long-GOP MPEG samples in our example.

- **Sound item:** The sound item contains sound elements that contain predominantly sound essence data bytes—e.g., the BWF sound samples in our example.

- **Data item:** The data item contains data elements that are neither picture nor sound, but continuous data. There are no data elements in our example.

- **Compound item:** The compound item contains compound elements that are intrinsically interleaved. DV essence is a good example of this. The stream of DV block contains an intrinsic mix of picture sound and data.

Tracks, Generic Containers, and Partitions

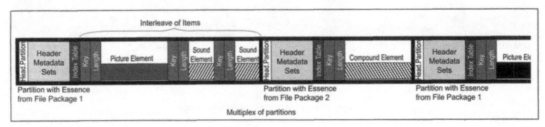

Figure 2.14 Interleaving, multiplexing, and partitions

Within the content package, the essence items and elements are said to be *interleaved*, as shown in Figure 2.14. A single file package describes a single generic container. If the generic container has a single stream of stereo essence elements, then the file package will have a single track to describe them. If the generic container has a single stream of picture elements, then the top-level file package will have single track to describe them.

What happens if a file has more than one file package? In this case there will be more than one generic container. We need to be able to *multiplex* together different file packages, which themselves may be interleaved. In order to separate the different stored generic containers, MXF inserts *partitions* between them. Each partition marks a point in the file where header metadata may be repeated, index table segments may be inserted and data for a different generic container may start.

Since the original design of MXF, it has been recognized that it is good practice to place only a single "thing" in a partition. Although the MXF specification allows each partition to contain header metadata *and* index table *and* essence, current wisdom advises that a partition should contain header metadata *or* index table *or* essence.

Mapping Documents

Generic Container Mapping Documents	
SMPTE 381M	Mapping MPEG Streams into the MXF Generic Container
SMPTE 382M	Mapping AES3 and Broadcast Wave Audio into the MXF Generic Container
SMPTE 383M	Mapping DV-DIF Data to the MXF Generic Container
SMPTE 384M	Mapping of Uncompressed Pictures into the Generic Container
SMPTE 385M	Mapping SDTI-CP Essence and Metadata into the MXF Generic Container
SMPTE 386M	Mapping Type D-10 Essence Data to the MXF Generic Container
SMPTE 387M	Mapping Type D-11 Essence Data to the MXF Generic Container
SMPTE 388M	Mapping A-law Coded Audio into the MXF Generic Container
work in progress	Mapping JPEG2000 into the MXF Generic Container
work in progress	Mapping VBI and ANC data into the MXF Generic Container

Figure 2.15 Mapping documents

In order to be able to achieve successful interchange, there must be a standardized way of encapsulating and describing commonly used essence types in the MXF specification. Many documents, known as *mapping documents*, have been created to define precisely the mechanisms required to place essence into the MXF generic container and the appropriate metadata to be placed in the header metadata. Figure 2.15 shows the mapping documents that had been created at the time this book went to print. Our example requires the mapping documents SMPTE 381M to map the long-GOP MPEG into the generic container and SMPTE 382M to map the Broadcast Wave stereo audio into the generic container.

Index Tables

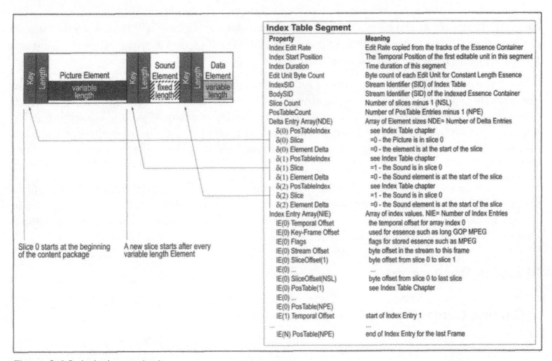

Figure 2.16 Indexing content

Now that the essence data has been mapped into the generic container and described by the header metadata, it is useful to be able to perform random access within the file so that efficient partial restore (i.e., picking out a portion of the stored material), scrubbing (moving quickly forwards and backwards through the material), and other operations can be performed. Figure 2.16 shows the basic *index table* structures provided within MXF to allow a time offset to be converted to a byte offset within the file. The richness of MXF makes the index table design rather complex. The index tables have to cope not only with an MXF file containing a single generic container with simple constant-sized elements, but also with MXF files containing multiple multiplexed generic containers with interleaved elements of variable length.

This gives rise to the structures shown in Figure 2.16. Subtleties of indexing content are covered more in Chapter 12 and in each of the essence-mapping chapters.

Generic (Non-Essence) Streams

There are certain types of data and essence that don't fit well in the generic container. These types of data are referred to as *generic streams* and may include things like "bursty" KLV data streams, text documents, and other large miscellaneous lumps of data that need to be included in a file.

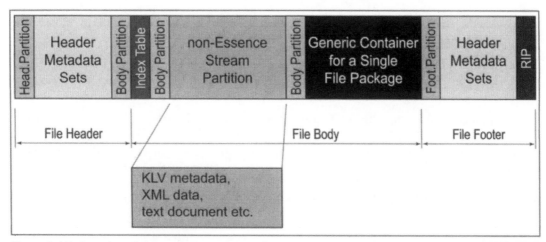

Figure 2.17 Generic stream container

A *stream container* has been defined that allows this sort of data to be included in an MXF file and associated with the header metadata. One of the key features of this sort of data is that the MXF index table structure either does not work or is extremely inefficient for indexing the content.

Identification and Numbers

The last part of this chapter is dedicated to some of the numbering schemes and principles that are used in MXF to link the whole file structure together. The most important number used in MXF

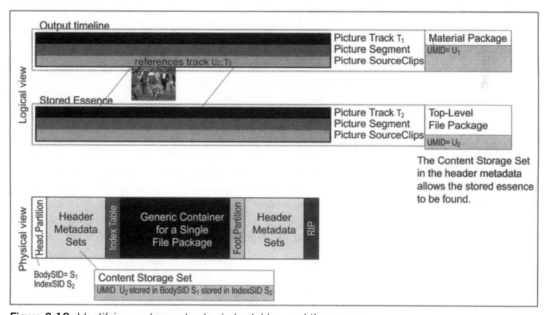

Figure 2.18 Identifying packages, tracks, index tables, and the essence

is probably the *Unique Material ID* or UMID. This is a number, specified in SMPTE 330M, that uniquely identifies a piece of material

As can be seen in Figure 2.18, the UMID is used to identify a package. The file package represents the stored material and has a different ID to the material package that represents the played material, even though, in an OP1a file, the material played may seem identical to the material stored.

Tracks are identified by their *TrackID*—a number that is unique within the scope of a package. To uniquely identify any tracks, you need both the UMID of the package and the TrackID. The UMID is also used to associate a top-level file package with a generic container and its index table. UMIDs and TrackIDs are part of the MXF data model and form part of the structural metadata that binds an MXF file together. If an MXF file is exported to some non-KLV physical representation, such as XML, then UMIDs and TrackIDs form part of the exported data.

At the physical level, *StreamID*s (SIDs) are used to identify logically separate streams of bytes. This parameter is not part of the MXF data model; it is a device used at the physical level to hold the file together. Each generic container is identified by a *BodySID*. Each index table is identified by an IndexSID. By convention, no two SIDs in a file can have the same value. If an MXF file is exported to some non-KLV physical representation, such as XML, then SIDs are **not** exported because they are only a device for holding the physical MXF file together. There is considerably more detail about SIDs and TrackIDs in Chapter 3.

Data Types

In order to handle MXF properties in a structured way, each property is associated with a data type. Some of the common data types are shown in Figure 2.19. Some of these data types are simple, such as the commonly used 8-bit unsigned integer (Uint8). Other data types are more complex, such as an *array*. This is a structure holding a list of data elements where the order has some significance. Each element of data in an array has the same data type and therefore the same number of bytes of storage. A similar data type is a *batch*. A batch is stored in an identical fashion to an array, but the order of the elements has no special significance.

MXF is intended to be used by people who speak different languages and write with different character sets. For this reason, 16-bit Unicode characters (UTF-16) are used wherever possible for stored text. In order to be efficient for storage, strings in MXF can exactly fill the KLV that holds them—e.g., the KLV for "hello" would have a length field of 10. However, this is not always a good approach for application writers, so it is also possible to terminate strings with a null character—e.g., the length field for "hello" could be set to 128, and the bytes stored would be 0x00,0x68, 0x00,0x65, 0x00,0x6c, 0x00,0x6c, 0x00,0x6f, 0x00,0x00, <116 random bytes>. With this approach, it is possible to change strings from "hello" to "goodbye" without having to rewrite the whole header metadata to make space for the two extra characters.

Data Model

We have mentioned in a couple of places the term *data model*. The structural metadata forms part of the MXF data model that is basically the definitive set of relationships between the various

Basic Types in MXF

Type	Meaning
BER length	A length value in bytes used to code a KLV triplet.
Boolean	1-byte value: zero == FALSE, non-zero == TRUE
Int8	Signed 8-bit integer.
Int16	Signed 16-bit integer.
Int32	Signed 32-bit integer.
Int64	Signed 64-bit integer.
Length	Int64 value of the length (duration) measured in edit units.
Package ID	A UMID to uniquely identify a package or a zero value used to terminate a reference chain.
Position	Int64 time value used to locate a specific point along a track.
StrongRef	"One-to-one" relationship between sets and implemented in MXF with UUIDs.
UInt8	Unsigned 8-bit integer.
UInt16	Unsigned 16-bit integer.
UInt32	Unsigned 32-bit integer.
UInt64	Unsigned 64-bit integer.
UL	Universal label (SMPTE 298M).
UMID	Unique material ID (SMPTE 330M).
UUID	Universally unique identifier according to ISO 11578.
Version type	Uint16 version number (major*256 + minor).
WeakRef	"Many-to-one" relationship between sets implemented in MXF with UUIDs.

Figure 2.19 Basic types—UMID, UL, UUID, UTF-16 strings, array, batches

metadata sets and properties used in MXF. The data model for MXF is derived from the AAF data model that is fully described in Chapter 13. Nearly all the metadata discussed in this book forms part of the data model, and a variety of diagrams will be used to express the different relationships between the various properties. One of the types of diagram is called UML (Universal Modeling Language) that shows pictorially the relationships between different properties and

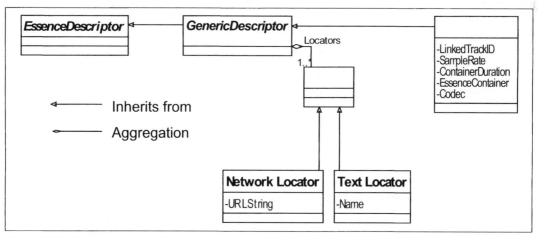

Figure 2.20 Data model extract

classes. Figure 2.20 on the previous page shows part of a UML class diagram that demonstrates some of the properties of MXF descriptors. The *parent* class or *super* class is on the left, with the name EssenceDescriptor in italics. This means that the super-class is "abstract" or, in other words, you never use it directly. You always use a subclass of an abstract class.

The arrow symbol shows which subclasses inherit from which superclasses, and the arrow with the diamond on the end shows aggregation. This is where the property of one class (or set) is itself one or more classes (or sets). The name on the line indicates the name of the property in the super-class, and the number at the end of the line shows how many of that property are required.

In MXF, the mechanism for implementing aggregation is via the use of references and instance UIDs. There is more about strong and weak references in Chapter 3. Within MXF, the basic method can be explained by referring to the Sound Essence Descriptor set in Figure 2.10. The first property is called the Instance UID. This is a 16-byte number that uniquely identifies this instance of the set within the MXF file. In order for the package to reference this set, there is a property in the package called *Descriptor*. The value of this property will be the same as the Instance-ceUID of the Sound Descriptor set in order to make the reference.

Figure 2.10 also shows a property called Generation UID. This is a special property that links to an identification set as shown in Figure 2.21.

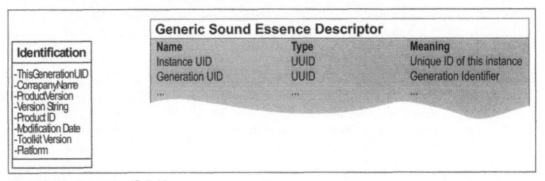

Figure 2.21 Generation ID linking

When an MXF file is modified, the application that modifies the file should create a new identification set, identifying itself as the creator of the most recent version of the file. Previous identification sets are not removed from the file. All MXF sets contain an optional generation UID property as shown in Figure 2.21. The value of this property is set to the same value as the ThisGenerationUIDproperty in the identification set; this identifies the application that wrote this metadata. In this way, MXF is able to create an audit trail of which applications created what metadata in the file.

Summary of MXF Documents

This completes the quick run through the basic concepts of MXF. The final Figure 2.22 shows the documents that had been standardized and those that were in progress at the time of writing this edition of the book. The status of these documents will change over time.

Number	doc	status
On the SMPTE CD-ROM in SMPTE directory		
SMPTE 377M	MXF File Format	Standard
SMPTE 378M	Operational Pattern 1a	Standard
SMPTE 379M	Generic Container	Standard
SMPTE 380M	Descriptive Metadata Scheme 1	Standard
SMPTE 381M	Mapping MPEG into MXF	Standard
SMPTE 383M	Mapping DV (&DV-based) into MXF	Standard
SMPTE 384M	Mapping Uncompressed into MXF	Standard
SMPTE 385M	SDTI-CP compatible system Item	Standard
SMPTE 386M	Mapping D10 into MXF	Standard
SMPTE 387M	Mapping D11 into MXF	Standard
SMPTE 388M	Mapping A-law audio into MXF	Standard
SMPTE 389M	Reverse Play	Standard
SMPTE 390M	Operational Pattern Atom	Standard
SMPTE 391M	Operational Pattern 1b	Standard
SMPTE 392M	Operational Pattern 2a	Standard
SMPTE 393M	Operational Pattern 2b	Standard
SMPTE 394M	GC System scheme 1	Standard
SMPTE 405M	GC System scheme 1 Elements	Standard
On the SMPTE CD-ROM in EG directory		
EG41	Engineering Guideline	Engineering Guideline
EG42	DMS Engineering Guideline	Engineering Guideline
At www.smpte-ra.org		
RP210	Metadata Dictionary	Standard
Class 13-14	Private number spaces	Registered UL number spaces
UMID	UMID registries	Registered UMID number spaces
In the Final Proof Reading stages of publication		
-	-	-
With the Standards Committee		
SMPTE 382M	AES - BWF audio	
-	-	-
In Trial publication on the SMPTE website - subject to change		
-	-	-
In Technical Committee Ballot - subject to change		
SMPTE 407M	OP3ab	-
SMPTE 408M	OP123c	-
SMPTE422M	Mapping JPEG2000	-
-	Generic Stream container	-
	XML Representation of Data Models	-
RDD9	Sony Interop Spec - MPEG Long GOP	-
-	MXF- XML Encoding	-
-	MXF Mapping for VBI Ancillary Data	-
-	MXF on Solid-State Media Card	-
SMPTE423M	MXF Track File Essence Encryption	-
SMPTE416	D-Cinema Package Operational Constra	-
-	dCinema Track File Specificaiton	-
Unballotted Working Drafts - subject to change		
---	---	---

Figure 2.22 MXF documents at the time of publication

3 Physical and Logical Structures within an MXF File

Bruce Devlin

This chapter is organized as an alphabetical reference to the terms and concepts used within MXF. Chapter 2, a general overview of MXF, can be read from start to finish and introduces all the terms explained in this chapter. Indeed, it is assumed that the reader is familiar with those terms before diving into the detail of this chapter. Chapter 3 is intended to be read on a section-by-section basis and provides further explanation of the individual concepts. It also allows individual sections to be referenced by implementers and specification writers. If you feel this chapter is missing any detailed explanations, please contact the publisher or the author to request additions for any future revision of this book.

This chapter contains several UML diagrams. These are introduced in Chapter 2 and explained in more detail in Chapter 13, where they are used more fully to explain the MXF data model. This chapter covers the following subjects (arranged in alphabetical order):

AAF	Continuous decoding of contiguous essence containers	Dark
Data Model	Descriptors	Essence—Internal
Essence—External	Generic Container	KAG

KLV (& BER)	Locators	Material Package
MXF Encoder & Decoder	Operational Patterns	Origin
Package	Partition	References—Strong, Weak, Global
Random Index Pack (RIP)	Run-In	Sets, Items (properties)
Source Package	Source Reference Chain	SIDs—BodySID & IndexSID
Structural Metadata	Time	Timecode
Timeline	Tracks	Types
Universal Labels & Registers	UMID	User Metadata

AAF

Definition: AAF is the Advanced Authoring Format.

Description: The Advanced Authoring Format specification is controlled by the Advanced Authoring Format Association. Within the association, users and manufacturers develop open interchange solutions that solve real-world business problems and create new business opportunities for content creation, production, post-production, and rich media authoring.

AAF shares the same data model as MXF, although, for historical reasons, there is a difference in terminology for some of the sets and properties. A full description of the MXF data model and its relationship to AAF is given in Chapter 13.

Continuous Decoding of Contiguous Essence Containers

Definition: SMPTE 392M: Operational pattern 2a, 2b, or 2c qualifier informing MXF decoders that playout without additional processing is possible.

Description: Operational patterns are fully described in Chapter 4. Sequencing or playlist functionality is intended to be provided by the operational patterns in column two of Figure 4.1. For many essence types, this is a trivial issue: one merely sends the stream of bytes, in the order they appear in the file, to a decoder codec. An example of such a structure is shown in Figure 3.1 on the next page.

There are certain essence types, however, that rely on predictive coding in order to achieve high compression ratios or alternatively employ buffer models that must be respected for continuous playback. Examples of this sort of essence are:

- Long-GOP MPEG
- H.264
- SMPTE VC-1 video
- MP3 audio
- AAC audio

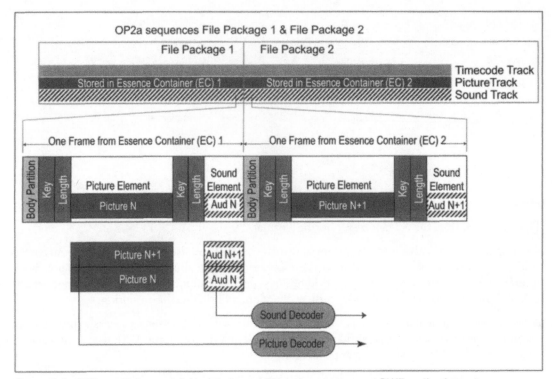

Figure 3.1 OP2a multiplex containing interleaved DV and uncompressed BWF audio elements

If these essence types are contained in MXF using a standardized or a private mapping, then care needs to be taken when constructing an OP2x multiplex. In order to create a system as shown in Figure 3.1, the application that created the MXF file must be sure that any buffer/prediction conditions required at the start of the second essence container(s) are satisfactorily established at the end of the first essence container(s). This is shown in Figure 3.2, where each essence element requires some form of splice processing before the byte stream can be delivered to the essence decoder and/or after the decoded byte stream exits the essence decoder.

Why two splice processors? This depends on the nature of the splice and the capabilities of the decoders. For long-GOP MPEG 2 video, it may be possible to arrange for closed GOPs at the end of EC1 and the start of EC2 with the correct number of frames and the correct buffer conditions. This may eliminate the need for Splice Processor 2 in the video chain.

The audio chain, however, may have fixed-duration, compressed audio-frames where the splice point occurs part way through the last audio frame in EC1 and the first audio frame in EC2. In order to process the splice correctly, the two audio frames must be decoded, audio samples discarded, filtered, and then presented to the output.

If any splice processing is required, then the OP qualifier bit 4 must be set to 1, indicating "no knowledge of the inter-SourceClip processing is available." (See Chapter 4 for a discussion of operational pattern qualifier bits.)

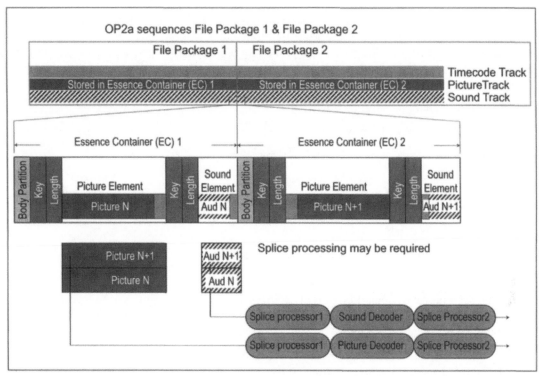

Figure 3.2 OP2a multiplex containing interleaved long-GOP MPEG and compressed BWF elements

Dark

Definition: Dark refers to any property, set, element, or value unknown to an application at a given time.

Description: The derivation of the word *dark* came from a discussion during the design of MXF where one contributor remarked. "This means you could have an MXF file with a few kilobytes of essence, but gigabytes of metadata that you would not be able to understand. It's like Dark Matter in the universe: You know it has to be there, but you don't know what it's for." From that point onwards, the term *dark metadata* has been used to describe unknown metadata.

Why should we care about dark metadata, or dark essence, or dark anything? One of the key points of MXF is that it should be extensible. This means that we should be able to create new MXF encoders that create files with new properties and sets. When these files are read by older encoders, the meaning of these sets will be unknown or dark.

The concept of dark data may occur for other reasons. A vendor who creates a store-and-forward device based on MXF is unlikely to implement the full functionality of an MXF-based editor. A store-and-forward device probably only needs to be able to identify the UMIDs within the packages and some basic MXF sets. There will be a lot of metadata in the file that the device will not be able to recognize and will thus be forced to treat as dark.

Dark essence is likely to occur when new essence types are added to MXF either via a public or a private specification. It is important that the essence description rules are followed by MXF encoders to ensure that the correct essence identification ULs are included in the file (see Descriptors in this chapter). MXF decoders can be designed to act on these descriptors to see if codecs are available to operate on the essence.

Other examples of dark data can be easily listed:

- Unexpected values to well-known MXF properties

- Unexpected properties in well-known MXF metadata sets

- Unexpected sets in well-known MXF structures

- Unexpected sets that appear not to be linked to the other sets in MXF

- Unexpected essence data

- Unexpected partition types

- Unexpected data types

Any of the examples above could be caused by an SMPTE extension to the MXF specification, a private addition to the MXF specification, or simply failure to implement the whole specification by a device.

The rule for handling dark data by devices is quite clear: **preserve dark data**. If you don't know what it is, don't delete it. A simple example of this is the addition of a new class to the data model that links into the data model as shown in Figure 3.3 and explained in more detail in Chapter 13.

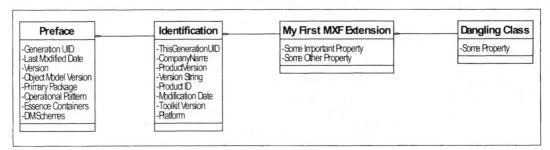

Figure 3.3 Addition of a new class to the data model

The desired result of the extension is that some new complex property is added to the Identification set. In the KLV domain, the new set will be inserted as a new local-set coded property in the Identification set. This is shown in Figure 3.4.

How should an MXF decoder treat this extension? The first action will be the discovery of the new tag value in the Identification set. The MXF decoder will look this value up in the Primer Pack and the MXF decoder will discover that it has no knowledge of the UL it represents. The MXF decoder knows that this property is dark, and that it should not infer anything else about it.

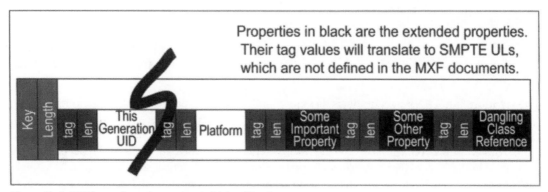

Figure 3.4 KLV encoding of an extended Identification set

When the MXF decoder discovers the KLV key for "My First MXF Extension" and the KLV key for "Dangling Set," then it has to decide that these are dark KLV triplets because it does not know the meaning of the KLV keys and has no way of linking these sets into the data model shown in Figure 3.3.

An MXF decoder that is able to look up the data type of the property may be able to discover that it is a reference (strong or weak) to a set. It may try to "help" by looking inside the dark sets it encounters to try and resolve the reference. This is very dangerous behavior and should not be attempted. The Instance UID creation algorithm guarantees that new Instance UIDs will be unique, but there is no requirement to prevent emulation of Instance UIDs in Dark metadata sets. Although the MXF decoder may discover some property in the "My First MXF Extension" set that appears to resolve the reference from the Identification set, the MXF decoder cannot know this for certain and, in real systems, this could prove a "false positive match" that would lead to other system problems in parsing the file. Even if this were done, the MXF decoder would have no way of determining the reference to "Dangling Set" and so this dangerous application behavior is of little practical use and should not be performed.

Applications that modify MXF files should be prevented, if possible, from modifying existing Instance UIDs. Instance UIDs constitute the linking mechanism between sets, and inadvertent modification of these numbers could cause dark sets to become accidentally unlinked and therefore lost to the applications that are able to parse and interpret the dark data.

It is strongly recommended to MXF application writers that mechanisms be included to allow "lightening" of the darkness. This means permitting the addition of structure and property information to an application that allows, at the very least, the resolution of dark references to ensure the integrity of the linked data within the MXF fie. This is often performed by the addition of run-time dictionaries that are written in XML and that describe the syntax and structure of the new properties. This will allow applications to have more robust dark-data-handling strategies.

At the time of writing, a working group of SMPTE is looking at the issues involved in lightening the darkness in an MXF file. It is anticipated that the solution to this problem will improve interoperability and will improve round tripping with AAF and XML applications.

Data Model

Definition: A data model defines what information is to be contained in a database/application, how the information will be used, and how the items in the database/application will be related to each other.

Description: The MXF data model is described in detail in Chapter 13. The data model is based on the AAF data model, although many of the terms and properties have different names. Each property in the MXF data model is registered in the SMPTE Metadata Dictionary RP210. Sets of properties are registered in the SMPTE Groups Register, and the data types of the properties are registered in the Types Register. From a basic relational and syntactical standpoint, the MXF data model can be constructed by inspecting the various SMPTE registers and constructing a model of the related groups of properties used in MXF. The semantic meaning and nuances of the use of these properties are given in the written SMPTE specifications.

Why is it done this way? Partly because of the historical order in which the documents were created, and partly to create a normative document chain without circular references. To illustrate the point, consider the MXF Descriptors (see Descriptors in this chapter). In the MXF File Format Specification (SMPTE 377M), each of the descriptors specified in the document has its

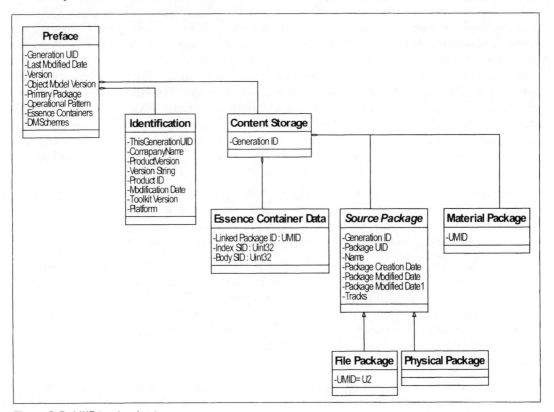

Figure 3.5 MXF top-level sets

KLV key given in one of the tables. New descriptors are defined in other MXF documents such as the audio-mapping document, SMPTE 382M. For each of the essence types mapped into MXF, an identifying Universal Label was defined that acted as a short cut to allow decoders to "fast fail" if they couldn't handle the essence types. These labels are defined in the File Format Specification and also in mapping documents, such as SMPTE 382M. Because these are abstract labels, these values are also copied into the SMPTE Labels Register RP224 that holds a list of all the labels, **but this is not the normative definition**. The normative definition is the original mapping document. This is important if errors or divergence are ever found in the values; then it is the underlying (mapping) documents that take precedence. They feed into the registries, and from these we can find the data model by inspection.

At present, the data model is inferred rather than explicitly defined. There are several reasons for this, including the fact that all the SMPTE registers were not finished at the time that MXF was standardized. Work is under way to rectify this and little "loopholes," such as the fact that the Universal Labels for the essence types have a register but there is no equivalent for the KLV keys, need to be fixed. Without a register, there is a small chance that a new document author may reallocate an existing key. This would be **bad**. Until such time as a full set of registers exists, the best guide to the data model is Chapter 13 of this book.

The top level of the data model is shown as a UML diagram in Figure 3.5. Further diagrams can be found in this chapter and in Chapter 13.

Descriptors

Definition: Descriptors are used to describe essence stored in or referenced by an MXF file.

Description: In an MXF file, stored essence is described by the top-level file package. The Essence Descriptors are used to uniquely identify the essence to be retrieved/decoded/displayed. The relationship between the descriptors in SMPTE 377M (File Format Specification), SMPTE 381M (MPEG mapping) and SMPTE 382M (audio mapping) are shown in the Figure 3.6 on the next page.

You can see how the arrangement of the descriptors is categorized to allow different generic sorts of essence to be described and specific extensions to be created as subclasses of the generic descriptors. There is a single descriptor associated with each file package. If there is more than one track in the package, then the descriptor will be a *Multiple Descriptor*, which in turn has a list of SubDescriptors—up to one per track. The FileDescriptor::LinkedTrackID property of each descriptor is set to the TrackID of the track within the file package that it describes.

- The abstract superclass EssenceDescriptor is never used directly—hence it is *abstract*. It is also the parent of all the descriptors—hence it is a *superclass*.

- The GenericDescriptor adds the Locators property. This allows hints about the location of external essence to be buried within the file. More on this under Locators in this chapter.

- The FileDescriptor adds generic properties for essence which is (or has been) stored in files—e.g., FileDescriptor::ContainerDuration.

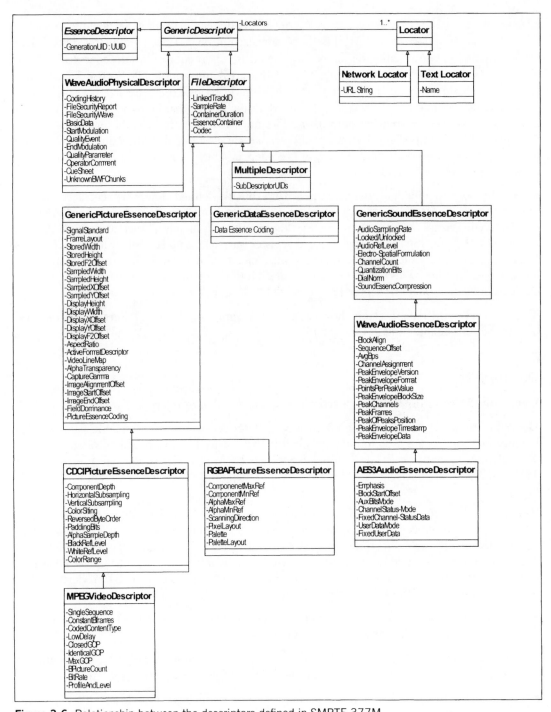

Figure 3.6 Relationship between the descriptors defined in SMPTE 377M

- The GenericPictureEssenceDescriptor adds generic properties that are common to rectangular images—e.g., GenericPictureEssenceDescriptor::DisplayWidth.

- The next picture-related subclass splits into pictures that are RGBα based and pictures that are color difference based (e.g., YCbCr). SMPTE 381M further extends the CDCI (Color Difference Component Image Descriptor) with MPEG properties that are useful for MPEG systems.

- At present, there are no specific data essence types defined within MXF and there is only Generic Data Descriptor defined.

- The GenericSoundEssenceDescriptor contains the generic properties of Sound Essence.

SMPTE 382M extends the GenericSoundEssenceDescriptor to handle metadata associated with Broadcast Wave and AES3 audio. The WaveAudioEssenceDescriptor adds properties that are defined in the Broadcast Wave extensions to the wave audio format. At the time of writing, the Audio Engineering Society (AES) is working to harmonize the different variants of the Broadcast Wave Format (BWF) that exist around the world. The AESAudioEssenceDescriptor adds extra properties unique to AES audio streams. Finally, the WaveAudioPhysicalDescriptor holds metadata that is required to recreate the original BWF file. Specifically, there is a mechanism where unknown chunks that are found in the original BWF file can be stored in the MXF WaveAudio-PhysicalDescriptor.

The smallest block on the diagram is also one of the most important—the MultipleDescriptor. When an essence container is created by interleaving a long-GOP MPEG picture element (SMPTE381M) and a Broadcast Wave element (SMPTE 382M), two different essence descriptors are required, one for each essence element. Unfortunately, a file package only has a single EssenceDescriptor property. This is where the multiple descriptor comes in; its only property is an array of SubDescriptorUIDs, which is a list of the Instance UIDs of the essence descriptors for each of the elements.

Essence—Internal

Definition: KLV wrapped video, audio, or other data that is used/referenced by the MXF file containing them.

Description: This section looks at the linking and usage of internal essence in MXF. The header metadata within the MXF file describes the synchronization, sequencing, structure, and type of the essence stored in the file. There are a number of "magic numbers" that are used to link the essence to the header metadata. MXF requires that each essence container in a file is described by a top-level file-package. In addition, each essence container within a file must be stored in its own partitions. This then requires a linkage between the file package and the essence container partitions. This link is defined in the EssenceContainerData set as shown in Figure 3.7. This relates the UMID of the file package to the StreamIDs (SIDs) found in the partitions and the index tables. More details of UMIDs, SIDs material package, and source package can be found in this chapter.

It is now necessary to connect the tracks of the file package to the individual elements of the essence container. This is done by linking the Track-Number property of the track to the last 4 bytes of the KLV key of the element as shown in Figure 3.8. The precise rules for this linkage are defined in the MXF Generic Essence Container Specification SMPTE 379M.

In order to find the correct frame/sample of essence within the essence container, it is necessary to use index tables to convert a temporal position value to a byte offset value. Index tables are fully described in Chapter 10, but how do you find the index table?

This is linked using the IndexSID value which is

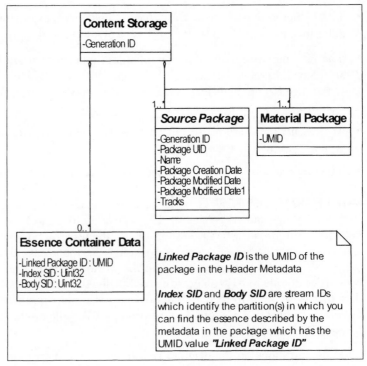

Figure 3.7 Linkage between the essence container and the top-level file package

obtained as shown in Figure 3.9. SMPTE 377M allows index table segments to exist in the same partition as the essence container they index. Since the writing of the standard, common practice

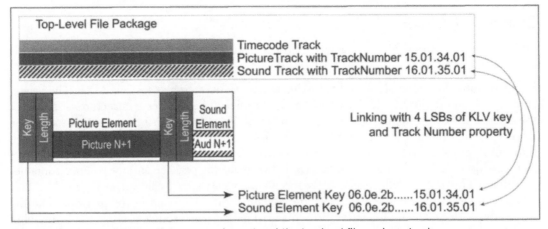

Figure 3.8 Linkage between the essence element and the top-level file package track

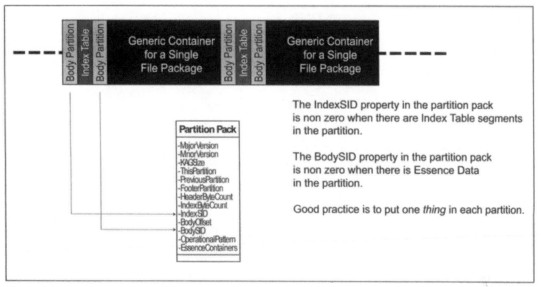

Figure 3.9 Linkage & placement of index tables to essence containers

is to put a single "thing" in a single partition. Good practice is to place index table segments in their own partition with the correct IndexSID value as shown in Figure 3.9.

Essence—External

Definition: Video, audio, or other data essence that is external to the MXF file referencing them.

Description: This section looks at the linking and usage of external essence in MXF. The MXF specification is a bit light on normative text that defines how to use external essence, so this section is split into two parts—(1) external essence contained in a separate MXF file, and (2) external essence in some other file type.

The one thing common to both external essence cases is the procedure to find the essence. Let's assume that there is a material package track that references a top-level file-package track with UMID U_1 and TrackID T_1. How do you locate the essence?

If there is an asset management, library, or content management system available, then this should be used to look up U1 and find the essence. Why? These systems are designed to manage and track live information, whereas any information stored in the file is old and possibly out-of-date location information. The unique reference to the file package is the UMID U_1. Once the value of U_1 is allocated, it is forever associated with that version of the essence, whether it is located inside or outside the file with the material package. A worked example of finding and synchronizing external essence is presented in the audio Chapter 6.

If no such system is available and there is no file package in the MXF file then, in all likelihood, the link to the essence has been lost.

If there is a top-level file package with UMID U_1 and a track with TrackID T1 in the file, then it can be inspected for *Locators* in the file descriptor for track T_1 (see Descriptors Figure 3.6 in this chapter). These locators can be used as *hints* to find the essence. Use these locators as explained in the locators section in this chapter to discover the essence if possible.

External Essence Contained in an MXF File

When the essence is in an external MXF file, all the linking mechanisms described in the "Essence—Internal" section of this chapter apply—i.e., each material package track references the UMID of the file package and TrackID of the track. The difference is that the file containing the top-level file package with the referenced UMID is in a different file to the one containing the material package.

External Essence Contained in Some Non-MXF File

This topic is not covered directly in SMPTE 377M, and so the text in this section reflects current thinking and is not a tutorial on how the specification actually works.

Let's assume that one of the location mechanisms can locate the essence and the EssenceCompression property of the essence descriptor correctly identifies the coding of the essence. An MXF

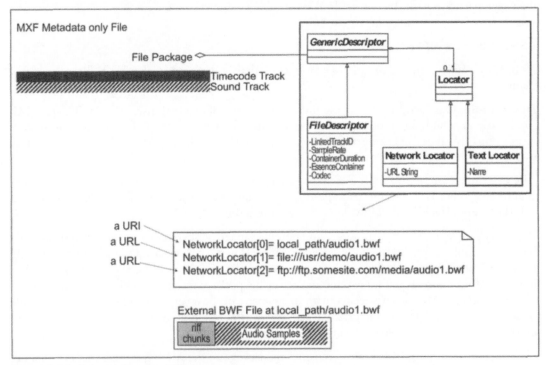

Figure 3.10 External Broadcast Wave essence

decoder should ensure that the actual essence found in the file is the same as that indicated by the PictureEssenceCoding or SoundEssenceCompression properties. If this is not the case, then this is an error.

The EssenceDescriptor and the track information should correctly describe the external essence file. All the duration properties and picture/sound descriptor properties should correctly identify the external essence. Any index table in the file will be able to convert time offsets into byte offsets. Recent work on external essence highlighted the fact that there are certain external essence file types (e.g., Broadcast Wave) where the essence has a constant number of bytes for each edit unit. This would suggest that the simplified index table structure in SMPTE 377M could be used. Unfortunately, there is usually a header at the start of the file. In SMPTE 377M-2004, there is no parameter that allows this header to be skipped. Recent work has identified a solution where an optional property is added to the index table to fix the problem. This property defines the number of non-essence bytes that exist at the start of the file.

As an example, Figure 3.10 shows an MXF metadata-only file that references an external broadcast wave file. Note that the URI in the Locators refers to a relative file location, whereas the URLs refer to absolute locations.

Generic Container

Definition: The generic container is the method for placing essence in an MXF file, defined in SMPTE 379M.

Description: One of the requirements in the design of MXF was that it should be agnostic of the underlying compression type. One mechanism that helps make this possible is the creation of the generic container. SMPTE 379M allows MXF applications to be written that work at the MXF/KLV level and can process the essence container without necessarily having to know what type of essence is in the essence container. The generic container categorizes essence into five categories:

- System elements
- Picture elements

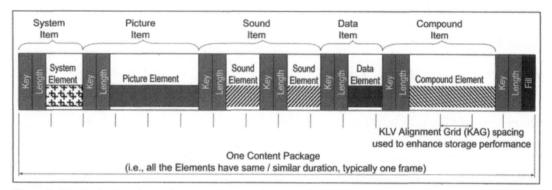

Figure 3.11 Content package, items, and elements

- Sound elements

- Data elements

- Compound elements

To simplify processing, each of these element types must be grouped together into Items. Groups of contiguous items with the same time duration are referred to as content packages. This is shown in Figure 3.11.

The generic container specification also defines the two major wrapping modes that are used in MXF:

- Frame wrapping

- Clip wrapping

Frame wrapping is the most common mode, and each content package has the duration of a single video frame. Clip wrapping is the wrapping mode where there is a single element for the entire content of the file. The duration of the file is the same as the duration of each of the individual elements. These two wrapping modes are shown in Figure 3.12, and other wrapping modes are defined in the SMPTE 381M MPEG mapping document for specialist modes such as GOP wrapping.

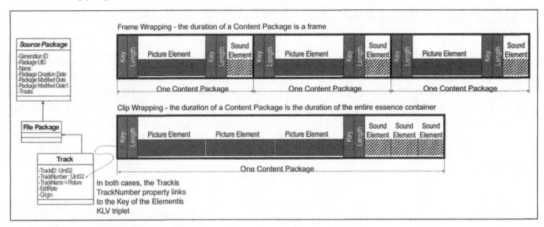

Figure 3.12 Frame and clip wrapping

Each element is linked to the metadata via the least significant 4 bytes of the key of the element's KLV triplet. In the case of frame wrapping, there is a key associated with each frame of essence and with clip wrapping, there is a single key for all the picture content, and a separate key for each stored channel of sound content.

When there are multiple elements from the same track, they must be adjacent to each other and in time order. Assuming the essence has a constant number of bytes per element, and is indexed accordingly, there are several simultaneous requirements that must be met when this is done:

1. The KLV key must have the correct least significant 4 bytes to link to the track.

2. Each element must have an identical number of essence samples and same number of bytes.

3. Each element must represent the same time duration.

4. Each element should have byte 16 correctly set—the essence element count from SMPTE 379M. When elements link to the same track, it is important to read the entire text from SMPTE 379M:

Byte 16 of the Element's KLV key shall be used to define the value of the element number in the range 00h~7Fh. It shall be set by the encoder to be unique amongst the elements in any one Item. In most cases, the element number will be increment by one for each new essence element in sequence within an item. For a given essence element, this value shall be constant within the entire generic container (even when new elements are added). This is to maintain track linking.

This final provision is important because changing the element's KLV key by incrementing byte 16 according to the first half of the rule would unlink the element from the corresponding track.

KAG

Definition: The KAG is the KLV Alignment Grid—a performance optimization technique.

Description: To create efficient MXF systems that involve storage, it is important to be able to define the byte alignment of the stored data. Many storage media such as hard disks are organized in fixed-size sectors and system speed, and efficiency can be improved if applications read and write integer numbers of sectors to fetch essence. MXF, however, is a generalized file format and there is no single sector size that is the optimum for all applications. Uncompressed HD applications work best with very big sectors; however, this can become very inefficient for low bitrate streams such as audio.

MXF defined a property called the *KLV Alignment Grid* (KAG). It is a UInt32 property of the Partition Pack and defines the desired byte alignment of the start of essence elements within a partition. It is possible to have many partitions in a file, each with a different KAG size, but this is not recommended. Higher operational patterns (particularly those in the "b" row) may have different essence containers, each of which has a different optimal KAG. For example, Figure 3.13 shows a partition with high data rate picture essence and another with low date rate sound essence. For overall system performance, there should be an integer relationship between all the KAG values, and the file overall should respect the smallest of these KAG values.

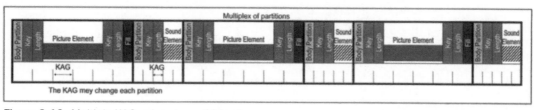

Figure 3.13 Multiple KAG values in an OP1b file

The KAG is, however, a performance accelerator that applies to each partition in the file. There are occasions when the KAG may not be respected, and when this happens, an MXF decoder should still decode the file; however, performance may be impaired.

KLV (& BER)

Definition: Key Length Value (KLV) coding is the lowest level protocol for encapsulating data in MXF. It is defined by SMPTE 336M.

Description: Key Length Value coding is the lowest level coding used in MXF. Each and every element, property, set, and "thing" in MXF is KLV coded in one way or another. Figure 3.14 shows the structure of a KLV key. It is composed of 16 bytes and should be treated as a dumb number.

It is important to note that when an MXF parser is in "KLV context"—i.e., it is expecting a KLV key—there are times when byte 9 will not have the value $0D_h$. This is because the defined key may well be the definition of a private KLV triplet. Figure 3.15 shows an example of a private KLV triplet being inserted between two known MXF triplets.

The private KLV triplet allows companies and organizations who have registered their own number spaces with SMPTE to be able to define structure (sets and groups) as well as individual

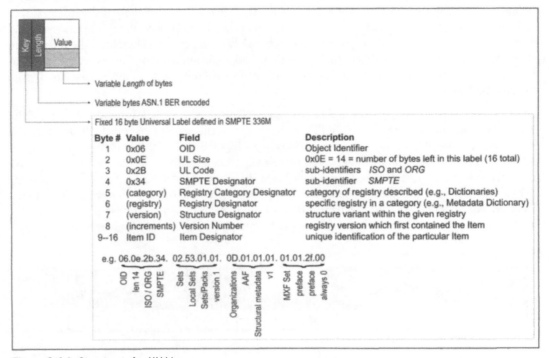

Figure 3.14 Structure of a KLV key

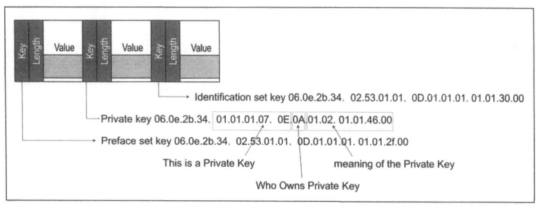

Figure 3.15 Private KLV triplets

KLV properties. Only two of the set coding schemes defined in SMPTE 336M are used in the MXF specification—local sets, and defined- (fixed-) length packs.

Local set coding replaces 16-byte keys with 2-byte tags to reduce the amount of space required to create a KLV triplet. In MXF, 2-byte length values are used in local set coding in addition to the 2-byte tag values. On the plus side, this is efficient in terms of storage space and CPU processing; however, it limits the size of properties which may be local set coded to 65535 bytes. Figure 3.16 shows local set coding as used in MXF.

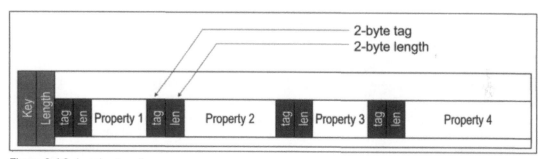

Figure 3.16 Local set coding

In a set, the order of properties is not defined, and each property has a length definition to allow a KLV parser to skip unknown elements. A pack structure, however, requires all the elements to be in a defined order, and in addition, a fixed-length pack does not signal the pre-known length of each individual property. This structure is used to contain the properties that describe partition metadata.

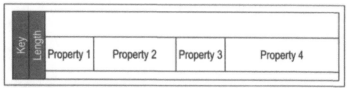

Figure 3.17 Fixed-length pack coding

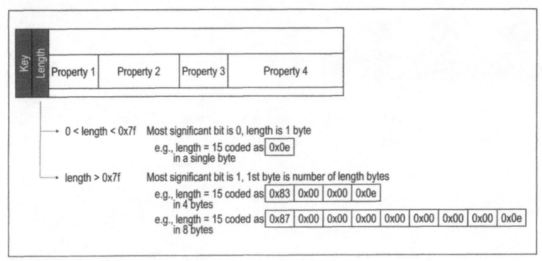

Figure 3.18 BER-length coding

MXF needs the flexibility to create KLV triplets that contain value fields of a few bytes as well as value fields of billions of bytes. The length field of the KLV triplet needs to be able to cope with these two extremes. For this reason, the length field is ASN.1 BER encoded as shown in Figure 3.18.

Locators

Definition: Locators are a property of the generic descriptor to hint at the location of external essence.

Description: Why are locators a hint rather than the knowledge of where the external essence file is? It is likely that once the information is written into the MXF file, the location of the external essence may move without the original referencing MXF file being updated. An MXF decoder should search for the essence in the order that the locators are placed into the array. The order of the locators is important.

There are two different types of Locator—a Network Locator that may be a URN or a URI, or a Text Locator, which is a text string intended for humans to read and act on. Examples of Network Locators are:

URL file://
A URL starting with file:// is treated as a fully qualified file path in accordance with RFC1738. If an MXF application supports external essence, it must support the file:// protocol and all reserved characters must be escaped—e.g., the space character ' ' is escaped to '%20.'

URL ftp://
A URL starting with ftp:// is treated as an external file available via the ftp protocol in accordance with RFC1738. The support for ftp:// is optional.

URIs

If a Network Locator string does not match any known URL protocol, then it is treated as a file path relative to the MXF file that contains the Locator. These relative URIs (RFC2396) must be supported by MXF applications supporting external essence.

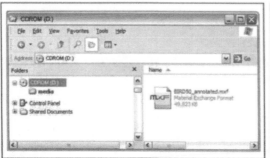

Figure 3.19 MXF file on a pressed CD-ROM

Figure 3.20 External essence files for Figure 3.19

Example

A demo CD is pressed which has a small MXF file containing metadata and has external metadata in a sub-folder as shown in Figure 3.19.

The video locators for the MXF file in Figure 3.19 would be like this:

Network Locator 1   media/Bird50_annotated.m2v

Network Locator 2   ftp://some.url.com/testfiles/Bird50_annotated.m2v

Text Locator 3   video essence file moved from CD-ROM sub-folder "media"

Note that the intention of the TextLocator is to present the text string to the user so that it might be helpful to the operator or the user. The audio Locators for the MXF file in Figure 3.20 would be like this:

Network Locator 1: media/Bird50_annotated.wav

Network Locator 2: ftp://some.url.com/testfiles/Bird50_annotated.wav

Text Locator 3:   audio essence file moved from CD-ROM sub-folder "media"

The media sub-folder is shown in Figure 3.20.

Here are some well-formed Network Locators:

absolute file path as a URL	file:///home/bruce/mxf/mxfa007c.mxf
escaped file path as a URI	file%20name%20with%20spaces.m2v
relative file path as a URI	mxfa007c.mxf
relative file path as a URI	../mxfa007c.mxf

Here are some bad Network Locators; they are all illegal:

relative file path as a URL is invalid—should be URI	file://mxfa007c.mxf
non-escaped file path as a URI	file name with spaces.m2v
absolute file path as a URI is invalid—should be URL	/home/bruce/mxf/mxfa007c.mxf

Material Package

Definition: The material package defines the *output timeline* of the MXF file. It synchronizes the stored essence.

Description: The material package is defined in SMPTE 377M. It corresponds to the *MasterMob* in AAF. Like all packages, the material package is a collection of tracks. Each of the essence tracks in the material package references a track in a top-level file package that, in turn, describes stored essence. The material package may also contain descriptive metadata tracks. These describe the essence "played out" by an application that "plays" the material package.

The precise relationship between the material package and the top-level file packages is governed by the operational pattern of the file. The precise choice of operational pattern is application specific, although there are rules laid down in the MXF File Format Specification mandating that the file must be described by the simplest operational pattern that can describe the file. The way in which the relationship is implemented is described in the Source Reference Chain section of this chapter.

There must be at least one timecode track in the material package that is continuous. Accordingly there may be other timecode tracks present in the material package, but their precise use is application specific.

Since the publication of SMPTE 377M-2004, a ZDD issue has arisen where there is common practice in the AAF community. Track number(s) within a material package should be assigned in accordance with the AAF Edit Protocol specification. TrackNumber is the *output channel number* that the track should be routed to when "played." Typically, for each kind of essence data definition within the material package, TrackNumber starts at 1 and counts up.

For example, in the case of a material package with one video track and two audio tracks, the TrackNumbers would be 1, 1, 2 respectively.

The material package can contain descriptive metadata (DM); however, it is the choice of the application whether there is:

a) A reference created from the DM Track in the material package to the DM Track in the file package.

b) A copy of the file package's DM is placed in the material package.

There are occasions when the material package is not the PrimaryPackage in the file. The OP-Atom specification effectively "demotes" the importance of the material package because this specialized operational pattern is primarily for content storage and not for content synchronization. The

Preface::PrimaryPackage property determines which package should be the primary package to be played out by a play command given to an MXF decoder.

MXF Encoder & Decoder

Definition:

MXF encoder: A device that creates or modifies an MXF file.

MXF decoder: A device that decodes, parses, reads, or plays an MXF file.

Description: The concept of MXF encoders and MXF decoders was useful in describing the desired semantics of the MXF specification. It is a much more useful concept, however, to application writers and equipment developers. MXF is agnostic of essence type, and compression type, and metadata scheme. This forces developers to write applications that separate the handling and synchronization of the essence at the system level from the low-level decoding and pixels handling.

Why is this important? As TV, film, and multimedia production moves increasingly toward file-based methodologies and workflows, the users of the content don't want to know whether the video was MPEG, uncompressed, or compressed. The creative process of telling the story and setting the mood should be independent of technical storage format used for the individual essence elements.

MXF provides the tools for managing the synchronization of the different essence components without needing to know how they are coded. An MXF encoder describes the type of essence using file descriptors and describes the synchronization with the different tracks in the material package(s) of the file. An MXF decoder selects the desired material package, then follows the source reference chain until it discovers the synchronization of the essence described in one of the top-level file packages.

MXF allows different language versions of a creation to exist in a single file. An MXF encoder will store the audio samples for each of the different languages in the file as different top-level file packages. The MXF encoder will create a material package for each of the different language variants that will reference the video track and the appropriate audio tracks for that language. An MXF decoder will select the appropriate material package and will follow the source reference chain until it can find which video samples are synchronized with which audio samples for a given language.

MXF provides a descriptive metadata plugin. This allows applications to be written that can handle descriptive metadata synchronized along the essence timeline. An MXF encoder application can, itself, have plugins that define the metadata properties and relationships (e.g., via XML). This allows MXF modification applications to manage metadata without explicitly knowing the syntax of each and every property in all MXF files at the time the MXF modification application was written. MXF decoders are able to parse files even if they do not understand the KLV triplets that wrap the descriptive metadata properties. The application is able to determine the synchronization with the essence and to give information about where information may be found about the descriptive metadata by inspecting the KLV keys and classifying them according to the SMPTE classifications (SMPTE registered, public, private, experimental). Applications can also be written that use XML to describe new metadata schemes; these are loaded into the application at run-time, rather than compiled into the application at the time it is written. This allows MXF decoder applications to be "enlightened" as to the meaning of the descriptive metadata without the application having to be rewritten.

MXF provides a separation between how the file is stored and what the file is intended to represent. An MXF encoder may take a simple OP1a file that synchronizes a video track and an audio track, and it may choose to store it in a number of physical forms:

- Frame wrapped with no partitions for simplistic "tape replacement" functionality;

- Clip wrapped with no partitions for simple NLE functionality;

- Essence stored in external OP-Atom files for simple NLE functionality;

- Frame wrapped with 1 partition per frame for fault tolerance in lossy transmission environments;

- Frame wrapped with stuffing to create constant bitrate streams for easy indexing; and

- Video internal to the file, but audio external to the file for easy replacement of audio tracks.

An MXF decoder instructed to play back the file would exhibit no difference between any of these physical storage mechanisms. The MXF structural metadata instructs the decoder how to synchronize the different essence streams during playback. The actual physical arrangement of the bytes should make no difference to the decoder.

Operational Patterns

Definition:

> Generalized operational pattern: a constraint on the functionality of MXF defined in SMPTE 377M.

> Specialized operational pattern: a constraint on the functionality of MXF to achieve a specific purpose.

Description: MXF is a toolkit of functionality designed to do a number of tasks in the broadcast, film, and media worlds. In order to achieve interoperability and give implementers the chance to build equipment at a reasonable cost, operational patterns were created to constrain the functionality of MXF. Chapter 4 in this book is entirely dedicated to operational patterns, so a reference summary will be given here. The grid below shows the matrix of generalized operational patterns.

Generalized operational patterns constrain the relationship between the material package and the top-level file packages. Traveling to the right or downwards in the matrix implies more random access and more sophistication in both the MXF encoder and the MXF decoder.

Note that a generalized operation pattern does not restrict the essence to being internal or external, nor does it restrict the interleaving to being frame wrapped (and hence probably streamable) or clip wrapped (and hence probably not streamable). Generalized operational patterns are

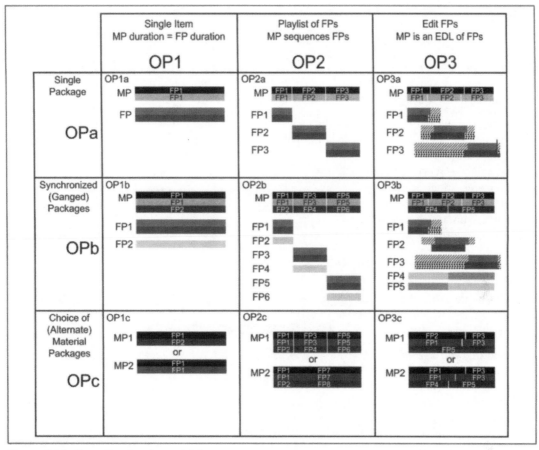

Figure 3.21 Operational pattern matrix

intended to limit the functionality of MXF to broad classes of applications rather than specific applications.

Specialized operational patterns are designed to restrict MXF to a specialized set of operational conditions. They are not the same as an application specification. Specialized operational patterns restrict the functionality to a specialized class of applications. At the time of publication of this book, only one specialized operational pattern has been specified. This is operational pattern Atom—SMPTE 390M.

An OP-Atom file is essentially a mono-essence file intended as an essence container for non-linear editing systems. The Primary Package property of the Preface Set references the top-level file package. The essence is always inside the OP-Atom file, and even if the essence is intrinsically interleaved (such as DV), then there will only be a single track associated with a single descriptor in the file package. OP-Atom files always have complete index tables and are intended for applications where capture (digitization or recording) of the file is completed before the file is used.

Origin

Definition: The property of a track that identifies its zero point in time.

Description: The origin of a track is a property that makes it easy for an MXF application to move the relative synchronization of one track against another. Figure 3.22 below shows a video track and an audio track that both have an origin of zero.

The video and the audio described by the picture track and the sound track are synchronized. Now imagine that extra material is ingested (digitized, captured) at the start of the stored audio essence.

The total duration of the stored audio essence is now greater than the stored video essence. Moreover, the synchronized audio sample is no longer at the start of the stored essence. We need to update the metadata in order to describe this state of affairs, which is shown in Figure 3.23.

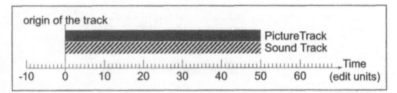

Figure 3.22 Tracks with zero origin

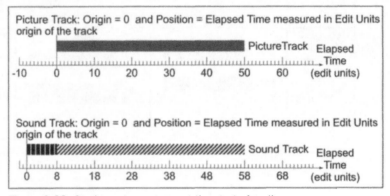

Figure 3.23 Storing extra essence at the start of a clip

It is clear that the elapsed time along the timeline from the start of the stored essence—i.e., the position—is no longer the correct parameter to describe the synchronization point. We need to define an offset to make this correct. This offset is the origin property of the track and corresponds to the position of the synchronization point when Origin is zero. In Figure 3.23, the value of Origin should be +8 in order to restore synchronization. This is shown in Figure 3.24 where material package Origins are always zero.

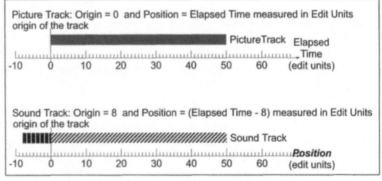

Figure 3.24 Restoring synchronization with origin

Package

Definition: A collection of synchronized tracks.

Description: A package is a collection of synchronized tracks. Each track may have a different EditRate and maybe even different durations. The package groups the tracks together, synchronizes them and identifies them with a UMID. MXF has three different sorts of packages:

- **Material Package** This package synchronizes the output "played" by an MXF player. Tracks in the material package reference store content in the top-level file packages.

- **Top-Level File Package** This package describes the content actually stored in the file (or that is externally referenced by it). MXF encoders should create one track for each of the stored essence elements. The tracks within the top-level file package describe the timing of the essence (via origin, duration, and edit rate). The relationship between the tracks in the package describe the synchronization of the different stored elements.

- **Lower-Level Source Packages** In MXF, the lower-level source packages describe the derivation of the essence stored in the file. This allows an MXF file to keep within it the history of where the essence came from. No stored essence is referenced at this level.

The precise relationship between the material package and the top-level file package(s) is described by the operational pattern. The referencing of one track by another is called the *source reference chain*, both of which are described elsewhere in this chapter.

The *Preface* of the MXF File contains an optional property called *PrimaryPackage*. The precise use of this property can be governed by a specialized operational pattern as explained at the end of the material package section of this chapter. By convention, this property identifies the package with the UMID used to identify this file. This is also the package that is "played" when an application chooses to play the file. If this optional property is omitted, the material package is assumed.

Partition

Definition: The smallest unit of an MXF file that can be individually parsed and decoded.

Description: A partition is an MXF physical structure that allows the file to be chopped up into manageable parts. Partitions can be inserted for error recovery purposes; they can be inserted to separate different generic containers within the file; they can be inserted to simplify processing of index tables; they can be inserted to contain generic data that is not a continuous stream—e.g., subtitles.

Each MXF file must always contain a header partition. This is the first partition in the file and its presence in the first 64kByte of a file indicates that the file is an MXF file. Usually, the Partition-Pack that starts the header partition will be the first bytes in the file, but sometimes the file may contain a *run-in*. In this case the start of the header partition must be searched for.

Nearly all MXF files will contain a *footer* partition. This partition is used to close the file and indicate that it had been successfully written to disc/tape/storage. In the middle of the file, the partitions are called *body partitions* and are used, for example, to divide up the different essence groups that are stored in the generic containers.

The rules of MXF state that each generic container in an MXF file has to be in its own partition. This means that an OP1a file can be contained in a single partition. An OP1b file which, by definition, has at least two file packages and at least two generic containers must therefore have at least two partitions.

A partition starts with the PartitionPack. This physical structure contains properties about the contents of the partition, but is not actually part of the header metadata. The properties are given in Figure 3.25.

The HeaderByteCount and IndexByteCount properties are given to allow MXF decoders to rapidly detect (and skip if necessary) any header metadata or index table segment that may be in the partition. The BodySID and IndexSID are described more fully in the SIDs section of this chapter. The BodyOffset property is used for essence parsing and indexing. It is a number that defines how many bytes have so far been written into the file for this essence container. This is important because an MXF file may contain several essence containers that are multiplexed together, each of which has a number of interleaved essence elements. Tracking the BodyOffset for each of the essence containers allows an MXF file to be re-multiplexed to optimize physical storage, without having to modify any of the header metadata or index tables. The OperationalPattern and EssenceContainer batch are fast look-up mechanisms intended to allow MXF parsers and decoder applications to determine the complexity of the file, and what it contains, without having to parse the entire header metadata.

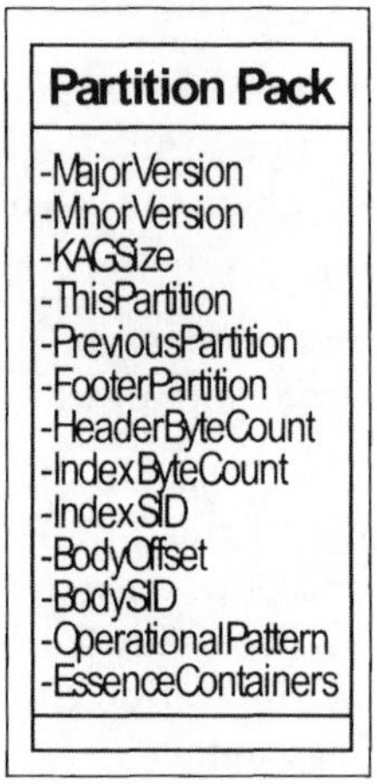

Partition Pack

- MajorVersion
- MinorVersion
- KAGSize
- ThisPartition
- PreviousPartition
- FooterPartition
- HeaderByteCount
- IndexByteCount
- IndexSID
- BodyOffset
- BodySID
- OperationalPattern
- EssenceContainers

Figure 3.25 The Partition Pack

After the Partition Pack, there may be a fill KLV and then there will be the Primer Pack that is a lookup table for all the local set tags used in the file. The Preface Set follows the Primer Pack and then all the other sets of the header metadata follow in no particular order. Current wisdom states that it is good practice to only put one "thing" in a partition. SMPTE 377M says that you can have one or more index table segments in a partition, followed by generic container data. In practice it is best to have header metadata **or** index table segments **or** generic container data in a partition. In the case of the Generic Data Partition (described in Chapter 10), no index table segment is permitted. These preferred arrangements are shown pictorially in Figure 3.26.

There are many properties of the header metadata and of the PartitionPack that require knowledge of the end of the file. The PartitionPack::FooterPartition is one such property and gives the byte offset of the footer partition relative to the header partition (i.e., it cannot be filled in until the position of the footer partition is known). In an application such as an MXF camera, it is impossible to know what value to put in these properties until the file is closed; so what do we do?

MXF provides signaling for an *open partition* and a *closed partition* in the KLV key of the Partition Pack. "Open" means that the position of the footer is not known and that many properties of the

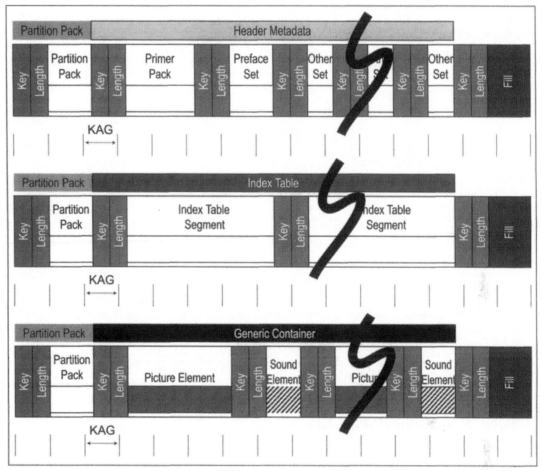

Figure 3.26 Order of items in a partition

header metadata are default values or guesses or just plain wrong. "Closed" means that the file has been correctly closed and all the MXF information has been correctly filled in.

There is an extra complication. There are devices that know how to make MXF files, but may not be able to correctly fill in all the information, even when the file is closed. Consider an MPEG Transport Stream demultiplexer. It is able to look at the MPEG Transport Stream metadata and is able to demultiplex the streams into valid MXF generic containers with video and audio elements. It may, however, encounter a private data stream. Although many of the properties of the stream are known, it is not possible to fill in an MXF File Descriptor unless the precise nature of the stream is known. Discarding the stream is not a practical proposition, so MXF provides another categorization of partition known as *Complete* or *Incomplete*.

A Complete Partition is one in which all the required properties of the header metadata were known and completed when the file was written. The partition may be open (i.e., we didn't know where the footer partition was) or it may also be closed (i.e., the file-write operation is completed and the footer partition position is known—if it exists).

An Incomplete Partition is one in which some of the required properties of the header metadata could not be filled in. It may be that the *duration* property could not be filled in because an essence parser was not available when the file was written. It may be that there are properties of the file descriptor that could not be completed.

Files are said to be *errored* if required metadata properties are incorrect or missing. In order to preserve some distinction between "incomplete" files and errored files, "best effort" properties are identified in the MXF File Format Specification (377M). These are the only properties that are allowed to have distinguished values to indicate an Incomplete Partition. These distinguished values have been specially chosen so that they would never occur in a Closed/Complete MXF file (e.g., a negative length value (-1) used to signal an (unknown) length value). Any other MXF required property that is not correctly filled in will result in an errored file. The signaling of Closed/Complete/Open/Incomplete is done in the KLV key of the partition pack. Errored files are not defined by SMPTE 377M.

In order to find the correct metadata in a file, an MXF decoder must search for a closed and complete partition. Most MXF files will have this in the footer or the header. The footer is the most likely place to find the correct metadata because it is usually the first chance an MXF encoder has to store the correct values of all the durations. Well-behaved MXF encoders will correctly fill in the footer so that it is closed and complete and then proceed to go back in the file and fill in the header metadata in all the other partitions in the file, starting with the header partition.

References—Strong, Weak, Global

Definition: A strong reference is a one-to-one relationship implying ownership. A weak reference is a many-to-one reference (e.g., a lookup in a table). An external reference is one that cannot be resolved within the MXF file.

Description: There are many ways in which relationships between data can be written down. Let's consider a very simple example: We want to create some data about a `person`, and we need to represent their address. As a first attempt, we give the `person` some properties called `street`, `city`, and `country`. Unfortunately, this doesn't capture the fact that these properties encapsulate the concept of an `address`. As a second attempt, we create a property called `address`, which itself has a `street`, `city` and `country`. This can be written down in several ways as shown in Figure 3.27

The first representation uses UML (Universal Modeling Language). It shows a class called `person` that aggregates (the symbol ◇——) a class called `address`. The `address` class has properties called `street`, `city`, and `country`. The numeral "1" on the aggregation symbol indicates that there is one and only one class called `address` that is aggregated by the `person` class. This is a strong reference from the person class to the address class. This strong reference also indicates ownership of the address class.

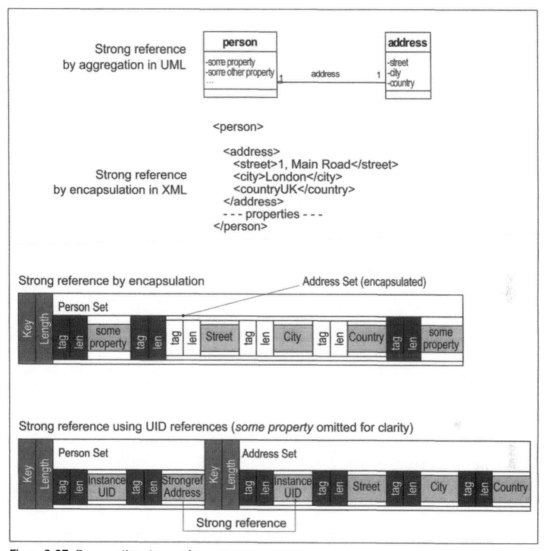

Figure 3.27 Representing strong references

The second representation is in XML. It shows an XML element called `person` that has an XML element, which is a complex type, called `address`. The `address` element is encapsulated (and thus owned) by the XML element called `person`. This is equivalent to the UML example above.

The next example shows a possible equivalent encapsulated structure implemented in KLV. The outer KLV is for the Person Set. The first tag-length is for the "some property" element. The next tag-length should encapsulate the entire Address Set except that **this structure is not allowed in MXF.**

MXF does not allow encapsulation (embedding) of one KLV set in another set, nor one tag-length value in another. In order to implement the Strong Reference in MXF, an Instance UID is generated in the person set and this is referenced by the Strongref Address, as shown in the last example in Figure 3.27.

In real life, however, a person may have more than one address, and, in addition, each address may have more than one person associated with it. One way to solve this would be to create a list of persons and a list of addresses. Each person would have a weak reference into the list of addresses. The reference is *weak* because there is no ownership associated with it. Finally, there may be a number of addresses that are well known and are resolved by looking in some external address book.

So how does this relate to MXF? The *Preface* is the root to all the other sets in an MXF file. The complete strong reference chain can be found by starting here. The preface contains a strong reference to the EssenceContainerData that, in turn, contains a strong reference to each of the packages. Because a strong reference is a one-to-one relationship implying ownership, this gives a strong indication as to how the structure may be represented in languages such as XML.

Examples of weak references within MXF are within Descriptive Metadata Scheme 1; for example, Participants of a scene have weak references into Organizations (to which they belong). It is not necessary for the Organization set to be within the same framework as the Participant set. This gives it a weak reference (global) quality—i.e., resolving the reference may involve looking outside the framework or even outside the file—for example, into an external database.

There is another sort of weak reference used in MXF—the Data Definition. This can be considered as a weak reference into a defined registry or dictionary. For example, a SourceClip has a property called *DataDefinition*. The value of this property references a dictionary where the property is defined (e.g., SMPTE RP210).

Random Index Pack (RIP)

Definition: The Random Index Pack (RIP) is a partition lookup table found at the end of an MXF File.

Description: The Random Index Pack provides a quick and easy method to find all the body partitions in an MXF file. Its structure is shown in Figure 3.28 on the right.

All the body partitions are listed in the RIP if it is present. To determine that it is there, the last 4 bytes of the MXF file are read, This is the offset backwards into the file where the random index pack key will be found. If it is not found at this location then the file does not contain an RIP.

The random index pack only lists body partitions (including generic data partitions). If a partition contains only index table segments, then it is not listed in the RIP. Common practice is to place index table segments in a partition just before the content, or just after the content. The complete list of segments can be rapidly built by inspecting the RIP and then reading the partition packs listed, then checking the *PreviousPartition* property of those partition packs. As a reminder, the properties of the partition pack have the following meaning:

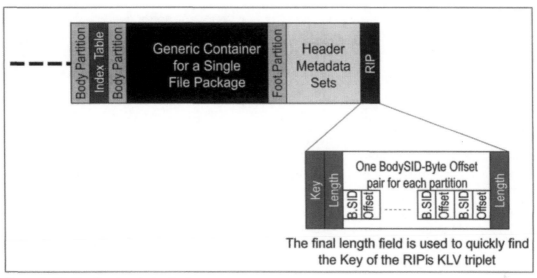

Figure 3.28 The Random Index Pack

ThisPartition	The absolute byte offset of the start of the partition (assuming no run-in).
PreviousPartition	The number of bytes in the previous partition.

The RIP can be considered as a catalogue of the ThisPartition values for all the partitions with a non-zero BodySID. If there are partitions containing only index table segments, then their Byte Offsets will not appear in the RIP, but must be calculated. If there are no such partitions, then all the values of $ByteOffset_{PartitionN}$ will appear in the RIP.

$BodyOffset_{PartitionN}$	The "ThisPartition" value found in Partition N
$PreviousPartition_{PartitionN}$	The "PreviousPartition" value found in Partition N

$$ByteOffset_{bodyPartition(N-1)} = ByteOffset_{PartitionN} - PreviousPartition_{PartitionN}$$

If this $ByteOffset_{bodyPartition(N-1)}$ does not appear on the RIP, then it does not contain any body essence and is either a header metadata repetition or an index table partition.

All these offsets are absolute offsets measured from the end of the run-in (usually the beginning of the file) and are not the same as the BodyOffset property described in the Partition section of this chapter.

Run-In

Definition: The run-in is the portion of the file before the KLV of the header partition pack.

Description: Most MXF files start with the partition pack of the header partition. Sometimes, however, an MXF file must be disguised to look like a different file type. This can be done through the use of the run-in—a sequence of up to 65536 bytes at the front of the file that precedes the first partition pack. This means that all MXF files start at the first byte of the first partition pack in the file. The run-in is not considered to be part of the MXF file and is ignored.

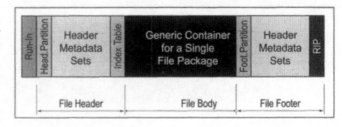

Figure 3.29 Position of the run-in

Figure 3.29 shows the position of the run-in in the file. The use of the run-in is restricted to specialized MXF operational patterns. This means you cannot label a file as, for example, OP1a, and still use a run-in.

There is no requirement in MXF for a decoder that is limited to operational patterns as defined in SMPTE 377M to support the run-in (see Chapter 4 for descriptions of OP1a through to OP3c). Its use should be limited to applications where the MXF decoder behavior can be predicted.

Summary of Run-In Restrictions

- Only to be used in specialized operational patterns

- Shall not contain the first 11 bytes of the Partition Pack key (06.0e.2b.34)

Example:

Camouflaging an MXF audio file as a WAV file to allow native WAV editors to open MXF files for backwards compatibility. More details of WAV and chunks are given in the audio Chapter 6.

The resultant physical structure of the file looks like this:

```
<fmt chunk>  <other chunks>  <private chunk [MXF HEADER]> <data
chunk  NNNNNNNNNNN>
```

All the initial chunks form part of the run-in. The private data chunk is used to camouflage the MXF header, and the data chunk contains the actual data samples.

Note that the last few bytes of the MXF header have to be carefully constructed to be able to hide the initial bytes of the data chunk header. A special KLV triplet would be required with the following properties:

Key   16-byte identifier

Length   BER-coded length value = sizeof(sample data) + sizeof(data chunk header)

Value   <data chunk header>

Sample data

Remember—this can only be used as part of a specialized operational pattern! Don't expect it to work with all the decoders out there in the wild.

Sets, Items (Properties)

Definition: A set is an unordered collection of MXF items (properties).

Description: MXF uses SMPTE 336M local set coding to group together properties within a set. The individual properties are referred to as *items* within the MXF suite of documents, but in most cases people refer to them today as properties. All KLV coded local sets in MXF use 2 bytes for the tag and 2 bytes for the length.

The MXF File Format Specification does not actually define the MXF data model; however, the KLV set structure is intended to be a physical representation of an MXF class instance. The MXF data model is not specifically written down in SMPTE 377M; however it was derived from the AAF data model. There is more information on this in Chapter 13.

There are several issues that are important to know about MXF KLV sets:

- Properties in MXF sets are unordered.

- Optional properties need not appear in a set.

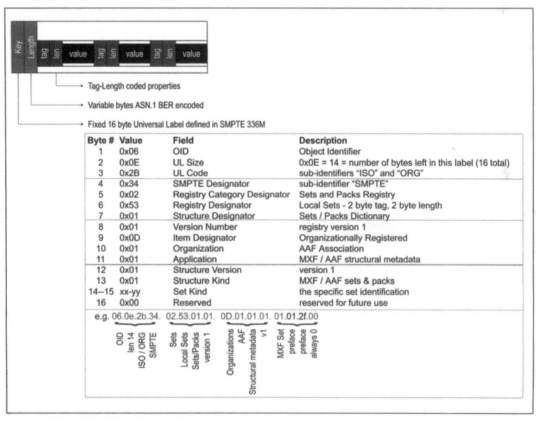

Figure 3.30 MXF-defined local set key structure

- Best-effort properties should appear in a set and are either set to the required value or are set to their distinguished value.

- The tags of a local set are shorthand for the full UL. The mapping for each file is defined in the Primer Pack of that file.

- The local set tags of a header metadata set must appear in the primer pack.

- The local set tags of an index table segment do not appear in the primer pack.

An MXF-defined local set will have a key that corresponds to the structure defined in SMPTE 336M, and the definitions in SMPTE 377M. This is shown in Figure 3.30 on the previous page.

When new set structures are added to MXF, they may be formed in the same way, or they may be registered in the class 13, class 14, or class 15 number space. This means that KLV parsers should not rely on the fact that all local set keys are formed in the same way as Figure 3.30. Figure 3.31 below shows a privately registered local set (class 14) and an experimental local set (class 15).

It can be seen from Figure 3.31 that companies registering their own number space with SMPTE have complete freedom in setting bytes 11 trough 16 of their private data area. The only obligation that the company has is to publish the top level hierarchy to SMPTE (i.e., the meaning of byte 11 of the label).

Source Package

Definition: An MXF source package describes stored essence or historical essence.

Description: Source packages are split into two different subclasses—file packages and physical packages. A file package describes essence stored in an MXF file. A physical package describes

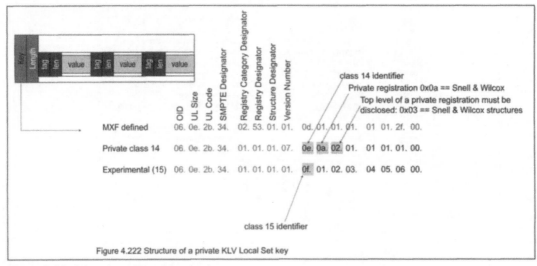

Figure 4.222 Structure of a private KLV Local Set key

Figure 3.31 Privately registered local sets

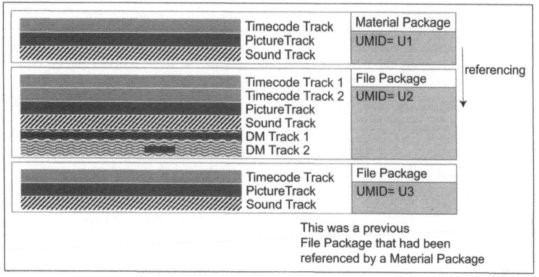

Figure 3.32 An MXF file showing packages and UMIDs

the essence before it entered the MXF domain. Confusingly, if a file were once a Broadcast Wave audio file, it is described using a physical descriptor before it enters the MXF domain. Once the essence has been wrapped in MXF, it is then described using a file descriptor.

In an MXF file, all the top-level source packages in the source reference chain are file packages. In an MXF file, only the top-level source packages reference actual stored essence, all the other source packages, which are lower in the source reference chain, describe the historical derivation of the file. The referencing mechanism is described in the Source Reference Chain section below.

The file descriptor associated with the top-level file package describes the essence stored in the file (more information in the Descriptors section).

The relationship between the material package and the top-level file package is defined by the generalized operational pattern of the file.

MXF applications that modify the essence in a file should create new packages for the modified stored essence. The older packages drop down a level so that what was a top-level file package now becomes a lower-level Source Package. A worked example of this is shown in the partial restore example in the Source Reference Chain section. The relationship between the packages is shown in Figure 3.32.

Source Reference Chain

Definition: The relationship between packages is known as the source reference chain.

Description: MXF allows tracks in one package to reference tracks in other packages—the goal being to allow the full derivation of essence in a file to be stored within the file. The mechanism by which this is achieved is shown in Figure 3.33 on the next page.

The material package is at the top of the chain and synchronizes the stored essence described by the top-level file packages. Each track within the material package has a sequence of SourceClips that reference tracks within lower-level packages. The SourcePackageID property identifies the package UMID and the SourceTrackID property identifies the TrackID within that package.

The StartPosition in the SourceClip describes where in the referenced track the essence starts, and the duration property in the SourceClip describes how much of the referenced track is used. The units of these two properties are defined by the *EditRate* of the track. But which track—the referencing track or the referenced track? There is no requirement that these two edit rates be identical.

It may seem a little strange, but the units are actually those of the referencing track (e.g., material package in Figure 3.33) rather than the track being referenced (e.g., file package in Figure 3.33). Why? Consider the case where there is an MXF essence file being referenced by several MXF files (or AAF files). If the EditRate property of the referenced track were modified, then there would be no requirement to change the UMID, so the file would still be a valid reference target. If the units of the reference were defined by the Edit Rate of the

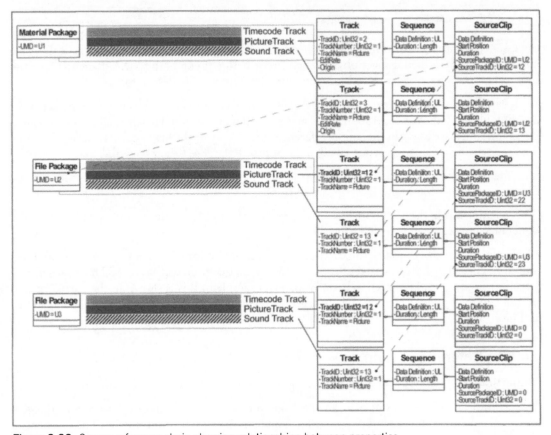

Figure 3.33 Source reference chain showing relationships between properties

target track, then it would mean that all the external MXF files would have to be modified to maintain the validity of the references. This is obviously not a practical way to build a system that allows external references.

The end of the source reference chain is identified when the SourcePackageID has the value 0. This property is shown in Figure 3.33 to be the property defining the package that is the target of the reference of the SourceClip. You can see that the last SourceClips in the chain have this property set to 0.

Consider an MXF file that has been stored in an archive as shown in Figure 3.32 in the lowest-level file package (known as a source package). Now let's perform a partial restore of the central section of the file. *To do this a new material package is formed and a new top-level file package is created, which describes the partially restored essence.* The new material package references the new top-level file package and Figure 3.34 shows the relationship between these new packages and the packages in the archived file.

The tracks in the new top-level file package reference the old material package. This allows the new file to contain the old material package UMID within the source reference chain. Why is this important? It is possible that the old UMID had been used in a database to reference some metadata/information about the archived file. Allowing a material package to appear in the middle of the source reference chain keeps this historical link, which would otherwise be lost, within the file.

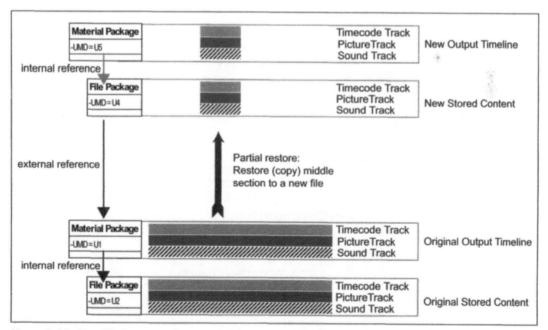

Figure 3.34 Simplified source reference chain when performing a partial restore (no descriptive metadata)

SIDs—BodySID and IndexSID

Definition: A SID is a StreamID—a unique identifier of a physical stream of bytes in an MXF file.

Description: The SIDs in a file are used to identify different streams of data within that file. The scope of a SID is the file, which means that the number space can be reused between different files.

A BodySID identifies essence within the file. Each generic container within an MXF file will have a unique BodySID value. If there are any generic data partitions within the MXF File, then these will have unique BodySIDs, too.

Each indexed generic container will have a unique IndexSID for the index table segments. Within any file, no IndexSID value will be the same as a BodySID value. No two BodySID values will be the same and no two IndexSID values will be the same.

The relationship between a top-level file package UMID, the BodySID, and its IndexSID is given in the EssenceContainerData set as shown in Figure 3.35. The position of the EssenceContainer-Data set within the data model can be seen in Figures 3.5 and 3.7.

Structural Metadata

Definition: The structural metadata relates to the structure and capabilities of an MXF file

Description: All the metadata defined in SMPTE 377M and all the mapping documents and operational pattern documents comprise the structural metadata. All the MXF-defined structural metadata is registered in one of the SMPTE registries. The structural metadata is "machine

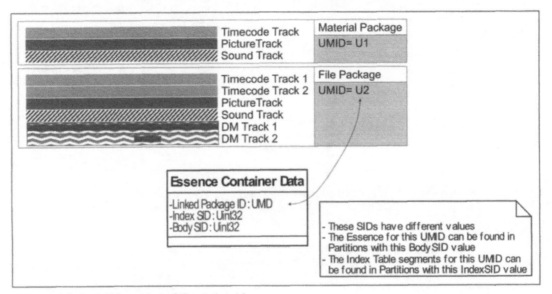

Figure 3.35 BodySID and IndexSID relationship

oriented" and is the first metadata to be found in the file. After the structural metadata, the descriptive metadata will be found.

The structural metadata is expressed in MXF as the relationship between all the various sets. When these relationships are written in a formal way, we end up with the structural part of the MXF data model.

Structural metadata in MXF is local-set coded with 2-byte tags and 2-byte lengths. The 2-byte length field means that each property must fit into a 64kbyte block of data. Future extensions to MXF may include data types that are bigger than this. It is expected that the stream data type will be used to carry this information in the file (see Types section in this chapter).

Time and Synchronization

Definition: Elapsed time within MXF is expressed by a *position* along a *track*.

Description: Timecode has been one of the most significant ways of describing time in the film and television world. It has its drawbacks, however, as a timebase within a file format. In any production, there may be several different values of timecode active at any one time, and so selecting the appropriate timecode becomes a production/post-production decision.

MXF uses a track to indicate the progress of time. Each track has its own timebase, whose units are defined by the track's EditRate property. A track does not itself have a duration property, but the sequence referenced by the track defines the duration of the content on the track.

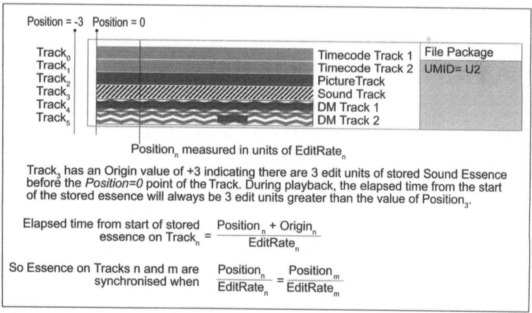

Figure 3.36 Position, Origin, and Edit Rate

The origin property of the track (see Origin above) allows one track to be offset relative to another so that synchronization can be correctly described.

In order for two essence samples to be synchronized, they need to be played out at the same time. This means that the normalized value of position along a track must be the same for both of the essence samples. Why normalized? This is because each track within a package may have a different value of EditRate. The equations are given in Figure 3.36 on the previous page.

Note that this equation applies within a package. See the section on source reference chain for information on how these values relate between packages. There is another example with external essence in Chapter 6.

Timecode

Definition: Timecode is defined by SMPTE 12M. In MXF it is represented in the structural metadata.

Description: MXF is a wrapper format. Its goal with timecode is to be able to correctly describe the timecode that was found in the stored essence, and to create new timecode in the output timeline. The ability to do this implies that there may be multiple timecode tracks in any package. Like any other track, a timecode track has an Origin, an EditRate, and a property that is a strong reference to a component such as a sequence or a SourceClip.

There is only one major restriction placed on timecode within MXF: The material package must have one timecode track that is a) continuous, b) lasts the duration of the material package, and c) has a timecode component referenced directly by the timecode track (not via a sequence).

When creating an MXF file, you cannot guarantee that any of the top-level file packages has linear timecode, so the material package mandates that at least one of the timecode tracks must be linear and continuous. Unfortunately, during standardization, we did not reach any agreement on what the start value should be, and so there is no start value mandated for the material package start code.

The start value is often the subject of a house practice. Setting the start value to 0:0:0:0 is widely regarded as a bad idea. Better values for the start timecode are:

- The same as the start timecode of the top-level file package (unless that is zero)
- 1:0:0:0 i.e., one hour
- 10:0:0:0 i.e., 10 hours

Good practice currently is to set the start timecode to be the same as the captured top-level file package. How is this actually stored? The timecode component set contains the timecode properties for the all MXF timecode tracks. The properties of the timecode component set and the representation of timecode tracks is shown in Figures 3.37 and 3.38 below. Note that the drop frame flag is a special timecode counting mode used for 29.97 frames/second material, which keeps the numeric value of timecode close to the time of day. Setting the drop frame flag to 1 gives a timecode value of 00:01:00:14, 42 frames after timecode 00:00:59:00. If the drop frame flag were 0, the result would be 00:01:00:12.

The timecode values at any given position along a track can be determined mathematically as is shown in Figure 3.38. Discontinuous timecode is represented by simply butting together individual timecode components. Note that a timecode track is always a timeline track, so there can never be any gaps or overlaps between the different timecode components.

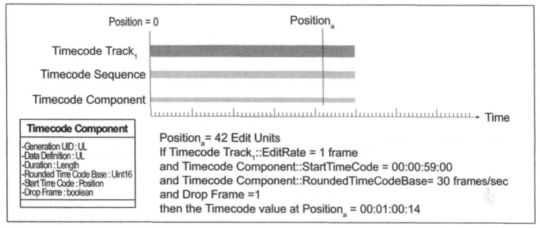

Figure 3.37 The Timecode Component

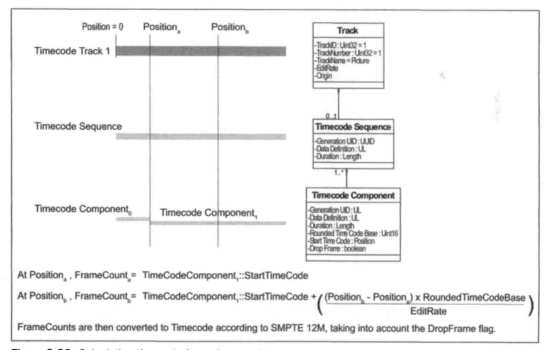

Figure 3.38 Calculating timecode for a given position

Tracks

Definition: A track describes the relationship between essence and time.

Description: Tracks in the material package describe the desired relationship between essence and the output timeline. Tracks in the top-level file package describe the relationship between stored essence and its timeline. Tracks in lower-level file packages describe where essence came from.

There are three different sorts of track in MXF:

- **Timeline Track**—This is used to describe continuous data such as audio essence and video essence. Throughout the entire duration of the track, there shall be no gaps or overlaps in the SourceClips or segments attached to it.

- **Event Track**—This is used to describe data that is time oriented, but discontinuous or "lumpy," such as descriptive metadata. Events on the timeline can be instantaneous (i.e., have no duration), can have gaps, or can overlap.

- **Static Track**—A static track describes data that is not time oriented (e.g., a static image). At present, MXF only uses static tracks for descriptive metadata.

The relationship between tracks in different packages is described by the source reference chain. The relationship between tracks and the essence they describe is given by the index tables and the TrackNumber property. As described in the section in this chapter on Essence, the TrackNumber

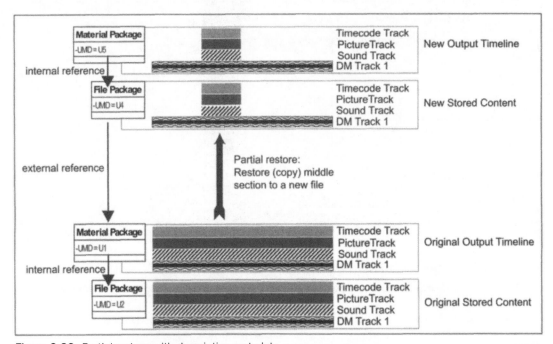

Figure 3.39 Partial restore with descriptive metadata

property of a top-level file package is numerically the same as the last 4 bytes of the KLV key used to wrap the essence within the file. This provides a linking mechanism that binds the header metadata to the stored essence.

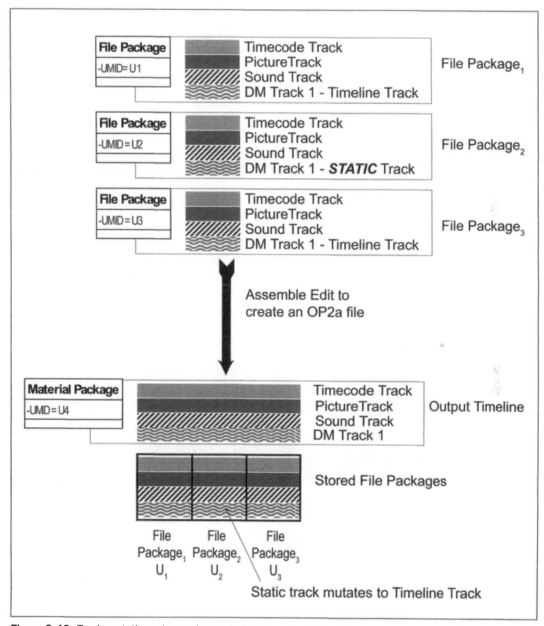

Figure 3.40 Track mutation when using metadata on a static timeline

Figure 3.34, which shows the source reference chain when performing a partial restore, displays only timeline tracks. The situation becomes a little more complicated when we consider the same situation with event tracks and static tracks that reference descriptive metadata.

The first problem to overcome is to decide which metadata should be retrieved from the partial restore. If the "in" point falls in the middle of a descriptive metadata event, should a new event be created which has half the duration? Is this a meaningful thing to do? The answer is sometimes yes, sometimes no—it depends on the metadata.

Likewise, there may be metadata on the timeline that is vital for the understanding of the scheme as a whole, but does not technically fall in the window of the partially restored content. The safest thing to do, for an application that does not "understand" the metadata, is for the partial restore to retrieve all the descriptive metadata from the entire timeline This is shown in Figure 3.39 (modified from Figure 3.34) on page 86.

Static descriptive metadata tracks bring their own set of interesting features. Consider filming at a location where there is a single production crew creating the audiovisual content. If you wanted to put some descriptive metadata into the file to capture the producer's name, it would seem reasonable to do this with a static track. All the content being shot on all the files is by the same crew, so the descriptive metadata is static for each of the takes—it does not vary with time.

Now what happens when that content is used as part of a larger production that was created with multiple crews? If we butt-edit two pieces of material together, as shown in Figure 3.40, we see that the descriptive metadata in the new file is no longer static, but changes over the timeline. This requires us to use a timeline track or an event track to represent the metadata. This process of changing the track type when processing an MXF file is known as *track mutation*.

Types

Definition: A data type defines the range of values a property may take and how it behaves (e.g., integer, boolean, UMID, etc).

Description: There are many data types used in MXF. The table below lists those commonly used, as well as information about the type.

Simple Types	
Data Type	Description
BER Length	A length value in bytes used to code a KLV triplet. BER (Basic Encoding Rules) length coding is described in the KLV & BER section of this chapter.
Boolean	1-byte true/false value. zero == FALSE, non-zero == TRUE For compatibility with older AAF SDK implementations MXF encoders should use the value 01_h for TRUE.
Int8	Signed 8-bit integer.
Int16	Signed 16-bit integer.
Int32	Signed 32-bit integer.

Simple Types	
Data Type	**Description**
Int64	Signed 64-bit integer.
Length	The Int64 value of a duration measured in edit units. Duration is the property and "length" is the data type. Negative values of this data type are reserved for indicating distinguished values and must never be used to indicate valid lengths.
Package ID	A UMID to uniquely identify a package or a zero value used to terminate a reference chain.
Position	The Int64 value used to locate a specific point along a track. Since properties of type position are relative to a chosen zero point, negative values may occur.
StrongRef	One-to-one relationship between sets and implemented in MXF with UUIDs. Strong references are typed which means that the definition identifies the kind of set that is the target of the reference.
UInt8	Unsigned 8-bit integer.
UInt16	Unsigned 16-bit integer.
UInt32	Unsigned 32-bit integer.
UInt64	Unsigned 64-bit integer.
UL	Universal label (SMPTE 298M). Several properties are of type UL, and they may be simple labels, or labels used as a weak or global reference. (See references section in this chapter.)
UMID	Unique material ID (SMPTE 330M). The UMID data type is used to identify packages. Only 32 byte basic UMIDs are used for this purpose.
UUID	Universally unique identifier according to ISO 11578.
Version Type	A Uint16 version number. The number is created from (uint8) major and (uint8) minor version numbers: Version_number= major_version*256 + minor_version.
WeakRef	Many-to-one relationship between sets implemented in MXF with UUIDs. Weak references are typed which means that the definition identifies the kind of set that is the target of the reference.
Compound Types	
Data Type	**Description**

Array	A compound type with multiple individual, ordered elements.
	The structure is:
	
	``
	Uint32 element_count
	Uint32 element_size
	        element1
	        element2
	        ...
	        element(element_count)
	``
	
	The data type of each element is defined by the array type. and the size of each element is fixed. There are some arrays in SMPTE 377M that have an element_count value written into the specification. It is very dangerous for MXF decoders to assume that value will be used in the actual file. There may be backwards-compatible extensions to MXF where the number might be different. It is the number found in the file that should always be used.

TYPES

Simple Types	
Data Type	Description
Batch	A batch is constructed in an identical fashion to an array. The only difference is that the order of the elements has no significance.
DataStream	A string of data or metadata elements. The type of data or metadata element and the length of the string are defined elsewhere.
Rational	A pair of Int32 values where the first is the numerator and the second is the denominator; e.g., for an aspect ratio of 4:3, the number found in the stream would appear as: `00.00.00.04.00.00.00.03`
Strings	Strings are created from individual characters defined either as ISO 7-bit characters (as used in SMPTE RP 210) requiring 1 byte per character, or as unicode UTF-16 characters requiring 2 bytes per character. In the case of UTF-16 characters expressing ISO 7-bit characters, an inspection of every byte will show each 2-byte pair as a null byte and a character byte. Byte order is specified as fixed big endian. The number of bytes allocated to this string is given by the KLV encoding. MXF encoders may wish to allocate space so that strings in metadata may be modified "in place." For example, the length field of the KLV may be set to 256, yet the string inside it may be very short and terminated by a zero valued byte/word.

Timestamp	A time and date item according to the Gregorian calendar constructed as:
	`Int16  Year`
	`UInt8  Month`
	`UInt8  Day`
	`UInt8  Hour`
	`UInt8  Minute`
	`UInt8  Second`
	`UInt8  ((mSec portion)/4)`
	
	A value of "0" for each and every field identifies a timestamp value of "unknown." This value should not be used unless unavoidable.

UTF-16	Unicode characters coded with 16-bits; i.e., 2-byte characters.
Compound Types	
Data Type	Description

ProductVersion	Constructed as follows (note that this differs from SMPTE 377M-2004 and agrees with the corrigenda text being proposed to SMPTE):
	
	`UInt16 major version number`
	`UInt16 minor version number`
	`UInt16 tertiary version number`
	`UInt16 patch version number`
	`UInt16 release version number`
	
	These describe the version of the tool that created or modified the file. The specific use of the first four values shall be defined by the tool. The "release" number is enumerated as follows:
	
	`0 = Unknown version`
	`1 = Released version`
	`2 = Development version`
	`3 = Released version with patches`
	`4 = Pre-release beta version`
	`5 = Private version not intended for general release.`

Simple Types	
Data Type	**Description**
Stream	The stream data type is identified by a StreamID, and is carried in MXF using the generic data partition (see Chapter 10). Stream data types are typically bulky and unable to fit within the 64k limit imposed by the MXF 2-byte tag and 2-byte-length coding.

Table 3.1 Data types used in MXF

Universal Labels, Registries, and Registers

Definition: The syntax and structure of Universal Labels are defined by SMPTE 298M. A registry is the organization responsible for registered information. A register is the container holding the registered information.

Description: Having made those reasonable formal definitions, the actual terminology used in common parlance is actually considerably looser. A universal label in MXF terms is a 16-byte number formed according to SMPTE 298M. Some ULs are used as KLV keys; others are used as properties (registered metadata); and others are used as values for properties. The important thing is that they are all registered.

Registered means that the number space is controlled and all numbers have been through some SMPTE process to control them. Figure 3.41 demonstrates the different classes of UL. Note that the public ones often have to go through a standardization committee "due process" before they can appear in the register. Private ones (class 14) are purchased in blocks by organizations, and class 15 are experimental ones that anyone can use for testing, but should never appear "in the wild."

The word "registry" is much misused. It is interchangeably used to mean:

- "SMPTE"—the organization responsible for registration.

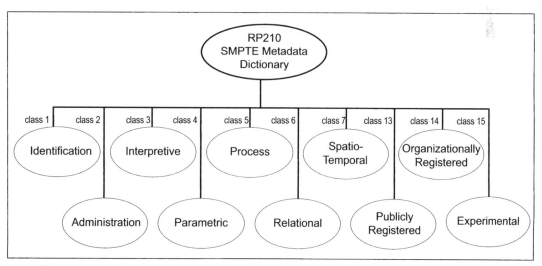

Figure 3.41 The different classes of registered metadata

- The controlling document that defines the structure and semantics of any given register.

- The register itself, which holds the actual data values.

There are several registers in SMPTE, each of which has a controlling document that defines each of the fields in the register, and how the number space for that register is used. Some of these registers were still in the process of being defined while this book was being written, so the information here may become a little out of date.

Register	Defining document	Name	Use
RP210	SMPTE 335M	Metadata Dictionary	Register of properties that have data types.
RP224	SMPTE 400M	Labels register	Register of language-independent labels: Class 1: Identification and location labels Class 2: Administration labels Class 3: Interpretive labels Class 4: Parametric labels Class 5: Process labels Class 6: Relational labels Class 7: Spatio-temporal labels Class 12: Compound labels Class 13: Organizationally registered labels for public use Class 14: Organizationally registered labels for private use Class 15: Experimental labels
Under development		Enumerations	For storing multi-lingual equivalents
Under development		Groups register	For collecting together the properties of registered sets
Under development		Types register	Register of data types of properties

Table 3.2 SMPTE Registration documents

UUID

A UUID (Universally Unique ID) is a 16-byte number that has been randomly generated according to the annex in ISO 11578 (rpc—remote procedure calls). UUIDs are used as dynamically generated unique numbers to bind the physical sets together. Set references are resolved by inspecting the Instance UID (Instance Unique Identifiers) of the target set (see Source Reference C).

There are cases in MXF where a property is of type UL, but the value one wishes to put there is entirely dynamic, or unregistered. It is valid for an MXF decoder to expect to find a UUID in this instance. An example of this could be the Product UUID in the Identification set or the Data EssenceCompression property in the generic data descriptor.

There are issues when a UUID is stored in a property of a UL. A decoder trying to differentiate between the two needs some way of identifying a UL from a UUID. All UUIDs have a 1 in the most significant bit of the "clk_seq_hi_res" word (byte 9), whereas all ULs have a 0 in the most significant bit of the first byte. If UUIDs are stored with a byte order that places the "clk_seq_hi_res" word first, then it is always possible to tell if the value is a UL or a UUID by examining the MSB of the first byte. This byte order also prevents the remote possibility of a UUID being stored that matches a registered UL.

EG41 gives the following guidelines:

- A UUID may be stored in a data field of type UL by swapping the top and bottom 8 bytes of the UUID (the most significant bit of the first byte of such a swapped UUID is always 1).

- MXF decoders should accept a swapped UUID in a place where a UL is expected.

NOTE—AAF uses a compatible byte-swap method for storing ULs and UUIDs in the same properties, which it defines as AUIDs.

UMID

Definition: The Unique Material Identifier is defined by SMPTE 330M.

Description: UMID provides for the globally unique identification of any audiovisual material. SMPTE 330M defines a basic UMID that provides a globally unique identification for audiovisual material made up from one or more material units. The basic UMID, however, has no embedded mechanism to distinguish between individual material units. In MXF the basic UMID is used to identify packages, whereas individual tracks provide the mechanism to identify the material units. This extra flexibility is vital to give MXF its sophisticated timeline description capabilities.

The basic UMID can be automatically generated. It does not require any registration or central authority to create UMIDs. MXF devices can manipulate and process MXF files without any central control mechanism. This allows autonomous behavior of devices to streamline workflows. An example of this is the case of ingesting material from a tape.

In nearly all applications, it is the UMID of the material package that is used to identify the file. In Figure 3.42, the UMID of the material package identifies what will be played out from the content stored in the single file called "ingest.mxf." This file was created by ingesting a tape with the content shown. An asset management system needs to track and manage the file based on this number. In this example, all the essence is stored in the single file irrespective of any cut detection or UMIDs that might have been found in the source tape.

In some applications, it might be preferable to create a file for each and every piece of content found on the tape. The goal is to create stand-alone MXF files for each of the pieces of content and to create a "stub" MXF file of a higher operational pattern to bind together the stub files.

In the example in Figure 3.43, life is a little more complicated. UMID1 identifies the Material Package of the file "ingest.mxf." This small file, however, does not contain any essence: It merely sequences the other files in order to play them out as though it were the case described in Figure 3.42.

Each of the small files "springbok.mxf," "roo.mxf," "sheep.mxf," and "cow.mxf" have a UMID for their material package and a UMID for their file package. An asset management system needs to track and manage each of those files individually. It needs to keep track of the material package UMIDs: $UMID_{springbok}$, $UMID_{roo}$, $UMID_{sheep}$, and $UMID_{cow}$. In some systems the overall sequencing file "ingest.mxf" may be discarded because this functionality is performed natively by the asset management and/or automation systems.

There is another (perhaps more common) example of Ingesting to a group of files in Chapter 6. The example in that chapter shows a group of files where each essence file contains only atomic essence. This means that there is one file for the video essence, another for the audio essence, etc. This physical storage scenario is becoming quite common.

Other identifiers are used in the industry to identify material, and MXF provides some support for them. MXF's intrinsic "dumb number" UMID is intended to be the primary way of identifying the file. Sometimes there is the need to provide extra identification within the file to associate it with a "house number," "work number," "production number," etc.

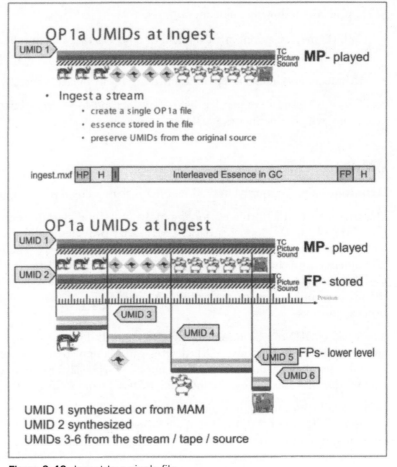

Figure 3.42 Ingest to a single file

This extra functionality was designed into MXF DMS-1 (SMPTE 380M) that specifically provides an identification set for containing such numbers. This is normatively defined in annex A.2.5 and D.5.2 of the DMS-1 specification and described below.

The basic structure of this descriptive metadata is:

Identification kind	string	e.g., UPN, ISAN
Identification value	string	the identifier
Locator	UL	machine description
Issuing authority	string	who issued it

Several of these identifiers can be included within an MXF file. They can be attached to specific audio/video tracks and may apply to only a portion of the timeline. This allows MXF to maintain

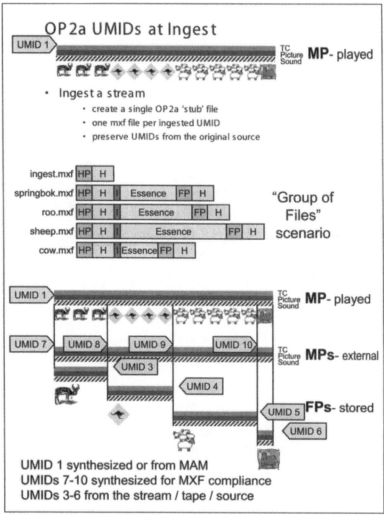

Figure 3.43 Ingest to a group of files

an audit trail of which parts of the timeline were derived from which original material.

An asset management system may choose not to track this additional information dynamically through the system. In principle, it is the asset management system's job to manage this information, and including it in the file perpetuates stale information.

4 Operational Patterns and Constraining MXF

Bruce Devlin

Introduction

Operational patterns are the way of controlling the complexity of MXF Files. Various names were tried during the design of MXF; for example, "templates" was rejected because it was already laden with expectations that differed depending on whether you came from a video or a software community. "Profiles" was rejected because there is a well-known video server with this name. "Operational patterns" was chosen because it had not already been used and conveyed the idea of the operational use of MXF. The design of the generalized operational patterns that appear in the MXF File Format Specification was governed by the desire to limit the complexity of encoders and decoders to acceptable levels. It was envisaged that specialist operational patterns would be created to cover the requirements of specific application areas such as non-linear editing and "live" file usage.

Generalized Operational Patterns

MXF was intended to be applicable to all parts of the multimedia content creation and manipulation chain. The goal was to create a file format that would be the equivalent of the BNC connector for streams. It would allow applications to speak to each other and it would allow facilities to be created using MXF as the interface of choice to connect together the various operational areas.

Because of this broad scope, there are many tools within the MXF suite of documents that are not applicable or not relevant to many designs. For this reason, the design committee looked at ways of simplification that would allow applications and devices of vastly different functionality and cost to interoperate. As already mentioned, these simplifications were going to be categorized as "templates" or "profiles," but these names were rejected in favor of *operation pattern* as this name did not come with any baggage.

Creating a number of useful operational patterns that scaled well was the next challenge. After several false starts, the relationship between the material package and the file package was chosen as the differentiating factor. This makes a lot of sense because the relationship has a large impact on the design of the MXF encoder and decoder. For example, the vast majority of MXF files will probably have a material package which says little more than "play out the entire file from start to

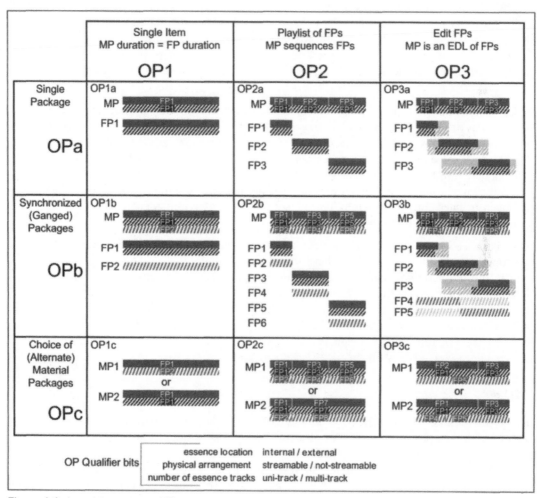

Figure 4.1 Ingest to a group of files

finish with all the video and audio tracks being presented to the listener." This is covered by the simplest of the generalized operational patterns—OP1a.

The next levels of complexity concern how playback of the file is controlled along the timeline. Playback could, for example, be represented by some kind of playlist where different parts of a file or files have to be played out one after the other. The most complex timeline involves full random access within the file with cut edits between the various segments that are played back. Any further timeline complexities such as blends, fades, wipes, and effects were acknowledged to be adequately addressed by the AAF specification.

The complexity of MXF usage is not, however, limited to cutting along the timeline; there is also the aspect of the number file packages active at any one time on the timeline. In the simplest case, there is only one MXF file or file package active at any stage along the timeline. The MXF timing model, however, is very sophisticated, and it is able to synchronize multiple active file packages—for example, to synchronize a video file with an external audio file. Finally, there is the versioning issue. If there are multiple versions of a file—for example, English, French, and Spanish versions—then it would be very convenient to be able to create a single file that described all the different versions, without having to store multiple versions of the common video.

At this point, the MXF problem space was defined, and the number of generalized operational patterns was defined. This gave rise to the (possibly familiar) operational pattern diagram on the opposite page (Figure 4.1). If you have trouble remembering which axis is numbers and which axis is letters, just remember that it is the **opposite** way around to Microsoft Excel! As author of the original diagram, I have to take the blame for this decision—the diagram was originally created late one night during a 5-day meeting where the discussions were quite heated. Once agreement had been reached on the principle, no one spotted the letter/number confusion possibility for another two years! By that time it was too late!

As you can see from Figure 4.1, the generalized operational patterns have been created to restrict the complexity of the devices which have to implement them. There are three generic flags (in byte 15 of the operational pattern UL) that apply to all of the generalized operational patterns. The first flag signals whether or not the essence for all of the file packages is located internally within the MXF File. The second signals whether the bytes have been arranged to allow the file to be streamable (i.e., the pictures can be seen synchronized with the audio while the file is being transferred). The third qualifier signals if there is more than one essence track within the file. If this qualifier is set to "0," then the file is *mono-essence* or *atomic*.

OP1a

This is the most common of the MXF files in existence today and is defined in SMPTE 378M. It was aimed at tape replacement or AVI file replacement applications. The most common files are frame wrapped with an interleave of audio and video. OP1a does not place any constraints on the physical partitioning of the file, and so there are a number of partitioning schemes in existence. Decoders should not be so fussy that they will not accept a file unless the partitions occur at some predetermined interval. OP1a has been very successful as a native storage format and not just as an interchange format, and there are a number of Tape, Optical, and Magnetic drives on the market that use OP1a on the surface of the storage medium.

OP2a

This operational pattern essentially creates a concatenation of individual OP1a files. It is less popular than some of the higher OP2 operational patterns, but does introduce a new and important concept via the addition of a new "inter SourceClip" qualifier bit. This new bit is part of the operational pattern UL as defined in SMPTE 392M. It is set to a "1" if no additional processing is required by an MXF decoder when playing across the "gap" between the different material package SourceClips referencing the individual file packages.

For uncompressed essence, most audio compression schemes, DV, and some intra-frame compression schemes, this bit will always be set to "1." For most long-GOP MPEG-2 streams, the qualifier bit will be set to "0" because it is not possible to concatenate two arbitrary MPEG streams and expect the MPEG buffers to match at the boundary. Naive playback would cause buffer overflow or underflow with spectacular visual consequences. Help is at hand, however, in that the MPEG stream can be prepared by "pre-splicing" the content so that the resulting file can be played without any stream processing being performed by the MXF playback device. The advice to MXF encoder writers is that pre-splicing should always be done unless the operational environment in which the MXF encoder is being used guarantees that the MXF decoder has the required splicing functionality.

OP3a

This operational pattern allows full cut-list playout from the file packages in the file. Random access is nearly always required in the MXF decoder in order to be able to play the file, and sophisticated decoding of essence formats, such as MPEG-2, may be required in order to provide seamless playback. OP3a is defined in SMPTE 407M.

OP1b

This operational pattern synchronizes multiple File Packages, all of which have the same length. This OP is defined in SMPTE 391M and is becoming much more important at the time of writing due to the creation of a proposal for an "MXF master file format" which can be used to manage content in a multilingual, multi-versioned environment. Some of the proposed details are given at the end of this chapter.

Due to the separation of the storage model from the metadata model in the MXF design, the actual essence could be inside the MXF file, or it could be external to the MXF file. In most uses, an OP1b file will reference all of its essence externally. The case where some or all of the essence containers are stored internally has not been widely implemented so far. The reason for this comes down to practical workflow issues. If you want to add an extra sound track to an existing multilingual asset, it is often easier to store an extra atomic MXF audio file with the existing atomic MXF files rather than take a long MXF file with internal essence and rewrite the entire file with the new file packaged linked inside it. This is shown in Figure 4.2 below.

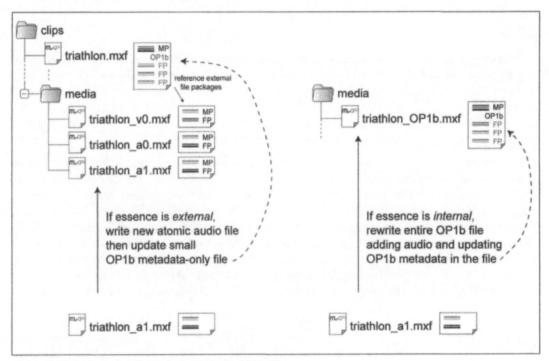

Figure 4.2 Adding an extra audio track to an OP1b file

OP2b

Operational pattern 2b is a combination of OP1b and OP2a and is defined by SMPTE 393M. It is essentially the result of concatenating a number of OP1b files. The actual essence can be stored internally or externally, and the "splicing" flag is present to indicate whether or not essence processing needs to be done by the decoder.

Although this format might seem useful for playout applications, it is likely that any device creating a playout file will "render" an OP2b file into an OP1b file in order to make a guaranteed playable file. Strangely, its more sophisticated variant, OP2c, is more popular.

OP3b

This operational pattern allows editing and synchronization of multiple file packages and is defined in SMPTE 407M. Although it looks attractive as a native format for editing applications, its lack of support for effects means that the Advanced Authoring Format (AAF) is more likely to be used.

OP1c

In row "c" of the table, there can be multiple Material Packages in an MXF File and all of the row "c" Operational Packages are defined in SMPTE 408M. Each of the material packages references a different set of File Packages and thus multiple versions of the content can be stored within a file. The simplest version of this is OP1c in which all of the file packages have the same duration and the material package acts as a file package selector. This can be very useful in a multilingual environment as explained throughout Chapter 6, and as shown in Figure 4.3 below.

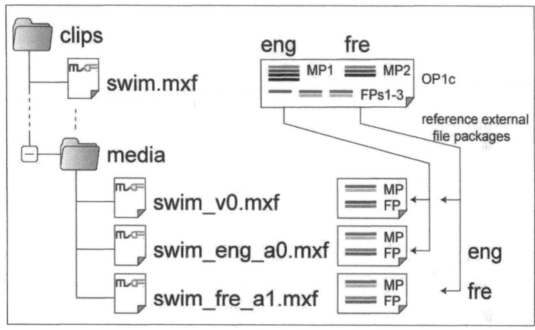

Figure 4.3 Creating a multilingual MXF package using OP1c

You will note from the diagram that the swim.mxf file contains identical copies of the file packages in the atomic essence files. The source reference chain links the material package tracks in swim.mxf to file package tracks within swim.mxf. These copies of file packages are identical in every way to the ones in the atomic media file, with the exception that they contain *Locators* to give a hint as to where the media files are actually stored. In a real operational environment, the location of the actual essence is likely to be governed by an asset management system.

The figure shows that the OP2c file contains two material packages. In the media folder, there are three atomic essence files, each of which has the same duration. In the case of the *eng* material package, MP1 selects the video essence file and the *eng* audio essence file. In the case of the *fre* material package, MP2 selects the video essence file and the *fre* audio essence file. Which file is played when an application is told to play the file depends on the operational environment of the application. In a playout environment, each server is often configured to select an appropriate

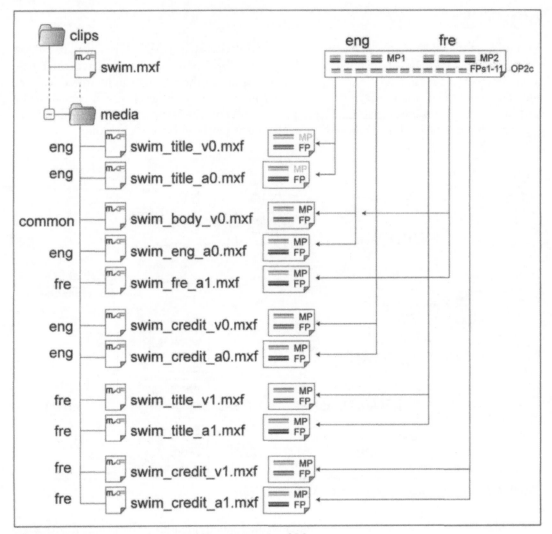

Figure 4.4 Creating a multilingual MXF package using OP2c

language variant for its output. In a user-oriented application, it would be "normal" to allow the user to select one of the material packages via some graphical user interface (GUI).

OP2c

OP2c is becoming popular in multi-versioned and multilingual environments. It allows MXF to define an asset that might have different titles and credits depending on the language. An example of this is shown in Figure 4.4. This example extends the idea of Figure 4.3 to have a common "body" video segment, and multiple versions of the titles.

As you can see from the figure, there are a lot more files now. Most people would require a rigorous file-naming convention in order to manage this number of files, and it would be tedious to keep the right versions coordinated. An asset management system, however, allows new title sequences to be added as discrete atomic essence files by means of a relatively minor update of the metadata-only OP2c file called swim.mxf in the clips folder.

New credits sequences can be added in the same way. The linkage of the MXF is achieved through UMIDs in the source reference chain (as explained in Chapter 3). Control of discrete files can be achieved through asset management and automation, with interfaces based on the UMIDs and filenames of the discrete atomic essence files.

OP3c

Beyond OP3c lies AAF functionality. OP3c adds together all the functionality so far discussed. It allows multiple versions of "cuts only" edit lists on multiple MXF essence files to be stored in a single MXF file. This would allow, for example, multiple censored versions of a multilingual asset to be packaged as a single file (internal essence) for distribution from a content creator. It could also be packaged as a collection of external essence files for a master archive. To date, this level of sophistication has not been deployed.

Specialized Operational Patterns—OP-Atom

Operational pattern Atom defines a tightly constrained file structure for a single track of essence. It is targeted as a material format for non-linear editing applications requiring high performance access to individual tracks of essence. The main features of an OP-Atom file are listed below:

- Within each OP-Atom file there shall be one top-level file package; this references the essence in the single essence container within the file.

- There shall be only one essence track in the top-level file package to ensure it is a mono-essence file.

- There shall be exactly one essence container and it shall only contain essence from a single instance of an MXF essence mapping. This essence container shall be internal to the file.

- Within each OP-Atom file there shall be one material package, which may have an unconstrained number of tracks and an unconstrained number of SourceClips within each track. This allows synchronization metadata to be held in the material package for a group of OP-Atom files. The grouping may be across the timeline (such as separate audio and video files generated from a synchronized audio-video source), along the timeline (such as where the entire essence will not fit on a single disc), or both. Using this approach, each OP-Atom file within a group contains the same material package, describing the structure of the complete audiovisual clip of which each OP-Atom file is a part. By including this material package in each OP-Atom file, the original clip metadata is always available with any individual essence file. This avoids the necessity for an additional metadata-only master MXF file, although one could be used to define new audiovisual clip associations.

- The OP-Atom universal label indicates the complexity of the material package. The range of defined values roughly equates to the material package complexity of generalized operation patterns OP1a to OP2b.

- The complexity of the material package does not affect basic decoding of an individual OP-Atom file because the Preface::PrimaryPackage property allows a simple decoder to jump directly to the top-level file package when parsing.

- There is no *run-in* used in OP-Atom files.

- The header partition shall be closed and complete. If the application must provide access to Atom-like material while it is still being recorded, such files should be labeled with the appropriate generalized OP identifier. When the recording is finished and a closed and complete header may be rewritten to the file, it may be appropriate to rewrite the OP label as OP-Atom.

- There shall be an *index table* in the *footer* and it shall not be sparse.

- There shall only be header metadata in the header partition (there shall be no header metadata repetitions).

- Each partition shall contain data from no more than one data stream.

- Each data stream shall be contained in a single partition. This condition was put in to allow for non-essence streams (such as subtitles and other stream data related to the essence) to be included in an OP-Atom file.

OP-Atom has become a popular format for some non-linear editing applications. It has also been incorporated into a camera which creates OP-Atom files on a removable medium, allowing direct editing without an ingest process.

Other Specialized Operational Patterns

In general, the proliferation of a wide number of specialized operational patterns is a bad thing. For each specialized operational pattern, a new label is required to define it. A general-purpose decoder might decide that an MXF file with an unknown OP label may well be outside its capabilities to decode because it does not understand the OP label. The fact that the file uses no extra facilities than those in OP1a cannot be conveyed to the decoder.

A decoder looking ONLY for a particular specialized operational pattern is limiting its interoperability range through design. This approach would to fly in the face of the interoperability creed:

"Be strict with the files you write. Be tolerant and accommodating in the files you read."

Application Specifications

In order to avoid this proliferation of specialized operation patterns, several companies have decided to create *application specifications* (AS). These are attempts a) to document the operational practice of an organization and b) to constrain the total number of options (and hence cost) associated with the use of MXF in a facility—yet at the same time preserving the flexible working practices that MXF makes possible.

To meet these goals, it is important that the scope of an application specification is carefully controlled. It would seem obvious that an AS would reasonably attempt to limit the number of compression formats used within a facility. It would not seem reasonable to reinvent mechanisms already standardized within MXF. As an example of the type of parameters that you would find in an Application Specification, here is a table of things to consider:

General	
Compliance	• All MXF file writers should comply strictly with the MXF File Format Specification SMPTE 377M and any other specification that forms part of the application specification. Constraining file creation should give performance/cost advantages. Constraining the physical properties of the written file, header metadata extensions, and vocabularies are all good practice. • MXF File readers and parsers should be tolerant of input files and should log errors and continue rather than abort.
Essence	
Video	• Constrain the underlying essence type to long-GOP MPEG, I frame, DV, etc. This would be the main essence type used within the facility for a certain time duration (e.g., 10 years). • Constrain the resolution of the master essence to SD and or HD. • Constrain the bitrates of the master essence. • Constrain the generation and location of proxies; e.g., in the Master MXF file, in a separate MXF file, on a separate proxy server, or made on the fly.
Audio	• How many channels should be included. • AES / BWF/compressed. • Interleaved or in a separate file(s). • Mono, multilingual as a single package, or as managed file groups.
Timecode	• Material Package only timecode is the master reference? • Or is capture timecode the master reference? • Or Camera timecode?
Partitioning	• Follow a shared storage, access-during-ingest model? • Insert MXF partitions for reacquisition of streamed files? • Encourage partial index tables during capture?
KAG	• Strictly enforced by file writers?
VBI / ANC	• Keep VITC in the file as VBI signal? • Maintain VBI/ANC in MXF standard format? • Maintain VBI/ ANC in server proprietary format? • Carry closed captioning? • Carry DVB subtitles? • Carry XML-based subtitle authoring information? • Carry other data /streams/embedded scripts/
Operational Patterns	
Zones	• One OP for the whole facility? • Match OP to the needs of each zone (news, archive, production)? • Specify OP conversion rules between zones for reliability? • Internal/external essence rules on a per-zone basis? • Versioning.

General		
Header Metadata		
Legacy	• Carry legacy House Numbers as well as UMIDs? • Support markin/markout? • Persist cue points in files?	
Descriptive Metadata		
DMS policy	• Use only SMPTE 380M – DMS-1? • Extend DMS-1 using name-value pairs only • Extend DMS-1 using private extensions from purchased SMPTE number space? • Map Existing Metadata schemes into DMS-1? • Create a private DMS, base on a purchased SMPTE number space?	
Vocabularies	• How are vocabularies and schemes managed over time? • Who has authority to add new properties or new values and what are the implications over time (backwards and forwards compatibility)? • Should metadata schemes and vocabularies be global or will zoning give better results? • How are assets labeled & what is the label scope? e.g., Program Number, UMID, and Asset Number are all related, often interchangeable, but are used for different things. • File-naming conventions don't substitute for identification with UMIDs.	

Table 4.1 Application Specification considerations

Case Study: The Master MXF File

As a result of looking at application specifications, and trying to build systems using only the tools in the standardized MXF documents, a group of interested parties got together and looked at the way in which shared storage systems were used to access MXF Files while they were being recorded. The scope was to try and create a master MXF file which could be used in an archive and was easy to convert into the right format at the right time in the right place within a facility.

The decision to create a group of file structures with atomic essence and OP1b, OP1c, or OP2c metadata files seemed to give the best flexibility while retaining 100% compatibility with the MXF specifications. Access to the atomic essence files while they were being recorded was important and this would also cover the case of an MXF camera that output MXF files on a streaming interface so that they would be usable while being recorded. The desires for the design were:

• Use only tools from OP1a to ensure the file was maximally interoperable.

• Ensure that the file was fully indexed.

• Ensure that partitioning rules were clear.

• Only one "thing" was stored in any one partition.

• The file-writing device did not have to random access in the written file (to allow FTP PUT and other protocols to be used for file writing).

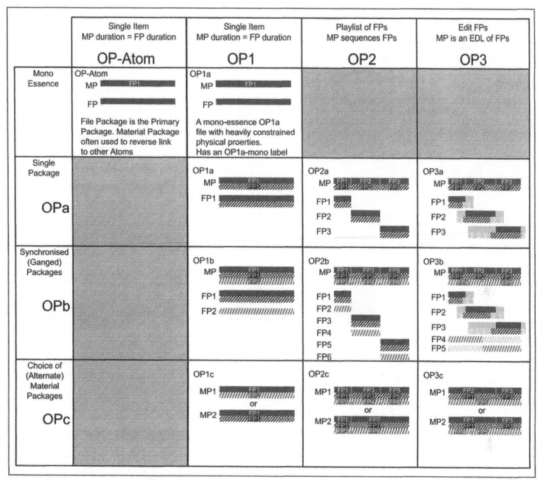

Figure 4.5 Operational Pattern Matrix with Atomic Essence Files

The resulting design placed the following restrictions on the MXF atomic essence file writer:

- Mono essence

- Frame wrapped

- Regularly partitioned

- Header partition contains only metadata

- Each body partition has metadata **or** index **or** essence

- Closed and complete in the footer partition

- Metadata repetition in the footer partition

- Distributed index tables

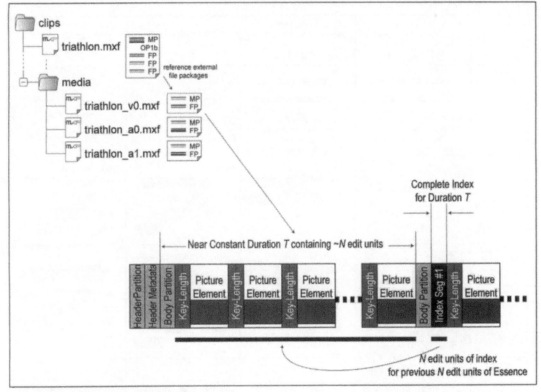

Figure 4.6 Atomic OP1a File Partitioning

- Signaled as OP1a (with mono-essence, streamable, internal essence qualifiers)
- Annotated with language metadata (when the essence is a specific language variant)
- Annotated with version metadata (when the essence is a specific version)

Despite these restrictions, the file remains 100% OP1a compatible and as such should be readable by any MXF application.

To see how this fits into the overall scheme of operational patterns, we can redraw the OP grid as shown in Figure 4.5.

The constrained OP1a file shares many properties with OP-Atom, yet allows more flexible partitioning. Whereas the primary package of an OP-Atom is the file package, the Preface::PrimaryPackage property of the OP1a atomic essence file is absent, leaving determination of the primary package to the application. An example of the file partition strategy is shown in Figure 4.6.

The figure shows the physical arrangement of the video atomic essence file. The file starts with a header partition that will be open and incomplete (as explained in Chapter 2), which indicates that the overall duration of the file is not yet known. The MXF file writing application chooses a duration

T and, if possible, fixes the number of edit units in a partition to a constant number N. This may not always be possible or desirable if long-GOP MPEG essence is being recorded with a dynamic number of pictures per GOP; hence the annotation "near constant duration T" in the figure.

Every time N edit units of essence have been recorded, an index segment is recorded; even if the essence is fixed bytes per essence (see Chapter 12—Index Tables). The index segment is a full index of all the essence in the previous partition. Optionally, an extra partition with a repeat of the header metadata may be inserted.

Constraining Descriptive Metadata

Once essence interoperability is achieved, the ability to add any descriptive metadata with free-form data values can lead to problems in the working of a system. The full topic of metadata interoperability is outside the scope of this particular chapter, but it is worth mentioning a few key points that are important when creating MXF constraints:

DMS Properties	
DMS-1 (explained fully in Chapter 11)	• Smpte 380M DMS-1 can be extended with name-value pairs. This is not very future proof, however, because the name-value pairs don't form a part of the overall data model and are hard to validate using tools such as XML schema. • DMS-1 can also be extended by adding extra properties to it that can be standardized, publicly registered, or privately registered. • The SMPTE Registration Authority *http://www.smpte-ra.org* allows organizations to register their own number space in the dictionary. Class 13 registrations are for public bodies to share their data. Class 14 are for private organizations, such as manufacturers, to define their own Universal Labels and to create their own Groups, Properties, Sets, and Simple Labels. It is up to the owner of that number space to manage it and publish as they see fit. The relationship between these classes is given in Figure 3.41. • Application specifications may be based on DMS-1 with a fixed list of extensions (which will probably vary over time as business practices change). • Application Specifications may also be purely based on a private DMS scheme. Mechanisms to publish these private schemes are needed if the metadata is ever to be interoperable between systems. One aspect of this is to publish the syntax of the scheme, for which XML schema is usually an adequate representation. Publishing the semantics so that automatic conversion and understanding can be achieved is a much trickier task. Some work along these lines is under way within SMPTE. Much work of this kind is under way in the IETF (Internet Engineering Task Force) where Semantic Web, RDF. and other technologies are still under development.
Metadata Extensions	• The MXF data model is a single inheritance hierarchy. This means that if there are two properties with the same meaning and same value, but appear in different parts of the hierarchy, then they are represented as different properties. For example, EditRate of a track and EditRate in an IndexTableSegment have the same meaning and same value, but have different Universal Labels. This feature of MXF can make it hard to model some descriptive metadata.
Vocabularies	• Many DMS properties take text strings or other free-form input. Constraining the values that can be entered into these free-form fields by creating a controlled vocabulary ensures metadata consistency and will improve the overall quality of searching in the metadata (assuming of course that the vocabulary is sufficiently broad to cover all the possible values, and sufficiently precise to ensure that there is not any ambiguity between the different values).

DMS Properties	
Language	• DMS-1 and other metadata schemes recognize that human-oriented metadata is best entered in the native tongue of the person entering the data. In a multilingual environment, it is likely that annotation may be in a different language to that spoken in the content. There is an example of this below.

Table 4.2 Application-Specific Descriptive Metadata considerations

Descriptive Metadata Usage Example for the MXF Master File

In a multilingual environment, it is important to know which track refers to which language. The structural metadata about the sound tracks and essence (e.g., in the EssenceDescriptors) does not carry language information and this needs to be carried as descriptive metadata. It is likely that the mechanisms for doing this will be standardized some time after this book is published. The examples below show one of the options for doing this. Constraining the way in which language is signaled is important to ensure interoperability in an MXF environment.

The technique used here takes the production framework from the DMS-1 metadata scheme (SMPTE 380M) because we are trying to convey information about the production as a whole. This framework is associated with a track in the file package of the atomic essence files because we are describing the stored essence within the file.

The production framework is referenced by a DM Track & DM sequence and DM segment (see Source Reference Chain in Chapter 3).

The production framework property that signals the language used for annotation (within the metadata) is the FrameworkExtendedTextLanguageCode. For technical annotation, this is set to eng for english annotation. This is important because machines match text strings, not concepts—

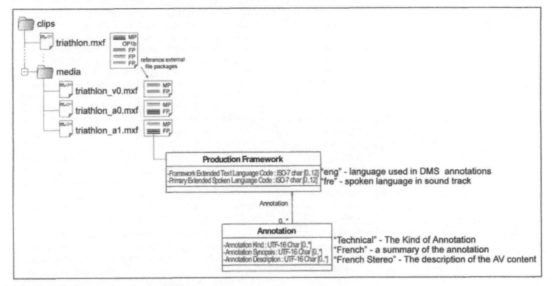

Figure 4.7 Annotating the multilingual atoms

a machine would not match *french* and *français*. The first being the english word for *french* and the second being the french word for *french*. Annotating in english allows string comparisons to be made. The FrameworkExtendedTextLanguageCode applies to the set in which it is found, as well as all the sets which are referenced by that set. This means that in the example below, the annotation sets as well as the production framework sets contain text in the english language.

The PrimaryExtendedSpokenLanguageCode property is used to indicate the spoken language.

Sometime, it is necessary to add a little more metadata, for example to indicate *french left*, *french right*, *french stereo*, *french signing*, etc. In this case, we use an Annotation set of the technical kind. The Synopsis property should have the full english name of the spoken language, and the Description property should contain the same value, followed by a space, and then the extra metadata as shown in Figure 4.7.

In order to identify the variants of a top-level OP2c file, a similar technique can be used as shown in Figure 4.8.

In this last example, the annotations should not refer to all the tracks in the material package. Instead, there should be an annotation for each track in order to ensure that audio channels can be differentiated by reading the metadata in the OP2c file without having to go and open all the individual atoms to check the descriptions.

The issues of operational patterns and constraining MXF will continue to evolve as MXF is rolled out into the content creation industry.

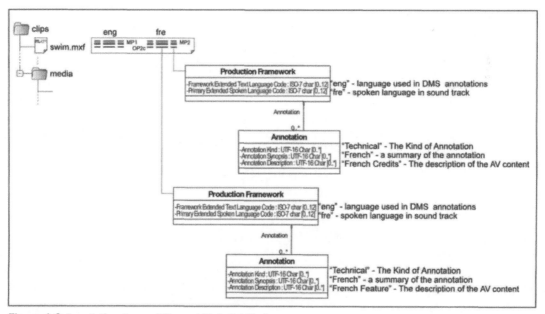

Figure 4.8 Annotating the multilingual Material Package

5 How to Put Essence into an MXF File

Jim Wilkinson

Introduction

This chapter will give a general introduction to the MXF generic container for the carriage of essence and metadata within the body of an MXF file. It starts with a description of the content model devised by the EBU/SMPTE Task Force and develops the requirements for a generalized essence container. It was from this generalized essence container that the MXF generic container evolved. The MXF generic container shares the same content model as used by SDTI-CP (SMPTE 326M), and the last part of this chapter explains how data from SDTI-CP can be mapped into the MXF generic container to provide a bridge from linear streaming devices to file storage devices.

The Generalized Content Model

The content model used in the generic container specification (SMPTE 379M) is based on the EBU/SMPTE Task Force Report that defines a content model as in Figure 5.1.

The Task Force report defines: "Content is composed of Content Packages which, in turn, are composed of Content Items, which are further composed of Content Elements." These *content packages* are convenient groupings of the various items where each item is a group of similar

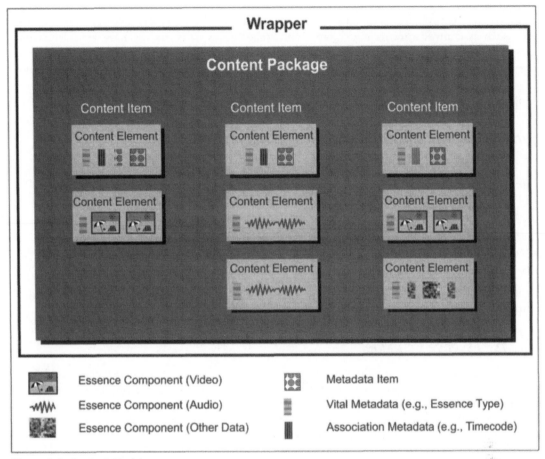

Figure 5.1 Content Model

element types. Although the term content package (CP) is also used in the SDTI-CP specification, the MXF generic container content package is a more generalized arrangement that retains backwards compatibility with the SDTI-CP content package.

The content model of the MXF generic container defines frame-interleaved content based on the following components:

- System item: includes system level descriptive metadata and content metadata;

- Picture item: includes one or more picture essence elements;

- Sound item: contains one or more sound essence elements;

- Data item: contains one or more data essence elements; and

- Compound item: contains one or more intrinsically interleaved elements (such as an interleave of DV-DIF packets).

The system item provides services for each content package through metadata elements and other data such as control information. Picture and sound items carry the primary video and audio elements that are often routed to specialist storage or processing equipment. The data item is used to carry data-centric elements such as subtitles and teletext data and is frequently created, processed, and stored on computer media. The compound item essentially carries mixed essence types that are intrinsically interleaved.

Why Picture and Sound, Not Video and Audio?

The term *picture* is a high-level abstraction that includes video, images, graphics, and other picture-related essence types. If the term *video* had been used, where would we put the other picture types? In practice, most essence-mapping documents will define the kind of picture essence intended and this will be mostly, but not exclusively, video.

Likewise, the term *sound* generally means *audio*, but there are other forms of sound that can be used in the sound item, including synthetic audio, MIDI data, and other data whose decoders will produce an audio output.

Note that all items in the content model are optional and their presence depends on specific implementations.

An MXF Essence Container

An MXF *essence container* provides the encapsulation of a particular type of essence. Its purpose is to allow the essence to be wrapped in KLV and to have associated with it an optional index table to allow rapid access to a given time offset within the essence. The essence container is structured to allow easy multiplexing with other essence containers and to allow identification of the decoding requirements needed to display/listen to/play/execute the content.

Every essence container specification provides for a unique SMPTE label for rapid identification of the contained essence type, as well as a method for encapsulating the essence in a KLV structure. Different essence containers may place restrictions on the interleaving of the essence data within the container to be compatible with existing applications. The SMPTE label at the beginning of the file allows decoders to make a fast go/no-go check of the essence type within the file.

An MXF file may contain more than one essence container and each essence container may contain different essence types. The precise number of essence containers and their relationships is constrained by the operational pattern with which the file complies.

How Is an MXF Essence Container Specified?

There are several specific questions that need to be asked when putting an essence container into an MXF file. These are notably:

1. What limitations (for example, essence length) are placed on the essence container when it is in an MXF file?

2. Are there interleaved variants of the essence container?

3. How do we KLV code the contents of the essence container?

4. How do we pad the essence containers to fit a chosen KAG size?

5. What do we do with the metadata embedded within the essence container?

6. How do we use index tables with the essence container?

The essence container and mapping specifications are basically answers to these questions. It is the intention of the essence container and mapping documents to restrict the choices of an essence container implementation sufficiently to allow interoperability between devices, yet with enough flexibility to solve real-world problems.

Essence Container Technical Requirements

As with all MXF components, an essence container must consist of a concatenated sequence of individually coded KLV packets, where each KLV packet meets the following requirements:

- Each KLV packet must comply with SMPTE 336M and the values of the keys must be publicly registered with the SMPTE.

- The size of the of each KLV packet must be defined in order to constrain what is required of compliant decoders.

MXF defines that all compliant essence container specifications must meet a number of technical requirements. These are listed below.

- The specification must include the byte order for the correct interpretation of multi-byte values. By default, all multi-byte values are assumed to be big-endian (network byte order).

- The essence container must be capable of carrying multiple essence elements that can be interleaved over a defined interleaving period or must be capable of being multiplexed in an MXF file using the partition mechanism. The interleave/multiplex duration is dependent upon the application, but should be the period of the minimum duration of usable picture essence, typically a picture frame period.

- The KLV packets of each interleave/multiplex duration should contain essence of essentially the same timing (for example, audio-video timing is rarely sample accurate). Special timing arrangements may be needed in the case of, for example, MPEG long-GOP coding using B-frame coding where there is an inter-frame dependency. This requirement allows simple editing and switching of the interleaved essence within the container.

- The essence container specification must be assigned a registered Universal Label value to uniquely identify the essence container type.

- The essence container specification must define the mechanism to identify track numbers for the purpose of identifying specific essence elements within the essence container.

- Individual essence container specifications should define how to index the essence elements with the essence container type for rapid searching.

- The essence container specification may define the use of the KLV Alignment Grid (KAG) to further aid rapid access to essence elements.

- The essence container specification may define the use of essence Descriptor(s) to describe essence elements within the essence container.

There is only one essence container defined for MXF to date and this is the MXF generic container. This generic container is intended to carry all the mainstream essence types available to date. It is very simple in operation, yet flexible enough to carry both compressed and uncompressed audio and video, including frame-reordered MPEG streams. The generic container specification does not define a complete essence container specification, but does define the model of how a specific essence container can be created. Individual mapping documents are needed to define precisely how each essence byte stream should be mapped into the MXF generic container.

The Design of the MXF Generic Container

The MXF generic container is defined by SMPTE 379M and is the only type of essence container defined so far for MXF.

The premise for the MXF generic container format is that of a general purpose essence data and metadata container for the containment of many different kinds of essence and metadata elements into a single entity by interleaving the data streams in a defined and time-synchronous manner (typically over a 1-frame duration). Associated mapping documents define the essence data and metadata elements that can be placed in the container. Some mapping documents may define complete mappings for an entire content package while others may simply define mapping of metadata or essence data into an element.

Each of these essence elements can be separately indexed in an index table and can also be linked to a track number in the header metadata. The track number is the metadata property that controls the way in which this essence element is used.[1]

The MXF generic container offers two forms of essence wrapping: *frame-based wrapping* and *clip-based wrapping*. Essentially, frame-based wrapping applies KLV coding to essence units based on the essence frame rate, and clip-based wrapping applies KLV coding to an essence clip. These serve most of the basic essence-wrapping requirements. However, there are sometimes special cases that are not solved using frame and clip wrappings. These are defined in individual essence mapping documents since, by definition, custom wrappings serve individual specific requirements. An example of a *custom wrapping* is KLV coded long-GOP MPEG-2 video essence over the duration of each GOP.

The initial specification of the MXF generic container included system, picture, sound and data items. During the development of the various mappings for the MXF generic container, the DV

---

[1] **Note:** When describing an essence container, the term *track* refers to a sequence of one or more essence elements and is analogous to tracks in a recorder.

container was found to be a special case that did not come under the umbrella of the existing model because the DV-DIF packet structure contains a mix of video, audio, and auxiliary packets that proved difficult to separate out into the components of the content model. Hence, an additional component was added to the data model specifically for essence that is essentially a mixture of indivisible essence types. This additional component is the *compound* item. With that extension, the MXF generic container could encompass all known essence formats within regular use in the content production industry. The MXF generic container comprises a contiguous sequence of content packages, each of which has up to five basic components known as *items*.

- A system item is a group of up to 127 metadata or control-data elements related to the container itself and may be related to the elements in the other four items below.

- A picture item is a group of up to 127 picture-essence elements. Each essence element in a picture item should contain a predominance of picture essence, although the element may contain metadata and other ancillary essence.

- A sound item is a group of up to 127 sound-essence elements. Each essence element in a sound item should contain a predominance of sound essence, although the element may contain metadata and other ancillary essence.

- A data item is a group of up to 127 data-essence elements. Each essence element in a data item should contain a predominance of data essence, although the element may contain metadata and other ancillary essence.

- A compound item is a group of up to 127 compound essence elements. Each essence element in a compound item should contain a mixture of essentially indivisible essence and metadata components that, as a group, do not match the intent of the picture, sound or data items.

Content Package Structure

When streaming an MXF file, it is desirable to limit the size of the buffers needed in the receiver to be able to display the material during transfer (this, in turn, reduces the overall latency of the system). To be streamable, a file will usually contain an interleaving of picture and sound elements. In many systems that use compressed sound material, it is likely that the smallest unit (or element)

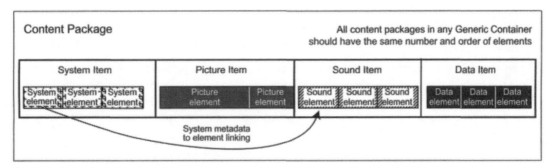

Figure 5.2 Logical structure of items and elements in a (interleaved) content package

of sound does not have the same duration as the field or frame duration of the pictures. These considerations underpin the requirements of a content package.

The guidelines below are intended to improve the chances of interchange when streaming, and refer to the placement of elements in the content package of the MXF generic container. The term *access unit* is borrowed from MPEG to indicate the smallest unit of content that can be allocated a time value. Figure 5.2 shows the basic structure of a content package that consists of different essence items where each contains different essence elements. The items can appear in any order, but all elements of the same type must be contiguous.

In each (interleaved) content package:

- There is one picture access unit.

- The synchronized sound sample should be in the first sound element in the same content package. This implies that the start position of the picture access unit should be equal to the start position of the sound element or fall within the duration of the first sound element.

- Sound elements should be placed in the content package until a sound element is found that overflows the duration of the content package and this then becomes the first sound element of the next content package. (Note that when the sound element duration is greater than the picture access unit, this results in content packages with no or zero length sound elements.)

- Any data element should start with the first indivisible unit of data where the start position of the video access unit is a) equal to the start position of the data element or b) falls within the duration of the first data element.

- Any data element should end with the unit of data whose start position on the timeline is not later that the start position of the next video access unit.

Note that the term *element* in the generic container is used both to refer to a single element within a content package and also as a general description of an element over the duration of the container.

Streamable Files

The guidelines above create files that are *streamable*, but may require large receiver buffers to synchronize the picture, sound, and data. Many compression specifications provide a lot of information on buffering and streaming, and creating a system with similar buffer characteristics is the goal here. For example, the MPEG-2 systems specification (ISO/IEC 13818-1) gives rules and guidelines for multiplexing the audio and video streams into either a program stream or a transport stream.

When streaming a file, the decoder is intended to display the pictures and recreate the sound while the file is being sent. The delay through the video and audio decoders is often not the same; therefore, buffering is required in the decoder to bring the sound and pictures into synchronization. This buffering is often in addition to any buffering required for compression decoding and basic demultiplexing of the streams.

The guidance given here is that an MXF encoder should create a stream as though it were creating the content for streaming using the underlying compression standard; the generic container content package guidelines above should be applied. This should result in a good compromise between low latency and KLV decidability.

Multiplexing vs. Interleaving

Multiplexing and interleaving are frequently used when describing an MXF file. What do these terms mean? A succinct description is as follows:

- Interleaving = combining tracks within an essence container.

- Multiplexing = combining tracks from different essence containers.

So an interleaved essence container is almost always frame wrapped with each content package containing the required audio, video, and other tracks. This is analogous to SDI operation, and an interleaved generic container has similar attributes to SDI. Indeed, as will be shown later, there can be a direct mapping between SDTI-CP and the generic container. It is possible for an interleaved generic container to be decoded "on the fly" without recourse to decoding the header metadata, a feature widely used in equipment that operates both with file storage media (for flexibility) and serial interfaces (for real-time audiovisual recording and replay).

A multiplex of essence containers will typically have each essence container containing only a single track. A typical multiplex of essence containers would partition each essence container over a defined duration, say 1 second, and then multiplex the essence container partitions. This is akin to the multiplex of MPEG PES packets into a program stream. There is clearly more flexibility with multiplexed essence containers compared to interleaved containers, and its use may be more appropriate with certain essence types such as long-GOP MPEG-2 coded video.

So interleaving and multiplexing allow more than one way to slice the cake, and their selection depends on the use-case requirements. It is likely that MXF files will use either interleaving or multiplexing but not both. Although the MXF specifications do not preclude multiplexing interleaved essence containers, many decoders might fail given the wide variety of possible essence container combinations.

Generic Container Guidelines

The MXF generic container specification has guidelines to ensure that MXF encoder implementations create consistent MXF files. These guidelines (see next two sections) should be followed wherever possible to improve interoperability, but there are known cases where individual guidelines cannot be met. These cases are documented in the individual essence mapping specifications where needed.

Frame-Based Wrapping

The frame in a frame-based wrapping may be a video frame, a video field, an audio block (e.g., a 192-sample group), a motion picture frame, or any other value that represents the basic sample unit of the primary essence component.

In a frame-based wrapping, there are usually multiple content packages in the essence container. If there is only one content package, it typically represents the contents of a single video frame (i.e., a "still" picture?). The frame or field duration is defined by the sample (or "edit") unit of the primary essence component carried by the content package.

An example arrangement of system, picture, sound, and data items in a frame-based wrapping is shown in Figure 5.3.

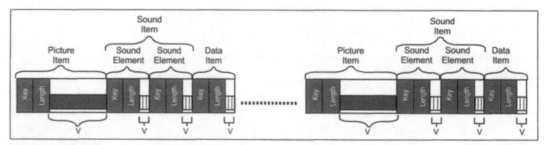

Figure 5.3 Example of frame-wrapping items and elements in the generic container

In any content package that has a system item, the system item identifies the start of the package. Where there is more than one essence element, there should be a system item in order to provide a reference point for in-line synchronization without the need to parse the whole file. Those files whose content packages do not include a system item must provide an alternate means to be able to locate the first essence element in the content package. Following any system item, each essence element of each essence item of a content package is added in a sequence. The sequence of items within a content package should be consistent over the sequence of content packages within an essence container. An example arrangement is shown in Figure 5.4. The system item is followed by one essence element in the picture item, two essence elements in the sound item, and one data element in the data item.

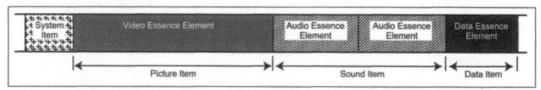

Figure 5.4 Example arrangement of system item, video, audio, and data essence elements in a content package

Frame-Wrapping Guidelines

The following guidelines apply to frame-wrapped essence:

- Each CP should have a constant number of elements;
- The order of elements in the CP should not change;
- Every element in the CP should have the same duration;

- Each CP should have one element that defines the primary timebase (usually the video);

- Each CP should have a duration that is an integer multiple of the atomic size of the underlying essence of the primary timebase (video frame, audio frame, audio block, etc.); and

- Synchronized elements should be grouped in the same CP.

Clip-Based Wrapping

In a clip-based wrapping, there is only one content package in the essence container. The duration of the clip may be one or more frames (or whatever is the basic sample unit of the essence).

An example arrangement of System, Picture, Sound and data items in a clip-based mapping are shown in Figure 5.5.

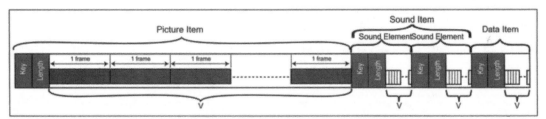

Figure 5.5 Example of clip-wrapping items and elements in the generic container

A clip-based wrapping may have more than one essence element. If so, the wrapping may include a system item to provide metadata for the essence elements and identification of the start of the essence container.

Clip-Wrapping Guidelines

The following guidelines should apply to clip-wrapped essence:

- Every element in the CP should have the same duration;

- Each CP should have one element that is the primary timebase (usually the video); and

- Each CP should have a duration that is an integer multiple of the atomic size of the underlying essence of the primary timebase (video frame, audio frame, audio block, etc.).

Since there is only one content package in a clip-wrapped generic container, the guidelines for the continuity of content packages in frame wrapping do not apply.

Picture, Sound, Data, and Compound Items

Each essence element is coded as a single KLV item, whether using frame-based or clip-based wrapping. The content package is therefore a sequence of one of more KLV packets contained within the duration of the content package.

Each KLV-coded element starts with a 16-byte element key value to identify the type of element and item, followed by a length field and completed by the element value itself.

Later chapters will explain specific essence mappings to the MXF generic container.

Generic Container System Item

The system item contains metadata elements that describe the operation of the content package and provides metadata related to the essence in the content package. It can include metadata elements linked to essence elements in the picture, sound, data and compound items. The system item may also include optional downstream control elements.

The system item comprises a sequence of up to 127 KLV packets where each packet comprises metadata elements or control data elements for support of different aspects of the content package. Depending on the requirements, each packet may be coded either as a local set, a fixed-length (FL) pack or a variable-length (VL) pack. The SMPTE key value defines the type of packet coding through the value of byte 6 of the key.

Figure 5.6 illustrates the system item data structure.

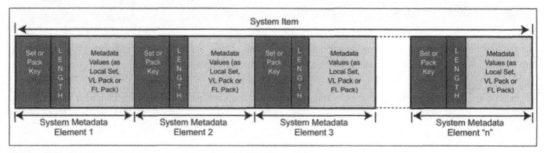

Figure 5.6 System item as a sequence of metadata elements

System Item Purpose

The system item may be simply the first system element that serves no purpose other than to identify the start of the content package. It may also be more complex. For this reason, the system item is defined by a scheme. One such scheme provides direct compatibility with SDTI-CP and this is described at the end of this chapter. A second scheme provides backwards compatibility with SDTI-CP but offers more capability for those instances of the generic container that require more functionality. This is also described at the end of this chapter.

If the content package has a single essence element, then a system item is neither required nor is it of very much use. However, for content packages that have more than one essence element, a system item, by default, should be present at the beginning of every content package in order that there is a defined starting point. The word "should" is used because there are applications where the first item in a content package can be determined by other means.

An example requirement for this extra capability is in the Sony XDCAM disc recorder that uses this extended system item along with proxy A/V items that are defined in 2-second access units.

The metadata contained in the system item may include local links that associate this metadata uniquely with its corresponding essence element. In many cases, metadata is embedded into each essence element (e.g., in the case of MPEG-2, the metadata is embedded in the various headers of the MPEG-2 essence bitstream). The external metadata link is supplied to provide metadata in addition to the essence bitstream. The system metadata can, for example, be a partial or whole extraction of embedded metadata extracted to provide quick access to key metadata without the requirement to re-parse the essence bitstream. The metadata can also be temporally sensitive, such as timecode information or camera coordinates.

System item metadata should only include that kind of metadata that is intimately linked to the essence in the same content package. It is not intended to provide metadata that is essentially static, that belongs in the header metadata. Examples of such system item metadata are those where the values will change for each access unit such as the extended UMID, timecode, and pan-scan vectors.

System Item Usage

Unlike the picture, sound, data, and compound items, which tend to be simple to define, system items can be complex in comparison. This section explains more about how a system item is used.

Within an MXF file, there are four potential locations for metadata (in order of preference):

- As part of the header metadata.

- As a separate data stream component in an MXF file.

- Intimately associated with the essence via the system item of a content package, as defined in this chapter.

- Embedded within the essence stream itself. Common examples are VITC (Vertical Interval Timecode) and AES-3 channel status data.

The order of priority of metadata use is subject to many constraints, but the following paragraphs provide some guidance.

As a rule, metadata is best placed in the header metadata wherever possible since that provides the greatest accessibility for all MXF readers. However, there are some limitations, such as metadata size (limited to 64KB) and mapping constraints during live file creation.

Bulky metadata, such as a frame-by-frame stream of timecode, can be extracted from the essence container and placed in an MXF file as a data stream. This offers ease of access that is slightly less than that provided by the header metadata, but is more accessible than parsing the contents of the essence container. At the time of writing, a new MXF specification for the carriage of such bulky metadata as a data stream is close to finalization.

Metadata that is created at the time of content creation may be presented together with a live stream of audiovisual content and, in this case, it is necessary to embed the metadata with the essence. This can be done by the traditional method of embedding in the essence stream itself, as with VITC and Channel Status metadata in AES-3. Both these methods of metadata carriage provide less access to the metadata than in a file environment. On the other hand, they are perfectly suited to live content creation that precedes the instantiation of a file.

Thus system item metadata and control data is intended only for that which is intimately associated with the content. Typical examples of metadata carried in the system item are:

- Timecode, as created by the content creation device. This could be a copy of the VITC or a single representation of the equivalent of VITC.

- Extended UMID (as defined by SMPTE 330M) that can be added by a device such as a camera enabled with a GPS (Global Positioning System) receiver that associates each picture with information comprising the date and time of content creation, the GPS coordinates, and the owner of the camera. The use of the metadata link mechanism in this GC System-item scheme allows multiple UMIDs to be created and maintained with the material. This may be used, for example, in sports where the microphone and camera locations may be different and may provide different UMID values according to the devices used to create the content, yet may be combined/mixed into one audiovisual stream for a contribution feed over a telecommunications or satellite link.

- The frame rate of the essence stream. This may be provided for those data streams that do not have another form of synchronization, such as an SDI/SDTI interface. This is useful for network transfers of the essence container only, where the header metadata is not carried.

The summary of this brief introduction is that metadata in the system item should only incorporate the metadata that is intimately linked to the content, most likely during the creation of live content. Metadata in the system item is more conveniently accessed than metadata embedded within the essence stream, but the system item is not intended as a replacement for the more easily accessed locations of the MXF header metadata area and the MXF data stream. In general, data originating at the essence layer should be copied to higher, more accessible layers. Systems that use this metadata should use the highest layer for ease of access and only access the lower layers if strictly necessary; for example, to copy a change of metadata from a higher layer through to lower layers in order to maintain data integrity.

Essence Container Identification

One of the requirements of an MXF essence container is to provide identification of the container. The MXF generic container provides this by defining it as an SMPTE-registered UL that identifies the essence container kind. Note that this use of an SMPTE UL is not as a key for KLV coding but simply as a 16-byte label.

The common framework for all SMPTE labels that identify an MXF generic container payload is illustrated in Table 5.1.

Byte No.	Description	Value (hex)	Meaning
1	Object Identifier	06	
2	Label size	0E	
3	Designator	2B	ISO, ORG
4	Designator	34	SMPTE
5	Registry Category Designator	04	Labels
6	Registry Designator	01	Labels Registry
7	Structure Designator	01	Labels Structure
8	Version Number	vv	Version of the Registry
9	Item Designator	0D	Organizationally Registered
10	Organization	01	AAF Association
11	Application	03	Essence containers
12	Structure Version	01	Version 1
13	Essence container Kind	02 01	MXF Generic Container Experimental MXF Generic Container for prototyping **only**
14	Mapping Kind	xx	Defines the kind of mapping
15~16	Locally defined	yy	Defined by the application specification

Table 5.1 Specification of the MXF generic container label

Byte 14 is defined by the appropriate generic container-mapping document and will have a value in the range 01_h to $7F_h$.[2]

This SMPTE label is used as the Essence Container property in the Partition Pack, in the Preface Set, and in the appropriate File Descriptor. This SMPTE label may also be present in the system item where the definition of the system item allows.

Note that the value of 01_h in byte 13 was used in an early experimental version of the generic container and is not used today.

KLV Coding of the MXF Generic Container

Essence Elements

This section describes the KLV coding of all essence elements that are part of the picture item, sound item, data item, or compound item.

Essence Element Key

The key structure for all essence element keys is defined in Table 5.2.

---

[2] All numbers are shown in 2-digit hexadecimal form; for example, "$7F_h$" for decimal 127.

Byte No.	Description	Value (hex)	Meaning
1	Object Identifier	06	
2	Label size	0E	
3	Designator	2B	ISO, ORG
4	Designator	34	SMPTE
5	Registry Category Designator	01	Dictionaries
6	Registry Designator	02	Essence Dictionary
7	Structure Designator	01	Dictionary Standard
8	Version Number	vv	Registry Version at the point of registration of this Key
9	Item Designator	0D	Organizationally Registered
10	Organization	01	AAF Association
11	Application	03	MXF Generic Container Keys
12	Structure Version	01	MXF-GC Version 1
13	Item Type Identifier	05 06 07 15 16 17 18	CP Picture (SMPTE 326M) CP Sound (SMPTE 326M) CP Data (SMPTE 326M) GC Picture GC Sound GC Data GC Compound
14	Essence Element Count	xx	See below
15	Essence Element Type	yy	See below
16	Essence Element Number	zz	See below

Table 5.2 Key values for picture, sound, data, and compound elements

Byte 13 of the key value identifies the essence item type.

- Values of 05_h, 06_h, and 07_h are reserved for essence item types defined in SMPTE 326M.

- Item type 07_h is known in SMPTE 326M as an auxiliary item, but is closely related to the data essence item of the MXF generic container.

- Values of 15_h, 16_h, 17_h, and 18_h are reserved for essence item types in the MXF generic container.

Each GC essence item can KLV code up to 127 essence elements (limited only by BER coding of each byte in an SMPTE UL). Should the number of essence elements in any GC item exceed 127, then there will be no further room for new element types under that essence item value. This is unlikely to happen in the short term; but if it does happen, there is room under byte 13 to define new values. For example, 25_h could be used to identify a picture item extension giving a further 127 values for new picture essence element types.

Byte 14 of the key value defines the number of essence elements in this item of the content package. A single essence element within an item will result an essence element count value of 01_h.

Byte 15 of the key value identifies the element Type as defined by either SMPTE 331M or by an associated essence-mapping document. Element type values are always constrained to the range 01_h~$7F_h$.

Byte 16 of the key value defines the value of the element number in the range 00_h~$7F_h$. It must be set by the encoder to be unique among all the elements in any one item. In most cases, the element number will increment by one for each new essence element in sequence within an item.

For any essence element, all four bytes must have a constant value within an instance of the generic container in order to maintain track linking (see below).

Essence Element Length

The essence element length is always BER coded. It is typical for the BER length to be 8 bytes, thus allowing a maximum length of 2^{56} bytes (or 72 Petabytes; $72*10^{15}$). This should be enough for all foreseeable image sizes and sequence lengths!

Essence Element Value

The details of the picture, sound, data, or compound-essence element value is defined in the appropriate mapping document.

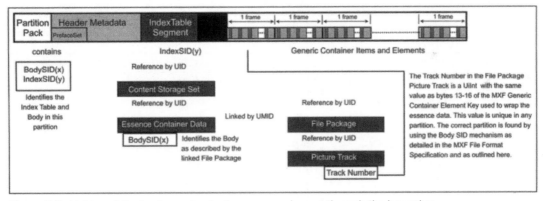

Figure 5.7 Linking of the track number to the essence element through the key value

Essence Element to Track Relationship

Each essence element in an essence container is described by a track in an MXF header metadata Package. This track will have an associated track number that is derived as follows:

The track number is a UInt32 value comprising bytes: "A.B.C.D" (most significant byte first). These byte values are assigned as follows:

A = Byte 13 of the element key value;

B = Byte 14 of the element key value;

C = Byte 15 of the element key value; and

D = Byte 16 of the element key value.

The assignment of values to these bytes, as defined above, ensures that each track referenced by the header metadata will have a unique number that is directly linked to the element key value.

Figure 5.7 on the previous page illustrates how the track number in the header metadata is linked to the track number derived from the essence key.

KLV Coding of System Elements

The system item is KLV coded as for the picture, sound, data, and compound items but, since the values are generally metadata rather than essence, there are some important distinguishing features as described next.

System Element Key

The system element key is defined in Table 5.3.

Byte No.	Description	Value (hex)	Meaning
1	Object Identifier	06	
2	Label size	0E	
3	Designator	2B	ISO, ORG
4	Designator	34	SMPTE
5	Registry Category Designator	02	Sets & packs
6	Registry Designator	xx (See SMPTE 336M)	Fixed-length Pack, Variable-length Pack or Local Set as required
7	Structure Designator	01	Sets & Packs Registry
8	Version Number	vvh	Registry Version at the point of registration of this Key
9	Item Designator	0D	Organizationally Registered
10	Organization	01	AAF Association
11	Application	03	MXF Generic Container Keys
12	Structure Version	01	MXF-GC Version 1
13	Item Type Identifier	04 14	CP-Compatible System Item (see SMPTE 326M) GC-Compatible System Item
14	System Scheme Identifier	xx	See appropriate System Item definition document

Byte No.	Description	Value (hex)	Meaning
15	Metadata or Control Element Identifier	yy	See appropriate System Item definition document
16	Reserved for use by metadata Element	zz	

Table 5.3 Key values for a system element

Within the system element, each group of metadata items can be coded as a fixed-length pack, a variable-length pack, or as a local set (see Chapter 1, KLV Coding). The choice of local set, variable-length, or fixed-length pack coding is defined by the metadata element or control data element specification. The method of coding will be reflected in the value of byte 6 of the key value.

The first metadata element of a system item must have a metadata element identifier (byte 15) value of 01_h. No other system item element can precede this element. This allows decoders to identify the unambiguous starting point of a content package.

System Element Length

Since the system elements are sets or packs, the length field is defined by the options allowed by SMPTE 336M. System elements typically use 2-byte or 4-byte length values. These are big-endian values (network byte order).

System Element Value

The value of a system item metadata element or control data element is a sequence of metadata properties coded as a local set, a variable-length pack, or a fixed-length pack as defined by byte 6 of the element key value. The definition of the properties in a metadata element or control data element will be found in the system item specification. There are two such specifications and these are described in Annex A at the end of this chapter. Note that if the system element is describing an essence element, then the method of linking the system element to the essence element(s) must be defined by the system item specification.

Element to Track Relationship

Each metadata element or control data element in a system item may optionally be described by a system track in a MXF header metadata package. This track will have an associated track number that is derived and linked to the system element using the same mechanisms as defined for essence elements.

Interfacing with Real-Time Stream Interfaces

MXF files may be directly created from standardized formats such as MPEG-2 system and elementary streams, AES3 data streams and DV-DIF packet streams. These formats may be mapped from one of several real-time interfaces such as SMPTE 259M (SDI), SMPTE 305.2M

(SDTI), SMPTE 292M (HD-SDI), or transport interfaces with real-time protocols such as IEEE-1394, ATM, IEEE802 (ethernet), ANSI fiber channel, and so on.

When a streaming file is captured, a file header is created and the essence is KLV wrapped on the fly. The data rate increases due to the KLV wrapping and addition of headers. Real-time streaming devices must ensure that any buffering requirements of a subsequent streaming interface are catered for with this change of data rate.

Conversion to and from the source format is always possible, but sometimes there will be loss of information. Not all streaming and storage formats are able to store the rich metadata constructs available in an MXF file. Often there will be a lossy data mapping where information in one format cannot be represented in the other. Eliminating this undesired loss is a function of the systems engineering that interconnects MXF and non-MXF systems. In many formats, research is being done to find ways in which MXF headers can be "tunneled" through the stream transport so that its use in an MXF system provides transparency as well as interoperability.

Annex A Specifications of the System Item Schemes

This annex describes the details of coding the two system items specified for the MXF generic container. Annex A.1 describes the SDTI-CP system item as used in the MXF generic container. Annex A.2 describes the system item—Scheme 1 that has been defined specifically for the MXF generic container and can provide system item support for a clip-wrapped generic container.

A System Scheme Compatible with the SDTI-CP Format

This section describes the system scheme defined in SMPTE 385M. This scheme was specifically designed to be compatible with that defined for SDTI-CP (SMPTE 326M) to allow for the Type D-10 (Sony IMX MPEG VTRs) to be mapped to MXF. This system scheme is implemented in the Sony eVTR (see Chapters 8 and 15) and provides only for the frame-wrapped generic container.

The MXF generic container uses the CP data structure, but can be made fully compatible with SDTI-CP by using the system item data defined by SMPTE 385M together with SMPTE 386M (the Type D-10 mapping standard).

SDTI-CP System Item

The SDTI-CP-compatible system item contains metadata that describes the operation of the content package in various modes and provides key metadata items related to the whole package. It can include metadata linked to essence elements in the picture, sound, and data items. Finally, the SDTI-CP compatible system item includes an optional downstream control element for future possible extension.

The SDTI-CP compatible system item is a combination of fixed-length pack and local set elements. Throughout the remainder of this annex, the SDTI-CP compatible system item will be called simply the "system item."

System Item Elements

The system item is coded as a sequence of up to six KLV packets, where each packet comprises metadata elements for different aspects of the content package. Figure 5.8 illustrates the system item data structure.

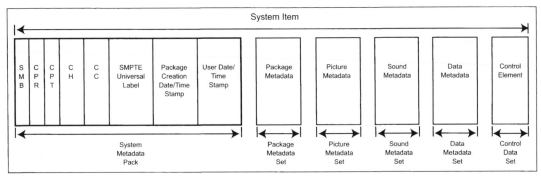

Figure 5.8 Elements of the SDTI-CP compatible system item

The elements are:

- A system metadata pack comprising a first 7 bytes and up to 50 further bytes (defined by the first byte of the pack).

- A package metadata set that provides metadata for all essence elements in the content package.

- A picture metadata set that provides metadata for any essence element in the picture item. The set includes identification to link the metadata item to a specific essence element in the picture item.

- A sound metadata set that provides metadata for any essence element in the sound item. The set includes identification to link the metadata items to a specific essence element in the sound item.

- A data metadata set that provides metadata for any essence element in the data item. The set includes identification to link the metadata items to a specific essence element in the data item.

- A control data set comprising only one data item that defines a downstream control element for the content package.

The system metadata pack is the first KLV packet in every content package. The content package metadata set is always present and immediately follows the system metadata pack. If there is no content package metadata, then the length field of the packet is simply zero.

The presence of each of the picture, sound, and data metadata sets and the control data set is determined by bits b3 to b0 of the first byte of the system metadata pack. Where one of these sets is present, its order in the sequence of sets is the same as the order of the sequence of picture, sound, and data items in the content package. This is intended to make it easier to match the system element to the essence element.

If a control data set is present, it must be the last KLV packet of this system item. To date, no control data set has ever been implemented.

There is a limit of one system, package, picture, sound, data or control element in the CP-compatible system item.

System Metadata Pack

Figure 5.9 illustrates the data structure of the system metadata pack.

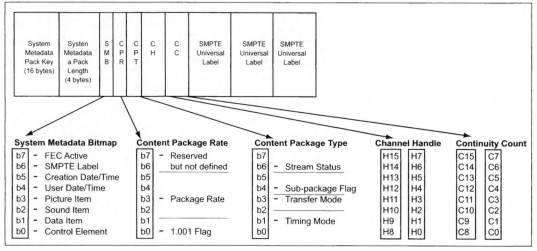

Figure 5.9 System metadata pack structure

Pack Key

The system metadata pack key is defined in Table 5.4.

Byte No.	Description	Value (hex)	Meaning
1	Object Identifier	06	
2	Label size	0E	
3	Designator	2B	ISO, ORG
4	Designator	34	SMPTE
5	Registry Category Designator	02	Sets & packs

Byte No.	Description	Value (hex)	Meaning
6	Registry Designator	05	Fixed length Packs
7	Structure Designator	01	Sets & Packs Registry
8	Version Number	01	Version 1 of the registry
9	Item Designator	0D	Organizationally Registered
10	Organization	01	AAF Association
11	Structure	03	MXF Generic container Keys
12	Structure Version	01	MXF-GC Version 1
13	Item Type Identifier	04	CP-compatible system item
14	System Scheme Identifier	01	SDTI-CP, Version 1
15	Metadata Element Identifier	01	System Metadata Pack
16	Reserved	00	

Table 5.4 Specification of the key for the system metadata pack

Pack Length

The system metadata pack length field uses 4-byte BER long-form encoding (83.xx.xx.xx).

Pack Value

The system metadata pack comprises up to 57 bytes defined as follows:

- A system metadata bitmap word (1 byte);
- A content package rate word (1 byte);
- A content package type word, including stream status flags (1 byte);
- A channel handle word (2 bytes);
- A continuity count word (2 bytes);
- An SMPTE universal label (16 bytes);
- A creation date/time stamp (17 bytes); and
- A user date/time stamp (17 bytes).

These component parts are briefly described in the following paragraphs. The full description of each component part can be found in SMPTE 326M (SDTI-CP).

The first component fields of the system metadata pack must be encoded as follows:

Core Fields

1. The system metadata bitmap:

   b7 = 0 (FEC not used)

b6 = 1 (SMPTE Universal label is present, see below)

b5 = 1 (creation date/time stamp is present)   [Note 1]

b4 = 0 or 1 (user date/time stamp)   [Note 1]

b3 = 0 or 1 (picture item present)   [Note 1]

b2 = 0 or 1 (sound item present)   [Note 1]

b1 = 0 or 1 (data item present)   [Note 1]

b0 = 0 or 1 (control element present)   [Note 1]

Note 1: The value depends on the application specification.

2. Content package rate: completed to reflect the correct value as defined in SMPTE 326M.

3. Content package type:

Stream status = 0, or 1~6 as required   [the first value is the default]

Sub-package flag = 0

Transfer mode = 0 (default value)   [Note 2]

Timing mode = 0 (default value)   [Note 2]

Note 2: These bits do not have the definition specified in SMPTE 326M and have no defined meaning in the MXF generic container. They must be set to the default value of zero.

4. Channel handle = 0 (default value).

5. Continuity count = modulo 65536 count as per SMPTE 326M. Note that the continuity count is not strictly required in many applications of an MXF file because the header metadata should correctly describe the timeline of the essence container. However, to maintain compatibility with the SDTI-CP system item definition, the continuity count must comply with SMPTE 326M.

SMPTE Universal Label

The SMPTE UL used in the system metadata pack identifies the MXF generic container and its payload. The value should be the essence container UL as defined in SMPTE RP224.

Creation Date/Time Stamp

A creation date/time stamp value should be entered in the system metadata pack according to SMPTE 326M. Note that the format of this item is defined by the first byte that has the metadata type value of "81_h" (timecode) or "82_h" (date-timecode) as defined in SMPTE 331M. In compliance with SMPTE 331M, of the 17 bytes available, only the first 9 bytes are used and the last 8 bytes are zero filled.

User Date/Time Stamp

A user defined date/time stamp value may be entered in the system metadata pack according to SMPTE 326M. The format of this item is identical to that described for the creation date/time stamp.

Package, Picture, Sound and Data Metadata Sets, and the Control Data Set

The first metadata set is the package metadata set that contains metadata for the package as a whole; such as, for example, a time code. This metadata does not require a "link" item as each metadata item of the set is related to the package as a whole rather than any individual part.

The subsequent metadata sets are picture, sound, and data metadata sets. They are only present if the associated picture, sound, or data item is present in the content package. Each metadata set has zero or more "link" metadata items that link each metadata item in the set to the associated essence element in the picture, sound or data item.

Note that each metadata item is coded in a metadata set with a local tag value for identification and a "link" metadata item that provides a unique link for subsequent metadata items to the associated essence element. This differs from the methods of linking defined for the header metadata.

Where present, the last data set is the control data set. Although coded as a data set, this set must contain only one control data item for compatibility with SMPTE 326M.

Each set is coded as a KLV local set. Figure 5.10 illustrates the basic structure of the package, picture, sound and data metadata sets and the control data set.

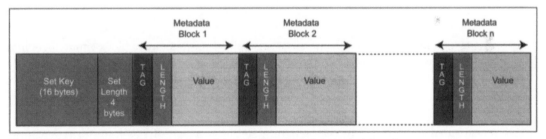

Figure 5.10 Structure for the package, picture, sound, and data metadata sets

Set Keys

The metadata and control data set keys are defined in Table 5.5.

Byte No.	Description	Value (hex)	Meaning
1	Object Identifier	06	
2	UL size	0E	
3	Designator	2B	ISO, ORG

Byte No.	Description	Value (hex)	Meaning
4	Designator	34	SMPTE
5	Registry Category Designator	02	Sets & packs
6	Registry Designato	Package, Picture, Sound & Data Metadata Sets = 43 Control data set = 63	Metadata sets (43h) = 1-byte tag, 2-byte length Control set (63h) = 1-byte tag, 4-byte length
7	Structure Designator	01	Sets & Packs Registry
8	Version Number	01	Version 1 of the registry
9	Item Designator	0D	Organizationally Registered
10	Organization	01	AAF Association
11	Structure	03	MXF Generic container Keys
12	Structure Version	01	MXF-GC Version 1
13	Item Type Identifier	04	CP-compatible system item
14	System Scheme Identifier	01	SDTI-CP, Version 1
15	Metadata Element Identifier	02~06	Package Metadata Set = 02_h Picture Metadata Set = 03_h Sound Metadata Set = 04_h Data Metadata Set = 05_h Control data set = 06_h
16	Metadata Block Count	xx	Number of metadata blocks in the Element (zero for the Control data set))

Table 5.5 Specification of the key for the system item sets

The package, picture, sound and data metadata sets embed the "metadata block count" byte into the set key to maintain compatibility with SMPTE 326M. The control data set does not require a "metadata count" byte and byte 16 is set to zero for just the control data set.

Set Length

Each metadata and control data set length field uses 4-byte BER long-form encoding (83.xx.xx.xx).

Although the SDTI-CP control set has data blocks with 4-byte length fields that can exceed the capability of 4-byte BER long-form encoding; in practice, the 16MB limit is more than sufficient.

Set Values

A metadata set comprises one or more metadata items. Each item of a set consists of a 1-byte tag followed by a 2-byte or 4-byte item length and completed by the metadata value. The item length is 2 bytes for data blocks in the picture, sound and data metadata sets, and 4 bytes in the control data set.

The common structures for data blocks in system item metadata sets are illustrated in Figure 5.11.

Tag Values

The tag value for any element in a metadata block is as defined in SMPTE 331M. Table 5.6 lists the tag values defined in SMPTE 331M-2004.

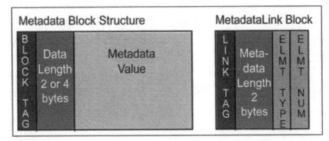

Figure 5.11 Structure for all metadata items (including the metadata link item)

Element Name	Item Name	Type Value (hex)	Description
Metadata link element	System item (metadata)	80	Used to link system metadata to picture, sound or data essence elements
SMPTE 12M time-code element	System item (metadata)	81	Contains a 16-byte field with 8 bytes of 12M time-code
SMPTE 309M date-time stamp element	System item (metadata)	82	Contains a 16-byte field with 8 bytes of 309M time and date information
UMID element	System item (metadata)	83	Contains a basic or extended UMID (32 or 64 bytes)
MPEG-2 picture editing element	System item (metadata)	84	Contains a data structure for MPEG editing. See SMPTE 331M for details
8-channel AES3 editing element	System item (metadata)	85	Contains a data structure for AES3 editing. See SMPTE 331M for details
Picture bit-stream splicing element	System item (metadata)	86	Contains a data structure with splicing information for MPEG video elementary streams with a GOP >1.
MPEG decoder buffer delay element	System item (metadata)	87	Used to support the low latency transfer mode of MPEG video elementary streams
KLV metadata element	System item (metadata)	88	For the carriage of any metadata that is KLV coded according to SMPTE 336M
AES3 non-audio metadata element	System item (metadata)	89	Describes individual channels of AES3 non-audio data in the 8channel AES3 element (type 10_h)

Table 5.6 Metadata, elements, and tag values

Metadata Link Item

Picture, sound, and data metadata items must be preceded by a metadata *link* item that provides a link between the metadata in the system item set and the associated essence element in a picture, sound, and data item. A metadata link item will occur at least as many times as there are essence elements to link. Each time a metadata link item is found, the metadata items that immediately follow will all refer to the linked essence element until the next metadata link item is found or the set is complete.

The value of the link metadata item is listed above in Table 5.6. In SMPTE 326M, the coding of this item does not include a length field. For consistency, this length field was added to the specification with the value of 0002_h.

Descriptors for CP-Compatible Metadata Elements

The appropriate header metadata package should have a descriptor for the "creation date/time" and "user date/time" item.

The definition of the descriptor for both date/time items follows in Table 5.7. This descriptor is a file descriptor as defined in the MXF format standard. The last four rows of this table are new metadata items added specifically for this date/time descriptor.

Item Name	Type	Len	Local Tag	UL Designator	Req ?	Meaning	Default
Date/Time Descriptor	Set Key	16		0D.01.01.01.01.46.00	Req	Defines the Date/Time Descriptor set	
Length	BER Length	Var			Req	Set length	
Instance UID	UUID	16	3C.0A	01.01.15.02	Req	Unique ID of this instance	
Generation UID	UUID	16	01.02	05.20.07.01.08	Opt	Generation Identifier	
Linked Track ID	UInt32	4	30.06	06.01.01.03.05	Opt	Link to (i.e. value of) the Track ID of the track in this Package to which this Descriptor applies.	
Sample Rate	Rational	8	30.01	04.06.01.01	Req	The field or frame rate of the Essence Container	
Container Duration	Length	8	30.02	04.06.01.02	Opt	The number of samples of the Essence Container (measured at the Sample Rate)	
Essence Container	UL	16	30.04	06.01.01.04.01.02	Req	The UL identifying the Essence Container described by this descriptor. Listed in SMPTE RP224	

Item Name	Type	Len	Local Tag	UL Designator	Req ?	Meaning	Default
Codec	UL	16	30.05	06.01.01.04.01.03	Opt	UL to identify a codec compatible with the Essence Container. Values are listed in SMPTE RP224	
Locators	Strong RefArray (Locators)	8+16n	2F.01	06.01.01.04.06.03	Opt	Ordered array of strong references to Locator sets If present, essence may be located external to the file. If there is more than one locator set an MXF Decoder shall use them in the order specified.	
Date/Time Rate	Rational	8	35.01	04.04.01.02.01	Opt	Defines the Date/Time rate where this differs from the essence container rate	Sample Rate
Date/Time Drop Frame	Boolean	1	35.02	04.04.01.02.02	Opt	TRUE if drop-frame is active	FALSE
Date/Time Embedded	Boolean	1	35.03	04.04.01.02.03	Opt	Is it embedded in other data?	TRUE
Date/Time Kind	UL	16	35.04	04.04.01.02.04	Req	Date/Time format kind. Values are listed in SMPTE RP224	

Table 5.7 Date/time descriptor

Mapping the SDTI-CP System Item to the MXF Generic Container

Mapping a fully implemented system item between SDTI-CP and the MXF generic container is a complex process. SMPTE 385M defines how to perform the conversion from the SDTI-CP system item to MXF in full detail. In the only implementation of SDTI-CP using the Type D-10 VTR, the mapping is actually quite simple as few of the features of the SDTI-CP system item were ever implemented. It may be possible that a fuller implementation may exist in the future but, for now, the conversion is actually straightforward. The full set of rules for conversion from

SDTI-CP to the MXF generic container are defined in sections 7 and 8 of SMPTE 385M and the reader should use this reference if full conversion is needed.

System Scheme-1

System Scheme-1 is a general-purpose system item that provides functionality and is a superset of the system item defined for SDTI-CP (SMPTE 326M). One of the key additions that make this a superset is the ability to include arrays of metadata items that can be used when the generic container uses clip wrapping.

The system item comprises a number of system elements. Each of these system elements contains metadata that is intimately related to essence within the same content package. The system elements are not intended to carry metadata that is to be described in the MXF header metadata. Neither are the system elements intended to carry metadata that should be carried in a non-essence data partition.

System scheme-1 (SMPTE 394M) defines a generic scheme for the GC system item that allows system elements to be added as required by an application. It is supported by SMPTE 405M which defines metadata elements and individual data items that are compatible with this GC system scheme-1.

In addition, SMPTE 389M defines a reverse play element that is compatible with this GC system scheme-1.

This system scheme defines a compatible superset of the SDTI-CP system item in that it provides a system item that can be used with all known generic container wrappings including clip wrapping. But, critically, this scheme can provide for a clip-wrapped essence container where the SDTI-CP compatible system item provides only for a frame-wrapped essence container. This system scheme-1 is a backwards-compatible extension to the SDTI-CP compatible system item.

Figure 5.12 illustrates the use of the system item in a content package.

In clip wrapping, one or more contiguous essence frames will be wrapped within a single GC essence element. Any GC system element must be capable of carrying any stream metadata that is associated with an essence element in a content package. Some stream metadata is present on

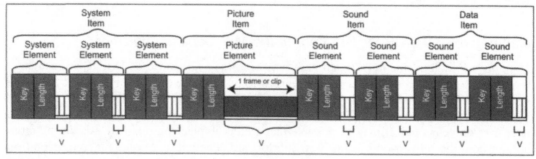

Figure 5.12 Illustration of a GC system item in a content package

a "per frame basis" and this needs to be mapped into a GC system element as a vector of values corresponding to the vector of frames within a GC essence element.

Because the system scheme-1 provides backwards compatibility with the SDTI-CP compatible system item, any elements that can be used in the SDTI-CP compatible system item can also be used in the system item defined in this scheme. However, this system scheme cannot generally be used where compatibility with SDTI-CP is required.

As noted before in this chapter, each system element may be coded as a local set or a fixed-length or variable-length pack.

GC System Scheme-1 Definitions

GC system scheme 1 comprises the following system element types as defined in Table 5.8.

Element Identifier	Element Name	Element Description
01_h	First Element	A System Element coded as a local set that contains metadata pertaining to the Content Package as a whole and is the first element in the System Item.
02_h	Subsequent Element	A System Element coded as a local set that contains metadata pertaining to the Content Package as a whole and is not the first element in the System Item.
03_h	Picture Item Descriptor	A System Element coded as a local set that contains metadata pertaining to any Picture Element in the Picture Item of the Content Package.
04_h	Sound Item Descriptor	A System Element coded as a local set that contains metadata pertaining to any Sound Element in the Sound Item of the Content Package.
05_h	Data Item Descriptor	A System Element coded as a local set that contains metadata pertaining to any Data Element in the Data Item of the Content Package.
06_h	Control Data Set	A System Element coded as a local set that contains control data pertaining to the Content Package.
07_h	Compound Item Descriptor	A set that contains metadata pertaining to any essence element in the Compound Item of the Content Package.
$08_h – 0F_h$	Reserved	Reserved.
$10_h – 7F_h$	Pack coded System Elements	A System Element coded as a SMPTE 336M compliant pack.

Table 5.8 Specification of the baseline elements in GC system scheme-1

Within the GC system scheme 1:

- The system item must start with a system element of type first element.
- There must be exactly one instance of a system element of type first element.
- There may be zero or more instances of the other system elements as required.

- The total number of instances of system elements must not exceed 127.

Other system elements not defined in Table 5.8 may be individually added by the creation of a separate document. SMPTE 389M (which provides the reverse play metadata) already adds a new element to the list in Table 5.8.

Element Keys

The key value of a system element is as defined below in Table 5.9.

Byte No.	Description	Value (hex)	Meaning
1~12	As defined in Table 5.4		See Table 5.4
13	Item Type Identifier	14	GC-Compatible System Item
14	System Scheme Identifier	02	GC System Scheme 1
15	Metadata or Control Element Identifier	See Table 5.10	As defined by Table 5.10 or by a separate document
16	Element Number	xx	Unique Element Instance Number (Always 00_h for the First Content Package Descriptor element)

Table 5.9 Specification of the set/pack keys for the system elements

The KLV-coded system element of type first element has the key value as defined in Table 5.7 above with byte 15 set to 01_h. It may have a KLV length field with the value "0" and hence the value field may be absent. The system element of type first element must be the first element within every essence container and it must only occur once within a content package.

Byte 16 is used to define the value of the element number in the range 00_h~$7F_h$. The system element of type "first element" uses the reserved value of 00_h. For all other instances of an element in the system item, the value must be set by the encoder to be unique amongst all elements in the system item. The use of this byte allows multiple system elements of the same kind within a content package. The unique element number allows, for example, multiple audio tracks to have several instances of a sound item descriptor each with metadata for one sound track.

All system elements that use local set encoding are coded using 2-byte local tags and either 2-byte or 4-byte lengths. Therefore, byte 6 of the set key has the values of "53_h" and "73_h" (as defined by SMPTE 336M). 2-byte lengths are typically used with frame-wrapping and 4-byte length with clip wrapping.

The tag values are defined by the system element specification. They have only the scope of the content package and are not added to the primer pack of header metadata (that is because these tags are part of the essence container, not the header metadata). The tag values must be selected to be unique and are either defined in SMPTE 405M or informatively copied into SMPTE 405M from the defining document.

Element Lengths

Element lengths are BER coded and typically have 4 bytes length (i.e. 83.xx.xx.xx).

Element Values

A system element of type *first element* or *subsequent element* relates to the content package as a whole.

All other system elements may optionally be linked to a specific essence element within the content package. This link is made via the essence track number such that the essence track number within the system element matches the 32-bit value comprising bytes 13, 14, 15, and 16 of the linked essence element key. This linking value (or batch of linking values) must be included in the appropriate system element value field to establish the link. By default, if no linking values are present in the system element, then the system element describes all essence elements of the associated type.

Note that this link value is identical to the essence track number as defined in the MXF generic container specification, but has only the scope of the essence in the content package within which it resides. It has no relationship to the header metadata track number property in a track in the header metadata.

Most (but not all) of the individual items within the system element sets or pack may be characterized as follows:

- Those that define a single value which describes some aspect of the essence element in frame-wrapping mode, or
- Those that define a single value which describes some aspect of the content in clip-wrapping mode, or
- Those that define a multiple value which describe some aspect of each frame of the content in clip-wrapping mode. These multiple values will typically be arrays so that the sequence of values in the array will relate directly to the sequence of frames in the clip.

Those individual items that define multiple values for use in clip-wrapping mode must constrain the first value in the system element to describe the first frame of the KLV wrapped essence element. Each subsequent value in the system element then relates the next frame in the essence element. The number of values in the system element will typically be equal to the number of frames in the essence element. The number of values in the system element must not exceed the number of frames in the essence element. However, the number of values in the system element may be less than the number of frames in the essence element.

Individual Data Definitions

In the following tables, individual metadata items are assigned with the following local tag value ranges:

"00.00$_h$" to "00.7F$_h$" are not used.

"00.80$_h$" to "00.FF$_h$" are reserved for individual metadata items defined in SMPTE 331M.

"01.00$_h$" to "7F.FF$_h$" are reserved for individual metadata items defined in this standard.

"80.00$_h$" to "FF.FF$_h$" are reserved for *dark* definitions defined elsewhere, either privately, or publicly.

CP-Compatible Individual Data Definitions

Table 5.10 defines the individual metadata or control data items that are compatible with SDTI-CP. The table defines a unique name, a data type, the length, the local tag value, the UL designator, the meaning and the standard on which this individual data item depends. The full 16-byte SMPTE UL value defined in SMPTE RP210 can be located from the UL designator value.

Unique Name	Type	Local Tag	UL Designator	Meaning	Standard
SMPTE 331M Metadata Items	See Table 5.6	00.xx$_h$ (where xx is the "Type Value" defined in Table 5.6.	See SMPTE 331M	See Table 5.6. The value of "xx$_h$" is the 1-byte local tag defined in Table 5.6 and ranges from "80$_h$" to a maximum of "FF$_h$." SMPTE 331M defines the SMPTE UL designator where needed.	SMPTE 331M

Table 5.10 Specification of SDTI-CP compatible individual data items

GC System Scheme Individual Data Definitions

Table 5.11 defines individual metadata or control data items that are compatible with the MXF generic container System Schemes, but not compatible with SMPTE 326M.

This table defines a unique name, a data type, the length, the local tag value, the UL designator, the meaning and the standard upon which this individual data item depends (where applicable). The full 16-byte SMPTE UL value defined in SMPTE RP210 can be located from the UL designator value.

Unique Name	Type	Length	Local Tag	UL Designator	Meaning	Standard
Frame Count	UInt32	4	01.01$_h$	07.02.02.01.01.01.00.00	The count of frames in either frame-wrapped or clip wrapped modes. In frame-wrapped mode, the value will be 1.	

Unique Name	Type	Length	Local Tag	UL Designator	Meaning	Standard
Timecode Array	T/C Array	$8+8n$	01.02_h	07.02.01.02.08.02.00.00	An ordered array of Timecodes with individual timecode packets as specified in Table 5.10 row 11.	SMPTE 331M
Clip ID Array	UMID Array	$8+32n$	01.03_h	01.01.15.0A.00.00.00.00	An ordered array of Basic UMIDs.	SMPTE 330M
Extended Clip ID Array	ExtUMID Array	$8+64n$	01.04_h	01.01.15.0B.00.00.00.00	An ordered array of Extended UMIDs.	SMPTE 330M
VideoIndex Array	VideoIndex Array	$8+15n$	01.05_h	04.04.04.03.01.00.00.00	An ordered array of Video Indexes. Each Video Index is a concatenation of classes 1.1, 1.2, 1.3, 2.1, and 2.2 as defined in SMPTE RP186 where each class is 3 bytes long. The CRCC bytes are not present in this data item.	SMPTE RP186
KLV Metadata Sequence	KLVMeta Sequence	$KLV*n$	01.06_h	03.01.02.10.06.00.00.00	A sequence of KLV metadata packets which shall have one KLV packet per frame in the sequence. Each individual KLV packet is specified in Table 1.10 row 18. Each individual packet may have a zero value where no metadata exists for the associated frame.	SMPTE 331M

Unique Name	Type	Length	Local Tag	UL Designator	Meaning	Standard
Sample Rate	Rational	8	30.01_h	04.06.01.01.00.00.00.00	The field or frame rate of the Essence Container (not the essence pixel clock rate). See SMPTE 377M.	SMPTE 377M
Essence Track Number	UInt32	4	48.04_h	01.04.01.03.00.00.00.00	Number used to link the System Item element to the essence track in the Content Package. See SMPTE 377M.	SMPTE 377M
Essence Track Number Batch	TrackNumberBatch	$8+4n$	68.01_h	01.04.01.04.00.00.00.00	An unordered list of Track Numbers used to link the System Item element to the essence tracks in the Content Package.	SMPTE 377M
Content Package Index Array	IndexArray	$8+11n$	68.03_h	04.04.04.02.06.00.00.00	An ordered array of index entries for each frame in this Content Package (see SMPTE 405M table 3 for details).	SMPTE 377M

Table 5.11 Specification of individual data items (dynamic)

6 Audio in MXF

Bruce Devlin

Introduction

MXF categorizes essence into picture, sound, and data. Sound essence covers uncompressed and compressed audio whether it be mono, stereo, multi-channel, or multilingual. MXF is intended for the interchange of complete or finished material. Although MXF can represent cut edits, it is not intended to be a full audio editing language, nor is it intended to be a full N channels from M sources crossbar-routing language.

As you will have seen in other chapters, MXF describes essence by using tracks and references. Figure 6.1 on the next page shows a typical *OP1a* file.

The material package sound track describes the output timeline that references the file package sound tracks. The file package sound track, in turn, is linked to a KLV element in the essence container via the FilePackage::SoundTrack::TrackNumber property, which will have the same value as the least significant 4 bytes of the KLV key. The actual essence is interleaved with the picture elements and is internal to the MXF file.

This referencing mechanism determines which audio content is played out. The subtlety comes in making it work in all the many and varied use cases that MXF addresses.

Before looking at specific audio examples, it is worth mentioning again the various MXF documents that are needed to understand audio:

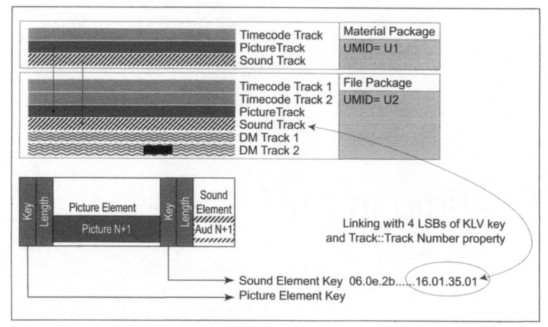

Figure 6.1 Locating the sound essence in a file

- SMPTE 377M—The MXF File Format Specification. This describes the tools available for describing and synchronizing the sound essence.

- SMPTE 379M—The generic container specification. This is the generic document that specifies how sound essence data is encapsulated in the file.

- SMPTE 382M—The AES/Broadcast Wave Mapping document. This specifies how AES audio frames and Broadcast Wave chunks are mapped into the MXF generic container.

- SMPTE 381M—The MPEG Mapping Specification. This specifies how MPEG compressed audio is mapped in to the MXF generic container and gives rules for aligning stored audio samples (MPEG or otherwise) with long-GOP MPEG content.

General Audio Usage

In the professional space, uncompressed audio is the most commonly used format, so we will use this to consider general issues concerning audio and then look at the specifics of AES format and Broadcast Wave format, followed by looking at compressed audio.

We talk about frame wrapping and clip wrapping in MXF. When there is synchronized video with the audio, what does the word *frame* actually mean? Common sense prevails here, and the word frame is a video frame. This means that frame wrapping is tied to the video frame as shown in Figure 6.2 on the next page.

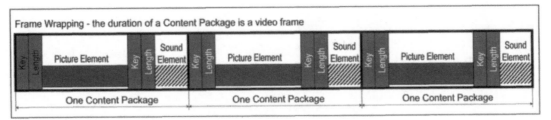

Figure 6.2 Frame wrapping with associated video essence

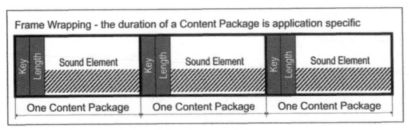

Figure 6.3 Frame wrapping in the absence of video essence

What about when an audio file is not associated with, and is not synchronized to, any video frames. What does *frame wrapping* mean in this case? At the time of writing, there is no hard and fast rule for this. It is common practice that a constant frame duration is chosen, and wrapping is performed with a constant number of audio samples within this duration as shown in Figure 6.3 above.

External Audio Files

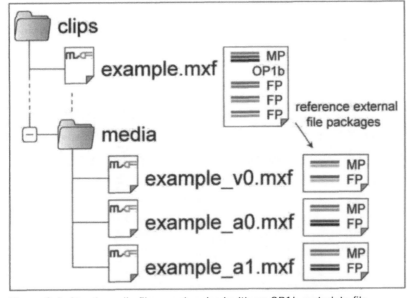

Figure 6.4 Atomic audio files synchronized with an OP1b metadata file

When an audio file is stored externally to the synchronized video stream, it is often the case that the audio file will be clip wrapped. This often occurs when atomic media files are created for synchronization by an OP1b (or higher) metadata file as shown in Figure 6.4.

As can be seen from the figure, the clips folder contains a file called example.mxf, This file is a metadata-only file whose

149

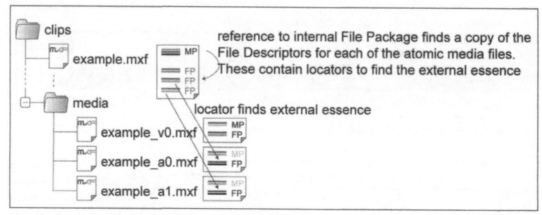

Figure 6.5 Linking to the external atomic audio files

material package references media files that are stored in the media folder. The media files, themselves, are atomic in nature—this means that they contain only a single file package with a single track, a single internal essence container and therefore can be considered as a mono-essence file.

There is a mono-essence file for each of the tracks in the material package of the example.mxf file in the clips folder. The source reference chain links the material package track to the file package track within the metadata-only file. This file package is identical in every way to the one in the atomic media file, with the exception that it contains *locators* to give a hint as to where the media files are stored. The linking mechanism is shown in Figure 6.5. Details of the low-level mechanisms are given in Chapter 3 in the Locators and Source Reference Chain sections.

This arrangement of audio files with a master video file is especially useful in a multi-language audio environment. The example shown in Figure 6.4 showed an OP1b master file with two audio tracks (e.g., English language and

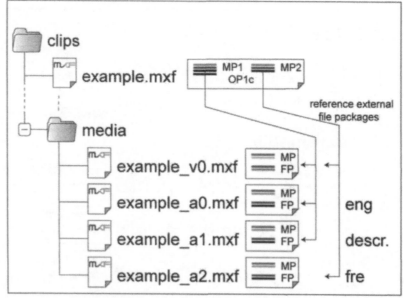

Figure 6.6 Multi-language audio files synchronized with an OP1c metadata file

audio description tracks). The principle can be extended for multi-language audio to create a file structure in which the addition or removal of extra audio languages is simple. This involves having an OP1c metadata-only file in the clips folder that contains a material package for each of the different language variants of the MXF asset. The media folder contains the different audio atomic files and the master video file to which the atomic audio files are synchronized. This is shown in Figure 6.6.

Synchronization

Before investigating how these media files are constructed, it is worth looking at the synchronization mechanism that ensures that the files are played out together. Chapter 3 gives the details of the source reference chain, and the meaning of *time* and *synchronization*. Here we will give an example of how they are used.

In Figure 6.4, we have an OP1b MXF file containing material packages with internal file packages that, in turn, reference external media files. The file packages of the media files are copied into the OP1b MXF file in order to use the Locator properties of the file package descriptor to find the essence. The first step to establish synchronization is to look at the material package. As you can see from Figure 6.7 below, we have a material package in the OP1b file that contains a timecode track: T_{m1}, a picture track: T_{m2} and two sound tracks: T_{m3} and T_{m4} (where the subscript "m" is used to denote the material package). None of these has an *origin* property (i.e., the origin is set to zero) and each track has a single SourceClip that lasts for the duration of the track. Let's assume that each of these tracks has an EditRate of E_{m1}, E_{m2}, E_{m3} and E_{m4}.

Two tracks are synchronized when the value of *position* along the track, divided by the EditRate of that track, is the same for each track; i.e., synchronization occurs when:

$$\frac{P_{m1}}{E_{m1}} = \frac{P_{m2}}{E_{m2}} = \frac{P_{m3}}{E_{m3}} = \frac{P_{m4}}{E_{m4}}$$

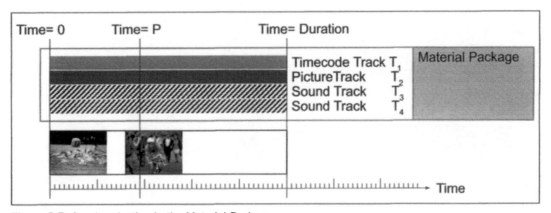

Figure 6.7 Synchronization in the Material Package

This, however, only gives synchronization in the material package. What we now need to find are the synchronized positions in the file package. For this we need to descend the source reference chain by inspecting the SourceClip properties of each track in the material package. For example, for material package Track 2:

SourceClipPos SCP_{m2} The SourceClip position within the material package measured in edit units of the material package E_{m2}.

StartPosition SP_{m2} The Start Position of the SourceClip in the referenced track, measured in Edit units of the material package E_{m2}.

Duration D_{m2} The Duration of the clip in the referenced track, measured in edit units of the material package E_{m2}.

SourcePackageID   The UMID of the file package that describes the content.

SourceTrackID   The TrackID within the file package of the referenced content.

Note that the referencing mechanism uses units of the material package and not the file package. Let's look at the case of track 1 in the material package, and assume it maps to track 1 of the file package.

We need to find the start position of the clip in file package edit units. This is because the index table is a lookup that converts between position (in file package units) and bytes offset within the essence stream. We know that Position/EditRate is equivalent for synchronized points on a timeline, and we are trying to find X—the equivalent position in file package units to P_{m2}.

$$\frac{X_{fp2}}{E_{fp2}} = \frac{(P_{m2} - SCP_{m2})}{E_{m2}} + \frac{SP_{m2}}{E_{m2}}$$

This formula states that the position in the referenced file package divided by the edit units of the track in that file package gives the elapsed time along that track. Likewise, the elapsed

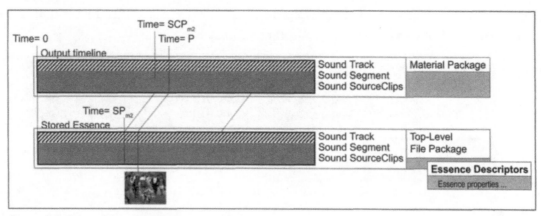

Figure 6.8 SourceClips that reference the middle of a track

time measured in material package edit units is given by the elapsed time from the start of the SourceClip added to the elapsed time of the start of the SourceClip within the destination file package. In the example of Figure 6.7 and in OP1a files, the value of SP_{m2} is always zero and the equation is trivial; however, in higher operational patterns, the SourceClip in the material package may be creating an *Edit Decision List* (EDL) and may therefore reference the middle of the file package. This is shown in Figure 6.8 on the opposite page.

Rearranging this equation gives:

$$X_{fp2} = \frac{E_{fp2}}{E_{m2}} \left(P_{m2} - SCP_{m2} + SP_{m2} \right)$$

Finally, to locate the essence in the file, we look up the position of the essence in the index table. If the picture essence is long-GOP MPEG-2, look up the byte offset using the index table mechanism explained in detail in Chapter 12.

Audio stored in an external atomic media file is almost always constant bytes per edit unit so the byte offset for track 3 can be simply calculated by multiplying X_{fp3} by the *EditUnitByteCount* in the index table and adding the *DeltaEntry* for the essence. This means that the byte offset in the essence container for the synchronized audio is as follows:

$$ByteOffset_3 = \left[\frac{E_{fp3}}{E_{m3}} \left(P_{m3} - SCP_{m3} + SP_{m3} \right) \right] \times EditUnitByteCount + DeltaEntry_{audio}$$

Describing Different Audio Tracks

Now that we can locate the synchronized samples in different files, we need to consider how to find the appropriate audio language in a multi-Language Audio OP1c file. This is done by adding a Descriptive Metadata Track to each of the file packages.

One proposal for doing this is to use SMPTE 380M—Descriptive Metadata Scheme 1, which is described fully in Chapter 11. The DM track has a single production framework and a single annotation set that describes the language appropriately. The FrameworkExtendedLanguage-Code property gives the language used for the subsequent entries in the sets. Usually this will be the letters *eng*. The PrimaryExtendedSpokenLanguageCode property is an ISO code that gives the actual spoken language—e.g., *fre* for *french* (assuming the text code was *eng*—if the text code was *fre*, then the language code is *fra*—see ISO 639 for the full tortuous details).

The extra annotation set is used to give the full name of the language and, in addition, extra information such as "*english* left," "*french* right," etc. At the time of writing, this proposal has not been finalized; however, the principals of full description are:

- Annotation::AnnotationKind—UTF-16 string technical.

- Annotation::AnnotationSynopsis—ish name of the spoken language with no leading or trailing spaces—e.g., *french*.

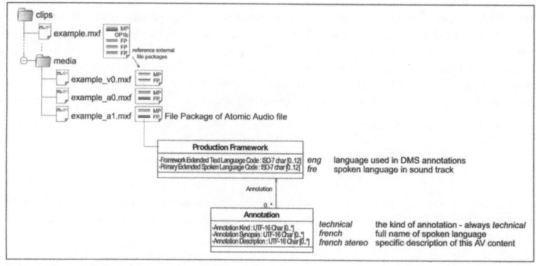

Figure 6.9 Annotation of multi-launguage audio

- Annotation::AnnotationDescription—value of the Annotation::AnnotationSynopsis field, followed by a single space character "0020," followed by additional metadata about the track in lower case. For example:
  - bars—when content is video color bars
  - slate—a slate signal for AV synchronization
  - title—a title sequence, probably preceding a feature
  - feature—the main a/v content
  - credits—a credits sequence, probably following a feature
  - black—the content is meant to be black
  - left—left channel
  - right—right channel
  - stereo—stereo signal
  - surround—surround sound signal
  - mono—mono audio signal

Any or all of these annotations may have a number appended; e.g., *french* credits 1 and *french* credits 2.

Placement of Audio Interleaved with Long-GOP MPEG

Chapter 9 describes the mapping of long-GOP MPEG in MXF. Synchronizing audio with long-GOP MPEG is a metadata-only issue when the external atomic media file strategy is used as shown above. When an interleaved OP1a file approach is taken, the placement of the synchronized audio within the file becomes an issue.

All mapping documents that have so far been standardized recommend that the picture data and the sound data in the element should be frame synchronized. The exception to this is long-

GOP MPEG, where reordering of the video frames takes place before display, and frame synchronization of the adjacent video and audio samples is not possible without reordering the audio, too. It should be noted that in MXF audio is NEVER reordered.

For the simple case of I-frame-only MPEG, there is no reordering to take place and the MPEG mapping document (SMPTE 381M) recommends co-timed content packages.

To make things more interesting, let's consider the case of a long-GOP MPEG file with 120 picture frames and a fixed GOP length of 12. This file will have 10 GOPs of video and will have 120 frames worth of audio. We will also assume that a video playback device will be able to play back all 120 frames. Figure 6.10 shows the first GOP in the sequence. This is a closed GOP that means that frames B_0 and B_1 can be decoded with only backwards prediction from frame I_2.

If we now look at the stored order of the frames, we can see that they are now not in the same sequence as the displayed order. The synchronized sound, however, is stored in its "displayed" order as shown in Figure 6.11.

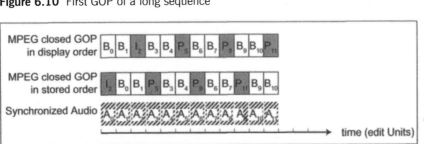

Figure 6.10 First GOP of a long sequence

Figure 6.11 First GOP of a long sequence-stored order

When we take into account the varying sizes of the different frames, we end up with the stored KLV structure as shown in Figure 6.12. A more complex example is given in Chapter 12, Figure 12.11.

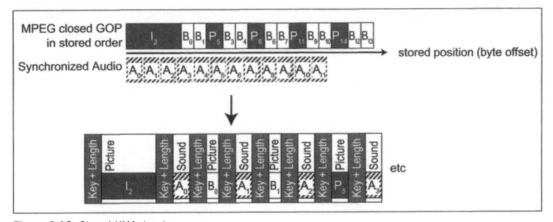

Figure 6.12 Stored KLV structure

Broadcast Wave Audio (BWF)

The Microsoft Wave Audio format (WAV) is a file format based on RIFF—The Resource Interchange File Format. This is an extensible file format where metadata and essence are carried in chunks that can be parsed when the chunk format is known, and skipped when the chunk format is not known. Mapping this format into MXF has the goal of trying to preserve the information contained in all the chunks, whether they are known standard chunks or whether they are opaque/dark/unknown chunks.

The actual audio essence samples are carried, unmodified, in the MXF file using Wave Audio Essence Elements. The essence samples may be uncompressed PCM, or compressed, and the actual format can be determined by looking at the SoundEssenceCompression property of the Wave Audio Essence Descriptor. For Broadcast Wave files, this is nearly always uncompressed PCM.

The two principal chunks of interest when mapping Broadcast Wave are the Format chunk <fmt> and the Broadcast Extension chunk <bext>.

The format chunk has the following structure:

```
typedef struct {
   UInt16 wFormatTag;
   UInt16 nChannels;
   UInt32 nSamplesPerSec;
   UInt32 nAvgBytesPerSec;
   UInt16 nBlockAlign;
   UInt16 wBitsPerSample;
} fmt-ck;
```

It carries metadata about the formatting of the audio samples and the individual properties are mapped directly into MXF as follows:

<fmt> chunk	MXF set :: Property	Meaning/Application
wFormatTag	WaveAudioEssenceDescriptor::Sound Essence Compression	The coding of the audio samples
nChannels	WaveAudioEssenceDescriptor::ChannelCount	The number of channels 1=mono, 2=stereo
nSamplesPerSec	WaveAudioEssenceDescriptor::SampleRate	e.g., 48000
nAvgBytesPerSec	WaveAudioEssenceDescriptor::AvgBps	This can be used to estimate playback buffers
nBlockAlign	WaveAudioEssenceDescriptor::BlockAlign	e.g., 2 for 16-bit samples, 6 for 20 & 24 bit samples
wBitsPerSample	WaveAudioEssenceDescriptor::QuantizationBits	The number of bits per sample

Table 6.1 <fmt> chunk mapping

For uncompressed PCM, the parameters above are related by the following formula:

$$BlockAlign = ChannelCount \times floor\left(\frac{QuantizationBits + 7}{8}\right)$$

where floor means "take the integer part closest to the value zero only." The reverse is also true:

$$ChannelCount = \frac{BlockAlign}{floor\left(\dfrac{QuantizationBits + 7}{8}\right)}$$

For compressed signals, however, ChannelCount and BlockAlign are independent and the ChannelCount property must be specified equal to the number of channels in the decompressed signal.

For audio data formatted according to SMPTE 337M - Format for Non-PCM audio and data in an AES3 Serial Digital Audio Interface—the number of AES channels (otherwise known as AES subframes) that are present in the essence data is given by the equation:

$$SubframeCount = \frac{BlockAlign}{floor\left(\dfrac{QuantizationBits + 7}{8}\right)}$$

Broadcast related metadata is carried in the <bext> chunk. At the time of writing, there were differences between the ITU and the EBU variants of the Broadcast Wave specification. The Audio Engineering Society took up the task of harmonizing the different variants, and there is a possibility that the coverage of the <bext> chunk by this book may become out of date as a result of that work.

The <bext> chunk carries the following metadata:

```
typedef struct {
  char Description[256];
  char Originator[32];
  char OriginatorReference[32];
  char OriginationDate[10];
  char OriginationTime[8];
  UInt32 TimeReferenceLow;
  UInt32 TimeReferenceHigh;
  UInt16 Version;
  UInt8 UMID[64];
  UInt8 Reserved[190];
  char CodingHistory[];
} bext-ck;
```

These individual properties are mapped into MXF according to the following table. In Broadcast Wave, the mappings are ISO-7 character strings, whereas in MXF, they are always UTF-16 strings. This means that round tripping from Broadcast Wave to MXF and back will always work, but not necessarily the other way round. This is a limitation of the Broadcast Wave format that cannot be rectified.

Status	\<bext\> chunk	MXF set :: Property	Notes
opt	Description	ClipFramework::Annotation::AnnotationDescription	
opt	Originator	ClipFramework::ContactsList::Person or ClipFramework::ContactsList::Organization	Mapping depends on whether the origina-tor is a person or an organization.
opt	OriginatorReference	ClipFramework::ClipNumber	This is an originator-specific ISO-7 chart
req	OriginationDate	FilePackage::PackageCreationDate	BWF format is "yyyy-mm-dd"
req	OriginationTime	FilePackage::PackageCreationDate	BWF format is "hh-mm-ss"
req	TimeReference (Low/High)	FilePackage::AudioTrack:: Origin	The value stored in MXF is actually the negative value of WAV TimeReference so that the sign of the Origin is correct.
	Version	(unused)	
req	UMID[0-31]	SourcePackage::PackageUID	
	Reserved	(unused)	The specified number of unused bytes.
req	CodingHistory	PhysicalPackage:: WaveAudioPhysicalDescriptor:: CodingHistory	This is text descrip-tion of the cod-ing history that is preserved in the Wave Audio Physical Descriptor.

Table 6.2 \<bext\> chunk mapping

In addition to these two important chunks, there may be other chunks that need to be preserved in the MXF file. This and other metadata that was present in the original file is carried in the Wave Audio Physical Descriptor (see Figure 3.6). Why is this a *physical descriptor* and not a *file descriptor*? This is because a broadcast wave file is not an MXF file and cannot be included as part of the source reference chain. The best we can do is to take the metadata that was in the original file and persist it in the MXF mapping and treat this as the root of a new source reference chain. This means that the file package that describes the mapped BWF essence can have a SourceClip referencing a lower-level Source Package that has a Wave Audio Physical Descriptor containing the metadata found in the file before it was mapped into MXF.

SMPTE 382M explicitly maps the Level Chunk \<lvl\> and the Quality Chunk \<qlty\>, but there may be other chunks that are defined and standardized within the WAV format after the stan-dardization of SMPTE 382M. These chunks are carried in the Wave Audio Physical Descriptor as shown in Figure 6.15. This is achieved by creating a Universal Label in the SMPTE metadata dictionary (RP210) for each of the properties of the new chunk. These are then carried as new optional properties in the physical descriptor. No new standardization process is needed because optional properties do not require the revision of the standard.

For example, to insert the <fact-ck> chunk property

```
DWORD dwHeadBitrate
```

into the WaveAudioPhysicalDescriptor, a data type corresponding to DWORD would be registered in the SMPTE Groups and Types Registry. Then, a SMPTE UL corresponding to the property `dwHeadBitrate` having the data type `DWORD` would be created in RP210. The primer pack mechanism in SMPTE 377M would be used to allocate this property a 2-byte dynamic tag that would then be used to insert the data value into the WaveAudioPhysicalDescriptor. An encoder or decoder wishing to use this property must know its RP210 UL.

Item Name	Type	Len	Meaning
Wave Audio Physical Descriptor	set UL	16	Defines the Wave Audio Physical Descriptor set (a collection of parametric metadata copied from the BWF <bext> and <qlty> chunks).
Length	BER Length	4	set length
All items from the Generic Descriptor in SMPTE377M (File Format Specification Table 17) to be included.			
CodingHistory	UTF-16 String	N	Coding History from BWF <bext> chunk
FileSecurity Report	UInt32	4	FileSecurityCode of quality report
FileSecurity Wave	UInt32	4	FileSecurityCode of BWF wave data
BasicData	UTF-16 String	Var	« Basic data » from <qlty> chunk
StartModulation	UTF-16 String	Var	« Start modulation data » from <qlty> chunk
QualityEvent	UTF-16 String	Var	« Quality event data » from <qlty> chunk
EndModulation	UTF-16 String	Var	« End modulation data » from <qlty> chunk
Quality Parameter	UTF-16 String	Var	« Quality parameter data » from <qlty> chunk
Operator Comment	UTF-16 String	Var	« Comments of operator » from <qlty> chunk
CueSheet	UTF-16 String	Var	« Cue sheet data » from <qlty> chunk
UnknownBWFChunks	Array of Strongref (Unknown Chunk sets)	8+ 16*N	An array of strong references to Unknown Chunk sets containing RIFF chunks that were found in the BWF stream, but were unknown to the MXF encoding device at the time of encoding. An array starts with a Uint32 number of items followed by a Uint32 length of item, hence overall length is 8 + 16*N.

Table 6.3 The Wave Audio Physical Descriptor—all properties are optional

If there are any unknown BWF chunks in the BWF file, then they should be carried in *Unknown-Chunk* sets as shown in Table 6.3 above. If one or more unknown chunks are encountered by an MXF encoder, then those chunks should each be stored as an unknown chunk set within the header metadata of the MXF File. The WaveAudioPhysicalDescriptor property, Unknown-BWFChunks, contains a strong reference to the Instance UID of all unknown chunk sets in the file that are associated with this essence. This allows all the unknown chunk sets to be found when parsing the stream.

AES Audio

The lowest-level representation of the AES3 interface is a sequence of *subframes*. Each subframe is intended to carry a single PCM sample, and contains 32 time slots, each of which can carry a single bit of information. A pair of subframes, each containing the PCM word of one audio channel, make up an AES3 frame containing two PCM words, one from channel 1 and one from channel 2. A sequence of 192 frames makes up a block. The 192 channel status bits for each

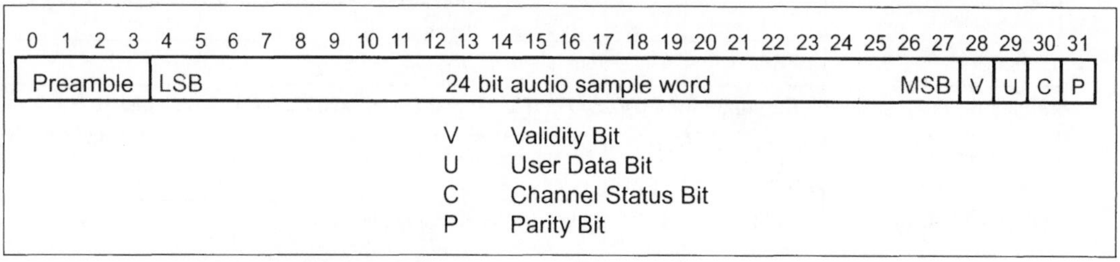

Figure 6.13 The AES3 subframe carrying audio

channel during a block make up the 192-bit (24-byte) channel status word for that channel. The standard usage of the 32 AES3 time slots is modified when conveying non-PCM data.

Only the actual audio samples of the AES3 are mapped into the essence container of the MXF file. Other data such as the *User Bits* and the *Channel status* bits are mapped into MXF user data (as described below). The wrapping of the essence is usually video-frame based when interleaved with video data, and clip based when stored as atomic essence for editing. Figure 6.14 on the opposite page shows frame-based wrapping and demonstrates the specific case of 20-bit samples from Figure 6.13 packed into 3 bytes per sample.

Mapping of the User Bits and the channel status bits requires that the MXF mapping application detects the Z preamble (E817$_h$) that occurs every 192 AES frames. This marks the beginning of the block structure used to organize the AES ancillary data.

One of the most common mappings of the channel status (C) bits is to take the block of 192 bits (24 bytes) and map them in a fixed fashion into the AES Audio Essence Descriptor FixedChannelStatus property. Likewise the UserData can be mapped into the FixedUserData property of the descriptor. The full AES Audio Essence Descriptor set is shown in Figure 6.15 on the opposite page. Note that most of the properties of the descriptor are optional, and in many cases the properties are not used

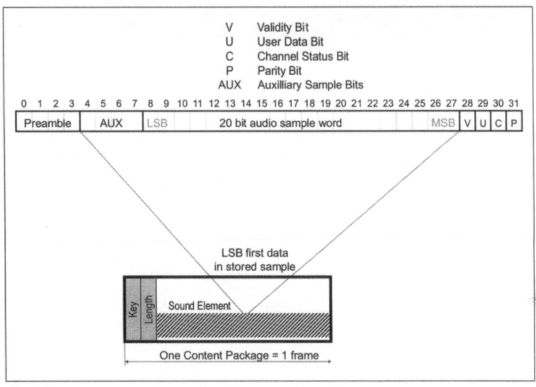

V   Validity Bit
U   User Data Bit
C   Channel Status Bit
P   Parity Bit
AUX Auxilliary Sample Bits

Figure 6.14 Frame wrapping of AES audio (20 bits per sample)

for a simple AES mapping. Some properties are mapped from a WAV audio source rather than an AES audio source.

Item Name	Type	Len	Local Tag	UL Designator	Req ?	Meaning	Default
AES3 Audio Essence Descriptor	Set UL	16		06.0e.2b.34. 02.53.01.01. 0D.01.01.01. 01.01.47.00	Req	Defines the AES3 Audio Essence Descriptor Set (a collection of Parametric metadata).	
Length	BER Length	4			Req	Set length.	
All items from the Sound Essence Descriptor							
BlockAlign	Uint16	2	3D.0A	04.02.03.02.01	Req	Sample Block alignment.	

Item Name	Type	Len	Local Tag	UL Designator	Req ?	Meaning	Default
SequenceOffset	Uint8	1	3D.0B	04.02.03.02.02	Opt	Zero-based ordinal frame number of first essence data within five-frame sequence (see 5.2).	
AvgBps	Uint32	4	3D.09	04.02.03.03.05	Req	Average Bytes per second (see 6.2).	
Channel Assignment	UL	16	3D.32	04.02.01.01. 05.00.00.00	Opt	UL enumerating the channel assignment in use eg. SMPTE 320M-A.	
PeakEnvelope-Version	UInt32	4	3D.29	04.02.03.01.06	Opt	Peak envelope version information (BWF dwVersion).	none
PeakEnvelope-Format	UInt32	4	3D.2A	04.02.03.01.07	Opt	Format of a peak point (BWF dwFormat)	none
PointsPerPeak-Value	UInt32	4	3D.2B	04.02.03.01.08	Opt	Number of peak points per peak value (BWF dwPointsPerValue).	none
PeakEnvelope-BlockSize	UInt32	4	3D.2C	04.02.03.01.09	Opt	Number of audio samples used to generate each peak frame (BWF dwBlockSize).	none
PeakChannels	UInt32	4	3D.2D	04.02.03.01.0A	Opt	Number of peak channels (BWF dwPeakChannels).	none
PeakFrames	UInt32	4	3D.2E	04.02.03.01.0B	Opt	Number of peak frames (BWF dwNumPeakFrames).	none

Item Name	Type	Len	Local Tag	UL Designator	Req ?	Meaning	Default
PeakOfPeaks Position	Position	8	3D.2F	04.02.03.01.0C	Opt	Offset to the first audio sample whose absolute value is the maximum value of the entire audio file (BWF dwPosPeakOfPeaks, extended to 64 bits).	N/A
Peak EnvelopeTimestamp	TimeStamp	8	3D.30	04.02.03.01.0D	Opt	Time stamp of the creation of the peak data (BWF strTimeStamp converted to TimeStamp).	none
PeakEnvelopeData	Stream	N	3D.31	04.02.03.01.0E	Opt	Peak envelope data (BWF peak_envelope_data).	None
Emphasis	Uint8 (enum)	1	3D.0D	04.02.05.01.06	Opt	AES3 Emphasis (aligned to LSB of this property).	00
BlockStartOffset	Uint16	2	3D.0F	04.02.03.02.03	Opt	AES3 Position of first Z preamble in essence stream.	0
AuxBitsMode	Uint8 (enum)	1	3D.08	04.02.05.01.01	Opt	AES3 Use of Auxiliary Bits.	000
ChannelStatusMode	Uint8 (enum) Array	8+N*1	3D.10	04.02.05.01.02	Opt	AES3 Enumerated mode of carriage of channel status data.	NONE
FixedChannelStatusData	Array of bytes	8+N*24	3D.11	04.02.05.01.03	Opt	AES3 Fixed data pattern for channel status data.	per AES3 minimum

Item Name	Type	Len	Local Tag	UL Designator	Req ?	Meaning	Default
UserDataMode	Uint8 (enum) Array	8+N*1	3D.12	04.02.05.01.04	Opt	AES3 Enumerated mode of carriage of user data, defined by AES3 section 4. (Aligned to LSB of this property.)	0 0
FixedUserData	Array of bytes	8+N*24	3D.13	04.02.05.01.05	Opt	AES3 Fixed data pattern for user data (see 8.3).	0

Table 6.4 AES Audio Essence Descriptor

Dolby E in MXF

Dolby E is a special case of mapping AES audio into MXF. First, we need to look at how Dolby-E is mapped into the AES stream. This is governed by SMPTE 337M: "Format for Non-PCM Audio and Data in an AES3 Serial Digital Audio Interface." As far as the AES stream is concerned, the Dolby E stream is data, and not audio. It is carried in AES frames as shown in Figure 6.15 .

SMPTE 382M is now used to map this data stream into the MXF essence container. Placing the essence into the file is pretty similar for both audio and data modes of AES. The precise data carried in the stream can be determined by the SoundEssenceCompression property of the General Sound Essence Descriptor in the file package of the MXF file (see Figure 3.6).

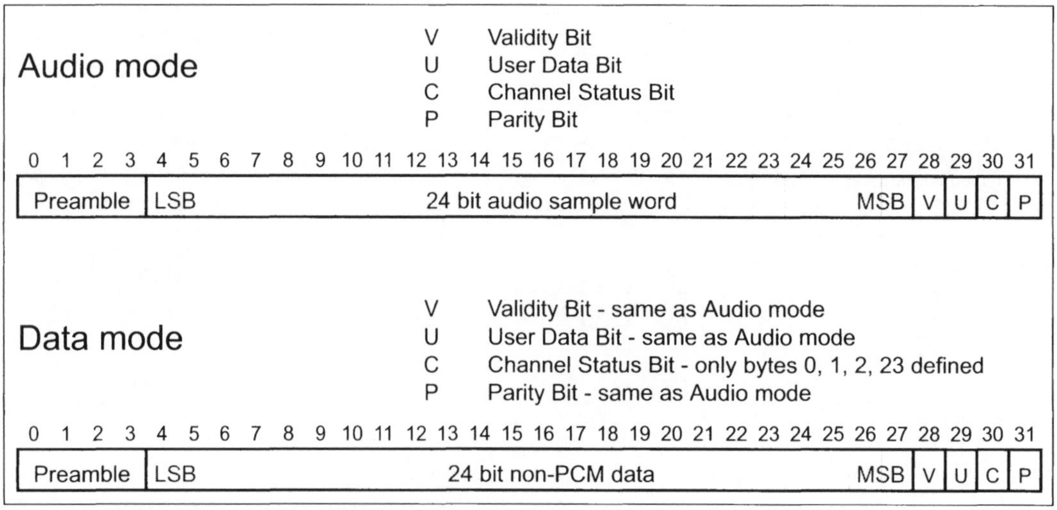

Figure 6.15 Carriage of data in the AES stream

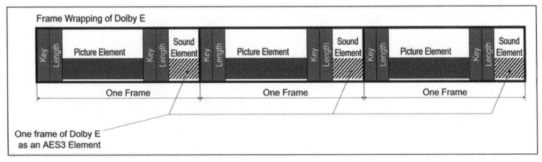

Figure 6.16 Embedding of the Dolby-E essence

Dolby E audio is intrinsically video-frame based and, as such, should be mapped into a frame wrapped MXF file. Figure 6.16 shows the basic frame-based KLV elements containing Dolby-E essence embedded in an AES stream.

All metadata mappings are the same as for putting AES into MXF, with the exception that

SoundEssenceCompression == 06.0E.2B.34.04.01.01.01. 04.02.02.02.03.02.1C.00

The UL value for this parameter can be found in the SMPTE Labels Registry RP224.

7 DV, DVC Pro, and DVCam in MXF

Bruce Devlin

Introduction

The generic mapping of the DV family of compressed streams into MXF is standardized in SMPTE 383M. There are several different variants of the DV specification in use both in the consumer space and in the professional space. The MXF mapping document, SMPTE 383M, concentrates on the similarities in the DV variants in order to present them to an MXF application as a single essence class. At the time of designing the MXF specification, there were several ways in which audio was handled within DV files which gave rise to long debates about *cheese*—but more of that later. Samples of DV MXF files can be found at *http://www.themxfbook.com/*.

DV Basics

DV is a DCT block based compression scheme that was originally designed for intra-frame coding with a fixed number of bits per video frame so that storage on a helically scanned tape was straightforward. The manufacturers of DV equipment made some variations between their equipment models that led to a number of different compression standards, all of which bear the title DV. Among these are:

- IEC61834-2 (1998-08), Recording—Helical-Scan Digital Video Cassette Recording System using 6.35mm Magnetic Tape for Consumer Use (525-60,625-50,1125-60 and 1250-50 Systems), Part 2: SD format for 525-60 and 625-50 Systems.

- SMPTE 314M-1999, TelevisionData Structure for DV-Based Audio, Data, and Compressed Video — 25 and 50 Mbps.

- SMPTE 370M-2002, Television—Data Structure for DV-Based Audio, Data, and Compressed Video at 100 Mbps 1080/60i, 1080/50i, 720/60p.

For most professional users of DV in MXF it is important to understand a few of the underlying differences between the standards. Before listing these, it is useful to go through some of the DV terminology so that the table in Figure 7.1, and the rest of this chapter, makes some sense.

Terminology

DV	Generic term used in this chapter to refer to any DV stream.
DIF	Digital interface.
IEC-DV	A DV stream compliant with IEC61834-2 (e.g., DV, mini DV, DVCam).
DV-Based	A DV stream compliant with SMPTE 314M or SMPTE 370M (DVC Pro, Digital S).
DV-DIF block	The smallest unit of a DV stream. A 3-byte ID followed by 77 bytes of data. There are many different types of DIF blocks, such as header, subcode, VAUX, audio, and video blocks.
DIF sequence	A specific sequence of DIF blocks as defined in SMPTE 314M.
DV-DIF data	A generic term for a number of DIF blocks.
DV-DIF frame	A generic term for all the DIF sequences that make up a picture frame.
DIF channel	A number of DIF sequences as defined in SMPTE 314M. For example, an MXF file with 50 Mbps DV-based content comprises 2 channels of 25 Mbps DV-based content.

The major difference between the different flavors of DV comes in the 625 chroma sampling as shown in Figure 7.1 below. In a 625 line IEC DV stream, the chroma sampling is 4:2:0, whereas in the DV-based stream, the chroma sampling is 4:1:1. There are more audio options available in

	IEC DV	25 Mbps DV based	50 Mbps DV based
525 line video chroma format	4:1:1	4:1:1	4:2:2
625 line video chroma format	4:2:0	4:1:1	4:2:2
Audio locked to video	Usually	Always	Always
Audio	48 kHz (16 bits, 2ch) 44.1 kHz (16 bits, 2ch) 32 kHz (16 bits, 2ch) 32 kHz (12 bits, 4ch)	48 kHz (16 bits, 2ch)	48 kHz (16 bits, 2ch)

Figure 7.1 Major differences between IEC DV and DV-based

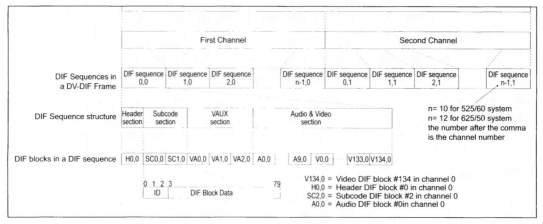

Figure 7.2 A 50 Mbps DV-based DV-DIF frame

the IEC DV variant, although in professional applications, running at 48kHz two channel within the DV-DIF stream is usually preferred.

In addition to the differences shown in Figure 7.1, there are differences of signaling, but these usually don't affect MXF wrapping. The issue causing most interoperability problems with DV is the handling of the audio. The DV standards define a coding method and a bitstream syntax of the

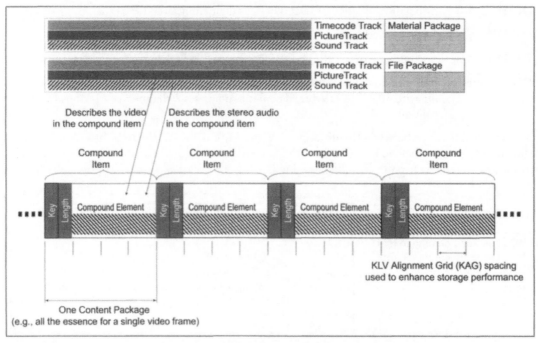

Figure 7.3 An MXF file with a frame-wrapped 25 Mbps DV-DIF sequence

DV-DIF sequence of video, audio and data DIF blocks and many DV editing applications work directly on the DV-DIF frame shown in Figure 7.2 for a 50 Mbps DV-based stream.

During the design of the MXF generic container, there was much debate over whether a DV-DIF frame should be wrapped as a picture element, or some new element. In the end, the verdict was that it should be wrapped up as a *compound element* on the grounds that the DV-DIF sequence was a compound element of video, audio and data DV-DIF blocks. A typical frame-wrapped MXF file with a 25 Mbps DV-DIF sequence inside is shown in Figure 7.3 on the previous page.

The material package references the video and audio described by the file package. In turn, the file package links to the compound item and indicates that the video is stored in the compound item, and the audio is stored in the compound item. This is achieved by setting the PictureTrack::Track Number property and the SoundTrack::TrackNumber property to be equal to the least significant 4 bytes of the compound element KLV key.

Keeping the audio in this format for editing, or manipulating the file is very inconvenient because audio DV-DIF blocks are shuffled in with the video and data DV-DIF blocks. There are four common actions to be performed with DV files:

1. Leave the audio where it is. This is the *Cheddar* cheese option as shown in Figure 7.3.

2. Unshuffle and decode the audio in the DIF blocks and erase the audio in those DIF blocks with silence—effectively erasing the audio to leave holes. This is the *Swiss* cheese option.

3. Unshuffle and decode the audio in the DIF blocks, but leave the original audio untouched where it was. There is the potential for the extracted audio and the DV-DIF block audio to get

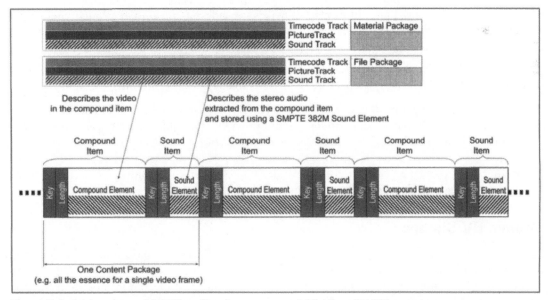

Figure 7.4 A blue cheese MXF File with a frame-wrapped 25 Mbps DV-DIF sequence

out of sync. This is known as the *blue* cheese option because the DV-DIF audio is left to go "moldy," and is shown for an OP1a file in Figure 7.4.

4. Store the video as a compound item in one atomic file, and store the audio separately in another atomic file. This is similar to the blue cheese option, and is becoming more popular at the time this book was written. The way in which the referencing works is described in Chapter 6.

The stereo audio in Figure 7.4 is extracted from the compound item when the MXF file is created and is stored separately in a SMPTE 382M compatible AES or BWF sound element. This sound element is explained in Chapter 6. Assuming no audio processing has been performed to the audio samples, it is likely that the main differences between the files shown in Figures 7.3 and 7.4 will be:

	Cheddar Cheese	Blue Cheese
SoundTrack::TrackNumber	Links to compound element	Links to BWF element
EssenceContainerULs in the Partition Pack	DV essence container UL only	DV essence container UL and BWF essence container UL
Descriptors	Multiple Descriptor Generic Picture Essence Descriptor Generic Sound Essence Descriptor	Multiple Descriptor Generic Picture Essence Descriptor Wave Audio Essence Descriptor
Index Tables	One entry in the Delta Entry Array	Two Entries in the Delta Entry Array

Table 7.1 Difference between DV wrapping options

The indexing of the DV content changes between the two storage methodologies. In the *Cheddar* cheese option, there is only one entry in the delta entry array because there is only one stored element in the essence container. There are, however, two tracks in the file package that refer to the same stored element. This, unfortunately, makes the indexing of audio in *Cheddar* cheese DV a special case. The index table for Figure 7.3 is shown in Figure 7.5.

Because DV is a fixed number of bytes per frame, no IndexTableSegment::IndexEntries are needed in the index table. The ByteOffset of each compound element in the essence stream can be calculated by multiplying the frame number by the IndexTableSegment::EditUnitByteCount.

Indexing and handling the *Blue* cheese variant is very similar to all the other MXF essence types, and is the preferred way of handling audio in MXF. The index table is very straightforward and is shown in Figure 7.6. There are now two entries in the IndexTableSegment::Delta Entry array, indicating the start position of each element. The overall constant length of a Content Package is now 149804 and is stored in the IndexTableSegment::EditUnitByteCount property. Further subtleties of indexing are discussed in the Chapters 6 and 12.

Atomic DV Storage

The P2 Camera format uses Atomic Clip-Wrapped DV MXF files stored on a solid state memory card. The audio associated with the DV-based video is stored in atomic audio MXF file. The association of the audio and video files is not controlled by an MXF file, but instead controlled by an external XML metadata file and a fixed directory structure. At the time of writing this book,

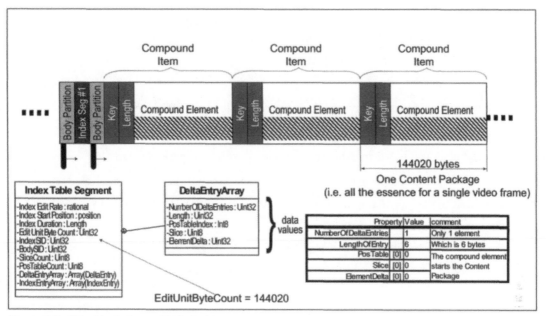

Figure 7.5 "Cheddar" cheese DV indexing

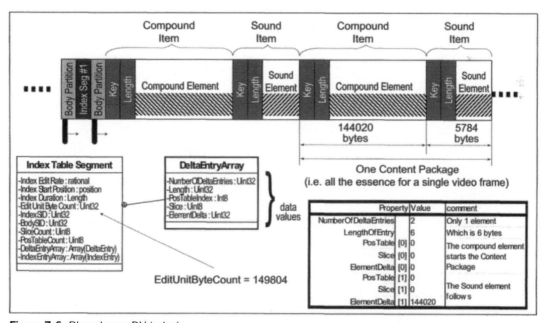

Figure 7.6 Blue cheese DV indexing

a SMPTE Recommended Practice was being created to describe the format in detail. The key features of the format from the MXF perspective are:

- Each essence file is stored using OP-Atom.

- Each essence file is clip wrapped.

- The video essence file is an atomic DV-based video file wrapped according to SMPTE 383M.

- The audio essence files are atomic AES audio files wrapped according to SMPTE 382M.

- No more than 16 audio essence files are associated with a single DV video file.

- Any audio blocks in the DV-based video file are ignored (and therefore "blue" cheese).

- Essence files are associated with each other via an external XML file and are organized into clips.

- The duration of each and every atomic essence file in a clip is the same.

- Further information on the P2 format can be found in Chapter 15.

8 D-10 and D-11 in MXF

Jim Wilkinson

This chapter introduces the reader to two mappings of the content from widely used VTR tape formats to MXF files. The first half of the chapter introduces those parts of the mapping that are common to both formats. The second half defines the details of the mappings for the type D-10 and type D-11 individually.

Introduction to the Type D-10 and D-11 Formats

The specification for the type D-10 format is defined by a suite of SMPTE standards The type D-10 uses MPEG-2 422P@ML video compression constrained to operate with intra-frame coding operating at data rates of 30, 40 and 50 Mbps. The audio recording offers four channels at 24-bit resolution or eight channels at 16-bit resolution. The type D-10 format is defined by two SMPTE standards:

- SMPTE 356M for the MPEG video compression and

- SMPTE 365M for the VTR format.

A recommended practice, SMPTE RP204 specifies an encoder template for the type D-10 format as comprising one MPEG-2 422P@ML video *essence element*, one 8-channel AES3 audio essence element, and one data essence element.

In addition, the type D-10 format uses the SDTI-CP data interface specified using the following two standards:

- SMPTE 326M for the SDTI-CP and

- SMPTE 331M for the SDTI-CP essence and metadata element definitions.

Again, SMPTE RP204 applies.

The specifications for the type D-11 format define a high definition VTR that records compressed pictures using 1920*1080 picture sources and four AES3 audio channels each at 24 bits/channel. type D-11 is defined by three SMPTE standards:

- SMPTE 367M defines the picture compression standard;

- SMPTE 368M defines the tape format; and

- SMPTE 369M defines a digital interface using SDTI.

Introduction to Mapping of Type D-10 and D-11 Formats into MXF

The type D-10 MXF essence mapping uses *frame wrapping* where each frame-based *content package* comprises the system, picture, sound, and *data items*. The system, picture, sound, and *data elements* are each of constant duration, so a very simple *index table* can be used that applies to all frames in the *essence container*. The KAG value is set to 512 bytes to match the block size for SCSI storage devices. This design has made it easy for existing type D-10-based VTR models to be upgraded to support MXF through a small adaptor card. SMPTE 386M defines the mapping of the type D-10 format into MXF.

Like type D-10, the type D-11 MXF essence mapping uses frame wrapping where each frame-based content package comprises the system, picture, sound, and data items. The system, picture, sound, and data elements are each of constant duration so a very simple index table can be used that applies to all frames in the essence container. The KAG value is again set to 512 bytes to match the block size for SCSI storage devices. SMPTE 387M defines the mapping of the type D-11 format into MXF.

In both the mapping of type D-10 and D-11 into MXF, the main requirement has been to provide for a simple bi-directional transfer of essence between the tape device and the MXF file format. Both type D-10 and D-11 tape formats provide tightly defined storage locations for the audio, video, auxiliary data, and control data. Therefore, when recording MXF versions of these formats, a special place has to be found to store the header information from the MXF file. In the Sony eVTR (IMX type D-10), the *header metadata* is stored in a 2-second portion of tape immediately preceding the start of the video recording. The header metadata is recorded in the audio sectors where the reliability of data reproduction is highest. This 2-second portion gives space for 500 KB of header metadata, which is more than enough space for most current metadata needs.

At the time of writing, there is no implementation of the type D-11 VTR (HDCAM), though operation could be reasonably expected to be similar to the type D-10-based eVTR.

Interleaving and Multiplexing Strategies

VTRs always operate using interleaving techniques defined either by the field or frame rate of the video. As a result, and to minimize buffer requirements, the MXF files described in this chapter use the same basic frame-based interleaving technique. This is especially true if the MXF files are created in real time from the VTR for output to a network port.

Once on a file server, the frame-based interleaving of the essence components could be subject to de-interleaving and separation for easier processing of the individual essence components. It could also be possible to create more complex files using *clip wrapping*, though a conversion process would be required.

It is important to note that, if any such de-interleaving process is carried out, any attempt to record an MXF file back onto the MXF-enabled VTR would require the frame-wrapped interleaved format defined in SMPTE 386M (for the type D-10 mapping into MXF) or SMPTE 387M (for the type D-11 mapping into MXF) to be faithfully recreated in order for the VTR to respond correctly. These devices will probably perform only limited checks on the file validity before recording. It will be up to the device that creates the file to ensure that the file structure faithfully follows the simple requirements of the MXF file interface to the VTR.

Use of Audio within Types D-10 and D-11

Both the type D-10 and D-11 formats record multiple channels of AES3 data. However, the formats differ in the number of channels and in the resolution of each sample. In both cases, the AES3 data may be compressed audio that is packed into the AES3 data format in non-audio mode. In this mode, both type D-10 and D-11 VTRs will automatically mute the replayed audio to prevent possible hearing damage.

An AES3 8-channel essence element is defined in SMPTE 331M and is used as the method of wrapping the audio for the type D-10 and D-11 mappings. This essence element predates MXF by several years but was designed to be file friendly.

The bitstream format of each channel of the 8-channel AES3 element is defined by the AES3 interface specification, (AES3-2003). Although the AES3 specification is limited to two channels, the SMPTE 331M 8-channel AES3 element was designed to carry up to eight individual channels of AES3 data transparently through SDTI-CP. Each AES3 channel may contain either linear PCM audio or data according to the AES3 specification.

The data format for an SDTI-CP 8-channel AES3 element is illustrated in Figure 8.1. The element data area contains AES3 audio or data samples for the period of the picture frame (or as close as possible to this period).

Up to eight channels of AES3 data are interleaved on a word-by-word basis; i.e., the first word (W) of each channel (Ch) is interleaved into the sequence:

W1 Ch1, W1 Ch2, W1 Ch3, W1 Ch4, W1 Ch5, W1 Ch6, W1 Ch7, W1 Ch8

W2 Ch1, W2 Ch2, W2 Ch3, W2 Ch4, W2 Ch5, W2 Ch6, W2 Ch7, W2 Ch8

In Figure 8.1, the channel number is defined by bits $c2$ to $c0$. These bits define eight states where "0" represents channel 1 and "7" represents channel 8.

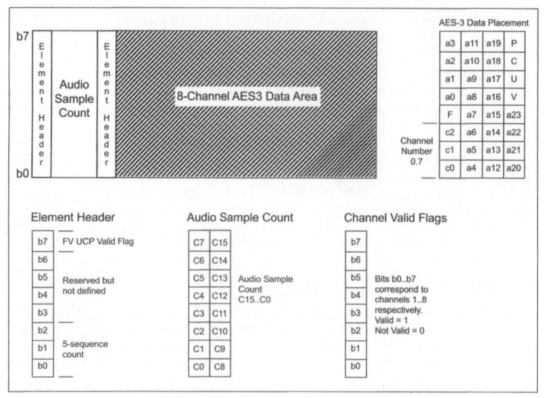

Figure 8.1 Format of the 8-channel AES3 element

The F bit indicates the first AES3 subframe of an AES3 block. This bit is "1" if the word is the start of the AES3 block, otherwise it is 0.

The 24 bits of the AES3 specification are directly mapped into bits a0 to a23. The V, U, C and P bits (validity (V), user (U), channel status (C) and parity (P) bits) are directly mapped as shown in Figure 8.1.

For the AES3 element header:

- Bit b7 indicates if the FVUCP bits are active. A value of "0" indicates that the FVUCP bits are not used. A value of "1" indicates that the FVUCP bits are valid and useable.

- Bits b6 to b3 are not defined but reserved for future use.

- Bits b2 to b0 define a 5-sequence count. In a content package based on the 525/59.94 system, the count is a (modulo-5 count + 1) value over the range 1 to 5. In a content package based on the 625/50 system, or any other system where the audio sample count is a consistent integer value over the content package period, the count is set to "0." Note that all AES3 data channels within the same element must have the same 5-sequence count number.

In the particular case of content packages based on 525/59.94Hz systems, the 5-sequence count defines one of the following sets of sample numbers per content package depending on whether it is frame or field based:

Sequence No.	30/1.001	60/1.001
1	1602	801
2	1601	801
3	1602	800
4	1601	801
5	1602	801

The audio sample count in Figure 8.1 is a 16-bit count in the range 0 to 65535 and represents the number of samples in each channel (i.e., the number of samples in each channel of the frame-wrapped essence element). All channels within the AES3 essence element must have the same sample count value.

The channel valid flag word has 8 bits, b0 to b7, which reflect the validity of the AES3 data in corresponding channels 1 to 8. A channel valid flag bit must be set to "1" if the channel contains valid AES3 data or else it is set to "0." A particularly important aspect is that the AES3 data area is always present for all eight channels whether valid or not.

This audio element thus defines a fixed allocation of data space for eight AES3 channels. Unused channels are flagged, but the size of the element remains constant no matter how many channels are in use. This is no problem for an interface with high capacity, but is wasteful of bandwidth and storage in an MXF file. It is, however, easy to implement in silicon as an SDTI payload. Although not specified as such, where the number of AES3 channels is less than eight, it is good practice to ensure that the channels are filled in the lowest numbered channels (i.e., if there are four channels, these would occupy the first four channel locations).

Mapping the SMPTE 331M 8-Channel AES3 Element to the SMPTE 382M AES3 Audio Element

As we have just seen, SMPTE 331M defines the 8-channel AES3 mapping for the type D-10 and D-11 formats and that this has a fixed size whether or not all eight available channels are filled with data. An alternative mapping is provided by SMPTE 382M, entitled "Mapping of AES and Broadcast Wave audio into the MXF *generic container.*"

SMPTE 382M (defined fully in Chapter 6) is more efficient in data capacity and is more flexible in regard of the number of audio channels and the bits per channel compared to SMPTE 331M. This flexibility is easy to manage in a purely file environment, but more difficult for interfacing with the real-time high speed SDTI.

Since the data carried by the 8-channel interface is AES3, it is possible to transparently map the AES3 data between the SMPTE 331M (SDTI-CP) AES3 element and the SMPTE 382M AES3 element with no loss of information. The essential operations required for this mapping are:

- Use only the valid channels from the SMPTE 331M 8-channel element as indicated by the channel valid flags.

- Extract a complete AES3 data block using the "F" bit as defined in SMPTE 331M.

- Extract the channel status data from "C" bits and use this data to find out the number of active bits per sample.

Note: An AES3 "data block" is a sequence of 192 audio samples. The definition of this data block and the meaning of the channel status bits within each data block is defined in AES3. The channel status bits define many key parameters of the audio samples such as professional/consumer use, sample bit depth, sampling rate, mono/stereo, and much more.

These basic operations now give sufficient information for the basic extraction of the AES3 data bits for mapping into the SMPTE 382M specification. Further extraction of the 'U' bit allows any "user" data to be used by the SMPTE 382M specification. Since the 8-channel AES3 audio element enables a lossless carriage of all the AES3 2-channel interface data, albeit in a somewhat modified form, all data from each channel can be mapped into the SMPTE 382M specification.

Operational Pattern Issues

Both the type D-10 and type D-11 mappings into MXF are constrained to OP1a when interfaced with the associated VTR. VTRs inherently cannot handle the more complex features of higher OPs.

These mappings into MXF also have other constraints within the general list defined by OP1a as follows:

- They use the simplest partition structure. On replay from a VTR, no *body partitions* are used. A VTR may, or may not, be able to accept MXF files that use body partitions.

- They do not record header metadata located in the *footer partition*. The recorder will probably not fail if it encounters such metadata, but any header metadata in the footer partition will simply be discarded.

- On replay of an MXF file from a VTR, the header metadata in the header partition will usually be complete, as the device will create a file of a defined length via the in-point and out-point definitions, and most header metadata values will be correct because they are predetermined.

- The header metadata sourced by a VTR will not define any lower-level source packages as it is generally the source itself. However, lower-level source packages may be present if the VTR has recorded the header metadata from a previous MXF file that added these packages.

- The OP qualifier bits (in byte 15 of the OP UL) will be set to "internal essence," "streamable," and "multiple essence tracks."

Of course, if these mappings are used as a source in another application, they may become a part of a more complex OP.

The specific limitations of the Sony eVTR family of products have been defined as a SMPTE registered document disclosure (RDD) document. The specific document is RDD-3, "e-VTR MXF Interoperability Specification."[1]

Use of Index Tables for Types D-10 and D-11 in MXF

One *index table segment* should be present in the MXF header partition. Repetition of this index table segment in a footer partition is optional.

The full definition of the format of index table segments is given in the MXF file format specification (SMPTE 377M) and in Chapter 12. This section describes the application of index tables to an MXF-GC (type D-10) essence container.

In particular, both the type D-10 and type D-11 mapping specifications define the use of fixed byte count mode where a single *index table* defines the length (in bytes) of all the content packages in the generic container. Furthermore, each essence element within every content package has a defined length (with appropriate use of the KLV fill item) to ensure that a single *delta entry array* is all that is needed. Any KLV fill items are treated as a part of the element that they follow and are not indexed in their own right. Note that the *index entry array* is not used for type D-10 and D-11 mappings because they both have fixed item lengths. Note also that an edit unit is the duration of one content package (i.e., one video frame).

The index table segment is constructed as follows:

Item Name	Meaning	Value
Index Table Segment	A segment of an Index Table	
Length	Set Length	
Instance ID	Unique ID of this instance	
Index Edit Rate	Frame rate of the type D-10 video	{25,1} or {30000, 1001}
Index Start Position	Byte address of first edit unit indexed by this table segment	0
Index Duration	Number of edit units indexed by this table segment (NSA)	0
Edit Unit Byte Count	Defines the length of a fixed size (content package) edit unit	>0
IndexSID	Identifier of the index table segment	
BodySID	Identifier of the essence container	

[1] Note: An SMPTE RDD is a service provided by SMPTE to enable manufacturers and users to publicly define a format or product that does not meet the requirements for SMPTE standards or recommended practices.

Item Name	Meaning	Value
Slice Count	Number of slices minus 1 (NSL)	0
Delta Entry Array	Map of elements in each content package (optional) (See Table 8.2)	
IndexEntry Array	Index from sample number to stream offset	Not encoded

Table 8.1 Index Table Segment set

Both the type D-10 and D-11 mapping specifications may use the optional delta entry array table. An example delta entry array table for system, picture, sound, and data elements is given below:

Field Name	Meaning	Typical Values	Comment
NDE	Number of Delta Entries	4	
Length	Length of each Delta Entry	6	
PosTableIndex	No temporal reordering	0	Element 0 e.g., System Data Pack Element
Slice	Slice number in index entry	0	
Element Delta	(Fixed) Delta from start of slice to this element	0	
PosTableIndex	No temporal reordering	0	Element 1 e.g., Picture Item
Slice	Slice number in index entry	0	
Element Delta	(Fixed) Delta from start of slice to this element	Len(system item + fill))	
PosTableIndex	No temporal reordering	0	Element 2 e.g., Sound Item
Slice	Slice number in index entry	0	
Element Delta	(Fixed) Delta from start of slice to this element	Len(system item + fill + element 1 + fill)	
PosTableIndex	No temporal reordering	0	Element 3 e.g., Data Item
Slice	Slice number in index entry	0	
Element Delta	(Fixed) Delta from start of slice to this element	Len(system item + fill + elements 1+2 + fill)	

Table 8.2 Structure of Example Delta Entry Array

General File Issues

File Descriptor Sets

The file descriptor sets are those *structural metadata* sets in the header metadata that describe the essence and metadata elements used in the type D-10 and D-11 mappings to MXF. File descriptor sets should be present in the header metadata for each essence element and for the system metadata pack element. The details of the file descriptors for each mapping are described in the sections describing the individual aspects of the type D-10 and D-11 mappings.

Mapping Track Numbers to Generic Container Elements

The number of essence tracks in the associated header metadata package must be the same as the number of essence elements used in these mappings. The *track number* value is derived as described in Chapter 3 and Chapter 5 (Essence Element to Track Relationship section).

The associated *header metadata* package should define one *metadata track* to describe the contents of the system metadata pack of the CP-compatible *system item* using the track number value described in Chapter 3 and the essence element to track relationship section of Chapter 5. This track can be used to describe the date/time components in the CP-compatible *system item* using the date/time descriptor defined in SMPTE 385M.

Essence Container Partitions

The type D-10 and type D-11 mappings both maintain each frame-based content package of the generic container as a separate editable unit with the contents of the system, picture, sound and data items in synchronism. As a consequence, if the essence container using this mapping is partitioned, then each partition must contain an integer number of content packages where each content package contains all the container items required. Note that such partitioning can apply only to a file on a server since the VTR formats do not support body partitions.

Specific Details of the Type D-10 Mapping

The MPEG-2 baseline decoder template specified by SMPTE RP204 provides for codecs operating with MPEG-2 4:2:2P@ML encoded pictures compliant to SMPTE 356M accompanied by an 8-channel AES3 data capability and a general data element. It specifies a codec capable of basic timing and transfer modes for SDTI-CP operation. The specification is a baseline that allows receiver/decoders to be designed with higher capabilities if and when desired.

This mapping is frame based and the order of items is assigned as system, picture, sound, and, optionally, data.

As previously mentioned, the reader should note that auxiliary items and elements in SMPTE 326M (SDTI-CP) are synonymous with data items and elements in the MXF generic container.

System Item Mapping

The system metadata pack and the package metadata set are required within each CP system item (as shown in Figure 5.8, elements of the SDTI-CP compatible system item). The presence of the *picture item*, *sound item*, *data item*, and control element is reflected by the setting of the system metadata bitmap as described in the Annex to Chapter 5 (see Annex Figure 5.9, system metadata pack structure).

The UL used in the MXF GC(type D-10) system item and in the MXF header metadata (partition pack, preface set, and *essence descriptor*) has the following value:

Byte No.	Description	Value (hex)	Meaning
1~13	See Table 5.1	-	As defined in Table 5.1
14	Type D-10 Mapping	01	Mapping compliant to SMPTE 356M and SMPTE RP204
15	MPEG Constraints: SMPTE 356M	01 02 03 04 05 06	50 Mbps, 625/50 50 Mbps, 525/60 40 Mbps, 625/50 40 Mbps, 525/60 30 Mbps, 625/50 30 Mbps, 525/60
16	Type: Template Extension	01 or 02	01 = template defined in SMPTE 386M 02 = extended template

Table 8.3 Specification of the MXF-GC(D-10) Essence Container UL

Picture Item Mapping

There is just one essence element in the MXF-GC picture item, which is a MPEG-2 4:2:2P@ML video elementary stream constrained according to SMPTE 356M. The KLV coding details are as follows:

Essence Element Key

The *essence element* key value is as follows:

Byte No.	Description	Value (hex)	Meaning
1~12	See Table 5.2	-	As defined in Table 5.2
13	Item Type Identifier	05	SDTI-CP compatible Picture Item
14	Essence Element Count	01	One Eessence Eelement present
15	Essence Element Type	01	MPEG2 422P@ML Element as defined in SMPTE 331M
16	Essence Element Number	nn	See Chapter 5, Essence Element Key section

Table 8.4 Key Value for the type D-10 Picture Element

Essence Element Length

The length field of the KLV coded element is 4 bytes BER long-form encoded (i.e., 83_h.xx.xx.xx).

Essence Element Value

The MPEG-2 4:2:2P@ML video elementary stream is per the definition in SMPTE 331M (section 5.1) with the encoded bitstream constrained according to the type D-10 MPEG-2 data stream specification (SMPTE 356M).

Per SMPTE 356M, the maximum bit-rate for this stream is 50 Mbps. When operating at 50 Mbps, the size (in bytes) per frame is:

For 525/60 operation: 208,541 bytes; and

For 625/50 operation: 250,000 bytes.

The MPEG-2 picture element comprises the MPEG video elementary stream (V-ES) for one video frame, together with all its MPEG-2 header information (including extensions), required to support the independent decoding of each picture.

An example V-ES bitstream is shown in Figure 8.2.

The MPEG-2 picture element should comply with SMPTE 328M (MPEG-2 elementary stream editing information). The following list of points summarizes that standard for the repetition of MPEG-2 GOP and sequence header information.

1. If the picture to be formatted is not an I-picture, then the data from the picture header code up to, but not including, either the next GOP or picture header is formatted into a block;

2. If the picture to be formatted is an I-picture, then the data from the sequence, GOP and picture headers up to, but not including, either the next GOP or picture header is formatted into a block;

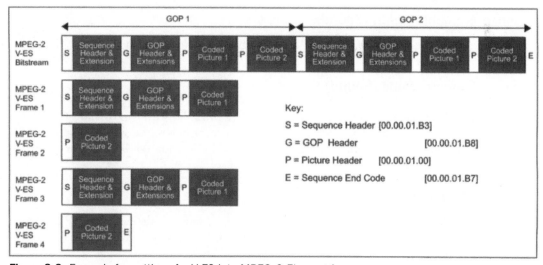

Figure 8.2 Example formatting of a V-ES into MPEG-2 Element frames

3. The sequence header information should be repeated at each I-picture with the informa- tion placed immediately prior to the GOP Header information. Thus information about the sequence is readily available following any editing process. If sequence header information were not repeated so frequently, then edit processes may easily remove this information making downstream processing more difficult or even impossible; and

4. A sequence end code must be retained with the end of the last picture in the sequence.

Sound Item Mapping

There is just one sound element in the MXF GC sound item which is the 8-channel AES3 element described earlier in this chapter.

Essence Element Key (Sound)

The essence element key value is as follows:

Byte No.	Description	Value (hex)	Meaning
1~12	See Table 5.2	-	As defined in Table 5.2
13	Item Type Identifier	06	SDTI-CP compatible Sound Item
14	Essence Element Count	01	One essence element present
15	Essence Element Type	10	8-channel AES3 Element as defined by SMPTE 331M
16	Essence Element Number	nn	See Chapter 5, Essence Element Key section

Table 8.5 Key value for the 8-channel AES3 sound element

Essence Element Length (Sound)

The length field of the KLV coded element is 4 bytes BER long-form encoded (i.e., 83_h.xx.xx.xx).

Essence Element Value (Sound)

The 8-channel AES3 element is as described in the Use of Audio within D10 and D11 section of this chapter. Active channels are filled with AES3 data according to the stream valid flag. The element data length varies according to 625/50 or 525/60 operation (and in 525/60 operation varies over the frame sequence as it has a 5-frame sequence).

Data Item Mapping

The D-10 GC data item may contain zero or more *data elements* as defined in SMPTE 331M section 7. If the data item has a variable length in each content package, then the end of the data item should be padded with the KLV Fill item to ensure that the content package size is constant so that a simple index table can be used.

Essence Element Key (Data)

The *essence element* key value is as follows:

Byte No.	Description	Value (hex)	Meaning
1~12	See Table 5.2	-	As defined in Table 5.2
13	Item Type Identifier	07	SDTI-CP compatible Data Item
14	Essence Element Count	nn	One or more essence elements present
15	Essence Element Type	Per SMPTE 331M, 20 = VBI 21 = Anc	Data Essence Element
16	Essence Element Number	xx	See Chapter 5, Essence Element Key section

Table 8.6 Key value for the data essence element

The types of data *essence elements* that could be used will have byte 15 having values in the range 20_h to $7F_h$ (using the tag values defined in SMPTE 331M section 7).

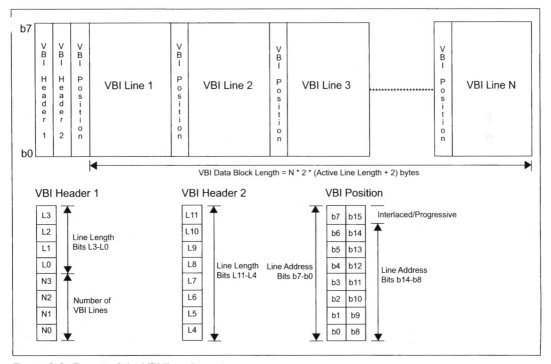

Figure 8.3 Format of the VBI line element

Essence Element Length (Data)

The length field of the KLV coded element is 4 bytes BER long-form encoded (i.e., 83_h.xx.xx.xx).

Essence Element Value (Data)

The permitted data essence types are those defined in SMPTE 331M section 7. Of particular interest are the values defined by auxiliary essence types 20_h and 21_h that define VBI line data and ancillary packet data respectively. Descriptions of these two values now follow.

VBI Line Element

The VBI line element carries one or more lines from the vertical blanking interval. It has a header that identifies whether the source is interlaced or progressive and a number to identify the number of VBI lines carried. Each VBI line is created from one line of the vertical blanking interval and each line starts with a VBI information word followed by the 8-bit words from the whole of the VBI line. Details of the VBI Line element structure are shown in Figure 8.3.

The order of the VBI lines are displayed on a viewing device.

Therefore, for an interlaced scanned system we get:

[VBI 1, 1st field], [VBI 2, 2nd field],

[VBI 3, 1st field], [VBI 4, 2nd field], and

[VBI 5, 1st field], [VBI 6, 2nd field].

And for a progressive scanned system, we get:

VBI 1, VBI 2, VBI 3, VBI 4, VBI 5, VBI 6.

In the VBI Header words:
1. Bits N3 to N0 of the first word define the number of VBI lines and the value range is 0 to 6.
2. Bits L3 to L0 of the first word, together with bits L8 to L11 of the second word, form a 12-bit count value that identifies the length of the VBI lines. It should be noted that all VBI lines in one element must have the same length.

In the VBI Position word:
1. Bits b14 to b8 of the second word and bits b7 to b0 of the first word form a line number in the range 0 to 32767. The line address number represents an absolute line number for both interlaced and progressive line numbering systems.
2. Bit b7 of the second word (P) is set to "0" for interlaced scan and "1" for progressive scan.

A line address value of "0" means that no line number has been defined. Any line address number outside the vertical interval period for the picture scanning system is invalid and could cause unspecified effects in receiving equipment.

File Descriptors for Type D-10 Mapping

The file descriptors in the tables below indicate property values, where appropriate. In all tables describing file descriptor sets in this section, the columns are defined as follows:

- Item name: the name of the property;
- Type: the defined type of the property;
- Len: the length of the value in bytes where known;
- Meaning: a description of the property;
- 525/60: default values for 525-line source video; and
- 625/50: default values for 625-line source video.

Note that the key, length, instance UID, and generation UID rows are not included for clarity. Note also that, for the case of properties in this section that are SMPTE labels (ULs), a full list of appropriate values is provided in the SMPTE labels registry, SMPTE RP 224.

Item Name	Type	Len	525/60	625/50
Linked Track ID	UInt32	4		
Sample Rate	Rational	8	30000, 1001	25,1
Container Duration	Length	8		
Codec	UL	16	Not used	Not used
Essence Container	UL	16	See Table 8.3	See Table 8.3
Picture Essence Coding	UL	16	See SMPTE RP224 under node 04.01.02.02.01.02.01.00	See SMPTE RP224 under node 04.01.02.02.01.02.01.00
Signal Standard	Enum	1	1	1
Frame layout	UInt8	1	1 (= I)	1 (= I)
Stored Width	UInt32	4	720	720
Stored Height	UInt32	4	256	304
StoredF2Offset	Int32	4	0	0
Sampled Width	UInt32	4	720	720
Sampled Height	UInt32	4	256	304
Sampled X-Offset	Int32	4	0	0
Sampled Y-Offset	Int32	4	0	0
Display Height	UInt32	4	243	288
Display Width	UInt32	4	720	720
Display X-Offset	Int32	4	0	0
Display Y-Offset	Int32	4	13	16
DisplayF2Offset	Int32	4	0	0

Item Name	Type	Len	525/60	625/50
Aspect Ratio	Rational	8	{4,3} or {16,9}	{4,3} or {16,9}
Active Format Descriptor (AFD)	UInt8	1	0	0
Video Line Map	Array of Int32	8+(2*4)	{7,270}	{7,320}
Alpha Transparency	UInt8	1	0 (False)	0 (False)
Gamma	UL	16	: 06.0E.2B.34.04.01.01.01 04.01.01.01.01.01.00.00	06.0E.2B.34.04.01.01.01 04.01.01.01.01.01.00.00
Image Alignment Offset	UInt32	4	0	0
Field Dominance	UInt8	1	1	1
Image Start Offset	UInt32	4	0	0
Image End Offset	UInt32	4	0	0
Component Depth	UInt32	4	8	8
Horizontal Sub-sampling	UInt32	4	2	2
Vertical Sub-sampling	UInt32	4	1	1
Color Siting	UInt8	1	4	4
Reversed Byte Order	Boolean	1	False (0)	False (0)
Padding Bits	UInt16	2	0	0
Alpha Sample Depth	UInt32	4	0	0
Black Ref Level	UInt32	4	16	16
White Ref level	UInt32	4	235	235
Color Range	UInt32	4	225	225
Locators	StrongRefArray (Locators)	8+16n	Present only if essence container is external to the file.	Present only if essence container is external to the file.

Table 8.7 CDCI Picture Essence Descriptor

Note: CDCI is defined in SMPTE 377M as "Color Difference Component Image."

Item Name	Type	Len	525/60-i	625/50-I
Linked Track ID	UInt32	4		
Sample Rate	Rational	8	{30000, 1001}	{25,1}
Container Duration	Length	8		
Codec	UL	16	Not used	Not used
Essence Container	UL	16	See Table 8.3	See Table 8.3

Item Name	Type	Len	525/60-i	625/50-I
Sound Essence Coding	UL	16	Not used	Not used
Audio sampling rate	Rational	8	{48000,1}	{48000,1}
Locked/Unlocked	Boolean	4	01_h (locked)	01_h (locked)
Audio Ref Level	Int8	1	0 (default)	0 (default)
Electro-Spatial Formulation	UInt8 (Enum)	1	Not encoded	Not encoded
Channel Count	UInt32	4	4 or 8	4 or 8
Quantization bits	UInt32	4	16 or 24	16 or 24
Dial Norm	Int8	1	Not encoded	Not encoded
Locators	StrongRefArray (Locators)	8+16n	Present only if essence container is external to the file.	Present only if essence container is external to the file.

Table 8.8 Generic Sound Essence Descriptor

Item Name	Type	Len	525/60-I	625/50-I
Linked Track ID	UInt32	4		
Sample Rate	Rational	8	{30000, 1001}	{25,1}
Container Duration	Length	8		
Codec	UL	16	Not used	Not used
Essence Container	UL	16	See Table 8.3	See Table 8.3
Data Essence Coding	UL	16	Not used	Not used
Locators	StrongRefArray (Locators)	8+16n	Present only if essence container is external to the file.	Present only if essence container is external to the file.

Table 8.9 Generic Data Essence Descriptor

Specific Details of the Type D-11 Mapping

The type D-11 mapping standard defines the generic container with a system item, a type D-11 compressed picture element, a 4-channel AES3 audio element, and optional auxiliary data elements in the data item.

The mapping (as specified in SMPTE 387) defines the mapping of the type D-11 data as seen on the SDTI data port specified by SMPTE 369M to the MXF generic container. The type D-11 data comprises packets of type D-11 basic blocks containing compressed picture data and auxiliary picture data as specified in SMPTE 367M (type D-11 picture compression and data stream format).

Four channels of 24-bit AES3 data are optionally mapped into the H-ANC space of the SDTI in compliance with SMPTE 272M. In addition, VITC may also be mapped into

189

the H-ANC space according to SMPTE 369M. The type D-11 mapping specification also covers the mapping of the audio and VITC data from the SDTI into the MXF generic container.

The type D-11 data stream packets are grouped into six equal data segments of which the first three data segments are mapped onto the first field of the SDTI and the last three data segments are mapped onto the second field of the SDTI, as shown in Figure 8.4.

Note that because the type D-11 format operates at 24-Hz and 24÷1.001-Hz frame rates as well as the conventional television rates of 25-Hz and 30÷1.001-Hz, the SDTI must operate at all frame rates to support synchronous stream transfers based on one frame of compressed HD picture data together with the associated audio data and VITC data packed into one frame of the SDTI.

Figure 8.2 illustrates the optional four channels of 24-bit AES3 data mapped into the H-ANC space. VITC data (named "auxiliary data" in Figure 8.4) may also be mapped into the H-ANC space.

Table 8.10 on the next page shows the core parameters of the SDTI at all the frame rates used by SMPTE 367M.

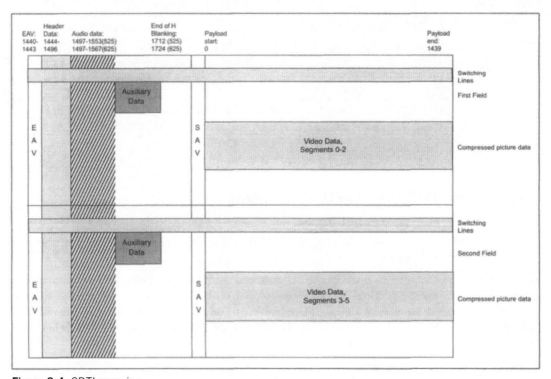

Figure 8.4 SDTI mapping

Frame rate of the Interface	24÷1.001Hz	24Hz	25Hz	30÷1.001Hz
Total number of Lines	525	625	625	525
Total number of samples per Line	2145	1800	1728	1716

Table 8.10 Total number of lines and samples per line for each frame rate of the interface

Type D-11 Data Structure and Mapping to the Generic Container

For each frame of the type D-11 SDTI payload, the data is divided into four components as follows:

- A metadata pack element followed by optional metadata elements whose values are extracted from ancillary data packets. These ancillary data packets are extracted from the H-ANC space as specified in SMPTE 369M.

- A mandatory *picture element* whose value comprises all six concatenated segments of the type D-11 compressed picture information (see SMPTE 367M). This component is mapped into a type D-11 element in the *generic container picture item*.

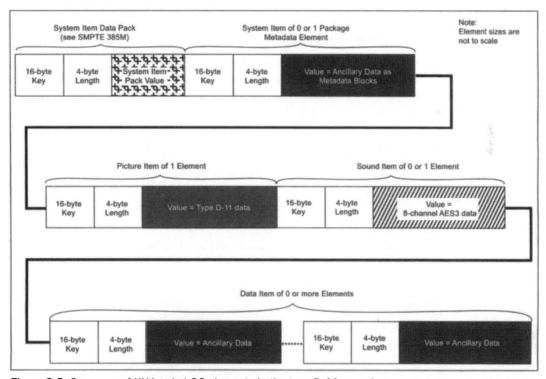

Figure 8.5 Sequence of KLV-coded GC elements in the type D-11 mapping

- An optional AES3 *sound element* whose value comprises all the AES3 data packets extracted from the H-ANC space of the SDTI as defined in SMPTE 369M. This AES3 data is mapped into an 8-channel AES3 element as defined in SMPTE 331M. Only four channels of the 8-channel element are used.

- Optional H-ANC data packet elements for the carriage of ANC data packets not carried by the *system item*.

The order of items in this frame wrapping is system, picture, sound, and data (if present).

The resulting KLV-coded packets for each frame are represented in sequence as shown in Figure 8.5.

Ancillary Data Packet Mapping

The type D-11 SDTI payload may optionally include auxiliary data coded as H-ANC packets. These H-ANC packets contain data that can be mapped into either the GC system item or the GC data item depending on the value of the H-ANC data ID word and the secondary data ID word (where applicable). Only those auxiliary data H-ANC packets carrying 8-bit data are supported in this mapping. 9-bit data is not supported. Figure 8.6 illustrates the "auxiliary data" H-ANC packet structure.

If the H-ANC packet "Data ID" word identifies a user data type that is metadata, then each packet payload is mapped into the system item as a package metadata element.

The H-ANC packet mapped to any GC (D-11) element removes the 3-word ancillary data flag (ADF) as this is specifically related to synchronization of the H-ANC packet in the SDTI. The GC (D-11) element mapping must include the CRC (cyclic redundancy check) word to provide some level of error protection.

Each element value is defined as the least significant 8 bits of each word from the following contiguous parts of the H-ANC data packet:

- The data ID word;

- The secondary data ID (or data block number) word;

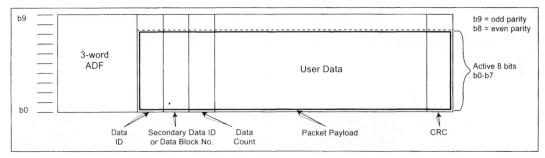

Figure 8.6 Ancillary data packet structure

- The data count word;
- The user data words; and
- The CRC word.

To reconstruct an H-ANC packet from the GC (D-11) element value, the 3-word ADF must be added and bits b8 and b9 of each word must be recalculated.

Note that any change to the user data words while in the MXF file domain will require a recalculation of the CRC check word according to SMPTE 291M.

System Item Mapping

The contents of the system item must comply with SMPTE 385M (see Appendix to Chapter 6). The system metadata pack and the package metadata Set are required. The presence of the picture item, sound item, data item, and control element depends on the setting of the system metadata bitmap.

SMPTE Universal Label (UL)

The UL used to identify the type D-11 essence mapping into MXF is as defined in Table 8.11.

Byte No.	Description	Value (hex)	Meaning
1~13	See Table 5.1	-	As defined in Table 5.1
14	Mapping Kind	03	Type D-11: SMPTE 367M compression and SMPTE 369M SDTI transport
15	Type D-11 Source Coding (1920*1080 picture size)	01 ~06	01_h = 23.98 PsF 02_h = 24 PsF 03_h = 25 PsF 04_h = 29.97 PsF 05_h = 50 I 06_h = 59.94 I
16	Type: Template Extension	01 or 02	01_h = template defined in this document 02_h = extended template

Table 8.11 Specification of the MXF-GC(D-11) essence container UL

Package Metadata Set

Metadata Element Key

The package metadata element key value is as follows:

Byte No.	Description	Value (hex)	Meaning
1~12	See Table 5.3	-	As defined in Table 5.3
13	Item Type Identifier	04	CP-compatible system item

Byte No.	Description	Value (hex)	Meaning
14	System Scheme Identifier	01	SDTI-CP, version 1
15	Metadata Element Identifier	02	Package metadata set
16	Metadata Block Count	xx	Number of H-ANC packets

Table 8.12 Key value for the type D-11 package metadata element

Metadata Element Length

The length field of the KLV coded element is 4 bytes BER long-form encoded (i.e., 83_h.xx.xx.xx).

Metadata Element Value

Where this set is present in the system item, it contains the 8-bit payloads of all auxiliary data H-ANC packets present on the SDTI that are identified as carrying metadata.

The 8-bit payload of each auxiliary data H-ANC packet is mapped into a sequence of metadata items as illustrated in Figure 8.3 above. Each metadata item comprises a local tag with a value of "21_h," a 2-byte length, followed by the 8-bit payload of the H-ANC data packet mapped into the value field.

Where more than one auxiliary data H-ANC packet is present in the frame period, they are mapped to the metadata element in the sequence as they appear in the frame. Metadata packets mapped from field 1 of the SDTI are followed immediately by metadata packets mapped from field 2.

The package metadata set will typically comprise two *metadata items* mapped from the payloads of two auxiliary data H-ANC packets, one in the first field of the SDTI and one in the second field. These typically contain only VITC data.

Picture Item Mapping

The *picture item* value comprises a single element that contains the compressed picture and embedded auxiliary data as defined by SMPTE 367M.

Essence Element Key

The *essence element* key value is as follows:

Byte No.	Description	Value (hex)	Meaning
1~12	See Table 5.2	-	As defined in Table 5.2
13	Item Type Identifier	15	GC Picture item
14	Essence Element Count	01	One essence element present
15	Essence Element Type	01	Type D-11 video as defined by SMPTE 367M
16	Essence Element Number	01	Normative value

Table 8.13 Key value for the type D-11 picture element

Essence Element Length

The length field of the KLV coded element is 4 bytes BER long-form encoded (i.e., 83_h.xx.xx.xx).

Essence Element Value

Each compressed picture data stream is divided into six equal segments, numbered 0 to 5 where each segment has an even channel and an odd channel as defined in SMPTE 367M.

All the packets from both channels of segments 0 to 2 are mapped into 212 lines of the first field of the SDTI and all the packets from both channels of segments 3 to 5 are mapped into 212 lines of the second field of the SDTI, as illustrated in Figure 8.4. The reader should note that the last of the 212 lines in each field are not fully occupied.

SDTI Payload Line Mapping

The transfer of the data from SDTI to the type D-11 element value in the picture item includes all the basic block data (see details below), but specifically excludes the first two words and the last two words of each SDTI payload line.

The first two words of each SDTI payload line contain the SDTI data type identifier word followed by a data valid word. In this latter case, a value of $1FE_h$ identifies the first line of the payload and a value of $1FD_h$ identifies all other payload lines. These words are discarded at the point of mapping from the SDTI to the type D-11 picture item value, but must be accurately recreated when mapping from a type D-11 picture item value to the SDTI.

The last two words of each SDTI payload line contain the payload CRC values. These words are discarded at the point of transferring from the SDTI to the type D-11 picture item value, but must be faithfully recreated when transferring from a type D-11 picture item value to the SDTI.

SDTI basic blocks from the even and odd channels are interleaved on a byte by byte basis for the SDTI mapping with the first byte from the even channel preceding the first byte from the odd

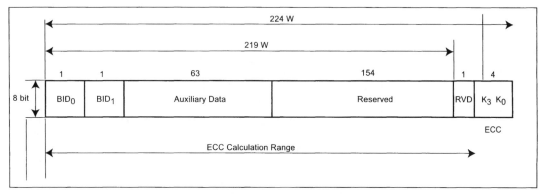

Figure 8.7 Addition of reserved word and ECC to an auxiliary basic block

channel. In the mapping to the MXF generic container, the basic blocks are maintained as individual blocks so that each basic block from the even channel precedes the equivalent basic block from the odd channel. The mapping from SDTI to MXF thus involves a remapping of each pair of basic blocks from byte interleaving to block interleaving.

Basic Block Mapping

Each segment comprises a first auxiliary basic block followed by 225 compressed picture basic blocks. The type D-11 compressed picture and auxiliary basic blocks conform to SMPTE 367M.

Four bytes of Reed-Solomon error correction code (ECC) are added to each basic block. Between the end of each basic block and the start of the ECC, a 1-byte reserved word is added, the default value being zero.

Figure 8.7 illustrates the addition of the reserved word and the 4-byte RS ECC to an auxiliary basic block while Figure 8.8 illustrates the addition of the reserved word and the 4-byte RS ECC to a compressed picture basic block.

The basic blocks are mapped into the 8 LSBs of the SDTI. Bits 9 and 8 of the SDTI are defined as parity check bits and these are discarded during the transfer from the SDTI to the type D-11 *picture item* value. The Reed-Solomon ECC words at the end of all basic blocks are discarded and the resulting space removed during the transfer from the SDTI to the type D-11 *picture element* value.

At the point of transferring basic blocks from the *picture element* value to the SDTI, the 4 Reed-Solomon ECC words must be recalculated and reinserted at the end of each basic block. Each byte is mapped to the least significant 8 bits of the SDTI and bits 8 and 9 recalculated as parity bits according to SMPTE 305M.

The *picture element* value comprises the basic blocks from all six segments of the two channels in a contiguous byte-stream. With the removal of the Reed-Solomon ECC words, the basic block size is reduced to 220 bytes. The length of the concatenated basic blocks must be calculated and entered into the *picture item* length field. The length of the element value is defined by

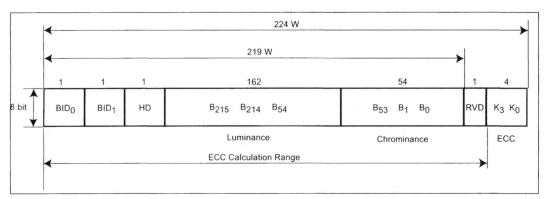

Figure 8.8 Addition of reserved word and ECC to a compressed picture basic block

2 fields per frame (2*3*226 basic blocks per field) with 220 bytes per basic block, giving a value of 596,640 bytes.

Sound Item Mapping

The *sound item* comprises one 8-channel AES3 element. For this mapping, only the first four channels are used.

Essence Element Key

The *essence element* key value is as follows.

Byte No.	Description	Value (hex)	Meaning
1~12	See Table 5.2	-	As defined in Table 5.2
13	Item Type Identifier	06	SDTI-CP compatible sound item
14	Essence Element Count	01	One essence element present
15	Essence Element Type	10	8-channel AES3
16	Essence Element Number	02	Normative value

Table 8.14 Key value for the 8-channel AES3 sound element

Essence Element Length

The length field of the KLV coded element is 4 bytes BER long-form encoded (i.e., 83_h.xx.xx.xx).

Essence Element Value

The element value is the 8-channel AES3 element described in this chapter, section: "Use of Audio within Types D-10 and D-11"). The first four channels are filled with AES3 data. The active data length will vary according the frame rate. Additionally, for the 29.97 Hz frame rate, the active data length varies over a 5-frame sequence.

Data Item Mapping

The SDTI may contain H-ANC data packets that have non-metadata payloads. Each such H-ANC data packet may optionally be mapped to a data essence element in the MXF GC (D-11) essence container. The data item value may contain zero or more essence elements mapped from those H-ANC data packets in the horizontal blanking area of the SDTI (those that have not already been mapped to the package metadata element in the system item).

For each frame, each non-metadata payload must be mapped in the order in which they appear on the SDTI. H-ANC data payloads from field 1 are followed immediately by H-ANC data payloads from field 2. If no non-system item H-ANC data packets are present on the SDTI, the data item is not included in the MXF generic container.

If the data item has a variable length in each content package, then the end of the data item should be padded with the KLV fill item to ensure that the content package size is constant to allow a simple index table to be used.

Essence Element Key

The data *essence element* key value is as follows:

Byte No.	Description	Value (hex)	Meaning
1~12	See Table 5.2	-	As defined in Table 5.2
13	Item Type Identifier	07	SDTI-CP compatible data item
14	Essence Element Count	nn	Defined as required
15	Essence Element Type	21	ANC packet payload
16	Essence Element Number	03 ~7F	Different from byte 16 of Tables 8.13 and 8.14. See Chapter 5—Essence Element Key.

Table 8.15 Key value for an ANC packet data essence element

Essence Element Length

The length field of the *essence element* is 4 bytes BER long-form encoded (i.e., 83_h.xx.xx.xx).

Essence Element Value

Each *essence element* value comprises the 8-bit payload of an H-ANC packet.

File Descriptors for Type D-11 Mappings

The file descriptors in the tables below indicate property values, where appropriate.

In all tables describing sets in this annex, the columns are defined as follows:

- Item Name: The name of the property;
- Type: The defined type of the property;
- Len: The length of the value in bytes where known;
- Meaning: A description of the property; and
- Default Value(s): Appropriate values for type D-11 mapping.

The key, length, instance UID, and generation UID rows are not included in these tables.

Item Name	Type	Len	Default Value(s)
Linked Track ID	UInt32	4	
Sample Rate	Rational	8	{24000,1001}, {24,1} {25,1}, {30000,1001}

Item Name	Type	Len	Default Value(s)
Container Duration	Length	8	
Codec	UL	16	Not used
Essence Container	UL	16	See Table 8.11
Picture Essence Coding	UL	16	See SMPTE RP 224 under node: 06.0E.2B.34.04.01.01.01 04.01.02.02.70.01.00.00
Signal Standard	Enum	1	4 (SMPTE 374M)
Frame layout	UInt8	1	1 (I) or 4 (PsF) (see SMPTE 377M E2.2)
Stored Width	UInt32	4	1920
Stored Height	UInt32	4	540
StoredF2Offset	Int32	4	0
Sampled Width	UInt32	4	1920
Sampled Height	UInt32	4	540
Sampled X-Offset	Int32	4	0
Sampled Y-Offset	Int32	4	0
Display Height	UInt32	4	540
Display Width	UInt32	4	1920
Display X-Offset	Int32	4	0
Display Y-Offset	Int32	4	0
DisplayF2Offset	Int32	4	0
Aspect Ratio	Rational	8	{16,9}
Active Format Descriptor (AFD)	UInt8	1	0
Video Line Map	Array of Int32	8+(2*4)	{21,584}
Alpha Transparency	UInt8	1	0 (False)
Gamma	UL	16	06.0E.2B.34.04.01.01.01 04.01.01.01.01.02.00.00
Image Alignment Offset	Uint32	4	0
Field Dominance	UInt8	1	1
Image Start Offset	UInt32	4	0
Image End Offset	UInt32	4	0
Component Depth	UInt32	4	10
Horizontal Sub-sampling	UInt32	4	2
Vertical Sub-sampling	UInt32	4	1
Color Siting	UInt8	1	4
Reversed Byte Order	Boolean	1	False (0)

Item Name	Type	Len	Default Value(s)
Padding Bits	UInt16	2	0
Alpha Sample Depth	UInt32	4	0
Black Ref Level	UInt32	4	64
White Ref level	UInt32	4	940
Colour Range	UInt32	4	897
Locators	StrongRefArray (Locators)	8+16n	Present only if essence container is external to the file

Table 8.16 CDCI Picture Essence Descriptor

Item Name	Type	Len	Default Value(s)
Linked Track ID	UInt32	4	
Sample Rate	Rational	8	{24000,1001}, {24,1} {25,1}, {30000,1001}
Container Duration	Length	8	
Codec	UL	16	Not used
Essence Container	UL	16	See Table 8.11
Sound Essence Coding	UL	16	Not used
Audio sampling rate	Rational	8	{48000,1}
Locked/Unlocked	Boolean	1	01_h (locked)
Audio Ref Level	Int8	1	0 (default)
Electro-Spatial Formulation	Uint8 (Enum)	1	Not encoded
Channel Count	UInt32	4	4
Quantization bits	UInt32	4	16 or 24
Dial Norm	Int8	1	Not encoded
Locators	StrongRefArray (Locators)	8+16n	Present only if essence container is external to the file

Table 8.17 Generic Sound Essence Descriptor

Item Name	Type	Len	Default Value(s)
Linked Track ID	UInt32	4	
Sample Rate	Rational	8	{24000,1001}, {24,1} {25,1}, {30000,1001}
Container Duration	Length	8	
Codec	UL	16	Not used
Essence Container	UL	16	See Table 8.11
Data Essence Coding	UL	16	Not used
Locators	StrongRefArray (Locators)	8+16n	Present only if essence container is external to the file

Table 8.18 Generic Data Essence Descriptor

9 MPEG, MXF, and SMPTE 381M

Bruce Devlin

Introduction

The generic mapping of MPEG streams into MXF is standardized in SMPTE 381M. The basic assumption behind the document is that many people have worked very hard within the MPEG community to create a set of standards that allow compressed content to be streamed and transported. SMPTE 381M reuses the concepts and some of the identifiers created by MPEG. This chapter will review some of the basic concepts within MPEG and how they are used in MPEG mapping document SMPTE 381M. Samples of MPEG MXF files can be found at *http://www.the mxfbook.com/*.

MPEG Basics

MPEG is most commonly associated with compression for television and DVDs. This form of MPEG coding is called *long-GOP MPEG-2*. This compression scheme was created in the early 1990s for video compression and forms one part of the MPEG suite of standards. There are many books that cover MPEG compression very well, and this short review only covers those aspects of MPEG that are important for the mapping into the MXF Generic Container.

The MPEG specification comprises a number of different documents:

ISO 11172   MPEG-1 standard in several parts

ISO 11172-1	MPEG 1 system stream
ISO 11172-2	MPEG 1 video coding
ISO 11172-3	MPEG 1 audio coding
ISO 138181	MPEG-2 standard in several parts
ISO 138181-1	MPEG 2 systems
ISO 138181-2	MPEG 2 video coding
ISO 138181-3	MPEG 2 audio coding
ISO 138181-9	MPEG advanced audio coding
ISO 15114	MPEG-4 coding standard
ISO 15114-2	MPEG 4 video coding
ISO 15114-3	MPEG 4 audio coding
ISO 15114-10	MPEG advanced video coding

MPEG Basics—MPEG Streams

MPEG-2 part 1 describes the mechanism MPEG uses to create Transport Streams and Program Streams for the distribution of synchronized video, audio, and data. The Transport Stream is widely used in the terrestrial, satellite, and cable transmission of digital television. The Program Stream is widely used for the distribution of multimedia files. Both of these mechanisms rely on the underlying concept of the Packetized Elementary Stream (PES) that contains the synchronization metadata for each of the multiplexed streams.

When creating a synchronized MPEG multiplex, a Packetized Elementary Stream is created for each of the component streams in the multiplex. Each Packetized Elementary Stream is then divided into a number of PES packets. The basic header information of each of these packets contains a StreamID to categorize the content of the packet and one or more *timestamps* to provide synchronization information for the stream.

MXF reuses the StreamID in the categorization of the content. The timestamp information is, however, not directly used: Any application creating an MXF file may need to use the PES timestamps to construct the correct MXF timing information in order to retain the synchronization of the original MPEG multiplex.

MPEG Basics—I-Frame MPEG

The simplest form of video coding is *MPEG I-frame coding*. In this case, each individual video frame is compressed independently of other frames and sent in the same order in which the frames will be displayed. Although this makes applications such as editing and random access easy to implement, it requires a comparatively high bitrate in order to compress images for any given picture quality.

I-frame-only content can be labeled and described more simply than long-GOP MPEG. In particular, a constrained form of MPEG, I-frame-only coding has been defined by SMPTE that takes into account the constraints imposed by recording the compressed signal using video tape recorders; this is known as the *D10* standard. The constrained D-10 variant of I-frame MPEG is mapped into MXF by its own specification: SMPTE 386M. If the D10 constraints are not met by the MPEG stream, then SMPTE 381M should be used to map it into MXF.

The terminology described in the long-GOP section below, also applies to I-frame coding. Specifically, the use of access units and the position of the headers remains the same.

MPEG Basics—Long-GOP

Long Group of Pictures (GOP) describes the predictive form of MPEG encoding. To explain the term group of pictures, it is first important to understand the basics of predictive coding. Figure 9.1 below shows the three different types of pictures that exist in MPEG. "I" pictures are those that can be decoded without using information from another picture. A "P" picture can be decoded using only information from a single picture that has already appeared in the MPEG stream (i.e., in the past). A "B" picture is one that can be decoded using information from one picture in the past and one picture in the future.

In order for a long-GOP MPEG stream to be easily decoded, the pictures are reordered between transmission and display. In MXF, it is the transmission order, as shown in Figure 9.2, which is stored on disc, rather than the display order of the images. The number of bytes allocated to each picture can vary greatly. This, coupled with the fact that MPEG does not require the number of

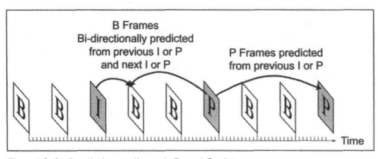

Figure 9.1 Predictive coding—I, P, and B pictures

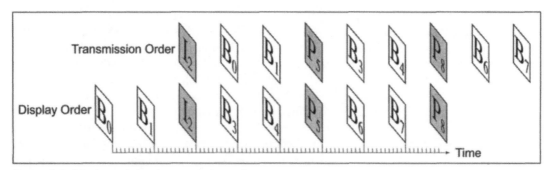

Figure 9.2 Display order and transmission order

B pictures to be constant, makes the creation of index tables challenging. The basics of MPEG index tables are covered in this chapter, and are dealt with more fully in Chapter 12.

The MPEG bitstream contains a number of headers that help identify different elements within the MPEG bitstream. A valuable concept defined in MPEG is the *access unit*. This is the data for an entire picture, along with the GOP header and any sequence header that precede it. These headers allow an MPEG decoder to determine the size of the picture and other parameters vital for the decoder to correctly recreate the image. The MPEG System Specification deals with the mapping of access units into transport and program streams using PES packets. SMPTE 381M takes the same approach and maps one or more MPEG access units into KLV triplets as shown in Figure 9.3.

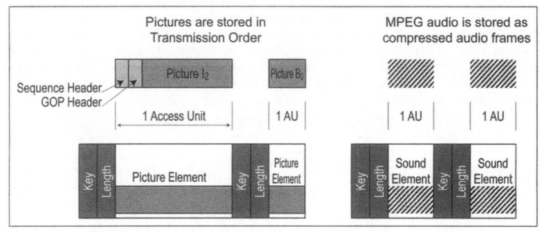

Figure 9.3 Mapping MPEG access units into KLV triplets

MPEG bistreams are intended for streaming; i.e., the pictures can be viewed and the sound can be heard while the bitstream is being transferred. MPEG defined a buffer model for the video and audio so that the decoders can know how much memory and how much delay they are required to provide when bitstreams are pushed at them. For broadcast applications, it is important to minimize the memory requirements of the decoder. However, MXF does not impose a buffer model, but instead provides rules for aligning synchronized pictures and sound within a generic container content package. This is because, even though MXF files are intended to be *streamable*, they are likely to be manipulated at the KLV level and are intended for professional applications, rather than for consumer applications where a *minimum decoder footprint* is the prime concern. The basic rule is that an MXF generic container content package should contain the audio sample that is synchronized with the video frame that would have been stored in the content package, if the video were in display order. This is a rather complicated rule, but it comes about because the designers of MXF did not want to have to change the audio storage strategy, which depended on the video stored order of the frames. It is for this reason that index tables are initially accessed

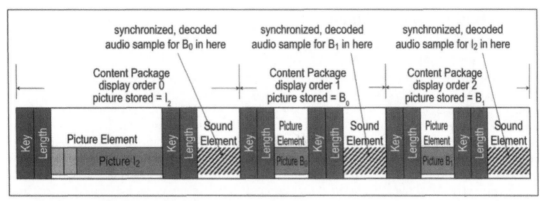

Figure 9.4 AV Interleave in an MPEG stream and an MXF generic container

in display order, and the audio is stored in the content package that would have contained the display-ordered video. This is shown in Figure 9.4.

Within an MPEG video elementary stream, the difference between MPEG-1 and MPEG-2 compression is identified by different sequence start code extensions. When wrapping within MXF, the difference is brought out in a subclass of the essence descriptor called the *CDCI descriptor*. (Color Difference Component Imagery Descriptor). In fact, many of the properties of the MPEG stream are brought to the MXF level in this descriptor. A full list of properties and how to fill them is given later in the chapter.

SMPTE 381M has been created so that streams created with no I-frames (often called *rolling refresh* streams) are supported.

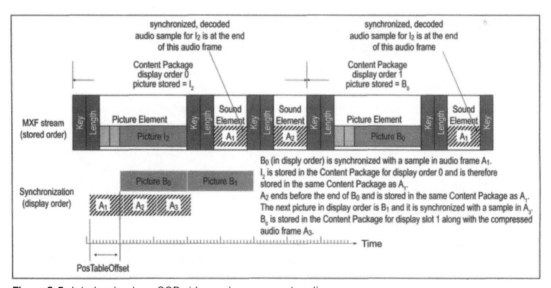

Figure 9.5 Interleaving long-GOP video and compressed audio

MPEG Basics—MPEG Audio

For the MPEG-1 and MPEG-2 standards, MPEG defined three compression schemes known as Layer I, Layer II, and Layer III. Audio Layers I and II use audio frames of a fixed-time duration. Unfortunately, the duration of these audio frames is not the same as the duration of video frames. When an interleaved audio-video stream is created, this difference in frame duration causes occasional irregularities in the pattern of audio and video frames. When the audio and video frames are KLV wrapped in frame mode according to the MXF rules, the temporal position of the first decoded audio sample of an audio frame will not coincide with the temporal position of the video frame. This can give rise to cumulative audio video sync errors when multiple random access jumps are made within the file. To prevent this, the MXF index tables have been designed with a special property called the *PosTableOffset* that explicitly tabulate any offset between the video and audio at the start of each content package. Tracking these offsets allows an application to track the cumulative offsets (synchronization errors) at each random access and thus, allows them to be compensated for. This is shown in Figure 9.5.

MXF Wrapping Strategies

The two modes recommended for MXF wrapping are *frame wrapping* and *clip wrapping*. MPEG, particularly long-GOP, has some difficult cases that need to be considered.

Frame Wrapping

In this mode, a content package is made up of an interleave of all the synchronized content for a given video frame. All video, audio, and ancillary data is KLV wrapped and, optionally, preceded by one or more *system elements* in a *system item*. The order of the elements must remain consistent throughout the file, and the index table is constructed according to Chapter 12. It is particularly important that if any one of the elements in the interleave has a variable length at any point in the file, then the index table must be sliced at that element according to the rules in Chapter 12.

Clip Wrapping

In this mode, each element of the interleave is stored, in its entirety, sequentially one after the other. For very long files, this can lead to index table number range problems if the bulky elements are stored before the shorter elements in the file.

Interleaving Strategies

I-Frame MPEG and AES/BWF Audio

There are several sorts of I-frame MPEG, almost all of which are frame wrapped in current implementations. One of the common types—D10 (SMPTE 386M) is coded so that each frame has a near constant number of bytes. Other I-frame variants, for example "constant quality coding" can have greatly differing numbers of bytes per frame. I-frame MPEG is not, in general, the same as fixed-

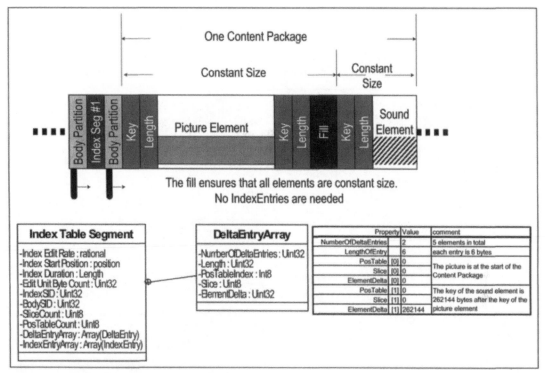

One Content Package

Constant Size

Constant Size

Body Partition | Index Seg #1 | Body Partition | Key | Length | Picture Element | Key | Length | Fill | Key | Length | Sound Element

The fill ensures that all elements are constant size.
No IndexEntries are needed

Index Table Segment

-Index Edit Rate : rational
-Index Start Position : position
-Index Duration : Length
-Edit Unit Byte Count : Uint32
-IndexSID : Uint32
-BodySID : Uint32
-SliceCount : Uint8
-PosTableCount : Uint8
-DeltaEntryArray : Array(DeltaEntry)
-IndexEntryArray : Array(IndexEntry)

DeltaEntryArray

-NumberOfDeltaEntries : Uint32
-Length : Uint32
-PosTableIndex : Int8
-Slice : Uint8
-ElementDelta : Uint32

Property	Value	comment
NumberOfDeltaEntries	2	5 elements in total
LengthOfEntry	6	each entry is 6 bytes
PosTable [0]	0	The picture is at the start of the Content Package
Slice [0]	0	
ElementDelta [0]	0	
PosTable [1]	0	The key of the sound element is 262144 bytes after the key of the picture element
Slice [1]	0	
ElementDelta [1]	262144	

Figure 9.6 I-frame MPEG with AES/BWF audio

length-per-frame MPEG coding. It is, however, quite likely that padding each picture KLV triplet with a fill triplet to give a fixed number of bytes/frame can result in a reasonably efficient storage format.

One of the most common strategies within MXF is to pad the I-frame picture element to a constant length, and then to have a constant length AES/ BWF element. This is shown in Figure 9.6. The index table can then be created to be a fixed-length table.

Long-GOP MPEG and AES/BWF Audio

Most Long-GOP MPEG with AES/BWF is frame wrapped. Figure 9.7 shows an interleave with two sound elements for each of the picture elements. Note the variable size of the picture elements and the corresponding slicing of the index table. The PosTable property of the index table is not required because the audio is not compressed.

Long-GOP MPEG and MPEG Audio

In this case, the PosTable property of the index table can be used to prevent any accumulation of timing errors. Figure 9.5 on page 205 shows the basic principle of the PosTable offset. Figure 9.8 on page 209 shows some examples of how the durations of video and audio frames relate for different video frame rates and 48kHz sampled audio.

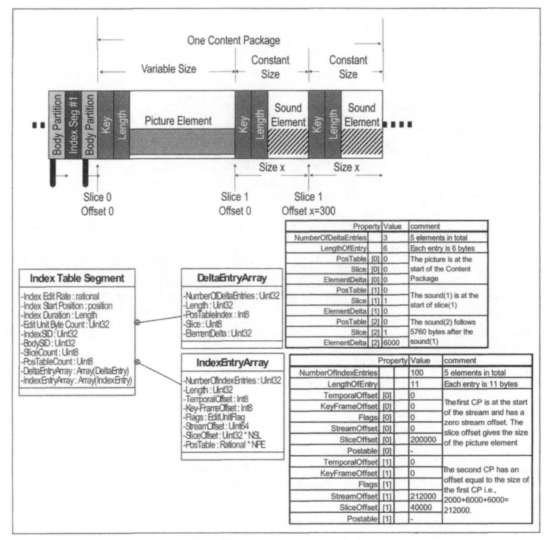

Figure 9.7 Long-GOP MPEG with AES/BWF audio

Other MPEG Streams such as Private Streams

SMPTE 381M relies on the underlying stream definitions in the MPEG-2 Systems document. This means that 381M can be used as a basis for the mapping of other stream types that may be defined by MPEG and contained in the MPEG-2 Systems layer. For many MPEG streams, such as MPEG-2 video and MPEG-2 audio, this is performed by identifying the content via the MPEG StreamID that would be used within the MPEG systems layer if the stream were being placed in a transport stream or a program stream. This StreamID is placed in the *essence container label* that identifies content wrapped via SMPTE 381M—the MPEG mapping document. This,

Video frame rate	frame duration	48kHz MPEG audio frame	minimum repeat (audio frames)	minimum repeat (video frames)	minimum repeat (duration)
23.98 Hz	41.708 ms	24 ms	1001	576	24.024 s
24.00 Hz	41.667 ms	24 ms	125	72	3.000 s
25.00 Hz	40.000 ms	24 ms	5	3	120 ms
29.97 Hz	33.367 ms	24 ms	1001	720	24.024 s
30.00 Hz	33.333 ms	24 ms	25	18	600 ms

Figure 9.8 Relationship between video frame rate and compressed MPEG audio frame size

is turn, is placed in the batch of essence container ULs at the start of each partition to provide a "fast fail" mechanism for essence identification.

Some essence types need more than a StreamID in the essence container UL to describe the essence. In fact, the intention of the essence container UL is a "fast fail" mechanism to give a quick identification at what is in the file (a list of the essence container ULs contained in the file is given in the partition pack). Certain ISO-MPEG and PrivateStream data essence types will require much more information for interoperable carriage in MXF. The correct place for this information is within the *essence descriptor* object. There may be required information for private streams, such as the MPEG-2 Registration Descriptor, which indicates the provenance of private stream types. To quote from the SMPTE-RA web site:

The registration descriptor of MPEG-2 transport is provided by ISO 13818-1 in order to enable users of the standard to unambiguously carry data when its format is not necessarily a recognized international standard. This provision will permit the MPEG-2 transport standard to carry all types of data while providing for a method of unambiguous identification of the characteristics of the underlying private data.

Carriage of information, such as that identified by the Registration Descriptor, should be performed by creating a new subclass of the appropriate essence descriptor with each property, new type, new group, and new enumerated value or enumerated value extension correctly registered in the appropriate SMPTE registry.

For decoding devices, the reverse is true. The StreamID field in the essence container UL batch indicates that a variant of the SMPTE381M mapping is in use. The essence descriptor will indicate the precise variant of essence that is mapped.

StreamID	Type
110x xxxx	MPEG1 audio stream number x xxxx (allocated from 0 on a per file basis) MPEG2 audio stream number x xxxx (allocated from 0 on a per file basis) ISO/IEC 14496-3 audio stream number x xxxx
1110 xxxx	MPEG1 video stream number xxxx MPEG2 video stream number xxxx ITU-T Rec. H.264 | ISO/IEC 14496-10 MPEG4-10 video stream number xxxx

Table 9.1 Some common StreamIDs

Some common StreamIDs are shown in Table 9.1. It is important to note that carriage of MPEG-2 and MPEG-4 can only be distinguished by looking at the PictureEssenceCoding parameter of the MPEG Descriptor (see Table 9.2 at the end of the chapter).

Multiplexing Strategies

Interleaving is the creation of content packages within a generic container by grouping elements into items (as shown for example in Figure 5.2). Multiplexing occurs when partitions are added to an MXF file to separate different essence containers within the file. This could be done for a variety of reasons that will now be explored.

Multiplexing for Error Resilience

MXF files containing MPEG, particularly long-GOP, are often created streamable/playable. If the file is to be transmitted over some link where errors may occur, or the transfer may be interrupted, it may be prudent to chop the file into a number of partitions. As explained in Chapter 3, a partition is the point in an MXF file where a decoder/parser can restart its decoding. Deciding how many partitions to insert into a stream to improve error resilience depends largely on what can be done as a result of detecting errors.

As an example, consider the case where a satellite broadcast of a file is taking place. If one of the reception sites fails to start the file capture process in time, the header partition containing all the header metadata would be lost and an MXF decoder would not be able to use any of the captured data until the next partition with header metadata was found. In an operational environment, this could be unacceptable. One way to protect against this would be to insert regular partitions into the transmitted file and to ensure that the header metadata was repeated in each partition.

How much overhead does this create? Again, this depends on the operational situation. If we assume that the file being transferred is 12Mb/s long-GOP with 3Mb/s of audio, we insert a partition pack with a repetition of the header metadata (512kbyte) every 10 seconds. This would give us:

$$\frac{0.5 \times 8}{10 \times (12 + 3) + (0.5 \times 8)} \approx 3\% \ \textit{overhead}$$

This is a fairly small overhead to ensure the maximum portion of the captured file that could be "lost" is limited to 10s.

Multiplexing for Higher OP Use

A "higher OP" is one higher than OP1a which, by definition, has more than one file package. When the essence for those file packages is stored internally, there will be more than one essence container. The MXF rules state that each essence container shall be stored in a different partition.

So what are the choices to be made when deciding on what multiplexing strategy should be used to multiplex the different partitions? Primarily, the choice comes down to streamable or not streamable. OP3x files are unlikely to be streamable because they require random access in order to play them back. For other operational patterns, making a file streamable depends on balancing delay requirements with buffer requirements. To be streamable, all the essence containers should be frame wrapped. The next requirement is to place the synchronized essence data for each of the essence containers close to each other in the file. The overhead involved in doing this depends on the precise mix of essence containers, but as an example, let's consider the following case:

Essence container 1 has 12Mb/s long-GOP interleaved with 3Mb/s BWF audio (*eng*—English)

Essence container 2 has 3 Mb/s of uncompressed BWF audio (*spa*—Spanish)

Essence container 3 has 3 Mb/s of uncompressed BWF audio (*fre*—French)

Each Partition Pack is 120 bytes

Multiplex all the essence containers at frame rate (30Hz—to simplify the math)

No repetition of header metadata or segmentation of index tables (to simplify the math)

The overhead is the size of three partition packs every frame:

$$\frac{3 \times 30 \times 120 \times 8 \times 10^{-6}}{(12+3)+3+3} \approx 0.4\% \ \textit{overhead}$$

Obviously, repeating header metadata will increase this overhead figure, and higher essence bitrates will reduce the overhead figure. This multiplex is shown pictorially in Figure 9.9.

Multiplexing for OP2x Contiguity

Operational patterns 2a, 2b, and 2c represent a playlist of essence containers. One of the qualifier flags of these operational patterns requires that the essence from the essence containers can be decoded by looking at a continuous stream of contiguous essence bytes. This is shown for an OP2a containing long-GOP MPEG in Figure 9.10 on the next page. In order to set this particular qualifier flag to "1," the bytes at the end of the first essence container must appear to be part of the same long-GOP MPEG stream as those at the start of the second essence container. Very often this will involve

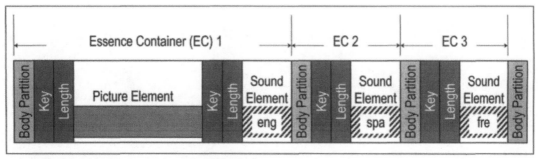

Figure 9.9 OP1c multiplex offering different audio languages

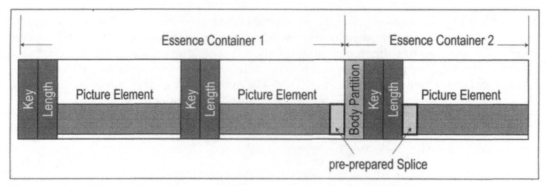

Figure 9.10 OP2a long-GOP playlist showing pre-computation of splice conditions

precalculating an MPEG splice at this join to ensure that the buffer conditions of the two streams are met. This is shown in Figure 9.10.

Multiplexing for Synchronization of Essence Containers OP1b and OP2b

In these operational patterns, individual file packages are synchronized using the MXF timing model. This is a specific case of the streaming example in the earlier sub-section entitled Multiplexing for Higher OP Use. The arrangement of the partitions in Figure 9.9 could equally represent an OP1b physical arrangement example.

OP2b brings with it the added complexity that partitions are required to segregate those essence containers which are synchronized across the timeline, as well as segregating those that represent the essence containers that are played out in sequence. This is shown in Figure 9.10—notice the point in the file where the first group of essence containers stops and the second group begins. For long-GOP MPEG, it is important that appropriate splice calculations be performed across the boundary.

Indexing Strategies

An index table allows an application to convert a time offset to a byte offset within the file. This allows applications to access any frame or sample within the file without having to parse the entire

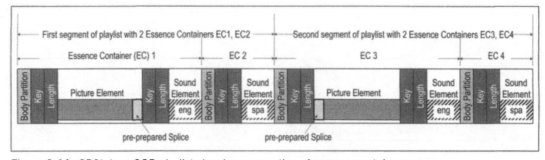

Figure 9.11 OP2b long-GOP playlist showing segregation of essence containers

file. The general concepts for the use of index tables are given in Chapter 2. Indexing of long-GOP MPEG is a tricky subject and full details of indexing are given in Chapter 12. This brief section will limit itself to the mechanism used to determine the location of long-GOP MPEG frames. A basic understanding of the following terms is needed:

DeltaEntry—Contains the basic indexing properties for each of the elements in the essence container. It is stored once per index table segment and contains properties such as the length of fixed-length elements and in which slice they occur.

IndexEntry—Contains the indexing details for variable length elements and is stored once per frame.

Slice—A technique where the IndexEntries only have to store the offsets for the variable length elements, and allows calculation of the fixed length elements.

The Basic Index Table for I-Frame MPEG

With I-frame MPEG, there is no reordering so the index tables are somewhat easier to construct than for long-GOP MPEG. Figure 9.12 shows the delta entries and the index table entries for the first 20 frames of the sequence. Note that in this example the audio is placed before the video in

Delta entry array has 2 items - Audio then Video

PosTable Index	Slice	Delta	
-1	0	0	audio element
-1	0	11540	video element

Index Entry Array for the first 20 Frames

frame #	size (bytes)	size +KLV	audio (bytes)	audio +KLV	Temporal Offset	Key Frame Offset	Flags	Stream Offset
1	25397	25417	11520	11540	0	0	0xC0	0
2	25985	26005	11520	11540	0	0	0xC0	36957
3	23929	23949	11520	11540	0	0	0xC0	74502
4	23785	23805	11520	11540	0	0	0xC0	109991
5	25068	25088	11520	11540	0	0	0xC0	145336
6	26000	26020	11520	11540	0	0	0xC0	181964
7	25169	25189	11520	11540	0	0	0xC0	219524
8	24995	25015	11520	11540	0	0	0xC0	256253
9	24478	24498	11520	11540	0	0	0xC0	292808
10	25601	25621	11520	11540	0	0	0xC0	328846

Figure 9.12 I-frame Index Table—Audio (CBE) with Video (VBE)

Delta entry array has 2 items ñ Video then Audio

PosTable Index	Slice	Delta	
-1	0	0	video element
-1	1	0	audio element

Index Entry Array for the first 10 Frames

frame #	size (bytes)	size +KLV	audio (bytes)	audio +KLV	Temporal Offset	Key Frame Offset	Flags	Stream Offset	Slice Offset
1	25397	25417	11520	11540	0	0	0xC0	0	25417
2	25985	26005	11520	11540	0	0	0xC0	36957	26005
3	23929	23949	11520	11540	0	0	0xC0	74502	23949
4	23785	23805	11520	11540	0	0	0xC0	109991	23805
5	25068	25088	11520	11540	0	0	0xC0	145336	25088
6	26000	26020	11520	11540	0	0	0xC0	181964	26020
7	25169	25189	11520	11540	0	0	0xC0	219524	25189
8	24995	25015	11520	11540	0	0	0xC0	256253	25015
9	24478	24498	11520	11540	0	0	0xC0	292808	24498
10	25442	25462	11526	11546	0	0	0xC0	328846	25462

Figure 9.13 I-frame index table—Video (VBE) with Audio (CBE)

the content package as placing the fixed size audio before the video in the stream makes the index table easier to construct as there is no need to slice the table.

Compare the same stream, but this time constructed with the video element before the audio element in the content package. This time it is necessary to slice the index table to find the start point of the audio. This is shown in Figure 9.13 for the first 10 frames of the same sequence shown in Figure 9.12. Note that there is now an extra column in the table that gives rise to an extra UINT32 for each frame in the file.

Index Table for Long-GOP MPEG

Long-GOP MPEG involves using the frame reordering mechanism in the index tables to convert between the desired display frame and the stored order within the file. Full details of the mechanism are given in the index tables Chapter 12. Here we will look at indexing a stream that has a 15-frame closed GOP with the following display order:

$\{ B_0\ B_1\ I_2\ B_3\ B_4\ P_5\ B_6\ B_7\ P_8\ B_9\ B_{10}\ P_{11}\ B_{12}\ B_{13}\ P_{14} \}$

We will consider the case where the video is frame wrapped and there is no other element interleaved with the video for simplicity. A closed GOP implies that the frames B_0 and B_1 are predicted entirely from frame I_2. Within the file, the frames are actually stored in transmission order, which is:

$\{ I_2\ B_0\ B_1\ P_5\ B_3\ B_4\ P_8\ B_6\ B_7\ P_{11}\ B_9\ B_{10}\ P_{14}\ B_{12}\ B_{13} \}$

Delta entry array has 1 items Video

PosTable Index	Slice	Delta	
-1	0	0	video element

Index Entry Array for the GOP

Display frame #		stored frame #	frame #	size (bytes)	size +KLV	Temporal Offset	Key Frame Offset	Flags	Stream Offset
B 0		I 2	1	145900	145920	1	0	0xC0	0
B 1		B 0	2	12268	12288	1	-1	0x33	145920
I 2		B 1	3	11244	11264	-2	-2	0x33	158208
B 3		P 5	4	50156	50176	1	-3	0x22	169472
B 4		B 3	5	8172	8192	1	-4	0x33	219648
P 5		B 4	6	8684	8704	-2	-5	0x33	227840
B 6		P 8	7	35820	35840	1	-6	0x22	236544
B 7		B 6	8	8684	8704	1	-7	0x33	272384
P 8		B 7	9	8684	8704	-2	-8	0x33	281088
B 9		P 11	10	35308	35328	1	-9	0x22	289792
B 10		B 9	11	8172	8192	1	-10	0x33	325120
P 11		B 10	12	8172	8192	-2	-11	0x33	333312
B 12		P 14	13	8172	34816	1	-12	0x22	341504
B 13		B 12	14	8172	8192	1	-13	0x33	376320
P 14		B 13	15	8172	8704	-2	-14	0x33	384512

Figure 9.14 Temporal reordering in the Index Table

The data values for the index table for this GOP are given in Figure 9.14. In order to find the location in the file of frame P5, we need to perform the following actions:

1. Look up the TemporalOffset for the frame with the frame number equal to the display frame number of frame P5—this position gives a TemporalOffset of -2.

2. Use the data for the frame that is two entries before this in the table (follow the grey arrow).

3. We can now see that this frame is:
   - 169472 bytes from the start of the stream
   - a P frame (flags = 0x22)
   - 3 frames from the Key frame (in stored order)

4. The number 169472 relates to the number of essence bytes in partitions with this essence container, not an absolute byte offset in the file. Further details are in Chapter 12.

Indexing with Fill

When an MPEG MXF file is created with fill KLV triplets, a decision needs to be made whether or not to index the *fill*. Generally fill would **not** be indexed because it is usually aligns with the content with the KAG boundaries. If, however, the index table is also used to provide an accurate count of the number of bytes for each and every picture, then it is possible to index the fill KLV triplets *in just* *the same way as a video or audio element is indexed.* Note that, if the fills are indexed, each and every fill needs to be indexed, even if a fill triplet is not needed at some point in the file.

MXF Application Interaction with Codecs

One of the goals in the design of MXF, was the creation of applications that could handle any kind of essence by acting only at the MXF/KLV level. For this to be possible, an MXF decoder will look at the essence container UL(s) (listed in the Preface) to see if the essence can be handled by the decoder. It will then look at the essence descriptor(s) within the top-level File Package to ensure that it is capable of finding a codec which can handle the contained Essence.

For this to work with long-GOP MPEG, it is vital that MXF encoders create MPEG essence descriptors with accurate and complete information in them. This will improve interoperability by giving MXF decoders the information they need to find the correct essence codec. Table 9.2 below (see also Figure 3.6) shows the properties of the MPEG Video Descriptor and where the properties can be found in the MPEG video stream.

Item Name	Type	Req ?	Meaning	Obtain From
MPEG Video	Set Key	Req	Defines the File Descriptor set	MXF defined key
Length	BER Length	Req	Set length	MXF defined length
Instance UID	UUID	Req	Unique ID of this instance	MXF defined UUID
Generation UID	UUID	Opt	Generation Identifier	MXF defined UUID
Linked Track ID	UInt32	Opt	This Descriptor is for the Track in this package with this value of TrackID.	MXF defined UInt32
SampleRate	Rational	Req	The field or frame rate of es-sence container (not the essence —pixel—sampling clock rate).	
Container Duration	Length	Opt	Duration of essence container (measured in Edit Units).	A file writer should write the best value it can write. If it cannot be completed, the Item should be omitted.
Essence Container	UL	Req	The essence container UL described by this descriptor.	These ULs are listed in SMPTE RP 224. Their definition is in SMPTE 381M and any docu-ments which extend SMPTE 381M.
Codec	UL	Opt	UL to identify a codec compat-ible with this essence container.	These ULs are listed in SMPTE RP 224 and identify the codec which made the content.
Locators	StrongRe-fArray (Locators)	Opt	Ordered array of strong refer-ences to Locator sets.	If present, the essence may be external to the file. The order of the locator sets is the order that an MXF Decoder should search for the essence.

Item Name	Type	Req ?	Meaning	Obtain From
Signal Standard	Enum	Opt	Underlying Signal Standard	This is usually known by the MPEG Encoder, but may not always be knowable by an MXF application. Exceptions are for MXF broadcast applications where well-known width, height, and frame rate values can be used to infer the underlying standard.
Frame Layout	Uint8	B.Effort	Interlace or progressive layout	The value in the descriptor is a static value for the file, whereas MPEG-2 can dynamically switch between field and frame coding. Unless the MXF application is certain that the content comprises only field pictures, then the value 0==FullFrame should be used.
Stored Width	Uint32	B.Effort	Horizontal Size of stored picture	SequenceHeader and SequenceHeaderExtension
Stored Height	Uint32	B.Effort	Vertical Field Size of stored picture	SequenceHeader and SequenceHeaderExtension
StoredF2Offset	Int32	Opt	Topness Adjustment for stored picture	This property should be the same as the TopFieldFirstFlag.
SampledWidth	Uint32	Opt	Sampled width supplied to codec	Omit or Set to the same as Stored Width.
Sampled Height	Uint32	Opt	Sampled height supplied to codec	Set to the same as Stored Height.
SampledXOffset	Int32	Opt	Offset from stored to sampled width	0
SampledYOffset	Int32	Opt	Offset from stored to sampled height	0
DisplayHeight	Uint32	Opt	Displayed Height placed in Production Aperture	Omit, unless it is known that vertical blanking has been encoded in which case set the correct value.
DisplayWidth	Uint32	Opt	Displayed Width placed in Production Aperture	Omit, unless it is known that horizontal blanking has been encoded in which case set the correct value.
DisplayXOffset	Int32	Opt	Offset from Sampled to Display Width	Omit, unless it is known that horizontal blanking has been encoded in which case set the correct value
DisplayYOffset	Int32	Opt	Offset from Sampled to Display Height	Omit, unless it is known that vertical blanking has been encoded in which case set the correct value.

217

Item Name	Type	Req ?	Meaning	Obtain From
DisplayF2Offset	Int32	Opt	Topness Adjustment for displayed picture	Omit—MPEG cannot represent this.
Aspect Ratio	Rational	B.Effort	Specifies the horizontal to vertical aspect ratio of the whole image as it is to be presented to avoid geometric distortion (and hence includes any black edges); e.g., {4,3} or {16,9}.	From the CodedFrame AspectRatio in the Sequence-Header.
Active Format Descriptor	UInt8	Opt	Specifies the intended framing of the content. Within the displayed image (4:3 in 16:9, etc.).	If it is known that the AFD is static in this sequence, then set to the correct AFD value, otherwise set to 4:3 or 16:9.
Video Line Map	Array of Int32	B.Effort	First active line in each field; e.g., {16,278}.	
Alpha Transparency	UInt8	Opt	Is Alpha Inverted ?	Omit—MPEG cannot represent this.
Capture Gamma	UL	Opt	Registered UL of known Gamma	Omit—MPEG cannot represent this.
Image Alignment Offset	Uint32	Opt	Byte Boundary alignment required for Low Level Essence Storage.	Usually 0
Image Start Offset	Uint32	Opt	Unused bytes before start of stored data.	Usually 0
Image End Offset	Uint32	Opt	Unused bytes after end of stored data.	Usually 0
FieldDominance	Uint8	Opt	The number of the field that is considered temporally to come first.	Omit—this property is invariant in MPEG, and most codecs are unable to change their behavior.
Picture Essence Coding	UL	D/Req	UL identifying the Picture Compression Scheme	Listed in RP 224 and defined in SMPTE 381M or one of its extensions.
Component Depth	UInt32	B.Effort	Number of active bits per sample; e.g., 8, 10, 16	8 for MPEG-1 and MPEG-2, extract appropriate information from FRext MPEG4-10.
Horizontal Subsampling	UInt32	B.Effort	Specifies the H color subsampling	2 for 4:2:2 MPEG & 4:2:0 MPEG.
Vertical Subsampling	UInt32	Opt	Specifies the V color subsampling	2 for 4:2:0 MPEG, omit for 4:2:2 MPEG.
Color Siting	UInt8	Opt	Enumerated value describing color siting	
ReversedByteOrder	Boolean	Opt	A FALSE value denotes Chroma followed by Luma pixels according to ITU Rec.601.	Omit—MPEG cannot change this.
PaddingBits	Int16	Opt	Bits to round up each pixel to stored size	Omit—MPEG cannot change this.

Item Name	Type	Req ?	Meaning	Obtain From
Alpha Sample Depth	UInt32	Opt	Number of bits per alpha sample	Omit—MPEG cannot change this.
Black Ref Level	Uint32	Opt	e.g., 16 or 64 (8 or 10-bits)	Omit—MPEG cannot change this.
White Ref level	Uint32	Opt	e.g., 235 or 940 (8 or 10 bits)	Omit—MPEG cannot change this.
Color Range	Uint32	Opt	e.g., 225 or 897 (8 or 10 bits)	Omit—MPEG cannot change this.
SingleSequence	Boolean	Opt	TRUE if the essence consists of a single MPEG sequence. False if there are a number of sequences.	This flag implies that the sequence header information is not varying in the essence stream.
ConstantBframes	Boolean	Opt	TRUE if the number of B frames is always constant.	Omit if unknown
CodedContentType	Enum	Opt	0= "Unknown" 1= "Progressive" 2= "Interlaced" 3= "Mixed"	An enumerated value which tells if the underlying content that was MPEG coded was of a known type. Set to 0 if unknown.
LowDelay	Boolean	Opt	TRUE if low delay mode was used in the sequence.	Omit if unknown
ClosedGOP	Boolean	Opt	TRUE if ClosedGop is set in all GOP Headers, per ISO/IEC 13818-1 IBP descriptor.	Omit if unknown
IdenticalGOP	Boolean	Opt	TRUE if every GOP in the sequence is constructed the same, per ISO/IEC13818-1 IBP descriptor.	Omit if unknown
MaxGOP	Uint16	Opt	Specifies the maximum occurring spacing between I-frames, per ISO/IEC13818-1 IBP descriptor.	Omit if unknown
BPictureCount	Uint16	Opt	Specifies the maximum number of B pictures between P- or I-frames, equivalent to 13818-2 annex D (M-1).	Omit if unknown
BitRate	UInt32	Opt	Maximum bit rate of MPEG video elementary stream in bit/s.	From sequence_header bit_rate property. Omit if unknown
ProfileAndLevel	Uint8	Opt	Specifies the MPEG-2 video profile and level.	ProfileAndLevelIndication in the MPEG-2 SequenceHeaderExtension. For main profile @ main level, the value is 0x48. For 4:2:2 profile @ main level, the value is 0x85.

Table 9.2 The MPEG video descriptor

10 Generic Data Streams, VBI, and ANC

Bruce Devlin

Introduction

Media files can contain many different types of associated data, and it is the job of MXF to synchronize and relate these different sorts of data in an extensible way. Over the years, there have been many ad-hoc solutions to synchronizing data with video and audio. Methods include hiding it in video blanking, carrying it inside *user bits* in the audio/video data stream, carrying it as a parallel data stream in a multiplex, or even printing it onto film near the sprocket holes.

The goal of MXF is to provide a common environment for the carriage of data, and a common approach to synchronizing it to the video and audio essence. In order to do this, the MXF designers recognized that there are different types of data to be transported, and different reasons why the data is transported. This has led to a number of different carriage mechanisms, optimized for the different data types.

- Essence-like or streaming data

- *Lumpy* or *non-streaming data*

- Opaque *ancillary data* carriage

Examples of streaming data include scene depth information, GPS positioning information, lens focal length information, etc. In these cases, there is a continuous stream of data synchronized to the video and audio. The temporal characteristics of the stored data are similar to the temporal characteristics of video and audio. This means that the data values may or may not change very much on a frame-by-frame basis, but there is always changing data to be stored—and it can be adequately contained in the file using the data element defined in SMPTE 379M, the Generic Container Specification. The metadata required is associated with a data track defined in SMPTE 377M, the MXF File Format Specification—and the data is indexed using a standard MXF index table. In fact, the data element and its metadata descriptions behave almost identically to a picture element or a sound element.

Examples of lumpy data include xml documents; bulky data sets associated with events such as picture analysis; time-stamped KLV data; and bulky metadata such as device or application settings that cannot fit in the 64kByte limit of the header metadata. It may also be the case that an application encounters unknown or *dark* data, which it is obliged to put into an MXF file, but has no knowledge of the temporal characteristics of the data. For this reason, SMPTE 410M defines a *generic stream* within MXF. The generic stream is a container for data that is associated with a StreamID (cf., BodySID and IndexSID). In MXF, the StreamID is an identifier that allows an application to uniquely match stored essence with metadata; it does not imply that the essence itself is streamed or streamable. So, despite the fact that the generic stream has a StreamID and is referred to as a stream, the word *stream* itself refers to the fact that, as far as the MXF application is concerned, it is just a stream of bytes, rather than some kind of essence with a linear relationship with time. This is pretty confusing, but there seems to be a shortage of appropriate words in the English language to describe the nuances of all these concepts!

Once the data has been contained in a generic stream, it can be described in the MXF metadata by referring to this StreamID. The mechanism is extremely simple and lightweight and is thus applicable for a number of different data types such as *opaque* ancillary data. In this context, the word opaque refers to the fact that the meaning of the data in the generic stream is unknown to the MXF application. The MXF application has, however, enough information to manage the data as an *opaque lump*.

The particular carriage mechanism described in this chapter for this form of data is not intended to replace the data elements defined within SMPTE 331M (Element and Metadata Definitions for the SDTI-CP), which are then used in the SDTI-CP compatible system item described in SMPTE 385M (Mapping SDTI-CP into Generic Container). Neither is it intended to replace the data elements for use in the Generic Container System Scheme 1 (as described in SMPTE 405M). This generic stream carriage is intended to allow the transport of opaque streams for compatibility with established formats and to facilitate the use of MXF for existing applications that use this data. In general, the application that created the file knows only that there are generic stream partitions present in the file. The nature and purpose of the data is often unknown to MXF creation application, but may be known to some plugin or helper application.

This chapter will only deal with the second and third data types in the list above. The GC data element is covered briefly in other chapters. Picture and sound elements are covered extensively in Chapters 2, 3, and the mappings chapters—Chapter 5 (general), Chapter 6 (Audio), Chapter 7 (DV), Chapter 8 (D10, D11), Chapter 9 MPEG, Chapter 16 (JPEG2000). The usage of the generic container data element can be derived from this information. If you are trying to put data into an MXF file, which could fit either into the generic container data element or into the generic stream, then it is up to the skill and judgment of the implementer to decide which of the mappings is likely to result in the greatest success for interchange and interoperability.

It is important to note that, at the time of writing, SMPTE 410M and the VBI/ANC data document had not completed the SMPTE ballot process. Despite the best efforts of the author, there is the chance that some of the information presented in this chapter will have changed as a result of the standardization process. If you are intending to implement or specify anything related to data in this chapter, you are strongly advised to obtain the latest version of the SMPTE specifications and consult them!

The Generic Stream

SMPTE 410M describes the *generic stream*. The goal was to create a *generic container* for non-timelined data that could be linked into the MXF header metadata. The goal was **not** to create a replacement for the generic container as defined in SMPTE 379M.

The generic stream is contained in its own partition within the MXF File. The partition is a form of *Body Partition* and, as such, can be easily located whenever there is a Random Index Pack in the stream. This is shown in Figure 10.1 below.

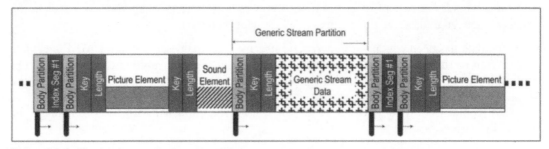

Figure 10.1 The basic generic stream partition

A generic stream partition follows the normal MXF rules that everything must be KLV coded. But there is always the case that the data may, in itself, already be KLV coded. What do we do? Add another layer of KLV outside the existing KLV? No—this would be inefficient and prone to implementation error. The whole goal of KLV coding is that the key should be sufficient to identify the payload regardless of the context in which that payload is found. It is therefore useful to categorize the payloads of the generic stream partition into those which are KLV coded and those which are not.

The data in the generic stream partition may a) be a continuous unbroken lump (e.g., a word-processed script) or b) have natural access units within it (e.g., rendered subtitle information). In the latter case, there are applications where improved performance can be achieved by storing the access units of the data stream physically close to the synchronized video and audio. It is therefore useful to be able to categorize the data to be stored in terms of being continuous or having access units.

The extensibility of the design also needs to be considered. It would be simple for the designers of the containment mechanism to force each and every data type to be registered with a registration authority, and an enormously long list of data types would have to be inspected by each and every MXF application. This would rapidly become unwieldy. Instead, the designers considered a model in which a generic implementation was considered. In this generic implementation, we consider that there is a KLV handler and a data handler in the application. The application needs to be able to find data within the generic stream partition, and it does this by knowing some offset (which may be a byte offset within the stream, time offset, depth offset, or other). This offset can be looked up in a data-specific index table, and the correct bytes within the data stream can be found. Once found, these data bytes are handed over to a codec which is able to parse and use these data bytes. This generic architecture is shown in Figure 10.2.

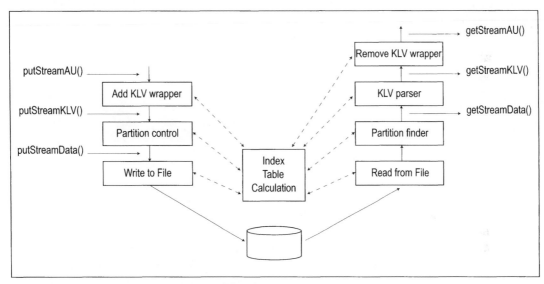

Figure 10.2 A generic data-processing architecture

The architecture shows that access can be achieved by an application at varying levels depending on the process that needs to be performed. Applications that treat a generic stream as opaque can access at the `putStreamData()` and `getStreamData()` levels. Other applications may need to manipulate data at the KLV level, and so a KLV interface is provided via `putStreamKLV()` and `getStreamKLV()`. Other applications may need to manipulate data via individual access units, in which case the `putStreamAU()` and `getStreamAU()` interfaces are likely to be used.

Given this architecture, we can now find a way to categorize the underlying data types and we are able to design systems that can handle this generic data at the MXF level. This means that the application only knows about the parameters defined in MXF, but is able to read, write, and locate generic data within the generic data stream.

The Stream Types

The three basic stream types are:

1. KLV-wrapped data.

2. Data that can be split on identifiable access units.

3. Contiguous data lumps with no identifiable access units.

These can be further subdivided to give useful handling rules for the different data types. It is important to note that the design of the indexing mechanism for the generic stream container is specific to each essence type, and there is no general design in the same way that there is an essence index specified in SMPTE 377M, The MXF File Format Specification. It is almost impossible to design a common index table that is simultaneously meaningful for encapsulated Word documents, XML timed text, and telemetry data. In the text that follows, some general guidelines are given for each stream type.

Type "A" Streams

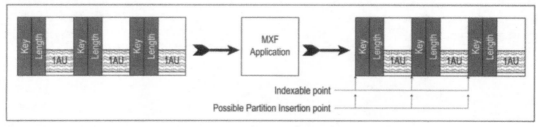

Figure 10.3 Type A data already wrapped as KLV

Type A streams are already KLV wrapped, an example of which is a series of timestamped KLV packets. An MXF application can handle the KLV triplets without having to know what the triplets mean. It can process the KLV data in the partition using *blind* rules—this means that it can hand KLV triplets to a stream API, or receive them from a stream API. The stream API can be configured with different partitioning rules to match the application requirements. This is independent behavior to that of processing and handling the actual KLV triplets.

Wrapping

No extra wrapping is necessary because the data already has KLV wrapping on it.

Indexing

Any indexing mechanism operates on the keys of the KLV triplets. The specific index table design converts the desired offset into the byte offset to the first byte of the KLV key. For example, a timeline-oriented KLV stream, such as timestamped KLV packets, could create an index table that associated the timestamp value with the byte offset of the first byte of key of that KLV triplet.

Like the SMPTE 377M Index Table Segment, it is recommended that the byte offsets in the index table are created relative to the partition. This allows the partitions to be moved around within the file without needing to recreate the index table and is different behaviour to that of indexing streams. This can be very useful when rearranging a file that has been created from a stream. Often the partitions will be multiplexed during capture, but it can be very useful to put all the data partitions in a batch at the end of the file.

Partitioning

Blind partitioning or repartitioning is possible. A partition can be inserted prior to any KLV key and the entire stream can be parsed and reconstituted using a KLV parser. An MXF application may combine or split partitions at will in order to repartition the file.

Application Behavior

The application writes individual KLV packets to the Stream API, which returns them as KLV packets. A well-behaved application should verify the integrity of the KLV packets returned from such an API. In the API in Figure 10.2, KLV data is returned through *both* the getStreamKLV() and getStreamAU() interfaces because the underlying access units were intrinsically KLV wrapped. The MXF system knows this because essence is flagged at a very low level as being intrinsically KLV wrapped or not as shown below.

Type "B1" Streams

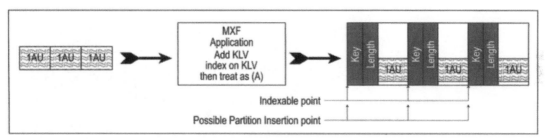

Figure 10.4 Type B1—data has access units—layered as though (A)

Type B streams have identifiable access units, an example of which is a series of configuration settings used while capturing a media stream. A type B1 stream handler writes data using the putStreamAU() API, but from then on manages the data in the MXF domain as though it were KLV wrapped. This has the benefit, for an MXF application, of making it appear like a type A stream for the purposes of managing the data stream.

Wrapping

Data is KLV wrapped on the access unit boundaries. It enters the MXF system via the putStreamAU() API. If this interface is passed the access units one at a time, then it need not have the intrinsic ability to parse the data. The data within the MXF stream is indexed and managed as though it were a type A stream with the exception that, when the data leaves the MXF environment, the KLV layer is removed.

Indexing

Index tables are created in the same way as index tables for type A streams.

Partitioning

Partitioning behavior is identical to type A partitioning.

Application Behavior

Type B1 streams are intended to give maximum compatibility with Type A streams. Data enters the MXF environment using the `putStreamAU()` interface, and is removed via the `getStreamAU()`.

Type "B2" Streams

Type B2 streams have identifiable access units, but are managed at the access unit level rather than the KLV level. This means that data enters via the `putStreamAU()` interface and leaves via the `getStreamAU()` interface. This type of stream is not as common as B1 or B3 and has few advantages.

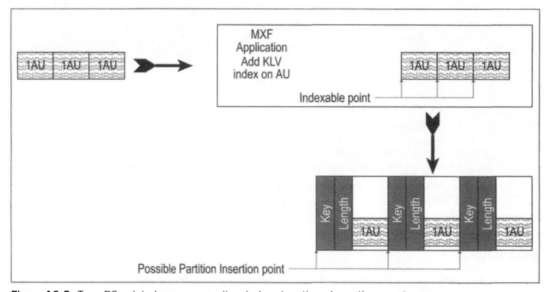

Figure 10.5 Type B2—data has access units—indexed as though continuous stream

Wrapping

Wrapping is the same as for a B1 stream.

Indexing

Each access unit is indexed individually where the byte offset in the table points to the first byte of access unit and not to the KLV that encapsulates it in the stream. This is a hybrid mechanism that "looks like" generic container frame wrapping but also "looks like" it is indexed as though the content were clip wrapped.

Partitioning

Partitioning rules are the same as type A streams.

Application Behavior

This type of stream is the most complex for an MXF application to handle. It does not behave like true KLV data (type A or type B1), nor as a clip-wrapped container (type B3). This means that special rules are required to handle this type of containment, and hence the chances of interoperability are significantly reduced.

Type "B3" Streams

Type B3 streams have individual access units, and are indexed on these access unit boundaries, but the entire data stream is contained in a single KLV triplet. This is similar to the generic container clip-wrapping method described in SMPTE 379M.

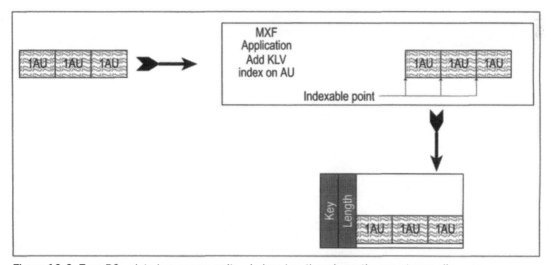

Figure 10.6 Type B3—data has access units—indexed as though continuous stream clip wrap

Wrapping

There is a single KLV that encapsulates the entire data stream. Creating a few KLVs that split the stream up into chunks is not recommended. The stream should either be wrapped with a KLV on every access unit **or** wrapped as an entire clip. Anything in between is not to be encouraged.

Indexing

Index tables are constructed to associate each access unit with the byte offset of that access unit within the KLV triplet. As there is one, and only one KLV triplet, this leads to a simple structure.

Partitioning

There is only one KLV triplet and it is located in a single partition. There can be no repartitioning without creating a type C stream.

Application Behavior

Data enters the MXF environment through the `putStreamAU()` interface and is retrieved through the `getStreamAU()` interface. This type of data stream leads to simple MXF handling and simple read-side processing. If the data stream itself is very large, then there may be write-side buffering issues that need to be solved if the data is received interleaved with other data, but has to be written as a single KLV in the file.

Type "C1" Streams

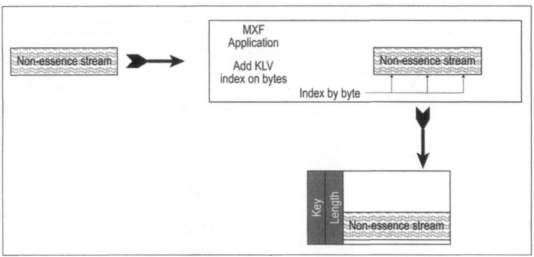

Figure 10.7 Type C1—data has no identifiable access units—indexed as though continuous stream clip wrap

Type C streams have no identifiable access units, an example of which is an XML document. Type C1 streams are contained in a single KLV and are indexed (if appropriate) according to the byte offset within the KLV stream.

Wrapping

There is a single KLV triplet that encompasses the entire data stream. Any other wrapping would create a type C2 stream.

Indexing

If indexing is appropriate, then an index table relates a position value to a byte offset value within the KLV stream. As in Type A streams, custom index tables are required.

Partitioning

As in the type B3 stream, no partitioning or repartitioning is possible.

Application Behavior

Applications handle the data as a large binary object of (possibly) unknown type. The same buffering issues apply as for type B3 streams. Data enters via the `putStreamData()` and is removed via the `getStreamData()` interface.

Type "C2" Streams

Type C2 streams have no identifiable access units but, for application reasons, splitting the chunk of data into partitions is desired.

Wrapping

In order to support multiple partitions, the data chunk is divided into chunks and each chunk is individually KLV wrapped. The strategy for KLV wrapping is either naïve— i.e., "stick a KLV wherever you want"—or depends upon a data stream parser that has knowledge of the intrinsic meaning of the data.

Indexing

Indexing is similar to stream type B2 and is highly stream dependent.

Partitioning

Once the data stream has been split into KLV triplets, partitions can be inserted in front of any KLV key.

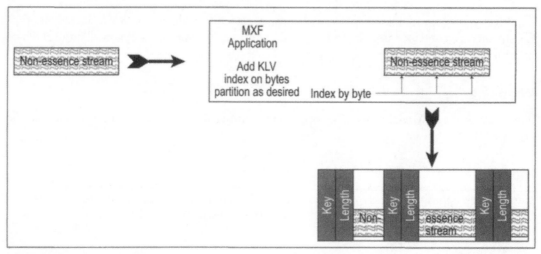

Figure 10.8 Type C2—data has no identifiable access units—partition as desired

Application Behavior

Application behavior has to be quite sophisticated for this type of stream. One example could be subtitling expressed as an XML file. The work for this particular standard is in progress at the time of writing, and the fine details of containing the file in the stream and mapping metadata have not been finalized. Key requirements are to be able to store XML locally to the audio video content in the file, and to be able to associate portions of the XML with the MXF timeline. Applications are likely to implement interfaces that live on top of the Data via the `putStreamData()` and are removed via the `getStreamData()` interface.

The Container

Having now decided what the different stream types are, we can provide appropriate low-level signaling to help a generic stream Application to process the data. A common KLV key is provided to wrap the data (i.e,. the generic data elements) within the partition. This KLV key has some low-level signaling that allows the interfaces described in Table 10.1 to be implemented:

Byte order of Data	Keep KLV with Data	Multi-KLV	Data wrapped by Access Unit	Wrapping Synchro-nized to Essence
Little-endian	Yes	Yes	Yes	Frame
Big-endian	No	No	No	Clip
unknown				unknown

Table 10.1 Signaling provided in the generic stream key

The low-level signaling forms part of the KLV key that allows the low-level KLV parsers to intelligently handle the data for the layer above.

The first level of signaling is big-endian, little-endian, or unknown-endian. This allows the creation of interfaces such as readInt32() to interface with getStreamAU() and to return an appropriate integer value. The case of *unknown endian* is intended to cover data streams that are coded as ISO-7 characters. In this case, there is no intrinsic endianness. Attempting a function such as readInteger() on such a data stream should at the least generate a warning function at the API layer that the underlying data may not match the expectations of the application.

The second layer of signaling instructs the lower layers to keep or discard the KLV layer. This signaling distinguishes type A streams from other data types. When "keep KLV with data" is asserted, APIs should always return KLV packets at the getStreamKLV() and getStreamAU() interfaces.

Multi-KLV signaling is intended to indicate whether a partition contains a single or many KLV triplets. This is a performance-enhancing flag that prevents the lower-level APIs from searching within a partition to find out if there are extra KLV triplets. This flag is rarely used by application code.

"Data wrapped by Access Unit" signals a type A or B1 or B2 type of stream. The flag indicates that each and every access unit in the stream has its own KLV wrapper. This will always be set to false for a type B3 or a type C stream.

The final flag indicates how the MXF encoder placed the generic stream partitions in the file. If there was intrinsic synchronization between the data stream access units and the audio-video stream, then it is possible to indicate that the generic stream partitions have been placed locally closed to the audio-video Generic Container Partition by asserting the "Wrapping synchronized to essence" flag. This flag can take the values:

- "Frame" to indicate that the generic stream partition is close to the frame-wrapped generic container essence;

- "Clip" to indicate that the clip-wrapped generic stream has some intrinsic synchronization to the clip-wrapped generic container; and

- Unknown to indicate that the synchronization is unknown.

Indexing the Content

Some generic stream data can vary along the timeline and may have structural metadata associated with it that describes temporal offsets. In order to identify which portion of the data is to be used, an index table must be constructed to associate the temporal offset with a byte offset within the file.

SMPTE 377M section 10 Index Tables are designed for data streams that are continuously present and have Constant Bits per Element (CBE) or Variable Bits per Element (VBE). These index tables are not appropriate for generic stream data and should not be used.

The index tables needed for a generic stream should have many of the features of the MXF Index Table:

- They should associate the Track Position with a Byte Offset.

- The ByteOffset should be the offset within the stream; i.e., only the payload of the partitions is considered when calculating the byteoffsets.

- Index tables should be relocateable without calculation; i.e., it should be possible for a generic stream's index table to be moved to another partition within the file without having to recalculate any of the parameters.

- It should also be possible to move a generic stream partition within the file without having to recalculate its index table.

- The index table should itself be a stream and identifiable with a StreamID. Because of this, the index table will live in a generic stream container and will have its own BodySID. Using an IndexSID is not possible.

Rules of the Generic Stream Partition

There are a number of rules associated with the generic stream partition that are given in the specification and explained here:

1. A generic stream partition shall include one or more KLV-wrapped Generic Data Elements. This is to ensure that no one reading the specification forgets to KLV wrap the data within the partition. This may seem obvious, but it is surprising how often this can be forgotten.

2. A generic stream partition shall contain data from a single generic stream. This keeps the metadata linking simple. A single SID is associated with a single generic stream. This prevents having to generate substream identifiers, which is just messy.

3. A generic stream partition shall not include any essence container, header metadata repetition, or SMPTE 377M index table segments. To keep parsing and multiplexing rules simple, it has been recognized that the original MXF design should have kept to the "one thing per partition" rule. This cannot be retro-fitted to the MXF standard at this late stage in the standardization process, but well-behaved applications should follow this guideline. For any MXF file that contains a single generic stream partition, this rule is in the specification—only a single "thing" can live in a partition when the generic stream partition is in use.

4. The order of the generic stream data elements is important and shall not be altered by any application treating the generic stream data elements as dark. This rule is to prevent any "helpful" application from corrupting data by making wrong assumptions about it. An obvious example is reading the data as big-endian and rewriting it as little-endian when, in fact, the application did not know the meaning of the underlying data.

5. The generic stream data elements may be placed in a single partition, or distributed over two or more partitions. This condition may be restricted by an operational pattern or other constraint. The generic stream partition specification merely defines the signaling of the different data types. It does not mandate how any individual stream should be handled. For this reason, this condition states that there may be some other restriction in force.

6. Each unique generic stream shall be assigned a BodySID value that is unique within the file. Different generic streams can thus be uniquely identified even if there are several generic streams distributed throughout the file. This keeps the number space of the BodySID unique.

7. If the Random Index Pack is present at the end of the MXF file, the generic stream partitions shall be included in the Random Index Pack. This rule forces the Random Index Pack to include the generic stream partitions. This is important for reading applications that rely on a random index pack to find the appropriate contents of the file.

8. Generic stream BodySIDs shall not appear within the EssenceContainerData set. This is to ensure that a generic stream is not considered as generic container-encapsulated essence.

SIDs

Stream IDs form a unique number space as outlined in Chapter 3. It is not allowed for any two BodySIDs, IndexSIDs, or any other SIDs to have the same value in a file in order to ensure proper management of the StreamID number space. When a file contains generic stream partitions, each partition is associated with a single SID. You cannot have essence and index information in the same partition when the generic stream partition is in use.

Repetition

Some generic stream data may be repeated within a file. In order to detect the start of a generic stream repetition, each repetition starts with a new generic stream partition pack. To identify this partition as the start of a repetition, the BodyOffset property of the Partition Pack is set to 0.

MXF applications shouldn't assume that each and every repetition is identical. It may be that the generic stream data set is repeated because the data set is a function of the file capture process and that the data set is growing as the MXF file is being created.

Using the Generic Stream for "Bulky" Properties

MXF uses 2-byte tags and 2-byte lengths for the local set coding of properties of metadata sets. Some metadata properties may be too large to fit into these 64kB Local Set tag-length-value triplets. For example, an MXF modification application may store its configuration as an XML document. The application may wish to prolong this configuration information within the Identification Set created during the modification of the file. This is because an Identification Set, as explained in the section headed Dark in Chapter 3, should be inserted every time a file is modified and is used in conjunction with the Generation ID. This identifies when metadata within the file was updated. For this example, we will assume that the XML document containing the configuration information can grow to be bigger than 64kBytes and thus the safest way of storing it in the file is by using the generic stream partition.

One solution is to register a property in a private SMPTE data class as shown in Table 10.1.

Item Name	Type	Len	Tag	UL Designator	Meaning
My Private XML doc key	Element Key	16	dynamic	06.0E.2B.34.1.01.01.07. 0E.XX.01.01.01.01.01.01	Identifies my XML document (property of a class 14 registration—company XX)
TLV Length	Uint16	2	-		Length of a BodySID
SID of XML doc	Uint16	2	-		The BodySID identifying the partition with the XML document in it

Table 10.2 Local set tag-length-value coding of a privately registered BodySID

This property would be added to the Identification Set that is created when the application modifies the MXF file. A partition would be created at the same time with the following Partition Pack Key:

06.0e.2b.34.01.01.01.vv 0d.01.05.DS.WS.00.00.00

where: vv -   indicates the version of the registry
         DS -   indicates the Data Signaling   = "0d"$_h$ (KLV not part of data, unknown endianness)

         WS—   indicates the Wrapping Signaling = "01"$_h$
                   (first byte of KLV has no special importance, may be more than 1 KLV, not Frame synchronized)

Within the Partition, there will be one or more KLV triplets containing the XML data as shown in Figure 10.9.

This example assumes that the privately registered class 14 KLV key of the XML document (06.0 E.2B.34.01.01.01.07. 0E.XX.02.01.01.01.01.01) is in the 02 number range of the private number space. The identifier was in the 01 number space (identified by byte 11 of the key).

Using the Generic Stream to Contain "Lumpy" Data Essence

Lumpy essence is the sort of data that may be discontinuous throughout the piece, or whose access units may have unpredictable start times (which may include overlapping of essence lumps), unpredictable durations, and variable bitrate. These sorts of essence do not fall conveniently into the framing structure that is dictated by the audio and video. Subtitling information, analysis information, and some telemetry data may fall into this category.

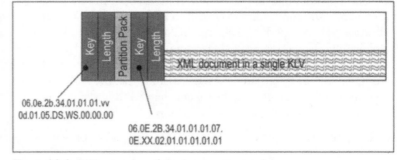

Figure 10.9 KLV wrapping of the lumpy essence data

As an example, imagine that some process is searching for a video feature. When this feature occurs, analysis data is stored to the lumpy essence partition. One possible implementation of this containment is as follows:

Here, a new KLV generic data element key has been registered in the private number space we used earlier. This KLV key wraps up access units of our lumpy essence. The payload also includes an ID—this might be a timestamp, unique ID, or some other value that can relate this physical KLV triplet to the header metadata or to an appropriate indexing structure.

In order to describe this lumpy essence from the header metadata, we could use an Event Track with subclasses of SourceClips/Segments. The subclassed SourceClips/Segments will have the appropriate 377M Event Properties (i.e., Start Position and Duration) in order to describe the lumps. Using an event track allows the lumps to overlap, to have gaps, or to have instantaneous durations. The subclassed SourceClips/Segments will need to refer to their indexing method.

In order to link specific subclassed SourceClip/Segment instances to the appropriate KLV-wrapped lumpy essence, an index table structure will be needed. This is likely to be a custom design as its performance will depend on the exact lumpy nature of the essence. The role of the index table is to convert

$$(packageID + trackID + start\ offset) \rightarrow (BodySID, ByteOffset, ID)$$

The precise design of this table depends on the nature of the essence. In addition to the index table, an essence descriptor may need to be defined for the essence type if there are parameters about the essence which need promoting to the MXF application.

Timeline Association of Generic Stream Data

The general design for linking the essence to the timeline metadata is described above. Generic stream data has a different temporal characteristic to video and audio. In general:

- The "packet" size of a generic stream is unpredictable.

- The arrival rate of "packets" is unpredictable.

- The duration of "packets" is unpredictable.

- The relationship between *temporal offset* and *byte offset* is neither linear nor monotonic.

It is recommended that event tracks are used to describe generic stream data as their temporal characteristics are similar. At the time of writing, work is being carried out within the AAF Association by one of the authors of this book to put in place the appropriate generic tools to associate lumpy essence contained in a generic stream partition with an MXF event track. The general guidance is given here:

- Create a DynamicClip for event tracks.
  - This is analogous to a SourceClip for timeline tracks (chapters 4 and 11).
  - The DynamicClip has the following properties:

- SourcePackageID—the UMID of the package describing the data stream.
- SourceTrackIDs—an array of TrackIDs describing the data stream.
- SourceIndex—a means of defining the start point of the data.
- SourceExtent—a means of defining the duration of the data.
- SourceSpecies—a means of identifying the stream's data type.

- Create a DynamicMarker for event tracks.
  - This is analogous to a DMSegment for timeline tracks.
  - The DynamicMarker has the following properties:
    - ToleranceMode—defines timing accuracy.
    - ToleranceWindow—defines timing accuracy.
    - InterpolationMethod—defines how to find the correct time offset.

Describing the Generic Data Stream Type

In order to know what the data stream contains, a Data Descriptor needs to be created. Two examples of this are shown in Figure 10.10.

Of particular interest is the ParsedTextDescriptor that is being designed to carry enough properties to link the metadata of the MXF timeline to the essence in the generic stream partition.

Opaque VBI and ANC

Within the television world, the analog *vertical blanking* has been used to carry extra data for many years. When MXF files are introduced into a TV workflow, it is often the case that the original *VBI lines* need to be recreated during the playout of an MXF file. However, MXF applications often do not need to know or understand the data within those VBI lines. The requirement is simply to carry them intact throughout the MXF environment and to ensure that they can be recreated correctly.

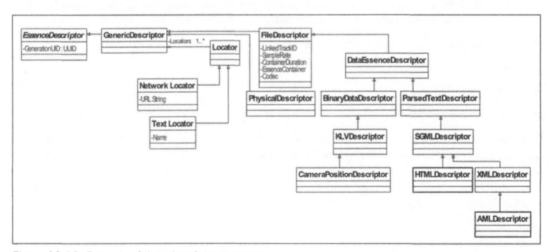

Figure 10.10 Example of data descriptor structure

In a digital TV environment, the same holds true for ancillary data packets (*ANC packets*) that can be found in both horizontal and vertical blanking.

VBI lines and ANC data packets have many applications. In some cases, this information can be encapsulated as standardized MXF metadata items. In other cases, this approach is not practical. For example, some stations and networks encode non-standard data in VBI lines. Attempting to write additional MXF standards to describe each of these applications was not practical. Adding a facility to MXF that supports opaque VBI lines and ancillary data packets is a better solution.

At the time of writing this book, the work had not finished its standardization process, and so the finer details of this section of the chapter may not agree with the SMPTE standard. The work within SMPTE describes the transport of VBI lines, and ANC data packets for standard definition television (525 and 625 line) and high-definition television. It also describes the encoding of additional information so an MXF decoder can place the VBI lines and ANC data packets at the proper location in a generated television signal.

Carriage of VBI and ANC in MXF

The goal of the carriage within MXF is opaque transport. We know that the VBI and ANC packets are broadcast within the (continuous) video signal, and, as such, the data will be timeline oriented. This means we can use the Generic Container Data Element to place the Data in the file as shown in Figure 10.11.

Within the generic container, the KLV key is used to link the essence to the header metadata (as described in Chapter 3). There is a single KLV triplet for VBI data and a single KLV triplet for ANC data in each generic container. Within each triplet, there is a data structure that describes how the various VBI lines/ANC packets are encoded. The standards were created with the goal of limiting the number of choices to improve the chances of interoperability.

VBI lines are PCM coded to a depth of 1 bit, 8 bits, or 10 bits as shown in Figure 10.12. The signaling of this coding is done within the data structure in the KLV triplet. Although it is technically possible to use a different coding for each and every VBI line, this practice is not to be recommended.

ANC packets may be 8-bit or 10-bit coding. In each mode, it is possible to indicate that a packet was in error. This may seem strange until you consider that the goal of the mapping was to create

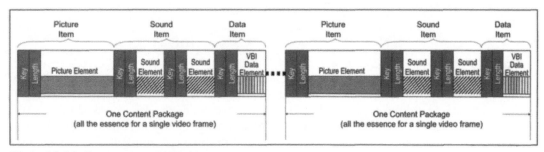

Figure 10.11 Frame-wrapped VBI data elements

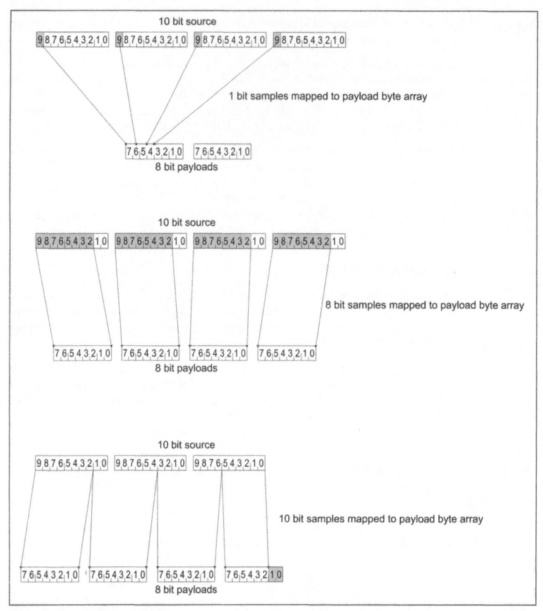

Figure 10.12 Coding of VBI lines in MXF

an opaque transport mechanism. If the device writing the MXF file received an errored ANC packet, what should it do? Correct it? If this is not possible, we don't want to end up in the situation where an errored ANC packet going into an MXF environment comes out of the other side looking as though it were not errored. This could lead to some very unpredictable system level results. For this reason *transparent* errored packet propagation has been enabled.

11 DMS-1 Metadata Scheme

Jim Wilkinson

Introduction

The MXF specification provides the mechanism by which a *descriptive metadata* (DM) *framework* can be plugged into the *structural metadata* part of the *header metadata*. These DM frameworks are a part of the header metadata and provide additional editorial value to an MXF file. The DMS-1 specification is defined in SMPTE 380M. Further information on using descriptive metadata in MXF is given in *engineering guideline* document SMPTE EG42.

A Short History of DMS-1

The descriptive metadata scheme, now known as DMS-1, started life as a short list of metadata items that were needed to replicate roughly the equivalent of a tape label. Inevitably, this list grew rapidly in an attempt to create a common initial framework of metadata items that might be implemented by manufacturers in order to achieve interoperability,

Work on defining a data structure for descriptive metadata within MXF started in February, 2000. This structure provided for *production*, *clip*, and *scene* sets. Production metadata applies to the production as a whole, clip metadata applies to the content as it was created or captured (e.g., where a scene was actually shot), whereas scene metadata applies to the editorial intent of individual scenes (e.g., where a scene is set).

By 2001, the three sets had become collections of sets (now known as frameworks) with the collections sharing several sets of the same kind in common relationships. During the period 2001–2002 there were several meetings focused on harmonization with the metadata attributes defined by the wide-ranging work of the P/Meta Group within the EBU. The discussions included fundamental issues around what should and should not be stored in an MXF file, because a MXF file might not be seen as an appropriate place to store some business metadata that might be transitory in nature. The harmonization resulted in a refinement of the sets retained within DMS-1 and removal of some sets that could be considered as transient, such as financial information.

During the period 2002–2003, there was work to harmonize DMS-1 with metadata schemes defined by MPEG-7 and also *TV Anytime*. The results were some refinements in DMS-1 and (in the case of MPEG-7) some better understanding of real-world requirements. MPEG-7 is a massive metadata scheme that contains very sophisticated content analysis metadata, much of which is beyond the immediate needs of regular program making. The harmonization with MPEG-7 was deliberately limited to focus on metadata that is closely associated with program production.

TV Anytime metadata is primarily targeted for content delivery to the consumer and, as the focus of DMS-1 is program production, only a part of DMS-1 provides metadata directly applicable for final distribution. However, in order to reduce the necessity for re-keying of data during the process of preparing material for final delivery, DMS-1 was further enhanced to maximize the compatibility with the TV Anytime metadata.

2004 saw the final tweaks and responses to user inputs and completion of the SMPTE ballot process on the DMS-1 documents. The process of developing DMS-1 had been long and had received much input from several interested parties. The result is a specification that covers most of the requirements for the content production industries. However, its apparent complexity may overwhelm some communities and this chapter aims to explain how it works and what it can do.

The Scheme in Outline

The core requirements that evolved over the development of DMS-1 are:

- To satisfy the basic needs for production and libraries in order to minimize re-keying of metadata during the production process.

- To use the provisions of the MXF *data model* for DM extensions through the DM Track mechanism defined in SMPTE 377M.

- To be usable by AAF applications (with the appropriate extensions).

- To interwork as far as practical with other metadata schemes such as MPEG-7, TV Anytime, and P/Meta.

DMS-1 follows a consistent modeling process that is the same as that used by the MXF structural metadata and is summarized as follows:

1. **Scheme:** A collection of *metadata frameworks* which, although essentially independent entities, are related through a common class hierarchy and may share resources.

2. **Framework:** A collection of related metadata objects (either as sets or properties) using an instance of a defined class hierarchy.

3. **Set:** A collection of properties that contribute in equal measure to an object whose overall value is greater than the sum of the individual properties.

4. **Property:** An individual item of metadata.

5. **Enumeration:** Metadata properties have defined types that may have defined values assigned for semantic meaning. Property enumerations may be numeric (and hence language independent), rigid textual (and language independent), or flexible textual (with values dependent on language, culture, application, or industry). In some limited circumstances, sets may also be enumerated, although this is not commonplace. Some examples of these enumerations are:

Model Number—"XYZ-123" (as a numeric enumeration).

Lens Type—"MAN-Focus" (as a language independent text string).

Role Name—"Best Boy" (as a flexible textual string).

The relationship between these layers is as follows:

1. A scheme may have one or more related frameworks.

2. A framework may have one or more sets. Where there is more than one set, they must each specify their relationship within the framework and their relationship with each other. For example, a framework may have three sets, A, B, and C. The framework owns sets A and B and set B owns set C. Thus the framework also owns set C, but only via set B.

3. A set may have one or more properties. Where there is more than one property, each property is generally considered equal in weight and of no defined order within the set.

4. Each individual property may have particular attributes such as:
   a) It may have specifically agreed values (either numeric or textual values).
   b) It may have minimum and maximum values (e.g., min= 16, max = 235).
   c) If a string property, it may have lower and upper limits to the string length.

DMS-1 defines four layers: scheme, framework, set, and property. It also provides the hook for property enumerations via the mechanism of a *thesaurus* that can be loaded dynamically by an application as required. This is a very powerful way to provide those standard text enumerations that are sensitive to language, industry, and local variations. Later in this chapter, there is a fuller explanation of the thesaurus.

Metadata Model

As explained, the MXF data model is constrained to be compatible with the AAF data model explained fully in Chapter 13. The modeling rules defined by the AAF specification are followed by DMS-1, as if the descriptive metadata were part of the AAF data model, in order to maximize the interoperability between MXF-based DMS-1 and AAF applications. These rules essentially revolve around a formal class model with a single-inheritance class hierarchy. However, as most of the classes in the DMS-1 specification are largely independent entities, the DMS-1 class hierarchy is a relatively flat structure. However, the object models for the production, clip, and scene frameworks tend to be tree-like in structure resulting from the way in which the class model provides for connections between the sets.

The common single-inheritance class hierarchy is used by all three frameworks and can be found in Annex A. In this annex, the individual framework object models expand the class inheritance hierarchy for clear understanding.

Wherever possible, the properties within any class have been chosen to be intimately related to the intent of any particular class. In several cases, there are classes that are very generic and are widely used. In particular, individual classes were extracted wherever it was determined that the properties could be repeated within any set. Thus a "person" can have many "addresses," and each "address" can have many "communications" (e.g., telephones).

The DMS-1 class hierarchy has several abstract superclasses designed to act as the common points in the hierarchy for the purpose of spawning subclasses. (Note: Abstract superclasses have no properties that can be instantiated on their own.)

Since AAF defines the individual properties of *Instance UID* and *Generation UID* at the highest level of the data model, all DMS-1 sets can include these properties and use them in the same way as used for the MXF structural metadata. However, all other properties in DMS-1 are unique within the AAF data model.

DMS-1 Frameworks

As mentioned earlier, the three essentially different *frameworks* for containing *descriptive metadata* sets are:

- **Production metadata:** describes the editorial identifiers that apply to the production as a whole.

- **Clip metadata:** describes the content as it was created or captured.

- **Scene metadata:** describes the editorial intent of the content.

DM frameworks give contextual meaning to a metadata set by logically grouping metadata sets used in the same context. For example, a metadata set that describes a location can be used within the *clip framework* to describe the real location (the actual location of the camera) or within the *scene framework* to describe the fictional location (where the scene is supposed to be set). Similarly, a name in the clip framework could be a participant's real name, whereas a name in the scene framework could be that of a fictional character (e.g., "Falstaff").

In the DMS-1 specification, the terms production, clip, and scene were agreed with several parties after lengthy discussions. There is no single word that can express the intent of these terms that is common across all the industries that might use the DMS-1 specification (music, video, file, etc.), so these terms need to be explained in detail to ensure consistent usage.

Essentially, they can be described as follows:

- Production information provides identification, label, and other metadata for the file as a whole. As such, this metadata is likely to change if a new production is created based on material taken from an already existing production.

- Clip information is provided to allow material to be described from the aspect of its capture or creation. This information is likely to be persistent whatever its use.

- Scene information provides metadata to describe the actions and events in the material in an editorial context (e.g., the location of the scene in a drama). This information is less likely to change in different usage as, once defined, it typically represents the material as annotated in the first production.

The data models of each framework are illustrated in the Figures 11.1–11.3.

Frameworks and Their Relationships to Packages

Where a DM framework is used in a *material package*, it provides information about the output *timeline* of the file.

Where a DM framework is used in a *file package*, it provides information about the material in the associated *essence container*.

If there are *source packages* present in the file, then the DM *framework* provides historical annotation of the material described by the source package.

Clearly, in the simplest case where a file has just one file package, the scene and *clip frameworks* associated with the essence container that is described by the file package may be copied to the material package and used to describe the output presentation. The *production framework* may be copied from the file package, or a completely new production framework may be created if needed.

If the essence container of an MXF file is copied to another MXF file, either in whole or as part of a larger production, then the DM frameworks present in the first file package may be copied into the second MXF file under its file package.

Using Frameworks in an MXF File

Each framework is referenced by a *DM segment* that associates it to particular times along certain defined tracks or all tracks.

The use of each *framework* will typically differ on a case-by-case basis as follows:

Production Framework

A *production framework* usually applies to all tracks of the package timeline.

- If referenced by a material package, it describes the file output as a complete entity and is regarded as the current production metadata. It will usually have the same duration as the

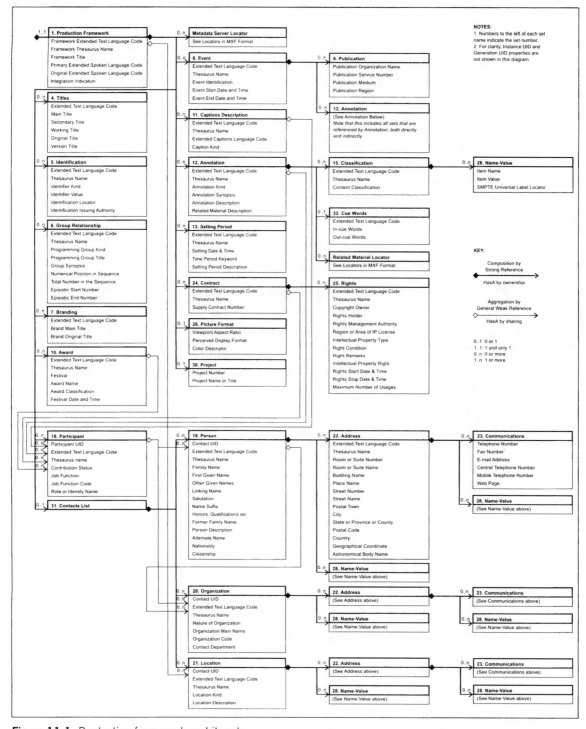

Figure 11.1 Production framework and its sets

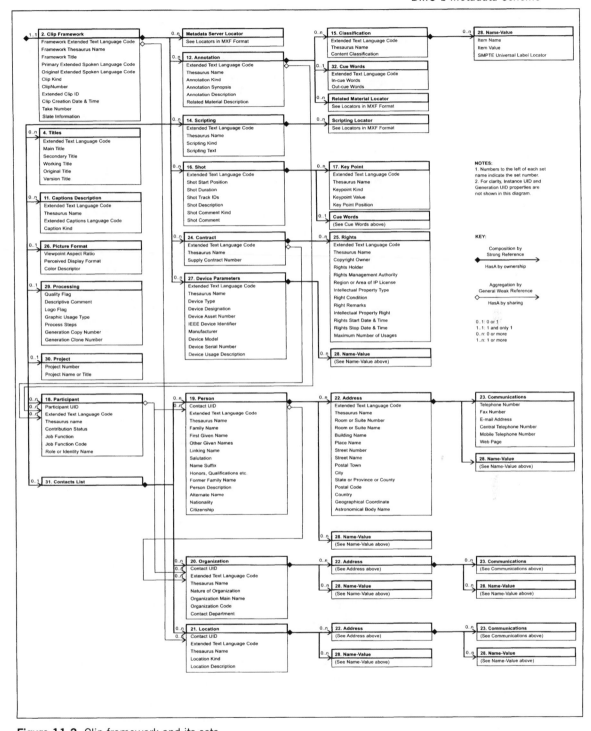

Figure 11.2 Clip framework and its sets

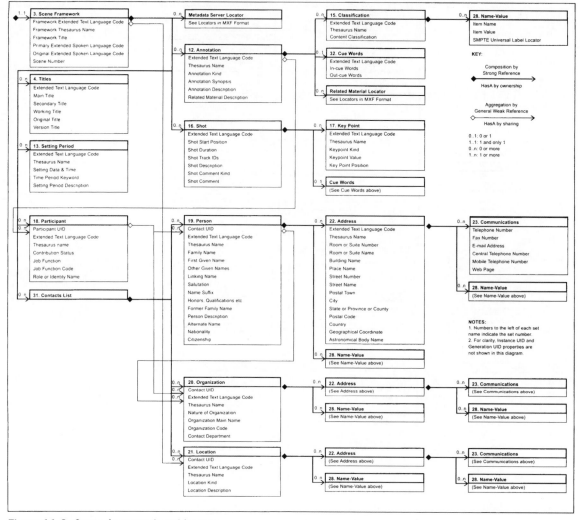

Figure 11.3 Scene framework and its sets

output timeline and apply to all tracks. In the case of files with operational patterns having alternate packages (see Chapter 4, Figure 4.1), there will usually be one *production framework* per material package in the file.

- If referenced by a top-level file package, it describes the material described by the file package. Thus, it will usually have the same duration as the associated essence container and apply to all tracks.

- If referenced by a lower-level source package, it describes the historical production information. It will usually have the same duration as the source material and apply to all tracks.

Clip Framework

A clip framework typically applies to a single essence track or a combination of essence tracks over a defined duration. Clip frameworks are typically contiguous along the timeline and may describe the picture and sound tracks with different frameworks. A clip framework is interpreted as follows:

- If referenced by a material package, it describes the clip information that is relevant for playout. This is a case where the *DM SourceClip* set is used to reference the clip information described by the file package.

- If referenced by a top-level file package, it will describe the clip information for the defined section of the associated essence container and typically represents the information captured at the point of creating or capturing the content (or copied from any source when appropriate).

- If referenced by a source package, it describes the clip information for the defined section of the source material that might be the original material as captured or created.

Scene Framework

A *scene framework* typically applies to a particular combination of essence tracks over a defined duration. Scene frameworks may overlap along the timeline or may even describe individual pictures. Consequently, there may be many scene frameworks referenced by any one package (material, file or source). Similar to a clip framework, a scene framework is interpreted as follows:

- If referenced by a material package, it describes the scene information as presented on playout. This is a case where the DM SourceClip set is used to reference the scene information described by the appropriate file package.

- If referenced by a file package, it will describe the scene information for the defined section of material in the essence container.

- If referenced by a source package, it will describe the scene information for the defined section of source material.

Using Frameworks in Editing Operations

Editing metadata is very similar to that of editing audio with video; it can be edited synchronously with the audio and video, or it can be stripped from the file and essentially rebuilt in coordination with the A/V editing process.

There are no clear rules for editing metadata at the time of writing this chapter. In general, the following can be considered as points to consider for metadata editing.

Production Framework

For many operations, this is likely to be newly created or recreated during editing, since most of the information in this framework is connected with the entire A/V content as a production entity.

Clip Framework

Clip metadata is most likely to be automatically created and recorded at the point of capture or creation. Since each clip framework is associated with a particular point or duration along the timeline, and may only apply to certain tracks, caution must be exercised in ensuring that the timing and track values are still relevant after editing. Of particular note is that the *shot* set has its own timeline and track set, so that individual frames and sounds can be logged for reference. (Note: The shot set is part of the clip and scene frameworks as shown earlier in this chapter.)

Scene Framework

Scene information is most likely to be created by editorial staff for logging purposes. Following its creation, the processing of scene metadata is likely to be similar, in many ways, to the processing of metadata in the clip framework (with the exception that the scene metadata resides on an *event track* that allows scene metadata to overlap or be discontinuous).

KLV Coding of DMS-1

A framework is coded as a sequence of KLV-coded data sets connected by strong (and weak) references. Every DMS-1 framework and set is a KLV coded *local set* that uses 2-byte *local tags* to identify individual items within each set.

A general illustration of the implementation of a framework is shown in Figure 11.4.

Most properties that are a part of the structural metadata have statically assigned 2-byte local tag values. All local tag values used by DMS-1 properties are dynamically assigned and stored in the *primer pack* where each 2-byte local tag value is mapped uniquely to the full SMPTE UL value as defined in the DMS-1 specification and registered in the SMPTE *metadata dictionary*.

Using the Primer Pack for Local Tag Assignment

The MXF format specification defines a primer pack that identifies all the local tags used for local set coding in the header metadata. Each local tag needs to be unique for each property and acts as an alias for the globally unique 16-byte UID that exists either as a publicly defined SMPTE metadata dictionary UL or as a privately defined UUID. Local tags are unique within the *partition* in which they are used. The function of the primer pack in each instance of header metadata in a partition is to ensure that all local tag values are unique within the header metadata.

With the exception of the instance UID and generation UID properties, all local tag values for DMS-1 are dynamically allocated for each partition. This means that, at each encoding, any local tag for any new descriptive metadata property must check first with the primer pack to ensure that both the local tag value and the UL have not previously been used.

In summary, the following rules apply to all DM schemes that use sets with 2-byte local tags.

1. All dynamic local tags for DMS-1 must lie in the range "80.00$_h$" to "FF.FF$_h$."

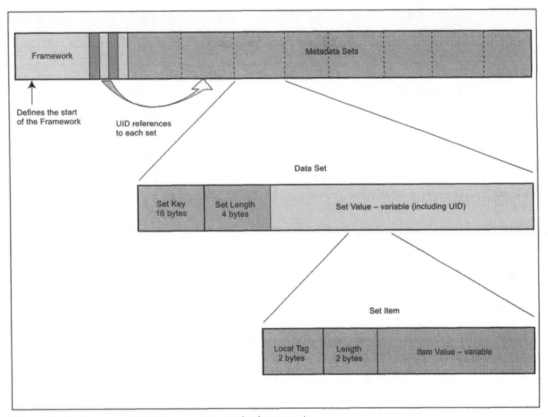

Figure 11.4 Three-level KLV data construct of a framework

2. For all statically allocated local tags, the associated UIDs that are defined for structural metadata or *index tables* cannot be used for descriptive metadata unless the property is inherited through the class inheritance mechanism. Where such a property exists (e.g., instance UID and generation UID), the local tag values are the same as the statically allocated local tags.

3. For each dynamically allocated local tag, the associated UID must be unique within the scope of the primer pack.

DMS-1 UL Identifier

The *preface set* of the header metadata contains a *DM schemes* property. This is an unordered batch of ULs that identify each DM scheme used in that instance of the header metadata. Since this DM Scheme defines DM frameworks that are not logically connected, but share a common data model, a UL is provided for each DM framework. For each DMS-1 framework present in the header metadata, the ULs as described in Table 11.1 on the next page must be added to the DM schemes property.

Byte No.	Description	Value (hex)	Meaning
1-12	See SMPTE 377M	06.0E.2B.34.04.01. 01.01.0D.01.04.01	As defined by MXF File Format Specification
13	Scheme Kind	01	MXF Descriptive Metadata Scheme 1
14	Scheme Version	02	Version 2
15	Framework Identification	01, 02 or 03	01h = Production Framework 02h = Clip Framework 03h = Scene Framework
16	Scheme Variant	01 or 02	01h = no extensions 02h = extensions present

Table 11.1 UL for DMS-1 frameworks

Byte 14 of the UL defines the version of DMS-1. Each new version of DMS-1 will increment the version number to identify that there are additions of new sets or properties. To maintain backwards compatibility with previous versions, any increase in the version number will only add new metadata sets or properties and will not change any part of any previous version.

The first published version of the DMS-1 specification started with the value 02_h. The earlier value 01_h was experimental only and is not valid.

To define whether the encoded descriptive metadata scheme lies within, or exceeds, the version defined, the UL has a scheme extension word defined in byte 15. This provides for those cases where an encoder has encoded metadata sets or properties that are classed as *dark* and that do not fall under any of the defined DMS-1 frameworks. Clearly, caution must be exercised to ensure that no unexpected or deleterious effects will occur at the decoder.

DMS-1 Set Keys

As stated above, all sets in DMS-1 are encoded as KLV local sets using 2-byte tag values and 2-byte length values and have a common structure for their UL keys as defined in Table 11.2.

Byte No.	Description	Value (hex)	Meaning
1~12	As defined in SMPTE 377M	06.0E.2B.34.02.53. 01.01.0D.01.04.01	MXF File Format Specification
13	Structure / Scheme Kind	01	Descriptive Metadata Scheme 1
14	MXF Set Definition	xx	See Table 11.3
15	MXF Set Definition	yy	See Table 11.3
16	Reserved	00	

Table 11.2 Key values for all DMS-1 frameworks and sets

Note that if any set is used for interchange with other metadata systems, *universal sets* (rather than local sets) may be required and for this, the value of byte 6 must be changed to a value of "01_h"

(from "53$_h$"). Furthermore, all local set tags should be set to the full 16-byte value based on the SMPTE metadata dictionary.

The definitions of bytes 14 and 15 of the keys for the descriptive metadata sets are given in Table 11.3.

Set Name	Byte 14	Byte 15	Annex A
Production Framework	01$_h$	01$_h$	A1
Clip Framework	01$_h$	02$_h$	A2
Scene Framework	01$_h$	03$_h$	A3
Titles	10$_h$	01$_h$	A4
Identification	11$_h$	01$_h$	A5
Group Relationship	12$_h$	01$_h$	A6
Branding	13$_h$	01$_h$	A7
Event	14$_h$	01$_h$	A8
Publication	14$_h$	02$_h$	A9
Award	15$_h$	01$_h$	A10
Caption Description	16$_h$	01$_h$	A11
Annotation	17$_h$	01$_h$	A12
Setting Period	17$_h$	02$_h$	A13
Scripting	17$_h$	03$_h$	A14
Classification	17$_h$	04$_h$	A15
Shot	17$_h$	05$_h$	A16
Key Point	17$_h$	06$_h$	A17
Participant	18$_h$	01$_h$	A18
Person	1A$_h$	02$_h$	A19
Organization	1A$_h$	03$_h$	A20
Location	1A$_h$	04$_h$	A21
Address	1B$_h$	01$_h$	A22
Communications	1B$_h$	02$_h$	A23
Contract	1C$_h$	01$_h$	A24
Rights	1C$_h$	02$_h$	A25
Picture Format	1D$_h$	01$_h$	A26
Device Parameters	1E$_h$	01$_h$	A27
Name-Value	1F$_h$	01$_h$	A28
Processing	20$_h$	01$_h$	A29
Project	20$_h$	02$_h$	A30
Contacts List	19$_h$	01$_h$	A31
Cue Words	17$_h$	08$_h$	A32

Set Name	Byte 14	Byte 15	Annex A
Reserved for Abstract Superclasses	7F$_h$	xx$_h$ (>00$_h$)	
DMS-1 Framework	7F$_h$	01$_h$	
Production/Clip Framework	7F$_h$	02$_h$	
DMS-1 Set	7F$_h$	10$_h$	
TextLanguage	7F$_h$	11$_h$	
Thesaurus	7F$_h$	12$_h$	
Contact	7F$_h$	1A$_h$	

Table 11.3 Values for bytes 14 and 15 of the DMS-1 framework and set keys

The 32 sets at the top of the table are concrete classes, meaning that they exist in the object model and may be present in a file. The seven sets at the bottom of the table are abstract superclasses, meaning that they are not present as individual sets in the object model, but their properties have been aggregated into the sets that form the object model. These abstract sets still have key values for use by AAF applications (and possibly by some MXF applications) that operate using classes rather than objects.

Using DMS-1 Sets

DMS-1 offers a number of sets that can be used flexibly to serve a wide variety of purposes. This section will explain how these flexible sets can be used in typical use cases.

All these sets are illustrated in the figures of the three frameworks illustrated earlier in this chapter.

Using the Contacts List Set

Each framework has a *contacts list* set. Each framework also has *person*, *organization*, and *location* sets that can be owned by the Contacts List by using a strong reference from the Contacts List set. Person, organization, and location are three categories of information that are widely used for contact information.

The aggregation structure (through referencing of other sets) allows the following combinations to be used:

- A participant may be a person, or an organization, or a person with an organization.

- A person may include reference to an organization.

- A framework may have a location (e.g., "UK—10 Downing St").

Using the Name-Value Set as a Flexible List

The *name-value* set is used in many places in DMS-1 as a means of extending certain sets with additional functionality by providing a list of names together with their values and unique IDs (where applicable). SMPTE properties should be used wherever they are available. This set is particularly useful for providing the ability to handle properties defined in legacy systems.

For example, the Person set can be supplemented with additional values as follows:

Name = "Eye Color"

Value = "Blue"

Name = "Sex"

Value = "Female"

The *classification* set defines a thesaurus name for the desired enumeration of a particular kind of classification (e.g., BIAB—British & Irish Archeological Bibliography).

For the example of the BIAB, a Name-Value set could provide the following additional details:

Name = "Classification Code"

Value = "6G:6H:7G:7H"

The reference to each name-value set is "typed" in order to maintain the single-inheritance hierarchy so that a reference from the classification set has a different (i.e., typed) reference from the person set.[1]

Descriptions of the MXF DMS-1 Sets

This section describes some of the characteristics and usage of DMS-1 sets explained on a case-by-case basis.

Titles, Group Relationship, and Branding

These are all language-sensitive sets since most of the property values are text based.

The titles set provides a number of different pre-assigned kinds of titles or names for the A/V content. This set could have adopted the structure: *title kind* plus *title value* as used in other DMS-1 sets. However, content titles are an important asset and it was felt that this was one set where pre-assigned title kinds was the best approach. Titles are language sensitive, so a language property is included in the set to define the set language if this differs from the language identified in the framework that owns this set. This language property is also provided (for the same reason) for many other sets in DMS-1.

The *group relationship* set is used to relate the framework with any associated groupings to which this A/V content may belong (e.g., *Onedin Line*, *The Waltons*). The *programming group kind* property allows the episodic context of the group to be defined; for example, as a program episode within a series, an item within a program, or a package within an item, etc.

---

[1] Note: If you don't understand the need to use a typed reference in order to maintain the single-inheritance hierarchy, don't worry about it! It will not affect your understanding of the remainder of this chapter.

The *branding* set is used to define any adoptive brand to which this A/V content may belong (e.g., *Sky Sports*, *Cartoon Time*).

Identification

This set is generalized so that it can provide for all kinds of production identification. The key enabler is the *identifier kind* that provides a name for the identifier (e.g., V-ISAN). An *identification locator* is an SMPTE UL that locates the kind of identifier in an SMPTE registry (where applicable). As with nearly all sets, there may be more than one instance of this set, thus allowing multiple identifiers where needed.

Event and Publication

The *event* set is provided to allow various different kinds of event associated with the content to be defined and includes a start date/time and an end date/time. The *event indicator* property defines the kind of event in industry-standard terms. The set can be used to define, for example, license start date/time, publication start date/time, repeat date/time, etc. The date and time format is human readable and uses the internet format that allows the definition of specified days, specified times (with time-zone information), as well as defining a single unique date/time event.

The optional *publication* set gives further details about any publication event, including publication medium (e.g., web, terrestrial broadcast, satellite broadcast, DVD, video-cassette, etc.). The term "publication" is intentionally broad to include all forms of publication and is not limited to any specific publication channels.

Award

This set provides historical evidence that the production has been given an award or honor by some institution. This provides useful information for archivists wishing to search for A/V material that has been the subject of particular awards.

Captions Description

This is another generic set that can be used to describe any kind of captions, be they *closed caption*, *subtitles*, or any other. The kind of caption can be determined from a text string defined in the appropriate thesaurus.

Annotation and Classification

The optional *annotation* set allows A/V content to be annotated and classified according to the rules adopted by libraries and archives. This set defines basic information such as a synopsis, an outline description of the A/V content, and a link to any related material. The kind of annotation can be determined from a text string defined in the appropriate thesaurus. The annotation set can be used to provide keyword support by defining the *annotation kind* as keywords and setting the *annotation description* to be the keyword string (typically as a space separated list of words).

The annotation set can have optional classification sets, each of which can identify the use of a knowledge management scheme such as "Marc," "BBC Lonclass," etc. The use of the name-value set permits a string of classifications to be made within a given scheme (each name-value set is used to define a single entry of cataloguing or classification data within a list).

Setting Period

The *setting period* set is an optional editorial component in the scene framework that can be used to describe the period in which the scene is set. The set provides for specific dates and times for relatively recent events and also provides a period keyword for past or future ages such as "Jurassic" or "Elizabethan."

Scripting

The *scripting* set is an optional component in the clip framework that can be used to contain any simple scripts associated with the clip. These may be camera, music, lighting or microphone scripts, as well as theatrical scripts. Since the KLV coding limits the length of properties to 64K, the script length is limited to 32K characters (UTF-16 using 2 bytes per character). Note that this instance of a script is formatted not as a document, but simply as a text string, so the length limit should not be a problem.

Shot and Key Point

The optional *shot* set is used within the scene and clip frameworks to describe the scope of a shot in regard of its start and duration and the tracks with which the shot is associated. The shot set gives only a simple high-level text description of the shot (e.g., "Shot of rider jumping Beecher's Brook at Aintree in 1955").

Key point sets can provide further information. The *key point kind* property is used to delineate different kinds of key points, for example: "*key words*," "*key sounds*," "*key actions*," "*key frames*," and other key point kinds as needed.

Participant

The *participant* set is used to assign a status of participation to an individual, an organization, or a group of individuals or organizations. This set relies on the *contacts list* described next.

Contacts List, Person, Organization, and Location

The contacts list set is a set that is used to own a contacts database comprising information contained in referenced person, *organization*, and *location* sets.

The person set, organization set, and location set include the option of referencing extra properties via name-value sets and the option of referencing addresses via *address* sets. Note that a person and an organization may have multiple addresses, although a location will typically have only one address.

Each address set (whether used by a person, organization, or location) may have multiple *communications* sets. Thus an organization set may have a list of several central telephone numbers simply by instantiating and referencing several communications sets with the appropriate properties and values.

Furthermore, a person may have not just an organization with his or her business contact details, but several instances of communications sets, each with a different mobile telephone number.

Contract and Rights

The optional *contract* set provides the minimum information needed to identify any persistent contractual information. It is only appropriate to embed in a file (and any copies that may be made of that file) contract details that are sufficiently persistent. It is not appropriate that this set be used where contractual details are transitory in nature. Any *rights* sets that are aggregated with a contract set should also only be used in files when the information is regarded as persistent and appropriate for duplication.

Image Format

The *aspect ratio* property in the *picture essence descriptor* set (which is part of the structural metadata) defines the aspect ratio of the essence as captured together with the *active format* descriptor that indicates the framing of the *active picture* within the viewable scanning raster.

The *image format* set within the descriptive metadata may be used in the production framework to identify the *viewport* aspect ratio, together with the *display format code* of the production as a whole. The viewport aspect ratio may differ from the aspect ratio defined in the picture essence descriptor.

The image format set is also present in the clip framework to provide for any case where the viewport aspect ratio of the clip diverges from the value given in the picture essence descriptor. The image format set should not be used in the clip framework unless it identifies some aspect of the image format not already defined in the picture essence descriptor.

Note: Aspect ratio can be a complex subject. In the above description, the term active picture means that area of the image which has viewable information—that is, it does not include any black bars that may be visible at the edges of the image (often seen when viewing a widescreen movie on a television). The viewport is total image area and includes any black bars that may be present at the edges of the image. The display format code is a digital code that defines how the active image is presented in the viewport (as full screen, pillarbox, letterbox, or other).

Device Parameters

The *device parameters* set is provided to identify the devices used in capturing or creating the A/V content in a clip. The list of property types is comprehensive, but since it can never be exhaustive, this set can reference as many name-value sets as required to provide a list of additional device parameters. The device parameters set provides many generic properties that are common to many items of equipment and it is not limited to video cameras. In conjunction with name-value sets, it can provide a list of parameters for an almost unlimited range of devices used in content creation.

Name-Value

The name-value set is a generic set used in many places to provide a list of names (of properties) and the value associated with each name. A name-value set contains information for a single name-value pair only.

Each item in a name-value list can have a name, a value, and a UL locator. The UL locator property is a SMPTE UL that can be used to locate the definition of the named item in a registry (where that exists).

A particular example of the use of the locator property is in the name-value sets related to the classification set of the production framework, where each name and value of the classification list is accompanied by an SMPTE metadata dictionary UL that uniquely identifies each item in the list (e.g., genre, target audience, etc.).

Processing and Project

These two sets provide extra information specific to the *clip framework*. The former identifies the number and type of processing steps that the clip may have undergone. This set includes the following information on a clip:

- Does it contain a logo?
- The intended use of a graphic (if it is a graphic).
- The number of processing steps and lossy/lossless generations of copying.

The latter provides information relating to the project that resulted in the MXF file.

Cue Words

The *cue-words* set is used to describe verbal or textual information used to help a production team correctly cue a program or program item. This will, for example, often be the closing words on a sound track.

Using DMS-1 in the Real World

Extending DMS-1

DMS-1 is written as an SMPTE *dynamic document* (see SMPTE 359M for detail of the dynamic document procedures). Rather than, as the name implies, something that can change from day to day, the rules of a dynamic document allow new components to be added as follows:

- A new set for use within the *frameworks*.

- A new (and unique) property within the sets.

The rules of SMPTE 359M provide for the timely and pertinent addition of entities to the existing document without the need to reconsider all that has been established in previous versions. There are various processes by which new entities can be added through a relatively simple registration procedure that bypasses the lengthy and full SMPTE "due-process" procedures. Any new additions to DMS-1 will be accompanied by an increment of the version number provided by the DMS-1 UL so that a new version can be easily identified.

In order to preserve backwards compatibility with existing files, existing sets and properties cannot be deleted. However, such entities can be deprecated after SMPTE's due-process balloting in order to prevent their further use. This would mean that encoders should not encode these deprecated entities and decoders can optionally treat them as dark. This policy of deprecation is usually reserved for entities that everyone agrees were mistakes and should not be perpetuated. Entities can be deleted in time, based on due-process agreement and a passage of sufficient time and notification of every party affected. Although an entity can be deleted, the use of version numbering ensures that, once an SMPTE UL or a key has been assigned by SMPTE, it is **never** reassigned to anything else and thus remains unique.

What Is the "Thesaurus" and How Is It Used?

A thesaurus (dictionary definition: a storehouse of knowledge, especially of words, quotations, phrases) is a list of defined terms that may be applied to text, numbers, ULs, or any other property that is defined as a list of recognized values.

A word with a similar meaning is "lexicon" (definition: a vocabulary of terms used in connection with a particular subject). However, the requirement here is for a term that encompasses a list of defined terms not restricted to a particular language. However, in certain communities, the word lexicon is used in the context that thesaurus is used in the DMS-1.

The optional thesaurus property in DMS-1 operates in a similar (but not identical) manner to the language property for sets: a framework thesaurus is defined as a default for all sets in the framework, but individual sets can override the default framework thesaurus with one specifically defined for this set.

A thesaurus, especially if text based, is very likely to be dependent not just on language, but on the industry in which the file is created and used. For DMS-1 it was decided that a thesaurus should be referenced by name, so that an application can dynamically load the thesaurus for the purpose of encoding or decoding. It is expected that an individual thesaurus will be created for a language, industry, organization, or even for an individual production and loaded by an application that can parse the thesaurus definition and present the user with the choices available for the operation required.

Because of the variable nature of the thesaurus values, the definition of values is beyond the scope of the MXF DMS-1. However, a common data format is needed for software to be able to parse the values and for this XML is an ideal candidate. The format should provide for unique identification of the thesaurus, the industry it serves, the language, optionally the organization, the name of the catalogue of values, and then the list of values. Note that a single thesaurus may serve many sets by listing all enumerations required by the sets in one file of composite catalogues.

Since the thesaurus will be loaded into the descriptive metadata software either dynamically at run-time or statically encoded into the software application, it may be coded in any appropriate form. XML is likely to be the preferred coding format for most application software, although it should be capable of using the Unicode text format to support any language as needed.

Below is a suggestion for the layers to be considered for the construction of a thesaurus in general terms:

Layer 1:   Thesaurus: {Specified: e.g., DMS-1}

Layer 2:   Community: {Specified: e.g Music Recording}

Layer 3:   Language: {Specified: e.g., International English}

Layer 4:   Set Name: {Specified: e.g., Production Framework}

Layer 5:   Property Name: {Specified: e.g., Integration Indicator}

Layer 6:   Property Values: {Enumerated:

e.g., "Album," "Track," "Compilation"}

How Will All this Metadata Be Created?

Much of the metadata in a clip framework can be pre-loaded into the memory of a camcorder or other content-creation device. We can also expect these devices to be able to automatically assign dates, times, and geo-spatial coordinates.

Back in production, software tools will be able to provide easy access for metadata entry into MXF/DMS-1. Such metadata entries might already be made into databases. The difference with MXF and DMS-1 is that some of this metadata can be entered into the file, thereby leaving the database to perform its vital role of content management rather than carriage of content-specific (and possibly time-dependent) metadata.

Of course, DMS-1 is powerful, but only insofar as users can enter as much, or as little, metadata as needed for their business. The capabilities of DMS-1 allow metadata entry to be made at any stage of the production process, including the point of archive.

Compatibility with Other Metadata Schemes (MP7, TVA, P/meta)

Relationship with MP7

MPEG-7 is a very large metadata description scheme that contains only a small part of the metadata needed by content producers, but a large part dedicated toward content analysis. While the content analysis metadata may be important for search tools, it has little current impact in normal video and audio productions. It was established at an early stage that there was a small overlap of metadata that was common to both MPEG-7 and DMS-1. It was also established that some of the MPEG-7 metadata that described content structure was already covered by the MXF structural metadata.

During 2002, a series of meetings were held with the aim of resolving the differences. The starting point was to break down the MPEG-7 XML code into a visual model that allowed easy comparison between the two metadata schemes. The analysis started with the removal of MPEG-7 types that were solely concerned with audiovisual analysis followed by the further removal of types that defined the audiovisual structure. This left a remainder of MPEG-7 types that could be more easily checked against the model of DMS-1.

The next stage was to compare like-for-like sets. This found several deficiencies in both DMS-1 and MPEG-7. For example, DMS-1 had no "astronomical body name" property in the address set! While it is unlikely that a real actor will have an address on the moon, such a property would be essential in the scene framework to describe a planet in space operas such as *Star Wars* and *Star Trek*. Likewise, similar but different, omissions were identified in MPEG-7.

Following detailed analysis of the MPEG-7 data model and its XML code, it was concluded that all areas of possible overlap between DMS-1 and MPEG-7 had been analyzed and actions taken to ensure DMS-1 omissions were corrected.

Relationship with TVA

The TVA (Television Anytime) specification defines the metadata that needed to be delivered with the content for the purpose of enhanced operations in the home environment, notably supporting the use of intelligent content storage devices. Some of the TVA metadata is carried through the production chain—for example, actors' names and the roles they played. Other TVA metadata is specifically created for the publication channel.

The TVA organization agreed to allow their metadata structure to be analyzed for the purpose of ensuring that any production metadata that they might need could be extracted from DMS-1. As with MPEG-7 metadata, there was a small, though significant, overlap of identical or similar metadata that needed to be carefully checked.

The TVA metadata is also coded as XML, so required work to format it as a data model. This resulted in a clear identification of those parts of the data model that were related to content production. The analysis indicated that a couple of minor additions to DMS-1 would provide all that TVA needed to prevent the need for data re-keying at the publication stage.

Relationship with P/Meta

P/Meta is an EBU metadata project that was based on the BBC SMEF[2] work using an entity-relationship (E-R) data model that defined data requirements for operations within the BBC.

---

[2] SMEF is an acronym for Standard Metadata Framework

P/Meta was coded using HTML that could be easily viewed in a web browser. It provided metadata that was essentially business related and of a type that would be expected to reside on a database and not embedded in a file. Nevertheless, there were several entities within P/Meta that were of sufficient stability that they could be considered as for inclusion in file-based metadata.

The work to start mapping between P/Meta and DMS-1 started in 2001 and continued with several meetings through to the end of 2002. The mapping proved difficult because the P/Meta "attributes" were considered as isolated entities that were not grouped into sets as in many other metadata schemes (DMS-1, MPEG-7, TVA, etc.). As with TVA and MPEG-7 metadata, there was overlap of certain P/Meta attributes with the properties in DMS-1, but many parts of P/Meta related to the MXF structural metadata and the remainder comprised metadata that had changing values best stored in a database.

MXF properties and P/Meta attributes were matched wherever possible; however, the effort met with limited success because of the considerable differences in the design approach.

Relationship with Dublin Core

The *dublin core metadata* intitiative (http://dublincore.org) is widely cited by archivists as the ideal way to describe content in libraries and archives and there is an expectation that this metadata classification can be used to catalogue and describe all kinds of content, including audiovisual content. DMS-1 has many parts that are close to the dublin core metadata and these are identified below. The table below is a non-exhaustive guide—only to aid the reader to understand how DMS-1 metadata may be categorized as dublin core elements and qualifiers. It should be noted that the DMS-1 Frameworks bind sets together and this binding has no direct equivalent in dublin core.

Set Number	DMS-1 Set	Dublin Core Element	Qualifier or Comments
4	Titles	Title	Includes "alternative" qualifier
5	Identification	Identifier	
6	Group Relationship	Relation	IsReferencedBy (the Group)
7	Branding	Relation	IsPartOf (a legal entity)
8	Event	Date	Valid (with start and end dates)
9	Publication	Publisher	
10	Award	None	
11	Captions Description	Description	Captions are a specialized form of text description.
12	Annotation	Subject	
13	Setting Period	Coverage	Temporal
14	Scripting	Description	There are many kinds of scripts that aid content production, such as lighting and sound stage scripts.
15	Classification	Type	
16	Shot	Subject	
17	Key Point	Subject	Key Point is a part of Shot.

Set Number	DMS-1 Set	Dublin Core Element	Qualifier or Comments
18	Participant	Contributor or Creator	Role is defined by the Participant set.
19	Person	Contributor or Creator	Person is an extension of Participant.
20	Organization	Contributor or Creator	Organization is an extension of Participant.
21	Location	Coverage	Spatial
22	Address	Contributor, Creator, or Coverage	Address is an extension of Person, Organization, and Location.
23	Communications	Contributor, Creator, or Coverage	Communications is an extension of Address.
24	Contract	Rights	
25	Rights	Rights	AccessRights qualifier. DMS-1 Rights set is an extension of Contract.
26	Picture Format	Format	Picture Format only defines a very small part of the Format element (see below).
27	Device Parameters	Out of scope	Defines the parameters used by the device used to create the content.
28	Name-Value	Out of scope	Used as a mechanism to add new properties to a set.
29	Processing	Out of scope	Provides a record of the processing applied to the content.
30	Project	Out of scope	Provides A/V project details.
31	Contacts List	Out of scope	An abstract element used to bind other elements.
32	Cue Words	Subject	Cue Words is an extension of Annotation and Shot.
-	-	Source	Source is covered by the hierarchy of MXF packages (Material Package references a top-level File Package; references a lower-level Source Package).
-	-	Audience	This element is not present in DMS-1.
-	-	Format	Defined by the Essence Descriptors.
-	-	Language	Many DMS-1 sets use the language element as an individual entity.

Table 11.4 Relationship of DMS-1 sets with Dublin Core metadata

Annex A DMS-1 Class Model

The figure on the opposite page gives the class structure of the scheme described in this chapter for the purpose of data modeling. The connecting lines in this figure show the inheritance hierarchy.

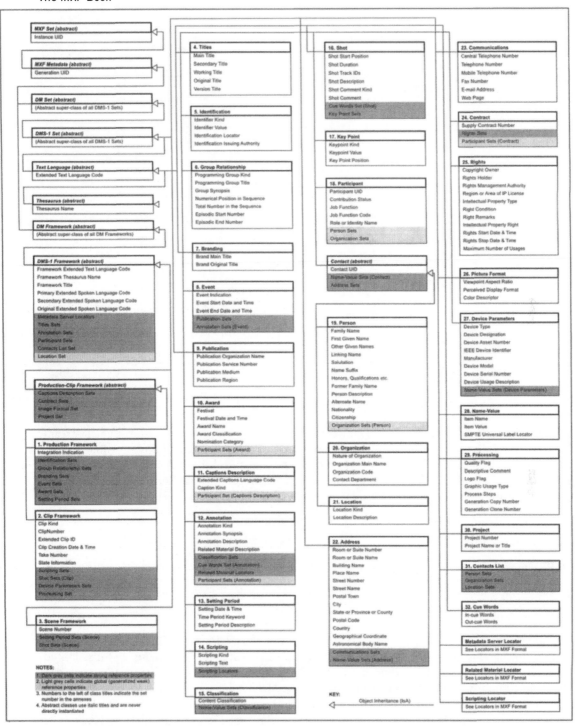

Figure 11.5 DMS-1 Class Model

12 Index Tables

Bruce Devlin

An *index table* allows an application to convert a time offset to a byte offset within a given stream in a file. This allows applications to access any frame or sample within the file without having to parse the entire file. The general concepts for the use of index tables were first introduced in Chapter 2. The detailed construction of index tables is given here. Further information for specific stream types such as MPEG and audio is given in the respective chapters.

Simple applications where index tables are required include:

- Trick mode playback
- Playout servers
- Editing applications
- Playback of OP3x files

The individual items within an index table are shown in Figure 2.16. These items will be discussed further during this chapter. In general, index tables can be split into segments and distributed through a file, or gathered together in a single location in the file; for example, in the header or the footer. There are various advanced features in the MXF index table design, such as slicing the index table to reduce its size when variable-length and fixed-length elements are mixed. Timing features, such as synchronization error prevention, are detailed along with slices in Chapter 9, where PosTable Offsets are discussed, as well as at the end of this chapter.

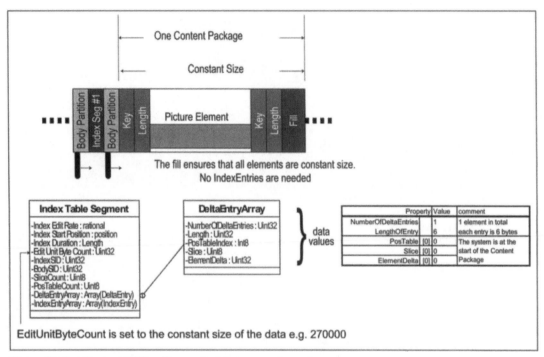

Figure 12.1 I-Frame MPEG with constant bytes per element

Essence with Constant Bytes per Element

Index table requirements vary according to the nature of the essence type being indexed. Simple essence which has a constant data rate per edit unit, such as uncompressed audio, can be indexed with a simple table which defines the number of bytes for each of the MXF edit units. This is stored in the IndexTableSegment::EditUnitByteCount property. An application can then calculate the byte offset within the file by multiplying the number of bytes per edit unit by the number of edit units:

ByteOffset = EditUnitByteCount * (Position + Origin)

Why has *origin* been included? This is because the value of origin indicates the number of edit units from the start of the stored essence to the zero value of *position* along any track.

Multiplexed Essence with Constant Bytes per Element (CBE)

There may be multiple channels of CBE audio multiplexed together giving a total interleave bitrate which is also CBE. Constructing an index table for this essence interleave is shown in Figure 12.2. In addition to the IndexTableSegment::EditUnitByteCount property shown above, we also store and make use of the *ElementDelta*. In the CBE case, this is the number of bytes from the start of the *content package* to the beginning of the data for that element.

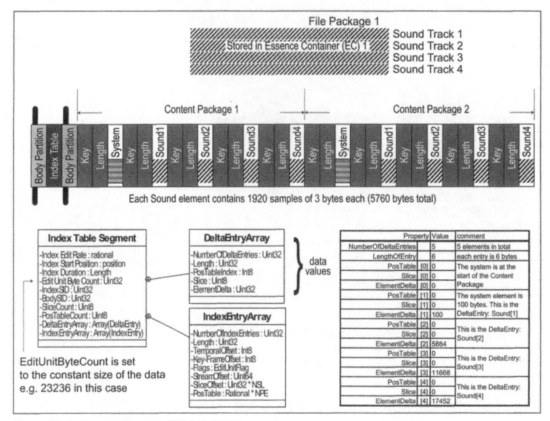

Figure 12.2 Construction of a CBE index table

As can be seen in Figure 12.2, we have a file package with four sound tracks inside it. Physically, these are stored as four sound elements with the start of a content package being indicated by a *system element*.

The first element in the content package is the system element, and so the IndexTableSegment :: DeltaEntry for this element is zero. The system element is 100 bytes long, and so the first of the sound elements is located at offset 100—as shown by DeltaEntry[1]. The second sound element is located at 100+sizeof(sound[1] including length of K and L) giving a DeltaEntry for this second element which is 5860 bytes. Similarly, the DeltaEntry for the third sound element is 11620 and so on.

Because each and every element is CBE, there are no index entries for this content package. The non-zero value of IndexTableSegment::EditUnitByteCount in the index table segment which indicates that only CBE tables are used.

When this property is non-zero, it is used to identify the (constant) number of bytes stored for each and every edit unit within the essence container. This makes the byte offset within the essence container for any element easy to calculate:

$$ByteOffset = EditUnitByteCount \times (Position + Origin)$$

As you can see, the index table shows that there are five indexed elements, each of which is CBE. However, the index table design does not tell you which delta entry is associated with which of the KLV wrapped generic container elements. In order to find this out, you have to parse one of the generic container content packages shown in Figure 12.2. SMPTE 379M (Generic Container Specification) states that the order of the KLV triplets shall always be the same in the stored file. This ensures that the order of the elements in the file agrees with the order of the entries in the DeltaEntry array.

Position of the Index Table Segments

The MXF specification, SMPTE 377M, states that an index table segment may appear:

- In a partition on its own;

- In a partition with a repetition of the header metadata;

- In a partition with its associated essence; and

- In the footer partition.

Current good practice is to put a single "thing" in a single *partition*. This means that index table segments should appear in a partition by themselves if this practice is followed. The index table as a whole is made up from one or more index table segments. In the CBE case above, there is likely to be only a single segment because the table is physically small and the position of the essence elements is deterministic.

In a VBE (Variable Bytes per Element) essence stream, we require an index entry for each and every VBE essence element in the stream because we cannot know a-priori the length of each frame. This may require a very large number of entries. What is not shown in Figure 12.2, is that index table segments are stored using local set coding. This means that the maximum size of the IndexEntryArray within a single segment is 64Kbytes (because MXF uses 2-byte tags and 2-byte lengths).

In order to construct an entire table in a single partition, it will be necessary to place several index table segments one after the other in the partition. The rules are quite simple:

- Only the index table segments with a given IndexSID can appear in a single partition.

- The IndexTableSegment::IndexSID property must be the same as the PartitionPack::IndexSID property (see Figures 12.2 and 3.9).

- If the index table segments are in the same partition as the essence, then the PartitionPack::IndexSID and the PartitionPack::BodySID must be related by an EssenceContainerData set as shown in Figure 3.7.

Relocating the Table

An important point about the index table design is that the byte offset entries are relative to the generic container and not relative to the file. Why is this? During the design of MXF, it was realized that the physical arrangement of the file should be independent of what the file was intended to represent. In addition, there may be several different possible physical arrangements of the bytes—each optimized for different applications.

For example, a common requirement is that index tables be distributed in small segments. This can occur when a device such as a camera is making a file. Cameras creating MXF files have the following limitations when creating index tables:

- Cameras don't know the duration of the file they are creating.
- Cameras cannot create index tables for content they haven't created yet.
- Cameras don't have enough internal storage to store an entire index table until the clip ends.
- Cameras have to flush index table segments periodically.

However, to use the file in a random access environment, it is often desired/necessary to group all the index table segments at the front or the rear of the file. This is shown in Figure 12.3. With the design of the MXF index table, this can be achieved by simple relocation of the segments in a new partition. No recalculation is needed because the ByteOffset entries within/relative to the partitions indexed by the rearranged index table segments remain unchanged by the reordering.

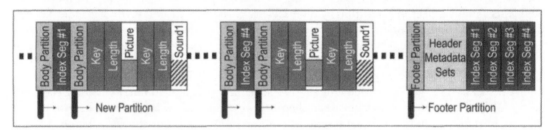

Figure 12.3 Relocating a segmented index table to the end of the file

In order to find the essence within the file, the correct partition containing the essence needs to be found. The "elapsed" number of bytes at the start of a partition for a given essence container is given by the `PartitionPack::BodyOffset` property as shown in Figure 3.9 in Chapter 3. It is this offset, rather than the absolute byte position in the file, that is indexed by the index tables.

Variable Bytes per Element

Not all essence types have constant bytes per element. Essence that is "almost" constant bytes per element, such as "fixed" bitrate MPEG coding, can have small variations in the actual number of essence bytes created for every frame. In order to make it truly fixed bitrate so that it can be indexed with a simple index table, KLV fill elements can be used to pad the essence. This is shown

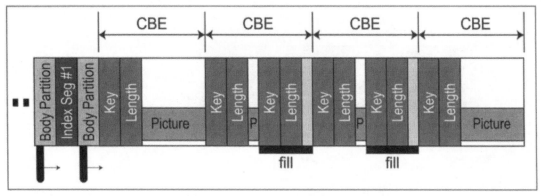

Figure 12.4 Using KLV fill elements to pad VBE essence to CBE

in Figure 12.4 where pictures 2 and 3 are padded to be the same length as pictures 1 and 4. In this case the IndexEntryArray is not present in the index table segment.

For many essence types, however, it is not appropriate to pad the data to CBE. Long-GOP MPEG, for example, can have vastly different numbers of bytes for different frame types. For indexing, there is little option other than to create an Index Entry that lists the stream offset within the generic container for each frame.

Single Component Case

The simplest case of a VBE index table is where there is only a single component in the generic container—for example a compressed video stream. The structure of the index table segment is different to the CBE case. The IndexTableSegment::EditUnitByteCount property is set to zero, which indicates that there will be IndexEntries. The DeltaEntry array is very simple: It contains a single entry with all the properties of the first array element set to 0 to indicate that the first (and only) element is in slice zero, at offset zero. Figure 12.5 on the next page shows the properties and values of the IndexEntry. The precise meaning of the properties will be introduced by example later in the text or in Chapter 9, where there are worked examples of essence reordering.

You can see that, in its most basic form, the index entry structure contains a list of IndexEntry::StreamOffset values. Each of these values gives the byte offset of the start of the frame relative to the start of the generic container—not relative to the start of the file.

It can become more complicated when the essence to be indexed is an interleave of CBE and VBE elements. In the most simplistic case, you could create an IndexEntry for each CBE element and each VBE element, but this would take rather a lot of storage space. You could imagine the cost of storing an IndexEntry structure for a file with a video element and 8 channels of audio stored as 8 elements. This would require 43 bytes per frame of storage (8 channels * UINT32 for each channel offset relative to the IndexEntry + 11 bytes for the IndexEntry itself), whereas the DeltaEntry, which describes the fixed length of each audio channel, would require only 48 bytes of storage to describe the channel offsets + 11 bytes per frame. For long sequences, this represents a significant improvement in storage and parsing efficiency.

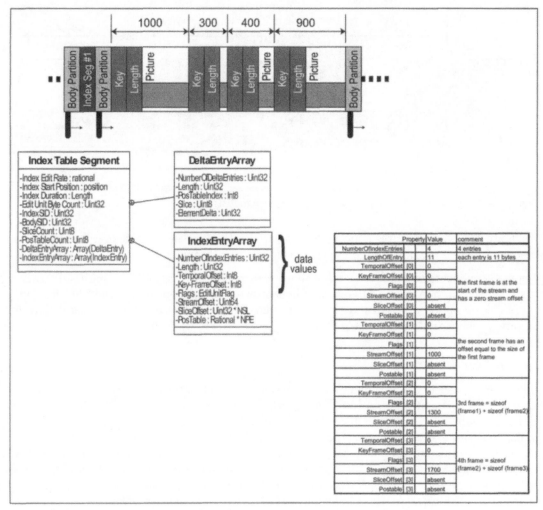

Figure 12.5 The Index Entry structure

This optimization, employed in MXF, allows the CBE element byte sizes to be described once in the DeltaEntry table, and there is an IndexEntry for each and every VBE element. This is shown in it simplest form in Figure 12.6.

Figure 12.4 has reduced the pictorial size of the key-length pair in order to fit more information on the page. You can see that each content package is now made up from a fixed-length CBE sound element and a variable-length picture element. Each IndexEntry tells us the start position of the content package, and the DeltaEntry array tells us the position of the different elements within the content package.

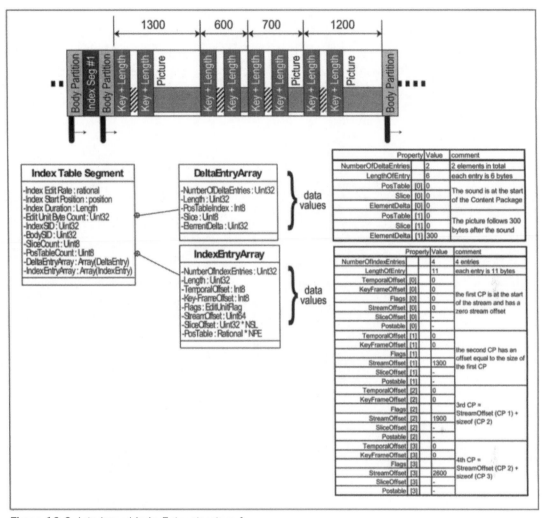

Figure 12.6 Interleaved IndexEntry structure 1

The DeltaEntry array has two entries in it. The first describes the sound element and the second describes the picture element. The sound element starts at an offset of 0 from the start of the content package—this is given by DeltaEntry[0]::ElementDelta = 0. The picture element starts at an offset of 300 from the start of the content package—this is given by DeltaEntry[1]::Element-Delta = 300.

This means that to find the byte offset of the picture element in the third Content Package, you would calculate IndexEntry[2]::StreamOffset + DeltaEntry[1]::ElementDelta= 2200 bytes from the start of the generic container.

271

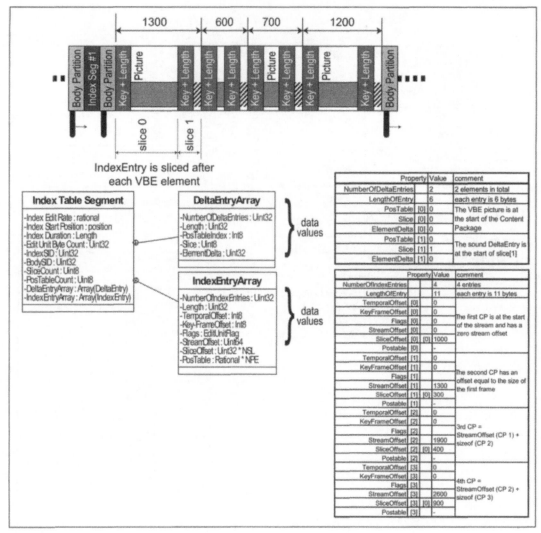

Figure 12.7 Interleaved IndexEntry structure 2

But what would happen if the order of the elements was reversed as shown in Figure 12.7? The first element of the content package is now VBE. In order to only store the CBE lengths in the DeltaEntry, we create slices in the index entry after each of the VBE elements. A slice in the index table means that the row labeled SliceOffset[x][s] now has a value in it. In other words, the offset from the IndexEntry::StreamOffset to the start of the essence at the beginning of slice[s] for frame [x] is SliceOffset[x][s]. Figure 12.7 shows the slice point after the picture element.

When the index table is sliced, the DeltaEntry[n]::ElementDelta property gives the offset from the start of the current slice to the start of the element. For the sound element in Figure 12.7, this is always zero because the sound element is the first element following the slice. In other words, DeltaEntry[n]::ElementDelta is the offset from the start of slice number DeltaEntry[n]:: Slice to the start of the element. This definition is consistent, even when the value for NSL or the "number of slices" is 0. So how do you know the value for NSL? It is simply:

$$NSL = \max\left(ElementDelta[n]::Slice\right)_{n=0}^{n=NumberOfDeltaEntries-1}$$

and stored in the SliceCount property of the index table segment.

In our example in Figure 12.7, the value for NSL is therefore 1 – in effect, *slice 0 is never counted!* This is verified by the equation above, and by inspecting the pictorial representation of the stored essence. The IndexEntry::SliceOffset property is a list of *NSL* Uint32 values giving the offset from the start of the Content Package to the start of the slice. In this example, IndexEntry:: SliceOffset corresponds to the number of bytes in the picture element.

Reordered Content

The complexity can increase even further with essence types such as MPEG2. In predictive coding schemes, such as MPEG-2, the stored order of the frames is not the same as the displayed order of the frames as shown in Figure 12.8. In order for an MPEG decoder to display a frame, it must have already received any frame from which predictions are generated. As you can see in the closed Group of Pictures (GOP) in Figure 12.8, this implies that the frame I_2 must be stored before the first 2 B frames, likewise the frame P_5 must be stored before the frames B_3 and B_4. The word "closed" refers to a GOP where no predictions are required from outside the GOP. (For example, in a non-closed GOP, the B frames B_0 and B_1 could have been predicted from the last P frame in the previous GOP before I_2.)

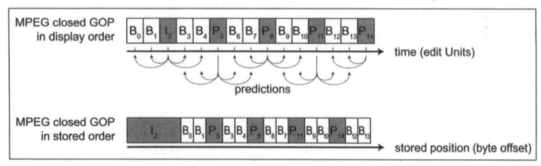

Figure 12.8 MPEG temporal reordering

The reordering required for any given stream depends on the number of B frames and the config- uration of the MPEG encoder. This means that the difference between stored and displayed order is not necessarily constant within the file. The only practical way to convert between displayed order and stored order is to tabulate the differences using the IndexEntry::TemporalOffset prop- erty as shown in Figure 12.9 on the next page.

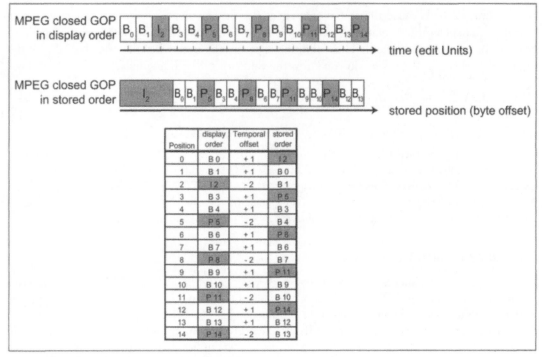

Figure 12.9 Reordering lookup

MXF IndexEntries are in stored order, but the MXF track is described in display order. It is therefore necessary to use the IndexEntry::TemporalOffset property to locate essence in its stored order when an application is seeking/indexing in display order.

For example, let's assume an application wants to seek to frame P_8 in the example of Figure 12.9. First it looks up the IndexEntry::TemporalOffset property for Position[8] and discovers the value "-2." In order to find the other parameters for the this frame, it must now look in the IndexEntry for Position [8-2]= Position[6]. It is important to note that the temporal offset must be applied first *before any other parameter is calculated*. Index tables in MXF always relate to stored order, not to displayed order.

This example is now expanded and the full IndexEntry and DeltaEntry can be seen in Figure 12.10 for the first five frames of the sequence. Reordering of the picture elements is indicated by the value -1 in DeltaEntry[0]::PosTable.

In MPEG, there are frames known as *anchor frames* or *key frames* and are the frames from which decoding should commence. In order to rapidly find the correct key frame, this property is stored in the IndexEntry. Note that this property refers to the key frame offsets between frames in stored order, not display order.

For example, if we wanted to decode the frame P_5, we would need to know where its key frame was stored. The first step is to find IndexEntry[5]::TemporalOffset. This tells us where the IndexEntry

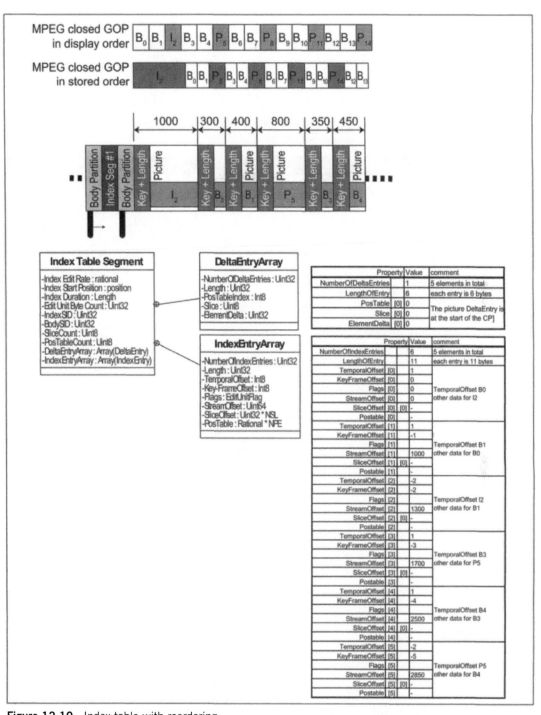

Figure 12.10   Index table with reordering

is stored for P_5. From the example in Figure 12.10, the property value is -2, so we know that all the properties for this frame are stored in IndexEntry[5-2] = IndexEntry[3].

In order to decode P_5, the key frame is given by IndexEntry[3]::KeyFrameOffset, which has the value "-3." We now know that if we start our decoding at IndexEntry[3-3]= IndexEntry[0], then we will successfully display P_5.

To help the decoding process, the MXF index table also stores flags that indicate the type of picture being decoded. These are given in the table below:

Bit	Function	Description
7	Random Access	This flag is set to "1" if you can random access to this frame and start decoding. Otherwise it is set to "0."
6	Sequence Header	This flag is set to "1" if the IndexEntry points to a frame including a sequence header. Otherwise it is set to "0." If the indexed content has a concept similar to the MPEG sequence header, but is called something different, then the mapping document for that content type will give details on how to set this flag.
5	Forward Prediction Flag	These two flags can be set in "precise mode," or in naïve mode. Precise mode can be useful to optimize decoder fetches when not all the bidirectional prediction options are used; e.g., in an MPEG-2 closed GOP environment.
4	Backward Prediction Flag	Naïve settings for Bits 5, 4 is identical to the MPEG FrameType bits 1,0 00== I frame 10== P frame 11== B frame In precise mode, the frames are inspected for their prediction dependencies and set as follows: 00== I frame (no prediction) 10== P frame(forward prediction from previous frame) 01== B frame (backward prediction from future frame) 11== B frame (forward & backward prediction)
3	Numerical Range Overload	Defined in SMPTE 381M. This flag was defined to cover the case when there are a large number of B or P frames between anchor frames, or when the temporal offset is very large. This flag is set to a "1" when either the value of TemporalOffset or the value of KeyFrameOffset is outside the range -128 > value > 127.
2	Reserved	
1,0	MPEG Picture type	I-frame 00 (no prediction) P-frame 10 (forward prediction from previous frame) B-frame 11 (forward & backward prediction) These bits are often identical to bits 5 & 4.

Table 12.1 MXF Index Table Flags

The final subtlety of the MXF index table is to compensate for lip-sync problems when streams contain interleaved video and audio of different frame durations. This can happen when, for example, MPEG-2 compressed video and MPEG2 compressed audio is interleaved and a number of random access "jumps" are made within the stream. The alignment differences between the smallest unit of audio and the video access unit are stored in the file in the *PosTableOffset structure*.

Figure 12.11 shows an example of interleaving MPEG-2 video and MPEG-2 audio access units (AU). The example shows 50Hz pictures because the alignment is simpler to illustrate. The same principle holds for 59,94Hz video, although the numerical values are less simple.

The figure shows that the MPEG-2 video frames have a duration of 40ms and the audio frames have a duration of 24ms. There are thus, 5 audio frames in the same duration as 3 video frames, as is shown in the top part of the figure.

The interleaving rules given in SMPTE 381M (MPEG Mapping into MXF) state that the audio access unit with the audio sample synchronized with the start of a video frame (in display order)

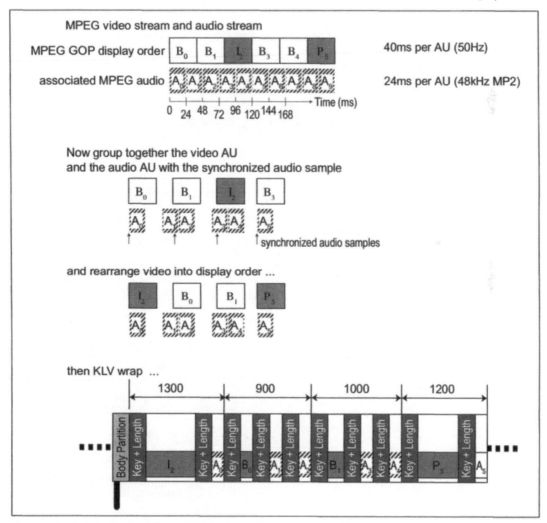

Figure 12.11 Interleaving MPEG video and audio

should be in the same content package as the video frame with the same stored position (i.e., before reordering). The next part of the figure shows how the video and audio access units are divided up in order to create this rule.

Once the reordering from display order to stored order takes place we now know which audio AUs and which video AUs should be stored together in the same content package. KLV wrapping is applied and the resulting KLV stream is shown at the bottom of the figure.

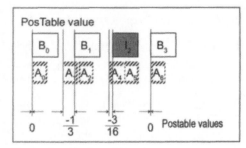

Figure 12.12 Postable values

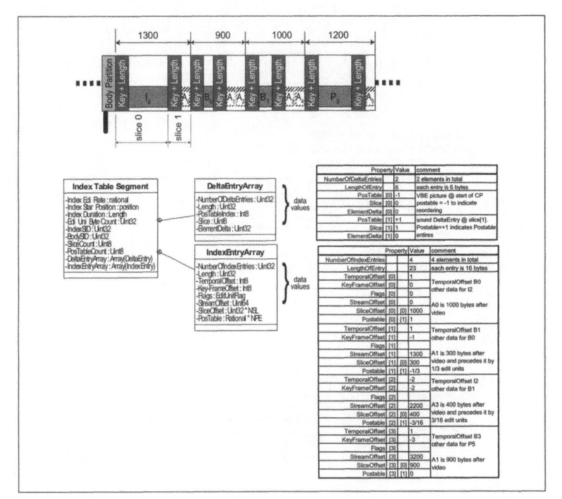

Figure 12.13 Interleaved reordered IndexEntry structure

As we mentioned earlier, the PosTable keeps a list of the time offsets between the start of the audio and the start of the video. Figure 12.12 takes the second part of Figure 12.11 and annotates it with the values of PosTable as a signed rational (Int32/Int32); e.g., -3/16 is coded as -3, 16.

Putting all of the information from Figures 12.11 and 12.12 into a single table gives us Figure 12.13—the complete index table with PosTable offsets for the KLV stream shown in Figure 12.12. Extending this to several channels of audio would require several PosTable entries—one per audio channel. Data elements may also require PosTable entries. This brings us to the end of this chapter on index tables.

13 The MXF Data Model in Context

Phil Tudor

Introduction

This chapter describes the MXF data model from the perspective of the AAF data model, from which it is derived. The MXF data model defines the data structures that can be included in an MXF file. An instance of a data structure in an MXF file is an *object*. An object has properties, which have a type and a value. The MXF data model defines objects by specifying a class model.

The MXF data model is expressed in terms that closely correspond to the video and audio domain. For example, it defines classes to hold metadata describing the material structure, format, derivation, and annotation; and classes to hold essence for file source material. The mapping of these objects into a file (or other persistent storage) is defined by a stored format specification. For MXF, the stored format is based on SMPTE 336M KLV encoding.

History of the MXF Data Model

The MXF data model is derived from the AAF data model, an insightful model created by Avid Technology for structuring source and editing metadata along object-oriented lines and used in the AAF file format.[1]

---

[1] Gilmer, Brad and Tudor, Phil et al. Chapter 6: "Advanced Authoring Format." *File Interchange Handbook for Images, Audio and Metadata*. Burlington, MA: Focal Press, 2004.

In 1998, the AAF Promoters, led by Avid and Microsoft, announced the AAF file format and participated in the EBU/SMPTE Task Force[2] to ensure that the AAF data model and file format would meet the requirements for standardized data transfer between authoring tools. By 2000, the independent, non-profit AAF Association had replaced the AAF Promoters and was responsible for developing and controlling the AAF specifications. The AAF Association's board of directors and membership include key authoring-tool and server manufacturers, user organizations, and developers. Significantly, several AAF Association members were also active Pro-MPEG Forum members.

When the Pro-MPEG Forum started to develop MXF as a format for transferring file–based material, there was an agreement among the membership to reuse the relevant parts of the AAF data model. Subsequently, at a plenary meeting of the Pro-MPEG Forum in Atlanta in May 2000, the Pro-MPEG Forum and AAF Association agreed to co-develop the MXF format.

The main areas of application for MXF were intended to be the transfer of completed programs, program segments, and source material. The main applications of AAF are the transfer of authoring, editing, and media-management metadata, and associated source material. It was recognized that there would be operational and functional simplifications if, through the use of a common data model, material could move between acquisition, authoring, and delivery domains while maintaining the relevant metadata.

MXF/AAF Zero Divergence Doctrine

The Pro-MPEG Forum and AAF Association agreed a design rule for creating MXF known as the Zero Divergence Doctrine (ZDD). This agreement works in two directions. Firstly, when MXF requires a feature that is already in the AAF data model, that feature should be directly reused. Secondly, when MXF requires a feature that is not already in the AAF data model, that feature must be designed in a way that could be added to the AAF data model, and therefore back to the AAF file format. The Pro-MPEG Forum and AAF Association agreed the ZDD at a joint meeting in Redmond, WA in May, 2002.

MXF reuses the parts of the AAF data model dealing with clips and source material. The parts dealing with compositions, effects, and the in-file dictionary of definitions are not used. The MXF format added new features to the data model for supporting a wider range of standardized essence formats and for supporting additional descriptive metadata features.

The AAF data model is defined by the AAF Object Specification.[3] The AAF Association actively maintains and revises the Object Specification to include features from the MXF data model. In this way, the MXF data model remains a complete subset of the AAF data model.

---

[2] EBU/SMPTE Task Force for Harmonized Standards for the Exchange of Program Material as Bit Streams. "Final Report: Analyses and Results." Available at http://www.smpte.org/engineering_committees/pdf/tfrpt2w6.pdf. 1998.

[3] AAF Association. "Advanced Authoring Format (AAF) Specification." Available at http://www.aafassociation.org.

Structure

Identifiers in the AAF Class Model

The AAF data model defines objects by specifying a *class model*. The AAF class model consists of definitions for classes, their properties, and property types.

Although classes, properties, and property types have names, they are primarily identified by unique identifiers. AAF uses a 16-byte unique identifier known as an *Authoring Unique Identifier* (AUID) for this purpose. The value of an AUID is either an SMPTE 298M Universal Label (UL)[4] or a UUID.[5]

An SMPTE UL is unique because it is allocated by a registration authority that ensures there are no duplicates. A UUID is unique because it is generated from elements based on date, time, device identifiers, and random numbers.

Through participation in SMPTE metadata standardization activities, the AAF class model has been registered in the SMPTE metadata registries. For each class, property, or property type that has been registered, an SMPTE UL has been allocated as an identifier. For each manufacturer- or user-specific extension that has not been registered in the SMPTE metadata registries, a UUID is used as an identifier.

As well as identifying classes, properties, and property types, an AUID may be used as a property value. For example, the DigitalImageDescriptor class has a Compression property of AUID type—the value of this property indicates the compression standard in use. For each standardized value, an SMPTE UL has been allocated.

Specifying the AAF Class Model

The AAF class model defines a class by specifying the following:

- Name of the class;
- Identifier (AUID) of the class;
- Parent class; and
- Concrete flag (true if the class is concrete, false if the class is abstract).

The AAF class model defines a property of a class by specifying the following:

- Name of the property;
- Identifier (AUID) of the property;

---

[4] Society of Motion Picture and Television Engineers. "SMPTE 298M: Universal Labels for Unique Identification of Digital Data." White Plains, N.Y. 1997.

[5] International Organization for Standardization/International Electro-technical Commission. "ISO/IEC 11578-1 Information Technology—Open Systems Interconnection—Remote Procedure Call. Annex A, Universally Unique Identifier." Geneva, Switzerland. 1996.

- Short local identifier of the property within a particular AAF file;

- Type of the property;

- Optional flag (true if the property is optional, false is the property is mandatory);

- Unique identifier flag (true if the property is the unique identifier for an object, false otherwise); and

- Class that contains this property.

The AAF class model defines a property type by specifying the following:

- Name of the type;

- Identifier (AUID) of the type; and

- Other details depending on the type.

The AAF class model is a single-inheritance class hierarchy. This can be seen in the definition of a class, which allows one parent class only. Similarly, the specification of a property allows it to belong to only one class (and its subclasses).

The class model allows concrete and abstract classes in the class hierarchy. A concrete class can be instantiated as an object, whereas an abstract class cannot.

The preceding definitions are part of the AAF meta-model—the model for building the data model. The ZDD requirement that new features required by MXF must be designed in a way that could be added to the AAF data model can be restated as saying that data model extensions required by MXF must follow the rules of the AAF meta-model.

Mapping between MXF and AAF Documentation

During the development and standardization of MXF, some changes in the documentation style were made, compared to the AAF Object Specification. Several kinds of change are worth mentioning here, to help the reader reconcile the two documents.

The AAF specifications maintain a clear separation between the data model and the stored format, on the grounds that the data may be mapped to several different stored formats to suit different applications. The MXF specifications combine the data model with the mapping to SMPTE 336M KLV.

MXF reuses only part of the AAF data model, not all of it. Specifically, some AAF classes are omitted from the MXF documentation and, for AAF classes that are reused, some optional properties are omitted. However, an MXF file may contain any object defined by the AAF data model. Objects in an MXF file that are not defined by the MXF data model are "dark" to certain kinds of MXF applications. The MXF data model classes presented in this chapter are those documented in the MXF specifications.

The inheritance hierarchy of the AAF model—a feature of the meta-model—is not shown in the MXF documentation. Instead, an approach is taken to present only the classes that could be instantiated as objects in an MXF file. Such classes are shown with all parent classes aggregated into a single class definition. This style of presentation appears to show the same property belonging to more than one class. Such properties actually belong to a common parent class.

The MXF documentation uses the term set to mean an object (that is, an instance of a class in a file). This follows the terminology used in the SMPTE 336M KLV encoding specification in which local set and universal set are defined as a serialization of a group of properties as a KLV packet.

The names of certain classes and properties taken from AAF are changed, although their meanings and unique identifications (AUIDs) are not changed. Because an MXF file identifies classes and properties by AUID, and not by name, the differences in naming are purely an editorial issue when comparing the MXF and AAF specifications. Some of the differences in class naming are shown in Table 13.1. This chapter uses the AAF names.

AAF Class Name	MXF Class Name
Header	Preface
Mob (Material Object)	Generic Package
MasterMob	Material Package
file SourceMob (contains a FileDescriptor, or sub-class)	File Package
physical SourceMob (does not contain a FileDescriptor, or sub-class)	Physical Package
MobSlot	Track
TimelineMobSlot	Timeline Track
EventMobSlot	Event Track
StaticMobSlot	Static Track
Timecode	Timecode Component
DescriptiveMarker	DM Segment
DescriptiveFramework	DM Framework
DescriptiveSourceClip	DM SourceClip
EssenceDescriptor	Generic Descriptor
DigitalImageDescriptor	Generic Picture Essence Descriptor
CDCIDescriptor	CDCI Picture Essence Descriptor
RGBADescriptor	RGBA Picture Essence Descriptor
SoundDescriptor	Generic Sound Essence Descriptor
PCMDescriptor	Wave Audio Essence Descriptor
AES3PCMDescriptor	AES3 Audio Essence Descriptor
BWFImportDescriptor	Wave Audio Physical Descriptor
DataDescriptor	Generic Data Essence Descriptor
EssenceData	Essence Container Data

Table 13.1 Differences in naming between MXF and AAF

Objects in an MXF File

Viewed in terms of the AAF class model, the objects within an MXF file are depicted in Figure 13.1, with a brief description of their purpose.

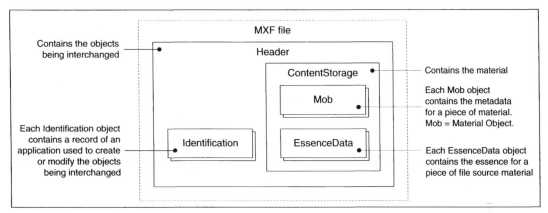

Figure 13.1 Objects within an MXF file

An important concept in the construction of an MXF file is *object containment*, in which one object logically contains, and is the owner of, another object or collection of objects. An object or a collection of objects can only be owned by a single object at a time, which allows tree-like structures of ownership to be constructed.

Object containment can be seen in Figure 13.1. At the highest level, there is one object in the MXF file: the Header. Within the Header, there is a collection of Identification objects and a ContentStorage object. Within the ContentStorage object, there is a collection of Mob objects and a collection of EssenceData objects. The Mob objects also contain objects, and so on. Object containment is also known as strong object reference.

In contrast to object containment, an object may reference another object or collection of objects without specifying ownership. This is known as weak object reference. An object can be the target of weak object references from more than one object. A target of a weak object reference must have a unique identifier so that a reference can be made to it.

An object reference, strong or weak, may be made to an individual object or a collection of objects. Collections are divided into two types: sets and vectors. Objects in a set have unique identifiers and are not ordered. Objects in a vector do not need unique identifiers and are ordered—the class model defines whether the order is meaningful for each vector.

The data interchanged in an MXF file is the tree of objects contained within it.

Unified Modeling Language in the AAF Class Model

The AAF Association Object Specification uses *Unified Modeling Language* (UML)[6] class diagrams

---

[6] Fowler, Martin. *UML Distilled: A Brief Guide to the Standard Object Modeling Language*. Boston: Addison Wesley, 2003.

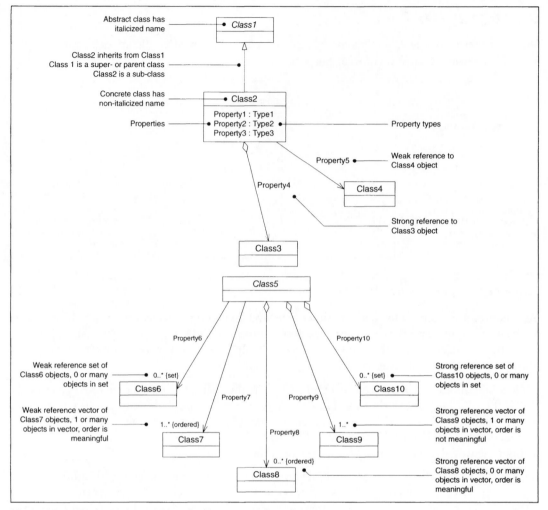

Figure 13.2 Key to Universal Modeling Language class diagrams

to depict the AAF class model. The UML class diagrams show the class name, properties, property types, object references and inheritance relationships. Figure 13.2 provides a key to the UML class diagrams used in the AAF Object Specification and in this chapter.

MXF Data Model Classes

Header

The Header class is shown in Figure 13.3. The Header contains the objects being interchanged—namely, an ordered vector of Identification objects that is a record of applications used to create

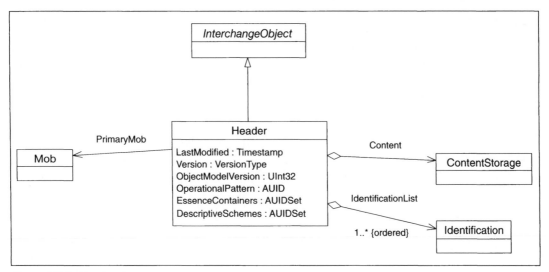

Figure 13.3 Header class

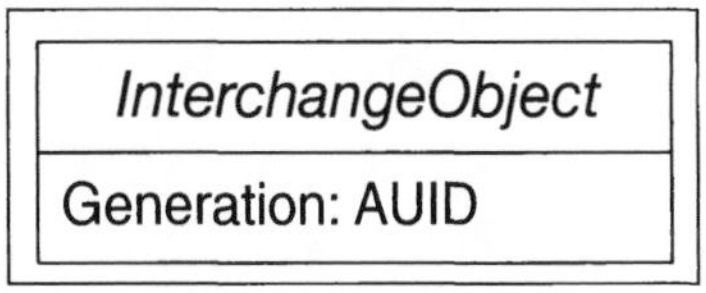

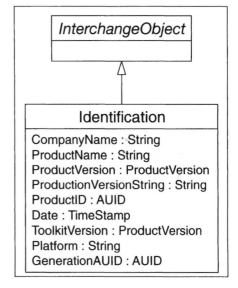

Figure 13.4 InterchangeObject class

or modify the MXF file; an optional weak reference to a primary Mob; and a ContentStorage object that contains the material metadata and essence.

The root of the inheritance hierarchy for Header and objects contained in Header is InterchangeObject. The InterchangeObject class is shown in Figure 13.4.

Identification

The Header contains a vector of Identification objects, which is a record of applications used to create or modify the MXF file. The Identification class is shown in Figure 13.4.

Figure 13.5 Identification class

When an MXF file is created and each time it is modified, an Identification object is added to maintain an audit trail. Any object in the Header can be linked to a particular Identification object, allowing the MXF file to record which application created or last modified the object. The link is made by setting the InterchangeObject::Generation property equal to the Identification:: GenerationAUID property.

ContentStorage

The Header contains a ContentStorage object, which contains the material metadata and essence. The ContentStorage class is shown in Figure 13.6. The ContentStorage contains a set of Mob objects, which hold the material metadata and a set of EssenceData objects, which hold the material essence.

Mob

The ContentStorage contains a set of Mob objects. Each Mob holds the metadata for a piece of material. The Mob class is shown in Figure 13.7. A Mob contains the material identifier (MobID), the material name and date and time of creation and modification. The material identifier is a 32-byte SMPTE 330M Unique Material Identifier (UMID).[7] Mob is an abstract class and has subclasses for different types of material: clip, file source, and physical source. The metadata for the tracks of material is in an ordered vector of MobSlot objects.

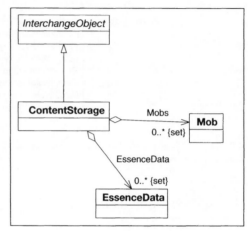

Figure 13.6 ContentStorage class

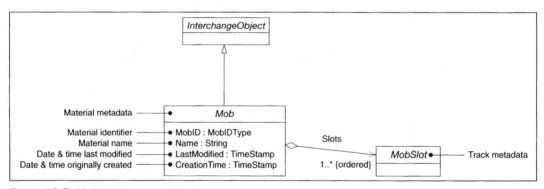

Figure 13.7 Mob class

MobSlot

The MobSlot class is shown in Figure 13.8. A MobSlot contains the track identifier (SlotID), the track name and any corresponding physical track number for the track. The physical track number can be used to link a MobSlot object to a specific input or output track on a device

---

[7] Society of Motion Picture and Television Engineers. "SMPTE 330M: Unique Material Identifier (UMID)." White Plains, N.Y. 2004.

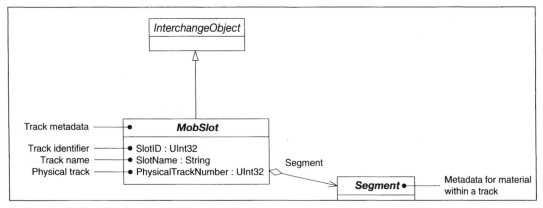

Figure 13.8 MobSlot class

(e.g., a value of 1 in a Picture MobSlot means the MobSlot object describes track V1). The track identifier is unique for each track within a Mob. Thus the combination of a material identifier (globally unique) and a track identifier (unique within a Mob) allows individual tracks to be globally referenced. MobSlot is an abstract class and has subclasses for different types of tracks. The metadata for the material within each track is in a Segment object. Segment is an abstract class and has subclasses for different kinds of material structure within a track.

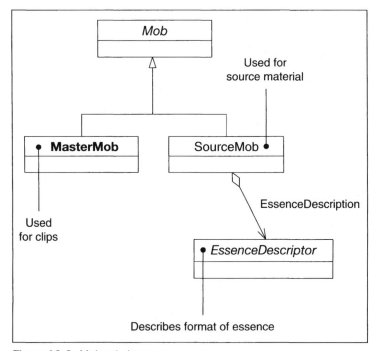

Figure 13.9 Mob subclasses

Types of Mob

Mob is an abstract class and has subclasses for different types of material, as shown in Figure 13.9.

A MasterMob describes a clip of material, collecting and synchronizing related source material and specifying how it should be output. The contained MobSlot objects describe the track layout, and their Segments reference the source material. The MasterMob provides a level of decoupling between the description of a clip and the source material for it. This provides flexibility for the arrangement of the sources (e.g., a MasterMob containing video and audio tracks might reference a separate file source for each track) and allows the clip to be associated with different source material during its lifetime if required (e.g., the source material for a clip might be changed from an offline proxy to online quality).

A SourceMob is used for file source material and physical source material. The contained MobSlot objects describe the track layout of the source, and their Segments describe how the source material was derived (e.g., a file SourceMob might be derived from a physical SourceMob).

A SourceMob contains an EssenceDescriptor object, which describes the format of the essence. EssenceDescriptor is an abstract class and has subclasses for different types of sources.

Types of SourceMob

The type of the SourceMob is determined by the class of the EssenceDescriptor it contains. Figure 13.10 shows the top of the EssenceDescriptor class inheritance hierarchy. A file SourceMob contains a concrete subclass of FileDescriptor and is used for a file source. A file source is one that is directly manipulated by the MXF application (e.g., video, audio, or data essence within an MXF file).

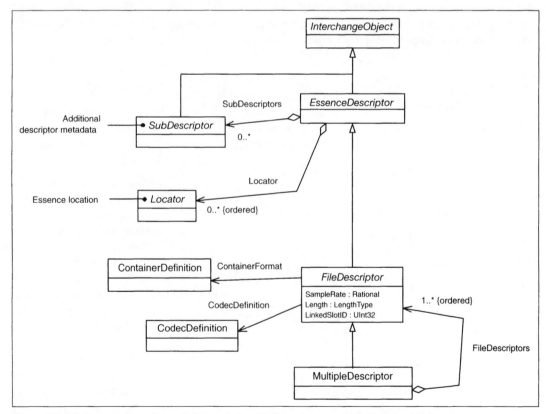

Figure 13.10 EssenceDescriptor, SubDescriptor, FileDescriptor, and MultipleDescriptor classes

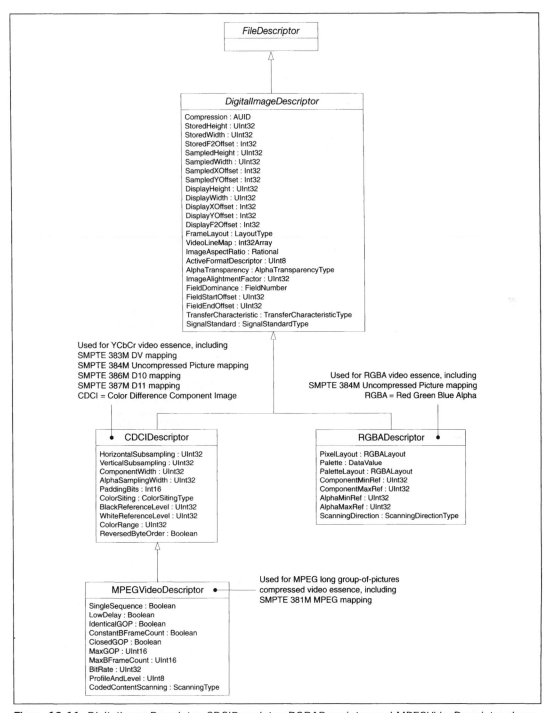

Figure 13.11 DigitalImageDescriptor, CDCIDescriptor, RGBADescriptor, and MPEGVideoDescriptor classes

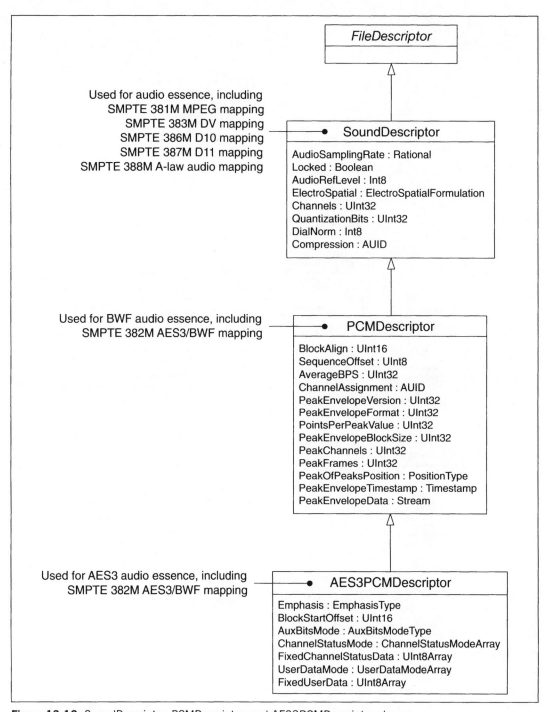

Figure 13.12 SoundDescriptor, PCMDescriptor, and AES3PCMDescriptor classes

Recall that, in the general case, the essence described by a SourceMob in an MXF file does not have to be stored within that file (although this is a requirement for certain Operational Patterns). A FileDescriptor has a weak reference to a ContainerDefinition and a weak reference to a CodecDefinition. The ContainerDefinition identifies the kind of file container the essence is in (e.g., an MXF file, an AAF file, or a plain file). The CodecDefinition identifies the codec that generated the essence. A FileDescriptor also contains the sample rate of the file source essence (for video, this is typically the picture rate) and its length in units of the sample rate.

A MultipleDescriptor contains a vector of FileDescriptor objects (that is, objects which are concrete subclasses of FileDescriptor) and is used when the file source consists of multiple tracks of essence. Each essence track is described by a MobSlot object in the SourceMob and a FileDescriptor object. The FileDescriptor is linked to the MobSlot by setting the FileDescriptor:: LinkedSlotID property equal to the MobSlot::SlotID property.

EssenceDescriptor has an ordered vector of Locator objects, which stores location information for the essence, when it is not stored in the MXF file. Locator is an abstract class and has subclasses for different types of locations. EssenceDescriptor also has an ordered vector of SubDescriptor objects, which may be used to store additional descriptor metadata that is not included in the defined EssenceDescriptor class hierarchy. SubDescriptor is an abstract class and has concrete subclasses for specific additional descriptor metadata.

Specifying Picture File Sources

The subclasses of FileDescriptor for specifying picture file sources are shown in Figure 13.11. CDCIDescriptor and RGBADescriptor are used for YCbCr and RGBA video file essence, respectively. The DigitalImageDescriptor::Compression property identifies the type of video compression (if any). MPEGVideoDescriptor is used for MPEG and MPEG-like long group-of-pictures compressed video file essence.

Specifying Sound File Sources

The subclasses of FileDescriptor for specifying sound file sources are shown in Figure 13.12. SoundDescriptor is used for audio file essence. PCMDescriptor is used for BWF audio file essence. AES3PCMDescriptor is used for AES3 audio file essence. The SoundDescriptor::Compression property identifies the type of audio compression (if any).

Specifying Data File Sources

The DataDescriptor subclass of FileDescriptor for specifying data file sources is shown in Figure 13.13. The DataDescriptor::DataEssence-Coding property identifies the type of data coding.

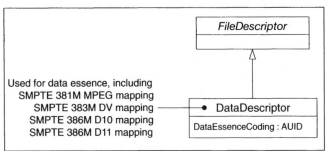

Figure 13.13 DataDescriptor class

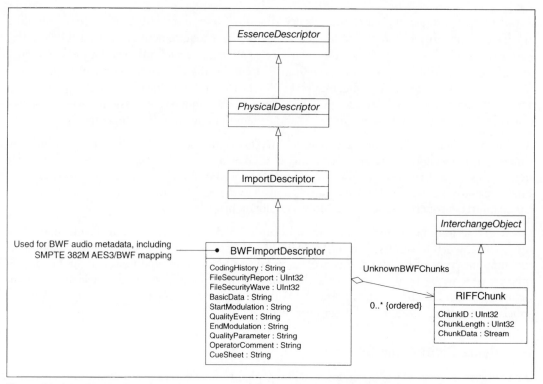

Figure 13.14 PhysicalDescriptor, ImportDescriptor, and BWFImportDescriptor classes

Specifying Physical Sources

The PhysicalDescriptor, ImportDescriptor, and BWFImportDescriptor subclasses of Essence-Descriptor are shown in Figure 13.14.

A physical SourceMob contains a concrete subclass of PhysicalDescriptor and is used for a physical source. A physical source is one that is not directly manipulated by the MXF application.

An import SourceMob contains an ImportDescriptor, or a subclass, and is used for a non-MXF file that was the source of an MXF file (e.g., a QuickTime video file that was the source for an import operation to create an MXF video file).

A BWFImport SourceMob contains a BWFImportDescriptor and is used for a BWF file that was the source of an MXF audio file. The BWFPhysicalDescriptor holds the BWF audio metadata that is not copied into the PCMDescriptor.

The AAF Object Specification also defines TapeDescriptor and FilmDescriptor for describing physical tape and film media sources respectively. A film SourceMob contains a FilmDescriptor and is used for a film source. A tape SourceMob contains a TapeDescriptor and used for a tape source. These classes are not currently specified in the MXF data model.

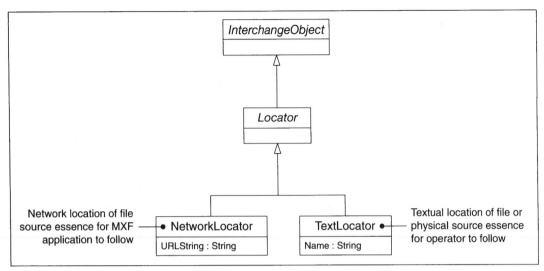

Figure 13.15 Locator subclasses

Types of Locator

The subclasses of Locator are shown in Figure 13.15. A NetworkLocator stores the network URL of file source essence for an MXF application to follow. A TextLocator stores a textual location of file source essence or physical source essence for an operator to follow.

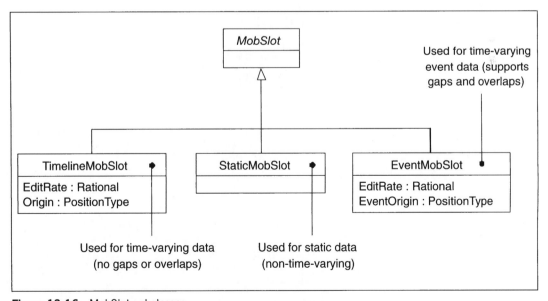

Figure 13.16 MobSlot subclasses

Types of MobSlot

MobSlot is an abstract class and has subclasses for different types of track, as shown in Figure 13.16. A TimelineMobSlot is used for time-varying data without gaps or overlaps, such as video and audio essence. An EventMobSlot is used for time-varying event data that may have gaps and overlaps, such as annotations occurring at specific times. A StaticMobSlot is used for non-time-varying data such as text.

TimelineMobSlot and EventMobSlot contain an edit rate that defines the time units (and hence, time precision) for the MobSlot and the contained Segment. A TimelineMobSlot contains an origin that defines the offset into the contained Segment of the zero time point—references into this TimelineMobSlot from SourceClip objects are deemed relative to this zero point.

Note that the edit rate for a TimelineMobSlot or EventMobSlot object is not necessarily the same value as the sample rate of the corresponding file source essence. For example, sound essence with a sample rate of 48000 kHz might be described by a TimelineMobSlot object with an edit rate of 25 Hz. The implication of this would be that the sound essence is being accessed in units of the picture frame rate.

Because a TimelineMobSlot has no gaps or overlaps, Segments within it do not need to specify their own starting time—it is implicit from the length of the Segments and their order. On the

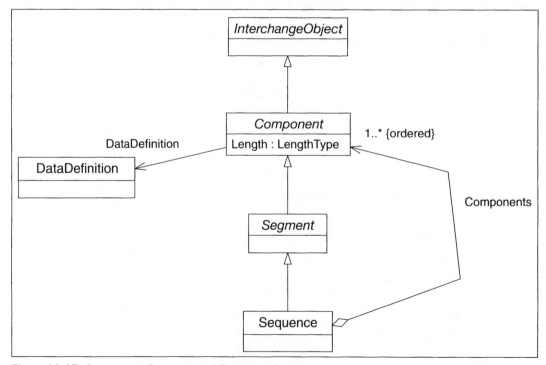

Figure 13.17 Component, Segment, and Sequence classes

other hand, because an EventMobSlot allows gaps and overlaps, Event Segments within it need to specify their own starting time.

The time-varying tracks within a Mob are synchronized. Although each TimelineMobSlot may have a different edit rate, its zero time point is timed with the zero time point of the other TimelineMobSlots in that Mob. A starting time specified by an Event Segment in an EventMobSlot is in units of the EventMobSlot edit rate, but it specifies a time relative to the zero point of all the TimelineMobSlots.

Types of Segment

The metadata for the material within each track is in a Segment object. Segment is an abstract class and has subclasses for different kinds of material structure within a track. Figure 13.17 shows the top of the Segment class inheritance hierarchy.

A Segment is derived from a Component. A Component has a length in time units defined by the containing MobSlot (where applicable), and a weak reference to a DataDefinition that defines the material type (e.g., picture, sound, or timecode).

A Sequence contains an ordered vector of Components. A Sequence is used when the material structure within a track consists of a number of different sections, such as a clip that references a number of sections of source material.

Specifying References between Material

A central part of the MXF data model is the idea of referencing between pieces of material, to describe how one piece is derived from another. Operational production processes are fundamentally about manipulating and assembling material to make new material, then manipulating and assembling that, and so on. The pieces of material in an MXF file (Mobs) reference one another to describe this derivation chain (or Mob chain). A typical derivation chain for a clip consists of a MasterMob (specifying a clip), which references file SourceMobs (specifying the file essence), which reference physical SourceMobs (specifying the source of the file essence). The derivation chain specified in an MXF file is as long as the processes it is describing.

The subclasses of Segment for specifying references are shown in Figure 13.18. SourceReference is an abstract class that enables a Segment in a MobSlot to reference a MobSlot in another Mob—the reference is made in terms of the referenced material identifier (MobID) and track identifier (SlotID). When a reference is

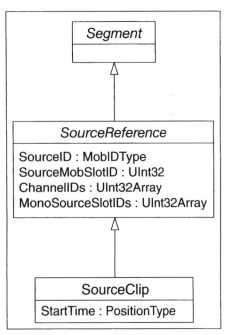

Figure 13.18 SourceReference and SourceClip classes

made to a MobSlot of a multi-channel material type (e.g., 5.1 surround sound), the ChannelIDs property specifies which channels are referenced. When a reference is made from a multi-channel MobSlot to multiple single channel MobSlots, the MonoSourceSlotIDs property specifies which MobSlots are referenced.

A SourceClip is a subclass of SourceReference that specifies a point in time in the referenced MobSlot. A SourceClip describes the notion that the value of this section of this MobSlot in this Mob is the value of that section of that MobSlot in that Mob.

The AAF Object Specification also defines a Pulldown subclass of Segment, which is used in conjunction with SourceClip to specify references between different rate tracks in mixed film and video scenarios. A Pulldown object describes the kind of pulldown (e.g., 3:2 pulldown), the direction (e.g., from film rate to video rate), and phase.

Specifying Timecode

The subclass of Segment for specifying timecode is shown in Figure 13.19. A Timecode object specifies a continuous section of timecode.

To specify a discontinuity in timecode, Timecode objects are placed in a Sequence—the discontinuity may occur at the junction between Timecode Segments.

A Timecode object has a weak reference to a timecode DataDefinition.

Source timecode is specified in a SourceMob. Output timecode for a clip is specified in a MasterMob.

The AAF Object Specification also defines TimecodeStream12M and Edgecode subclasses of Segment for SMPTE 12M timecode streams and film edge code respectively.

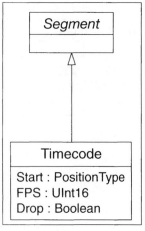

Figure 13.19 Timecode class

Specifying Annotations

The AAF data model provides several options for adding annotations to a piece of material, such as operator comments, user-specific data, and descriptive schemes of various kinds.

A particular area of development in MXF was to add descriptive metadata classes to the data model. The DescriptiveMarker and DescriptiveFramework classes are shown in Figure 13.20.

DescriptiveMarker is a subclass of CommentMarker and Event. Typically, DescriptiveMarker objects are placed in an EventMobSlot, and have a weak reference to a descriptive metadata DataDefinition. They have two functions: to specify what is being described, and to contain the description. The starting time and length of the DescriptiveMarker object specify the temporal extent of the description, and the DescriptiveMarker::DescribedSlots property specifies which of the essence MobSlots in the Mob are being described. The description is contained in a DescriptiveFramework object. A DescriptiveMarker object can also be placed in a Static-MobSlot, if the extent of the description is the entire Mob.

DescriptiveFramework is an abstract class. As new vocabularies of descriptive metadata, known as *descriptive metadata schemes*, are added, corresponding concrete subclasses of DescriptiveFramework will be defined. The abstract superclass for objects within a DescriptiveFramework is DescriptiveObject, shown in Figure 13.21. The descriptive metadata schemes used within an MXF file are identified in the Header::DescriptiveSchemes property.

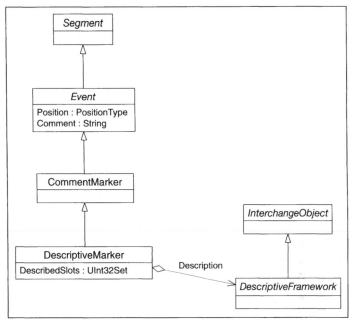

Figure 13.20 Event, CommentMarker, DescriptiveMarker, and DescriptiveFramework classes

The descriptive metadata scheme specified by SMPTE 380M Descriptive Metadata Scheme-1 (DMS-1), defines three concrete sub-classes of DescriptiveFramework, as shown in Figure 13.23, for production, clip and scene descriptive metadata. The descriptive metadata is structured according to the rules of the AAF meta model. The properties of the DMS-1 DescriptiveFramework classes are described in detail in Chapter 11.

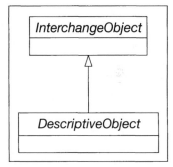

Figure 13.21 DescriptiveObject class

The DescriptiveSourceClip class, shown in Figure 13.23, enables a Segment in a descriptive metadata MobSlot to reference a section of a descriptive metadata MobSlot in another Mob. Typically, the referenced MobSlot would contain DescriptiveMarker objects. The two functions of a DescriptiveSourceClip object are to specify what is being described, and to reference some another Mob for the description.

EssenceData Class

An MXF file can contain essence for file source material. The essence may either be in the MXF file or held in an external file and referenced by the metadata. If the essence is internal, it is stored in an EssenceData object within the ContentStorage object. Each EssenceData object holds

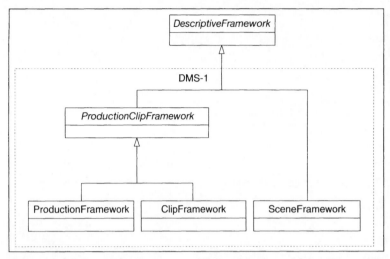

Figure 13.22 ProductionFramework, ClipFramework, and SceneFramework classes

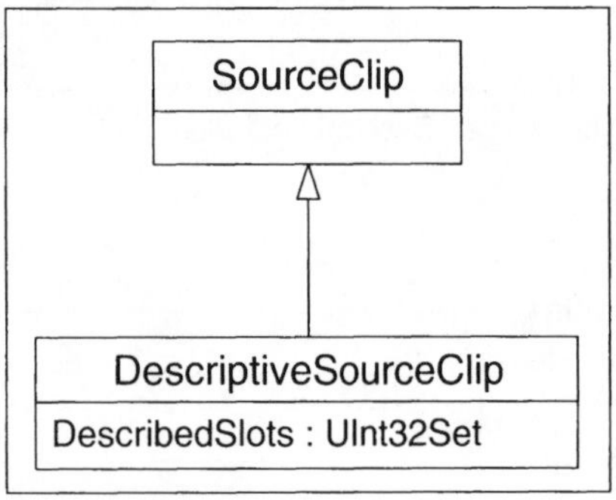

the essence for a piece of file source material. The EssenceData class is shown in Figure 13.24.

The essence may be of any kind (e.g., video, audio, or data) and of any compression type or uncompressed. The optional index table relates each essence sample to a byte offset into the essence stream.

The metadata for the piece of material, such as picture size, frame rate and compression type (if any), is stored in a file SourceMob. The file SourceMob and the EssenceData object have the same material identifier, because they are two facets of the same piece of material.

If the essence is held in an external file, the EssenceDescriptor of the file SourceMob will contain a Locator object for an authoring tool to follow to read the essence.

Figure 13.23: DescriptiveSourceClip class

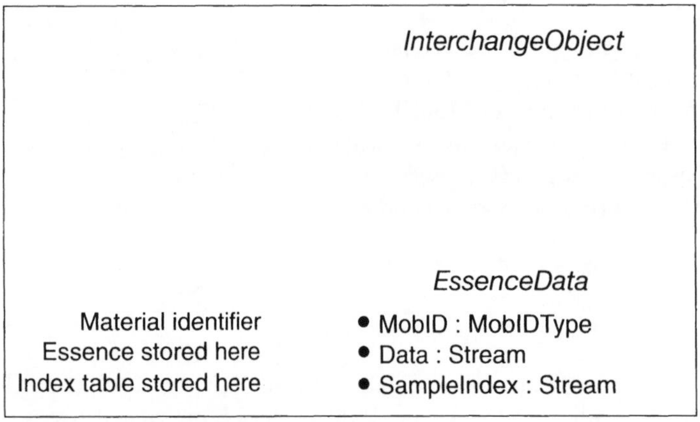

Acknowledgements

I would like to thank the BBC for permission to publish this chapter, and thank my colleague Philip de Nier for several mind-expanding conversations on models and meta-models (meta-meta-metadata). I would also like to acknowledge the contributions of Tim Bingham, Bruce Devlin, Oliver Morgan, and Jim Wilkinson for their work in keeping MXF and AAF closely aligned.

Figure 13.24 EssenceData class

14 The MXFLib Open Source Library

Matt Beard

Introduction

This chapter gives a basic introduction to the key principles of the MXFLib Open Source library. MXFLib is a fully featured library that allows reading, writing, and modifying of MXF files. It gives an easy-to-use interface to structural and descriptive metadata, as well as flexible essence-handling features and full indexing and encryption support.

The library can be downloaded from the project web page at: *http://www.freemxf.org.*

Intention

MXF is an advanced and "feature-rich" format that can be used in many ways throughout production, distribution, and archiving. However, its flexibility means that supporting MXF is not as simple as other more limited formats.

MXFLib is intended to help the uptake of the format by reducing the amount of time and effort required to add MXF support to applications. There are three main ways of using MXFLib.

As an Off-the-Shelf Library

MXFLib may be used unmodified to add MXF support. Most applications can use MXFLib in an unmodified form taking advantage of a full range of metadata and essence-processing features. This is the easiest way to get started with MXFLib-based development and, unless there are specific non-standard requirements, is generally the best option.

As a Starting Point for Proprietary Software

For applications that have unusual requirements or are tied closely to specific hardware, the library can be extended or modified. This can be as simple as adding proprietary essence handling classes or so far reaching that the source code is almost entirely rewritten. Of course the further the code moves from the standard library, the more difficult maintaining compatibility with the official version becomes.

As an Educational Tool

MXFLib may be used as a tool to help understand MXF, either in general terms or as the first step in developing a proprietary solution.

Licensing

As the main goal of MXFLib is the widespread support of the MXF format across the industry, an exceptionally open license was chosen:

```
Copyright (c) year, Copyright Holder(s)

This software is provided "as-is," without any express or implied warranty.

In no event will the authors be held liable for any damages arising from
the use of this software.

Permission is granted to anyone to use this software for any purpose,
including commercial applications, and to alter it and redistribute it
freely, subject to the following restrictions:

  1. The origin of this software must not be misrepresented; you must
     not claim that you wrote the original software. If you use this
     software in a product, an acknowledgment in the product
     documentation would be appreciated but is not required.

  2. Altered source versions must be plainly marked as such, and must
     not be misrepresented as being the original software.

  3. This notice may not be removed or altered from any source
     distribution.
```

This license allows the software to be incorporated into commercial or non-commercial systems free of charge without restriction. It also allows the source code to be modified freely and even redistributed in modified or unmodified form, as long the license itself remains unmodified (although the author of any modifications may add their name to the list of copyright holders of that version).

Design Principles

Platform Choice

A key design decision for MXFLib was to make it as easy as possible for the library to be used on a wide range of operating system/hardware combinations.

Language Choice

Although most people have their personal favorite programming languages, often for exceedingly good reasons, the choice of language for MXFLib was driven by a combination of the desire for the widest possible range of platforms and for the best run-time performance level. This quickly led to a choice between C and C++. C is available on a few more platforms than C++, and it sometimes performs fractionally better; however, the complexity of writing and maintaining such a complex system in C left C++ as the only viable choice.

The source code is currently written to support the following compilers:

- Microsoft Visual C++ 6 and Visual Studio .NET.
- GNU gcc (most recent versions).
- Any other ANSI C++ compiler that supports the C99 standard.

Abstraction of System Specifics

MXFLib is written to be platform independent with all system-specific code held in the file system.h. This is the only file that is permitted to contain any compiler or platform-specific macros or functions.

System.h holds definitions of generic type names, large file support, and access to a few other non-standard compiler features, such as those required to handle 64-bit integers or produce UUIDs.

Generic Type Names

Traditionally C and C++ variables have been sized in a platform-specific way. An *int* is often 4 bytes, but many compilers still use 2-byte ints and some use 8 bytes. Even the humble *char* is not guaranteed to be an unsigned 8-bit integer.[1]

MXFLib uses a set of exact-width integer types whose names match those used in the MXF specifications:

Int8, UInt8	8-bit signed and unsigned integers
Int16, UInt16	16-bit signed and unsigned integers

---

[1] C99 defines exact-width integers of the form int16_t; however, at the time the MXFLib API was defined, these were not widely supported and, at the current time of writing, they are still not universally available.

Int32, UInt32   32- bit signed and unsigned integers

Int64, UInt64   64-bit signed and unsigned integers

File I/O

ANSI C defines a standard set of file I/O functions that are adequate for most applications; however, they are limited to four gigabytes, which is insufficient for MXF. C++ streams have a platform-specific range that may be sufficient in some cases but, if used, could not easily be over-ridden if large-file support was only available through other mechanisms on a particular target system. In both cases, relying on standard I/O methods would rule out using MXFLib as an interface to non-standard hardware that has no convenient or efficient file-based interface.

MXFLib uses the following functions internally for file I/O and it is recommended that they are also used if an MXFLib application needs to access non-MXF files:

```
bool FileExists(const char *filename);
```
Determine if a file with a given name exists

```
FileHandle FileOpen(const char *filename);
```
Open an existing file for reading and/or writing

```
FileHandle FileOpenRead(const char *filename);
```
Open an existing file for reading only

```
FileHandle FileOpenNew(const char *filename);
```
Open a file for reading and/or writing, create the file if it does not exist

```
bool FileValid(FileHandle file);
```
Determine if a file handle relates to a valid open file

```
int FileSeek(FileHandle File, UInt64 Offset);
```
Seek to the given offset in an open file, returning –1 if the seek fails, else 0

```
int FileSeekEnd(FileHandle file);
```
Seek to the end of an open file, returning –1 if the seek fails, else 0

```
UInt64 FileRead(FileHandle file, unsigned char *dest, UInt64 size);
```
Read bytes from an open file, returning the number of bytes successfully read

```
UInt64 FileWrite(FileHandle file, const unsigned char *source, UInt64 size);
```
Write bytes to an open file, returning the number of bytes successfully written

```
int FileGetc(FileHandle file);
```
Read a single byte from an open file, returning the unsigned value, or –1 on error

```
bool FileEof(FileHandle file);
```
Determine if the most recent read from an open file was at or beyond the end

```
UInt64 FileTell(FileHandle file);
```
Return the position of the current file pointer of an open file, or (UInt64)–1 on error

```
void FileClose(FileHandle file);
```
Close a currently open file

Random Access v. Stream

MXF files may be large and it is not guaranteed that an MXF file is stored on a medium with full random access. The MXFLib library moves the file pointer as little as necessary and usually only forwards to skip over unused KLVs. Certain operations, like reading the file RIP, require seeking but, if necessary, these can be avoided at the application layer.

Streaming Media

A streaming storage medium, such as data tape, can be used with MXFLib by writing versions of FileRead(), FileWrite(), and FileSeek() that buffer a certain amount of data as it is read, allowing short backwards seeks to be performed without needing to rewind the physical medium. Providing the standard metadata and essence reading and writing methods are used, and random-access API calls, such as MXFFile::Seek() and ReadRIP(), are avoided in the application, the medium can be kept running forwards.

General Technology Choices

There are a number of key design decisions that shape the MXFLib library.

Smart Pointers[2]

Any software system that handles a large number of data items allocated at run-time needs to take special care to ensure that any memory allocated is released once it is no longer required, but also to ensure that no attempt is made to access memory once it has been released.

Such memory management is considerably simplified by the use of smart pointers. These manage reference counting of objects in memory and delete them when they are no longer referenced.

Example 1—Using Normal Pointers:

```
{
  Foo *Ptr1, *Ptr2;            // Pointers to objects of type "Foo"

  Ptr1 = new Foo;              // Ptr1 now points to a new Foo object
  Ptr2 = Ptr1;                 // Ptr2 points to the same Foo object

  delete Ptr1;                 // The object is deleted

  Ptr2->Use();                 // Error: Ptr2 now points to freed memory
}
```

In the above, trivial, example an object has been deleted too early—a pointer still exists that references the object and that causes an error later.

---

[2] The smart pointer class is based on code originally written by Sandu Turcan and submitted to *www.codeproject.com*. It is licensed as a part of the MXFLib library with kind permission of the author.

Example 2—Using Smart Pointers:

```
{
  SmartPtr<Foo> Ptr1, Ptr2;          // Smart pointers to two objects of type "Foo"

  Ptr1 = new Foo;                    // Ptr1 now points to a new Foo object
  Ptr2 = Object1;                    // Ptr2 points to the same Foo object

  Ptr1 = NULL;                       // Finished with Ptr1 pointer

  Ptr2->Use();                       // No error—the object still exists

}                                    // Object is deleted here
```

When the code is rewritten to use smart pointers, the error is removed. Rather than deleting an object when it is no longer required, the code simply stops referencing it either by the pointer being destroyed, or by changing it to point to some other object. In this case, Ptr1 is changed to point to NULL (a special case for a pointer that points to nothing). If Ptr1 were the only pointer referencing the object, it would be deleted at this point, but there is still one remaining reference from the pointer Ptr2 so it is not deleted. When Ptr2 goes out of scope, the pointer is destroyed and this releases the last reference to the Foo object, which is then deleted.

Often the relationship between a smart pointer and the referenced object is referred to as ownership. When more than one pointer references the same object, they have shared ownership. Once no pointer owns an object, the object is deleted.

The Following Example Shows a More Complex Flow of Ownership:

```
void TestFunc(void)
{
  // ItemPtr is a smart pointer to an object of type Item
  ItemPtr Ptr1;                      // Starts off as a NULL pointer
  ItemPtr Ptr2 = new Item("A");      // Ptr2 points to, and owns, a new Item called A
  ItemPtr Ptr3 = new Item("B");      // Ptr3 points to a second Item called B

  Ptr1 = Ptr3;                       // Item B is now shared by two
                                     // pointers: Ptr1 and Ptr3

  Ptr3 = NULL;                       // Now only Ptr1 owns Item B
  Ptr2 = Ptr1;                       // Now Item B is shared by Ptr1 and Ptr2
                                     // Ptr2 has released ownership of Item A so
                                     // it is deleted (it is now un-referenced)

}                                    // As Ptr1 and Ptr2 go out of scope
                                     // they each release ownership if Item B so
                                     // it is also deleted
```

Reference Counter Class

To enable the number of references to an object to be counted, the object must contain a counter that is incremented each time a new smart pointer references the object and decremented when the pointer releases ownership. Abstract super-class RefCount, from which classes must be derived, directly or indirectly, if they are to be owned by a smart pointer, achieves this reference counting.

For example, the Item class used above should be defined as follows:

```
class Item : public RefCount<Item>
{
  ...
};
```

Basic rules for using smart pointers:

- Smart pointers can only own objects that are derived from RefCount.

- Smart pointers can only reference objects created with "new."

- Never delete an object owned by a smart pointer (the pointer will do it).

- Smart pointers can be converted to/from standard pointers, but standard pointers are not "counted" and so may eventually point to freed memory.

- Use the naming convention: *xxx*Ptr is a smart pointer to an *xxx* object.

Use of stdlib Containers

The MXFLib API makes considerable use of simple stdlib containers for collecting related metadata. As well as using these containers as properties, a number of key MXFLib classes are derived from the container classes. The main container type used is the std::list, but std::map is also used where appropriate. Use is also made of std::pair, both directly and indirectly.

For example, an MDObject holds a single metadata object, but where this object is a container holding other objects, such as a KLV set or pack, it will need to hold some form of reference to the "contained" objects. This is achieved by the MDObject class being derived from a std::list<> of std::pair<UL, MDObjectPtr> allowing code such as the following:

```
MDObjectPtr ThisObject = GetSomeObject();

if(ThisObject.size() == 0)
{
  ProcessChildlessObject(ThisObject);
}
else
{
  MDObject::iterator it = ThisObject->begin();
  while(it != ThisObject->end())
  {
    ProcessChildObject((*it).second);
    it++;
  }
}
```

Note that the following naming conventions are also used by MXFLib:

- *xxx*List is a list of smart pointers to *xxx* objects
- *xxx*Map is a map of smart pointers to *xxx* objects

Error Processing

MXFLib does not throw exceptions. Errors are signaled by return values, and error and warning messages are passed to the application via a set of functions as follows.

```
void error(const char *Fmt, ...);
```
Display an error message

```
void warning(const char *Fmt, ...);
```
Display a warning message

The application need not display the messages produced, but they should be made available if practical. A command-line application may send all error or warning messages to stderr; an application with a GUI may display error messages in a window, or it may be more appropriate to write the messages to a log file. A number of items are worth considering when deciding how to handle MXFLib error and warning messages. Bad input data (such as a damaged MXF file or an incorrect dictionary) may produce numerous messages—if each message were to cause a new window to be shown, the user may not be too pleased. Some failures may not be easy to explain without making the content of the error messages visible. It may be possible to continue reading useful data from an MXF file even after warnings and errors have been produced.

A similar function provides a mechanism for passing debugging messages to the application:

```
void debug(const char *Fmt, ...);
```
Display a debug message

However, debug messages will only be passed to the debug function if the library has been compiled with symbol MXFLIB_DEBUG defined—this prevents code that builds debug messages appearing in release builds and so improves efficiency.

Basic Data Types

The following basic data types are used widely throughout MXFLib.

Position and Length

Both are Int64 types and are used for holding positions and lengths within a file in either bytes or edit units.

Rational

A compound type consisting of an Int32 Numerator and an Int32 Denominator. It can be constructed with no parameters, giving a value of 0/0, or by specifying both properties, as follows:

```
Rational EditRate(30,1001);          // Define 29.97Hz edit rate
```

DataChunk

DataChunk objects hold a memory buffer that can be read, set and resized as required. When the chunk is resized, the contents are preserved. This class is used to simplify memory management. Example usage:

```
// Make a chunk with a 16-byte buffer, but with no actual data yet
DataChunkPtr Chunk = new DataChunk(16);

size_t ChunkSize = Chunk->Size;        // Will be 0 as no data held

Chunk->Set(128, MemoryBuffer);         // Sets the contents of the buffer to be
                                       // 128 bytes copied from the location
                                       // of the supplied MemoryBuffer
                                       // The original 16-bytes will be freed
                                       // as a new 128 byte buffer is required

Chunk->Set(32, NewBuffer);             // Sets the contents of the buffer to be
                                       // 32 bytes copied from the location
                                       // of the supplied NewBuffer
                                       // The buffer will not be reallocated as
                                       // these 32 bytes will fit in the
                                       // existing 128-byte buffer

ChunkSize = Chunk->Size;               // Will be 32 as that is what was set
UInt8 *Buff = Chunk->Data;             // Will be the start of the buffer
```

Identifiers

There are a number of identifier types defined; each shares a common base template class called Identifier<SIZE> that supplies generic methods for setting, reading, and comparing the value as follows:

```
Identifier();
```
Build a zero-filled identifier

```
Identifier(const UInt8 *ID);
```
Build an identifier with a given value, whose size must equal SIZE

```
Identifier(const SmartPtr<Identifier> ID);
```
Build an identifier taking its value from an existing identifier

```
Set(const UInt8 *ID);
```
Set the value of the identifier; size must equal SIZE

```
const UInt8 *GetValue(void);
```
Get a read-only pointer to the identifier value

```
std::string GetString(void);
```
Get a human readable string containing the identifier value

```
Bool operator==(const Identifier& Other);
```
Compare the value of this identifier with another

UL

Universal Labels are represented by objects of class UL, which is derived from Identifier<16>, with the following additions:

- Operator==() compares the second eight bytes first as these are most likely to contain any differences.

- GetString() returns ULs in the compact SMPTE format.

- If the string appears to contain an end-swapped[3] UUID, GetString() returns it in the compact GUID format.

UUID

Universally Unique IDentifiers are represented by objects of class UUID, which is derived from Identifier<16>, with the following additions:

- The default constructor UUID() builds a new UUID according to ISO 11578.

- GetString() returns UUIDs in the compact GUID format.

- If the string appears to contain an end-swapped UL, GetString() returns it in the compact SMPTE format.

UMID

Universal Material IDentifiers are represented by objects of class UMID, which is derived from Identifier<32>, with the following additions:

- GetInstance() and SetInstance() methods get and set the instance number.

- GetMaterial() and SetMaterial() methods get and set the material number.

Metadata

The metadata-handling functions of MXFLib are written for ease of use rather than efficiency. Although performance has been a major design consideration, it has remained secondary to usability. This choice has been made because metadata handling forms a very small part of the workload when processing an MXF file, compared to essence handling.

---

[3] In MXF a UUID may be stored in a UL property by transposing the first and second eight bytes. Similarly, a UL may be stored in a UUID property by performing the same reordering. This is often described as end-swapping.

Run-Time Typing

As the MXF standard allows great flexibility in the type of metadata carried within an MXF file, including the ability to have public or private extensions to the data model, the metadata processing in MXFLib needs to be equally flexible. One of the ways this flexibility is achieved is by using run-time definitions for data types and structures. This allows new data types or sets to be added to an existing application simply by loading an XML description of the new type.

Metadata Objects/Values

When an MXF file is read or created by an MXFLib application, each metadata item within the file's header metadata is represented in memory by an object of class MDObject. These objects fall into two categories, MDObjects that hold a value (such as "KAGSize"), and MDObjects that are containers for other MDObjects (such as the "Preface" set).

If the MDObject is a container, it will hold a pair for each child object, containing a UL for the child and a smart pointer to the child object that can be accessed using std::list methods as per the following example:

```
MDObject::iterator it = ThisObject->begin();
while(it != ThisObject->end())
{
  MDObjectPtr ThisChild = (*it).second;

  ...

  it++;
}
```

If the MDObject represents a data value, it will be held in property Value, which is a smart pointer to an object of type MDValue. For example:

```
MDValuePtr ThisValue = ThisObject->Value;
```

Reading/Setting Metadata Values

Metadata values can be read or set as integers or character strings. In each case a translation is performed depending on the type of data held in the value object.

Integers can be read as 32- or 64-bit and as signed or unsigned. MDObject and MDValue share the following methods:

```
Int32 GetInt(void);
```
Read a 32-bit signed integer value from this object

```
UInt32 GetUInt(void);
```
Read a 32-bit unsigned integer value from this object

```
Int64 GetInt64(void);
```
Read a 64-bit signed integer value from this object

```
UInt64 GetUInt64(void);
```
Read a 64-bit unsigned integer value from this object

The following MDObject and MDValue method reads a string value:

```
std::string GetString(void);
```
Read a string value from this object

The string will be returned as a standard library string holding either an ISO 646 7-bit (ASCII) character string or a UTF-8 coded Unicode string. A UTF-8 version will only be returned from objects that contain a Unicode value. The return string can be tested with function IsWideString() to see if it contains any UTF-8 characters (if so, the function will return true).

Integers and strings can be set using the following MDObject/MDValue methods:

```
void SetInt(Int32 Val);
```
Set the value of this object from a 32-bit signed integer

```
void SetUInt(UInt32 Val);
```
Set the value of this object from a 32-bit unsigned integer

```
void SetInt64(Int64 Val);
```
Set the value of this object from a 64-bit signed integer

```
void SetUInt64(UInt64 Val);
```
Set the value of this object from a 64-bit unsigned integer

```
void SetString(std::string Val);
```
Set the value of this object from a string

It is not necessary to match the type of the set or get method with the underlying type of the metadata object, as appropriate conversions will be supplied where possible. Any integer metadata value can be set with any variant of the SetInt() method, providing the number is in the valid range for the function call and for the object being set. If a numeric metadata value is set using SetString(), the string will be parsed for a numeric value. Similarly, GetString() called on a numeric value will return a string holding the digits of the number. SetInt() and GetInt() calls on a string metadata value will set or get a single character, the first in the string.

For example:

```
// Get a smart pointer to a metadata object with a 64-bit signed integer value
MDObjectPtr Object64 = Get64BitSignedItem();

Int32 Value = 42;
Object64->SetInt(Value);                 // Object64 now holds 42 as a 64-bit int

UInt64 UValue64 = Object64->GetUInt64();  // UValue64 now holds 42

std::string Str = Object64->GetString();  // Str now holds "42"

// Get a smart pointer to a metadata object with a string value
MDObjectPtr ObjectStr = GetStringItem();

ObjectStr->SetInt(Value);                // ObjectStr now holds "*" (character 42)
```

If an MDObject is a container, such as a KLV set or pack, the contained objects can be read or set using similar set-and-get methods that also take the UL of the child object to manipulate:

```
Int32 GetInt(const UL &ChildType);
```
Read a 32-bit signed integer value from the specified child object

```
UInt32 GetUInt(const UL &ChildType);
```
Read a 32-bit unsigned integer value from the specified child object

```
Int64 GetInt64(const UL &ChildType);
```
Read a 64-bit signed integer value from the specified child object

```
UInt64 GetUInt64(const UL &ChildType);
```
Read a 64-bit unsigned integer value from the specified child object

```
std::string GetString(const UL &ChildType);
```
Read a string value from the specified child object

```
void SetInt(const UL &ChildType, Int32 Val);
```
Set the value of the specified child object from a 32-bit signed integer

```
void SetUInt(const UL &ChildType, UInt32 Val);
```
Set the value of the specified child object from a 32-bit unsigned integer

```
void SetInt64(const UL &ChildType, Int64 Val);
```
Set the value of the specified child object from a 64-bit signed integer

```
void SetUInt64(const UL &ChildType, UInt64 Val);
```
Set the value of the specified child object from a 64-bit unsigned integer

```
void SetString(const UL &ChildType, std::string Val);
```
Set the value of the specified child object from a string

If a set method is called with the UL of child that currently exists in the parent object, that child has its value set, otherwise a new child of the appropriate type is added and set to the given value. For example:

```
MDObjectPtr Header = new MDObject(ClosedHeader_UL);

Header->SetInt(MajorVersion_UL, 1);
Header->SetInt(MinorVersion_UL, 2);
Header->SetInt(KAGSize_UL, 256);
...
```

Note that each standard set, pack, and set or pack property defined in SMPTE 377M has a constant UL defined in MXFLib with the same name as used in that document, followed by "_UL"

An empty child object can be added to a container MDObject with the AddChild() method:

```
MDObjectPtr AddChild(const UL &ChildType);
```

If the parent object is an array or batch, there is no need to specify the type of the child as that can be inferred from the parent object's definition.

If a get method is called with the UL of a child that exists in the parent object, the value of that child is returned, otherwise 0 or "" is returned. This returned value may lead to the desired behavior. However, another value may be more appropriate when a child does not exist and this can be supplied as an extra parameter to the Get method call; for example:

```
MDObjectPtr Shot = GetShotSet();

std::string LangCode = Shot->GetString(TextLanguageCode_UL);
Position ShotStart = Shot->GetInt64(ShotStartPosition_UL);
Length ShotLength = Shot->GetInt64(ShotDuration_UL, 1);
std::string Description = Shot->GetString(ShotDescription_UL, "No description given");
```

If all four properties were omitted from the set, the above code would result in values of "", 0, 1, and "No description given," respectively.

If a metadata object is a *Best Effort* property from an *incomplete* partition, it may have a *distinguished value* to indicate that the actual value is unknown. This can be set or tested using the following MDObject methods:

```
bool SetDValue(void);
```
Sets this object to its distinguished value; returns true if successful

```
bool SetDValue(const UL &ChildType);
```
Sets the specified child object to its distinguished value; returns true if successful

```
Bool IsDValue(void);
```
Returns true if this object is set to its distinguished value

```
Bool IsDValue(const UL &ChildType);
```
Returns true if the specified child object is set to its distinguished value

If a metadata object has a default value defined, that value can be set with the following methods:

```
bool SetDefault(void);
```
Sets this object to its default value; returns true if successful

```
bool SetDefault(const UL &ChildType);
```
Sets the specified child object to its default value; returns true if successful

There are matching methods taking a smart pointer to a UL object (a ULPtr, or, to be more exact, for efficiency a reference to a ULPtr is passed):

```
Int32 GetInt(ULPtr &ChildType);
```
Read a 32-bit signed integer value from the specified child object

```
UInt32 GetUInt(ULPtr &ChildType);
```
Read a 32-bit unsigned integer value from the specified child object

etc.

It is also possible to use the name of a child object rather than a UL; however, only the UL is normative with the mapping between name and UL defined by a dictionary file. If an application loads a run-time dictionary that does not assign the expected names to objects, it is likely that the results would be undesirable.

Dictionary Files

An XML dictionary file containing the various MXF types, along with the set and pack structures described in SMPTE 377M, is included as part of MXFLib. This file, dict.xml, needs to be loaded at run-time in order for the library to function correctly. Having these definitions held in an XML file, which is parsed at run-time, allows modifications and extensions to be made by simply editing the dictionary file, rather than needing to change the application's source code. This file can be loaded using the LoadDictionary() function:

```
// Load the main MXFLib dictionary
LoadDictionary("dict.xml");
```

Further types and classes can be loaded from supplementary dictionaries after the main dictionary is loaded. This is especially useful for loading the sets used in descriptive metadata schemes, but may also be used to add other public or private metadata extensions.

```
// Load the main MXFLib dictionary
LoadDictionary("dict.xml");

// Load extra tape-archive locator metadata (private additions to NetworkLocator)
LoadDictionary("TapeLocate.xml")

// Load DMS-1 definitions
LoadDictionary("DMS1.xml");

// Load "My Broadcast Company" descriptive metadata definitions

LoadDictionary("DMS-MBC.xml");
```

In some applications, it may not be desirable, or even possible, to use run-time XML dictionaries. To allow for this. the dictionary data can be included at compile-time and loaded from within the application. It is not recommended that this compile-time dictionary system is used if an XML version could be a reasonable alternative; this is because it removes the possibility of modifying or extending the data without rebuilding the application.

MXFLib includes the dictconvert tool to convert an XML dictionary file into a C++ header file containing the corresponding compile-time definitions. These can then be loaded using an overloaded version of the LoadDictionary() function:

```
// Include the standard compile-time definitions
#include "dict.h"

// Load the main MXFLib dictionary from structures in dict.h
LoadDictionary(DictData);
```

Strong and Weak References

Some MXF metadata objects are linked to others using strong referencing or weak referencing. This referencing is managed through the following MDObject methods:

```
MDObjectPtr GetLink(void);
```
Gets a pointer to the referenced set

```
bool MakeLink(MDObjectPtr TargetSet);
```
Makes a link from this reference source to a target set

GetLink() returns a smart pointer to the set that is the target of the reference, or NULL if there is no reference. MakeLink() makes a reference from this object to the specified set, returning true if all went well. MakeLink() ensures that the target set has an InstanceUID property and copies its value to this object.

Note that you should never manually change the InstanceUID of a set, as this will break any existing reference linking.

The MXF File

Each MXF file is represented by an MXFFile object, which gives access to the key features of the file.

MXF files are opened and closed using the following methods:

```
bool Open(std::string FileName, bool ReadOnly = false);
```
Opens an existing MXF file; optionally opens as read only

```
bool OpenNew(std::string FileName);
```
Opens a new MXF file; any previous file is destroyed

```
bool Close(void);
```
Close this MXF file

When an existing MXF file is opened, the start of the file is scanned to see if there is a run-in. If one is found, it is read into the MXFFile object's RunIn property, which is a DataChunk.

The file pointer can be moved and read with the following methods:

```
int Seek(Position Pos);
```
Seek to the specified byte offset in the file—returns 0 if seek succeeded

```
int SeekEnd(void);
```
Seek to the end if the file—returns 0 if seek succeeded

```
Position Tell(void);
```
Returns the current byte offset within the file

Seeking within a file requires random access and so care should be taken if the application may be using a linear medium such as data tape. Note that if the file contains a run-in, byte offsets exclude the run-in, so the first byte of the header partition pack is always byte 0.

Random Index Pack

An MXF file may optionally contain a Random Index Rack and this allows for easier navigation of the file. If the file contains a RIP, it can be read using the following MXFFile method:

```
bool ReadRIP(void);
```
Read the file's Random Index Pack

This loads the Random Index Pack into the MXFFile's FileRIP property, giving easy access to the location of each partition. Note that reading the RIP will require random access to the medium containing the MXF file. Developers writing applications that may be using linear media should be aware that a call to ReadRIP() will cause a seek to the last byte of the file, even if there is no RIP.

The RIP class is derived from a std::map of smart pointers to PartitionInfo objects indexed by Position within the file. Each PartitionInfo object contains the following properties:

```
PartitionPtr ThePartition;
```
A smart pointer to the partition metadata, if currently in memory, or NULL

```
Position ByteOffset;
```
The location of this partition within the file

```
UInt32 BodySID;
```
The Stream ID of any essence in this partition

The information in the RIP is very useful for complex MXF files, and so it is possible to construct the same table for a file that does not contain a Random Index Pack. The following MXFFile method will scan the file to locate each partition and build a table in property FileRIP:

```
bool ScanRIP(void);
```
Scan the file to build a RIP; returns true on success

The easiest way for an application to acquire a RIP for an MXF file is to use the following MXFFile method, which will use ReadRIP() if the file contains a Random Index Pack, otherwise it will use ScanRIP() to construct one.

```
bool GetRIP(void);
```
Read the file RIP, or scan and build if required, returns true on success

Partition Metadata

Partition packs are represented by objects of class Partition. The Partition class manages any header metadata sets for this partition, a primer pack for the header metadata, and any index table segments. The pack itself is held in an MDObject, which is referenced by the Partition's Object property.

Partitions are read using the MXFFile ReadPartition() method. The following simple code reads the header partition and, if possible, the footer:

```
// Build an MXFFile object
MXFFilePtr File = new MXFFile;

// Open Test.mxf as read-only
File->Open("Test.mxf", true);

// Read the first partition in the file (the header)
PartitionPtr Header = File->ReadPartition();

// Read the footer location from the header partition pack
Position FooterPos = Header->(FooterPartition_UL);

// Smart pointer for the footer—NULL if not located
PartitionPtr Footer;

// Read the footer if the header locates it
if(FooterPos > 0)
{
  File->Seek(FooterPos);
  Footer = File->ReadPartition();
}
```

Partitions can be written using MXFFile method WritePartition():

```
// Build an MXFFile object
MXFFilePtr File = new MXFFile;

// Open a new MXF file called Test.mxf
File->OpenNew("Test.mxf");

// Build a new header partition in "Header"
...

// Write the header
File->WritePartition(Header);
```

The above code snippet writes a header partition, but without metadata. MDObjects are added to a partition object using the following Partition method:

```
void AddMetadata(MDObjectPtr NewObject);
```

AddMetadata() will add the specified MDObject, and any other MDObjects strongly referenced from it, to the partition. In standard MXF files, all MDObjects are strongly referenced, directly or indirectly, from the preface set so this is usually the only one that needs to be added.

The partition can now be written with its metadata as follows:

```
// Build a new header partition in "Header"
...

// Build new header metadata with a preface in "Preface"
...

// Attach the metadata to the header partition object
Header->AddMetadata(Preface);

// Write the header including metadata
File->WritePartition(Header);
```

Partition properties such as the current and previous partition positions and the count of header metadata bytes are automatically configured during the WritePartition() call.

If the metadata is changed after the objects are added to a partition, but before the partition is written, the partition will need to be updated using the following method:

```
void UpdateMetadata(MDObjectPtr NewObject);
```

Header metadata can be read from a partition using the ReadMetadata() method of a Partition object as follows:

```
// Read the first partition in the file (the header)
PartitionPtr Header = File->ReadPartition();

// Read the header metadata and report the number of bytes read
Length HeaderBytes = Header->ReadMetadata();
```

The metadata items read are added to two MDObjectList properties of the Partition. Every set or pack is added to the list AllMetadata, and those that are not the target of a strong reference are also added to the list TopLevelMetadata.

Finding and Reading the "Master" Partition

An MXF file contains a *master* instance of header metadata, which is the most up-to-date version and, when possible, should be the version used by an application reading the file. This master copy is usually located in the header partition; however, that partition may be flagged as open, in which case the file's footer partition will contain the master metadata. The following MXFFile method will locate and read the master partition.

```
PartitionPtr ReadMasterPartition();
```
Locate and read the partition pack of the partition containing the master metadata instance

ReadMasterPartition() checks the header partition; if it is closed, it is read and returned. Otherwise the footer is located and read; providing this footer partition contains metadata, the footer pack is returned.

Note that not only does this process require random access to the source file, but that a damaged or partial file may not contain a valid master partition, in which case ReadMasterPartition() will return NULL.

Higher-Level Metadata Classes

Standard MXF structural metadata components can be read and written as MDObjects. However, they can also be represented by classes that encapsulate the specific semantics of that set. Each of these higher-level classes contains an MDObjectPtr called Object that holds the basic metadata object and whose value is exposed by the same set-and-get methods used with MDObject. A brief description of each class follows.

Metadata

An object of class Metadata holds data relating to the top level of the structural metadata for a partition. Key Metadata methods are:

```
void SetTime(void);
```
Set the file modification time to the current time

```
void SetTime(std::string TimeStamp);
```
Set the file modification time to the specified time

```
void SetOP(ULPtr OP);
```
Set the operational pattern label

```
PackagePtr AddMaterialPackage();
```
Add a new material package (a package name and UMID can also be supplied)

```
PackagePtr AddFilePackage();
```
Add a new top-level file package (a package name and UMID can also be supplied)

```
PackagePtr AddSourcePackage();
```
Add a new lower-level source package (a package name and UMID can also be supplied)

A list of packages within the metadata is available as property Packages.

Package

Objects of class Package hold data relating to material and source packages. Key Package methods are:

```
TrackPtr AddTimecodeTrack(Rational EditRate, std::string TrackName, UInt32 TrackID);
```
Add a timecode track to this package (TrackName and TrackID may be omitted)

```
TrackPtr AddPictureTrack(Rational EditRate, std::string TrackName, UInt32 TrackID);
```
Add a picture track to this package (TrackName and TrackID may be omitted)

```
TrackPtr AddSoundTrack(Rational EditRate, std::string TrackName, UInt32 TrackID);
```
Add a sound track to this package (TrackName and TrackID may be omitted)

```
TrackPtr AddDataTrack(Rational EditRate, std::string TrackName, UInt32 TrackID);
```
Add a data track to this package (TrackName and TrackID may be omitted)

```
TrackPtr AddDMTrack(…)
```
Add a descriptive metadata track to this package; the parameters indicate the type of DM Track to add:

For a timeline DM track:
```
    Rational EditRate, std::string TrackName, UInt32 TrackID
```

For an event DM track:
```
    Rational EditRate, Length DefaultDuration, std::string TrackName, UInt32 TrackID
```

For a static DM track:
```
    std::string TrackName, UInt32 TrackID
```

In all the above methods TrackName and TrackID may be omitted

A list of tracks within the package is available as property Tracks.

Track

Objects of class Track hold data relating to a track within a package. All MXF tracks have exactly one sequence and so objects of class Track represent a track/sequence pair.

Key Track methods are:

```
SourceClipPtr AddSourceClip(Length Duration);
```
Add a SourceClip to a track (used with essence tracks), Duration may be omitted for "unknown"

```
TimecodeComponentPtr AddTimecodeComponent(Position Start, Length Duration);
```
Add a TimecodeComponent to a track, Start may be omitted for zero, Duration may be omitted for "unknown"

```
DMSegmentPtr AddDMSegment(Position EventStart, Length Duration);
```
Add a DMSegment to a track, EventStart should be omitted or set to −1 if not on an event track, Duration may be omitted for "unknown"

```
DMSourceClipPtr AddDMSourceClip(Length Duration);
```
Add a DMSourceClip to a track, Duration may be omitted for "unknown"

A list of SourceClips, TimecodeComponents, and DMSegments within the track is available as property Components.

SourceClip

Objects of class SourceClip hold data relating to a source clip within an essence track.

Key SourceClip methods are:

```
bool MakeLink(TrackPtr SourceTrack, Position StartPosition = 0);
```
Make a link to a specified track

```
void SetDuration(Length Duration = -1);
```
Set the duration for this SourceClip and update the track's sequence (-1 = Unknown)

TimecodeComponent

Objects of class TimecodeComponent hold data relating to a timecode component within a time-code track.

The most significant TimecodeComponent method is:

```
void SetDuration(Length Duration = -1);
```
Set the duration for this TimecodeComponent and update the track's sequence (-1 = Unknown)

DMSegment

Objects of class DMSegment hold data relating to a DMSegment within a descriptive metadata track.

Key DMSegment methods are:

```
bool MakeLink(MDObjectPtr DMFramework);
```
Make a link to a specified DMFramework

```
void SetDuration(Length Duration = -1);
```
Set the duration for this DMSegment and update the track's sequence (-1 = Unknown)

Using Higher-Level Metadata Classes

The higher-level classes, defined above, can be used to build structural metadata as follows:

```
// Define an edit rate of 25Hz
Rational EditRate(25,1);

// Define the length of the essence of 128 frames
Length Duration = 128;

// Build the metadata set
MetadataPtr Meta = new Metadata();

// Add a material package
PackagePtr MPackage = Meta->AddMaterialPackage("This file's material package");

// Add a timecode track to the material package
TrackPtr MTCTrack = MPackage->AddTimecodeTrack(EditRate);
MTCTrack->AddTimecodeComponent(Duration);

// Add a picture track to the material package
TrackPtr MPTrack = MPackage->AddPictureTrack(EditRate, "Picture Track (MP)");
SourceClipPtr MPClip = MPTrack->AddSourceClip(Duration);

// Add a file source package
PackagePtr FPackage = Meta->AddFilePackage("Main file package");

// Add a timecode track to the file source package
TrackPtr FTCTrack = FPackage->AddTimecodeTrack(EditRate);
FTCTrack->AddTimecodeComponent(Duration);

// Add a picture track to the file source package
TrackPtr FPTrack = FPackage->AddPictureTrack(EditRate, "Picture Track (FP)");
FPTrack->AddSourceClip(Duration);

// Link the material package picture track to the file source package picture track
MPClip->MakeLink(FPTrack);
```

Descriptive Metadata

Rather than a single descriptive metadata set, MXF allows different descriptive metadata schemes to be defined. Because of this there are no high-level classes defined for descriptive metadata, other than those that form the descriptive metadata tracks. This means that descriptive metadata must be constructed using MDObjects. The following example shows adding a simple DMS-1 production framework to the metadata created above:

```
// Add a timeline DM track, with a single DMSegment
TrackPtr DMTrack = MPackage->AddDMTrack(EditRate);
DMSegmentPtr DMSeg = AddDMSegment(0, Duration);

// Build a new production framework set
MDObjectPtr PFrame = new MDObject(ProductionFramework_UL);

// Populate the production framework properties
PFrame->SetString(FrameworkExtendedTextLanguageCode_UL, "EN");
PFrame->SetString(FrameworkTitle_UL, "My Production");

// Build a new titles set
MDObjectPtr TSet = new MDObject(Titles_UL);

// Populate the titles set properties
TSet->SetString(MainTitle_UL, "Birth of a File Format");
TSet->SetString(WorkingTitle_UL, "The MXF film");

// Add the titles set to the production framework
MDObjectPtr TSLink = TSet->AddChild(TitlesSets_UL)->AddChild();
TSLink->MakeLink(TSet);

// Add the completed production framework to the DM track
DMSeg->MakeLink(PFrame);
```

Note that there can be more than one Titles set in a production framework, so the TitlesSets property is an unordered batch of strong references to Titles sets. Because of this, the linking requires two AddChild() calls to be made. The first call adds the TitlesSets batch; the second call adds an entry to that batch, a smart pointer to which is returned as TSLink. Next the MakeLink() method is used to build the strong reference from the new entry in the TitlesSet batch to the actual Titles set.

Reading Higher-Level Metadata

When metadata is read from an MXF file using the Partition::ReadMetadata() method, it is held in memory as a collection of MDObjects. Once these have been read they can be parsed into higher-level objects using the following Partition method:

```
MetadataPtr ParseMetadata();
```
Build a set of high-level metadata objects for all the relevant MDObjects in this partition

Essence

Some essence-processing systems will require specialized software for reading and writing essence data—such as where the essence data is processed by hardware. In these cases, the standard MXFLib functions may be used for handling metadata and locating partitions, with custom code processing the essence. However, in the majority of cases, the standard essence reading and writing classes can provide a complete and efficient solution.

KLVObject Class

All essence reading and writing in MXFLib is based on the KLVObject class. KLVObjects represent the contents of a single KLV within an MXF file. As this KLV could be very large (especially with clip-wrapped essence), the value field is not always completely held in memory. Generally, when a KLVObject is read from file, only the key and length are loaded. This allows the item to be identified and decisions to be made about the handling of the value.

Key KLVObject methods:

```
ULPtr GetUL();
```
Returns a pointer to the UL Key of the KLV

```
Length GetLength();
```
Returns the length of the value field of the KLV

```
Length ReadData(Length Size);
```
Reads the first *Size* bytes of the value field

```
Length ReadDataFrom(Position Offset, Length Size);
```
Reads *Size* bytes of the value starting at *Offset*

```
Length WriteData(Length Size);
```
Writes *Size* bytes of data to the value

```
Length WriteDataTo(Position Offset, Length Size);
```
Writes *Size* bytes of data to *Offset* in the value

```
DataChunk &GetData();
```
Returns a reference to the DataChunk holding (a section of) the Value

```
UInt32 GetGCTrackNumber()
```
Returns the TrackNumber of this item if it is a GC Essence KLV

```
GCElementKind GetGCElementKind()
```
Returns the ElementKind of this item if it is a GC Essence KLV

Encrypted Essence—KLVEObject

Some MXF files contain essence encrypted according to the SMPTE 423M. These are read into KLVEObjects, a subclass of KLVObject.

Key KLVEObject methods, in addition to all KLVObject methods, are:

```
void SetEncrypt(EncryptPtr Handler)
```
Set the encryption handler to encrypt the contained essence

```
void SetDecrypt(DecryptPtr Handler)
```
Set the decryption handler to decrypt the contained essence

```
void SetPlaintextOffset(Length Offset);
```
Set the number of plaintext bytes at the start of the value

```
Length GetPlaintextOffset();
```
Get the number of plaintext bytes at the start of the value

With the decryption handler correctly set and initialized (see details below) calls to ReadData() and ReadDataFrom() will read the encrypted data, decrypt it, and place the decrypted data in the object's DataChunk. Similarly with the correct encryption handler, calls to WriteData() and WriteDataTo() will encrypt the data contained in the DataChunk before writing to the MXF file. This means that the KLVEObject will behave almost exactly as a KLVObject representing a plaintext version of the same essence. The only significant restriction is that if the value is read or written in chunks each one must follow the previous one exactly. Any attempt to issue calls to ReadData()/ReadDataFrom() or WriteData()/WriteDataTo() that either move backwards or skip forwards will cause an error to be issued and no data will be returned or written. This restriction is caused by the fact that most common encryption and decryption algorithms only work correctly if the data is processed sequentially.

Encryption/Decryption Handlers

Encryption and decryption routines are linked to KLVEObjects using encryption and decryption handlers. Each handler is derived from the Encrypt_Base or Decrypt_Base abstract super-class. The methods that need to be supplied by derived encryption classes are:

```
virtual bool SetKey(UInt32 KeySize, const UInt8 *Key) = 0;
```
Set an encryption key—return true if the key is accepted

```
virtual bool SetIV(UInt32 IVSize, const UInt8 *IV, bool Force = false) = 0;
```
Set an encryption Initialization Vector—return false if the IV is not set
If the IV can be chained from the previous block the IV will not be set, unless Force is true

```
virtual DataChunkPtr Encrypt(UInt32 Size, const UInt8 *Data) = 0;
```
Encrypt the data and return it in a new DataChunk—return NULL if unsuccessful

```
virtual bool CanEncryptInPlace(UInt32 BlockSize = 0) = 0;
```
Return true if a block of the specified size, or all possible sizes if BlockSize is zero, can be encrypted in-place

```
virtual bool EncryptInPlace(UInt32 Size, UInt8 *Data) = 0;
```
Encrypt data bytes in-place—return true if the encryption was successful

If the encryption algorithm can encrypt the data in the same buffer used to supply the plaintext, the process is likely to be more efficient; however, not all algorithms can be implemented practically in place, and so they will need to return the encrypted data in a new buffer. This is especially true if the size of the encrypted data may be different than the plaintext. Encryption handlers need to supply all the above methods, even if they do not support encryption in place; however, these should simply return false from EncryptInPlace().

The methods that need to be supplied by derived decryption classes are:

```
virtual bool SetKey(UInt32 KeySize, const UInt8 *Key) = 0;
```
Set a decryption key—return true if the key is accepted

```
virtual bool SetIV(UInt32 IVSize, const UInt8 *IV, bool Force = false) = 0;
```
Set a decryption Initialization Vector—return false if the IV is not set
If the IV can be chained from the previous block the IV will not be set, unless Force is true

```
virtual DataChunkPtr Decrypt(UInt32 Size, const UInt8 *Data) = 0;
```
Decrypt the data and return it in a new DataChunk—return NULL if unsuccessful

```
virtual bool CanDecryptInPlace(UInt32 BlockSize = 0) = 0;
```
Return true if a block of the specified size, or all possible sizes if BlockSize is zero, can be decrypted in-place

```
virtual bool DecryptInPlace(UInt32 Size, UInt8 *Data) = 0;
```
Decrypt data bytes in-place—return true if the decryption appears to be successful

The encryption and decryption handler super-classes also provide versions of methods such as SetKey, SetIV, Encrypt, and Decrypt that take a DataChunk or a DataChunkPtr as the parameter, but these are simply converted to calls to the UInt8 pointer versions and so don't need to be replaced in derived classes.

MXFLib contains a sample application, called mxfcrypt, that uses OpenSSL to implement SMPTE 423M encryption and decryption of MXF files.

Essence Reading—BodyReader

The MXF File Format allows a great deal of flexibility in the arrangement of essence within the file body. This can make reading the essence quite difficult, as there is no easy way to know in advance what essence to expect next. The solution is to use a *callback* system where handlers are defined for each essence stream that receive calls when data from the related stream is read from the file. Identification of essence data and dispatching callbacks to handlers is performed by objects of class BodyReader.

Read Handlers

When a BodyReader finds a partition containing generic container wrapped essence, it will select a GCReader object (generally there will be one GCReader per-BodySID in use) that will read each essence KLV and dispatch callbacks. The callbacks are directed to handler objects derived from class GCReadHandler_Base. These callbacks are in the form of calls to member function HandleData() whose prototype is shown here:

```
virtual bool HandleData(GCReaderPtr Caller, KLVObjectPtr Object) = 0;
```
Handle a "chunk" of data that has been read from the file

Parameter Object is a pointer to the KLVObject that represents the current essence KLV. The key and length will have been read, but the value will not have been read before the handler is called. Parameter Caller is a pointer to the calling GCReader. The handler can flag errors back to the calling GCReader and BodyReader by returning false from HandleData() this will cause parsing to stop and an error state to be passed up to the application.

Two key member functions of GCReader can be called using the Caller pointer; StopReading() will instruct the GCReader to stop reading the current partition and HandleData() will force a KLVObject to be handled as if it had been read from the file.

The ability to pass KLVObjects back to be handled again is key to the way encrypted data is read. The following code snippet shows how this can be achieved:

```
bool DecryptHandler::HandleData(GCReaderPtr Caller, KLVObjectPtr Object)
{
  // Construct a KLVEObject from the KLVObject containing the encrypted data
  KLVEObjectPtr KLVE = new KLVEObject(Object);

  // Set a decryption wrapper for this KLV
  Decryptor *Dec = new Decryptor;
  KLVE->SetDecrypt(Dec);

  // Set the decryption key
  Dec->SetKey( DecryptKey , DecryptKeySize );

  // Note: The decryption IV will be read from the KLVEObject automatically

  // Pass decryption wrapped data back for handling
  return Caller->HandleData(SmartPtr_Cast(KLVE, KLVObject));
}
```

Setting Read Handlers

Read handlers can be set for the whole body, for all KLVs in a specific Generic Container, or for each stream within each container. The following code snippets show each of these cases.

Whole Body Handling

```
// Set up a body reader for the source file
BodyReaderPtr BodyParser = new BodyReader(InFile);

// Set the a default handler for all essence KLVs
BodyParser->SetDefaultHandler(WholeBodyHandler);

// Create GCReaders for all containers
for_each(BodySID)
{
  BodyParser->MakeGCReader(BodySID);
}
```

Here a BodyReader is created and linked to a source MXF file. A handler (WholeBodyHandler) is set that will receive all essence KLVs found in the file. Finally GCReaders are built for all Body-SIDs of interest; this allows a subset of essence streams to be processed—any partitions found that contain essence of a BodySID for which there is no GCReader will be skipped.

Per-Container Handling

```
// Set up a body reader for the source file
BodyReaderPtr BodyParser = new BodyReader(InFile);

// Create GCReaders for all containers
for_each(BodySID)
{
  BodyParser->MakeGCReader(BodySID, Handler[BodySID]);
}
```

In this version no default handler is set for the BodyReader. Instead each GCReader is supplied with its own handler (in this case from an array).

Per-Stream Handling

```
// Set up a body reader for the source file
BodyReaderPtr BodyParser = new BodyReader(InFile);

// Create GCReaders for all containers
for_each(BodySID)
{
 BodyParser->MakeGCReader(BodySID);

 GCReaderPtr ThisReader = BodyParser->GetGCReader(BodySID);
 for_each(TrackNumber in BodySID)
 {
   ThisReader->SetDataHandler(TrackNumber, Handler[BodySID][TrackNumber]);
 }
}
```

Here each time a GCReader is built for a particular BodySID, handlers are added for each of the essence streams in that container. The handlers are set on a TrackNumber basis as this is the mechanism used for identifying essence streams in the MXF generic container. If any KLVs are encountered within the container that do not have a matching handler (or are not GC essence stream KLVs), then they will be discarded. This is not a satisfactory way to handle "unknown" KLVs in the body if the essence is being written to another MXF file—they may be useful data that is dark to this application. This can be solved as follows:

```
// Set up a body reader for the source file
BodyReaderPtr BodyParser = new BodyReader(InFile);

// Create GCReaders for all containers
for_each(BodySID)
{
 BodyParser->MakeGCReader(BodySID, DefaultHandler[BodySID]);

 GCReaderPtr ThisReader = BodyParser->GetGCReader(BodySID);
 for_each(TrackNumber in BodySID)
 {
   ThisReader->SetDataHandler(TrackNumber, Handler[BodySID][TrackNumber]);
 }
}
```

In this modified version a default handler is added to each GCReader that will receive all KLVs not handled by the per-stream handlers. Every KLV encountered within the container that does not have a defined per-stream handler will be sent to the default handler, even if they are not essence KLVs. The exception to this rule is Filler KLVs; these are never sent to the default handler. If there is a requirement to track filler, a separate handler can be defined per-body or per-container:

```
BodyParser->SetDefaultHandler(WholeBodyHandler);
BodyParser->SetFillerHandler(WholeBodyFillerHandler);
```

or:

```
BodyParser->MakeGCReader(BodySID, DefHandler[BodySID], FillHandler[BodySID]);
```

Encrypted Essence Read Handlers

Encrypted essence KLVs encountered in an essence container will not conform to the generic container key format and so will be included in those sent to the default handler unless a specific Encryption Handler is allocated. This can also be done on a per-body or per-container basis:

```
BodyParser->SetEncryptionHandler(WholeBodyEncryptionHandler);
```

or:

```
ThisReader->SetEncryptionHandler(EncHandler[BodySID]);
```

Note that unlike the default KLV handler and filler handler the encryption handler is not set during the GCReader constructor. This is because it is envisaged that in most cases there will only be one encryption handler per-body.

Reading the Essence Data

So far we have seen how to set up the essence read handlers, but no data has yet been read. This is performed by BodyReader function ReadFromFile(). This function will read all essence data from the next partition in the file (or the first partition if none has yet been processed). Note that the BodyReader maintains its own read pointer so moving to a different location is achieved by using BodyReader's own Seek() function rather than MXFFile::Seek(). However, BodyReader **will** move the attached MXFFile's read pointer during calls to ReadFromFile() and ReadData() or ReadDataFrom() on the resulting KLVObjects.

ReadFromFile() only processes a single partition and, providing there was no error, it will leave its read pointer at the start of the next partition pack. This allows metadata and index segments to be read from each partition pack in the body of the file if required. If an error occurs during the processing of a partition the read pointer is unlikely to be at the start of the next partition pack. This can be tested with function IsAtPartition() and the start of the next partition pack can be located with ReSync(). There may be valid reasons for a call to ReadFromFile() to abandon reading a partition that is not necessarily an error—these reasons can only be judged on a per-application basis.

The following code snippet shows the principle of reading essence from an MXF file:

```
for(;;)
{
  // If we are interested in the body metadata or index segments
  if(ReadingMetadata || ReadingIndex)
  {
    // Seek to the start of the current partition
    InFile->Seek(BodyParser->Tell());

    // Read the Partition Pack
    PartitionPtr ThisPartition = InFile->ReadPartition();

    // Read metadata if required
    if(ReadingMetadata) ThisPartition->ReadMetadata();

    // Read index segments if required
    if(ReadingIndex) ThisPartition->ReadIndex();
  }

  // Read and parse the essence
  bool Result = BodyParser->ReadFromFile();

  // Either end-of-file, an error, or the partition was abandoned
  if(!Result)
  {
    // If end-of-file we are all done
    if(BodyParser()->Eof()) break;

    // If an error or an abandoned partition skip to the next partition
    BodyParser->ReSync();
  }
}
```

Essence Writing

Essence Sources and Essence Parsers

EssenceSource Class

EssenceSource is an abstract super-class that defines the interface between the non-MXF essence world and MXF. It provides essence data in wrapping-unit-sized chunks as well as information to allow the BodyWriter to wrap the data in a generic container.

Key EssenceSource methods that must be defined:

- GetEssenceDataSize()—Returns the size in bytes of the next essence chunk to be wrapped.

- GetEssenceData (Size, MaxSize)—Reads the next Size bytes of next chunk to be wrapped.

- EndOfItem()—Returns true if last call to GetEssenceData() gave the end of a wrapping item.

- GetCurrentPosition()—Returns the position, in edit units, within the stream.

The following code snippet shows a simple EssenceSource:

```
// Simple essence source class that reads fixed-size data from a file
class SimpleSource : public EssenceSource
{
protected:
    Position CurrentPos;
    FileHandle File;

public:
    // Open the file when the source is created
    SimpleSource() : EssenceSource()
    {
        CurrentPos = 0;
        File = FileOpenRead("DataFile.dat");
    }

    // Close the file when all done
    ~SimpleSource() { FileClose(File); }

    // Essence from this source is always 1024-bytes per edit unit
    Length GetEssenceDataSize(void) { return 1024; }

    // Read the next chunk of data
    DataChunkPtr GetEssenceData(Length Size, Length MaxSize)
    {
        // Signal the end of data when all is done
        if(!FileValid(File) || FileEOF(File)) return NULL;

        // Make a new data chunk to hold the data
        DataChunkPtr Ret = new DataChunk(1024);

        // Read the next data
        Length Bytes = FileRead(File, Ret->Data, 1024);
        Ret.Resize(Bytes);

        // Exit with nothing if out of data
        if(Bytes == 0) return NULL;

        CurrentPos++;

        return Ret;
    }

    // Get the current position, in edit units
    Position GetCurrentPosition(void) { return CurrentPos; }
};
```

Note that this is a trivial example; there are a number of other functions required for a full EssenceSource class, and GetEssenceData() does not ensure that the returned data is no larger than MaxSize. However, it illustrates the principle and a genuine EssenceSource may be little more than twice as large.

EssenceSource objects can be written to provide essence from any source such as a hardware interface to a camera or a DirectShow stream but there is a special case for essence that originates in a file. Non-MXF essence files can be parsed by objects of the class EssenceParser, which provide an interface between those files and MXF via an EssenceSource.

EssenceParser Class

An EssenceParser will examine the contents of an open file and provide appropriate tools to parse the file, as well as details about the available options for wrapping that file—such as clip wrapping, frame wrapping, and line wrapping. This parsing is provided by EssenceSubParser objects—one for each type of essence file. MXFLib contains a number of EssenceSubParsers for types such as MPEG2 video elementary streams, Wave audio essence, DV audio/video essence, TIFF and DPX images. Other sub-parsers can be written and registered with the EssenceParser class via the AddNewSubParserType() static method.

There are two methods of specific interest when using EssenceParser.

IdentifyEssence(InFile)

Offers the open file to each of the registered EssenceSubParser types and returns a std::list of smart pointers to ParserDescriptor objects. Each ParserDescriptor object holds a smart pointer to an EssenceSubParser that is ready to parse the essence and a list of essence-streams identified within the file (some essence formats, such as MPEG Transport Streams, may contain multiple essence streams).

SelectWrappingOption(InFile, PDList, ForceEditRate, ForceWrap)

Takes the list provided by IdentifyEssence and optionally an edit rate and wrapping mode (such as FrameWrap) and configures an appropriate sub-parser to provide essence from the file for the specified wrapping. Returns a smart pointer to a configuration object holding a smart pointer to the EssenceSubParser and various other configuration details including an Essence Descriptor for the essence as it will be wrapped.

Once the EssenceSubParser is selected a call to its GetEssenceSource method will provide a pointer to an EssenceSource that will supply the parsed essence packaged for the selected wrapping.

The following code snippet shows how to use an EssenceParser to acquire an EssenceSource for a given file:

```
// Open the file to be parsed
FileHandle InFile = FileOpen("InputFile.dat");

if(!FileValid(InFile))
{
 error("Couldn't open input file\n");
 return false;
}

// Build an Essence Parser
EssenceParserPtr MainParser = new EssenceParser;

// Identify the essence
ParserDescriptorListPtr PDList = MainParser->IdentifyEssence(InFile);

// If no entries were returned we couldn't identify the essence
if(PDList.size() == 0)
{
 error("Couldn't identify the essence type\n");
 return false;
}

// Select an appropriate wrapping mode
WrappingConfigPtr WrapConfig = MainParser->SelectWrappingOption(InFile, PDList);

// If nothing was returned we couldn't identify the essence
if(!WrapConfig)
{
 error("Couldn't identify a suitable wrapping mode\n");
 return false;
}

// Get the EssenceSource
EssenceSourcePtr Source = WrapConfig->Parser->GetEssenceSource(WrapConfig->Stream);
```

Instantiating EssenceSubParser Objects Directly

If an application knows the format of an essence file and which EssenceSubParser can be used to parse that essence, it is possible to bypass the EssenceParser and avoid the inefficiency of letting other sub-parsers check the file.

It is still important to call the IdentifyEssence method of the sub-parser as there are numerous secondary effects of this call—such as building the Essence Descriptor metadata object.

Once the sub-parser has identified the essence in the file, the wrapping options must be set. This can be achieved by a call to method IdentifyWrappingOptions, which returns a list of available options, and method Use, which selects one of these options. An alternative method of choosing the wrapping option is to use the EssenceParser::SelectWrappingOption method. This will query the EssenceSubParser objects offered in the ParserDescriptorList and will select an appropriate wrapping option. In this case, there will only be one sub-parser referenced by the list. This option is especially useful if the EssenceParser::IdentifyEssence method may also be called.

The following code snippet shows how known essence types may be identified more efficiently by directly instantiating sub-parsers. Note also that the DV essence uses a non-standard sub-parser rather than the one supplied with MXFLib (another reason to call sub-parsers directly):

```
// Build an Essence Parser
EssenceParserPtr MainParser = new EssenceParser;

// List to receive the parser descriptors
ParserDescriptorListPtr PDList;

if( SearchString(Filename, ".mpg") )
{
 // Identify MPEG essence types
 EssenceSubParserPtr SubParser = new MPEG2_VES_EssenceSubParser;
 PDList = SubParser->IdentifyEssence(InFile);
}
else if( SearchString(Filename, ".dv") )
{
 // Identify DV essence types
 EssenceSubParserPtr SubParser = new MySpecialDVSubParser;
 PDList = SubParser->IdentifyEssence(InFile);
}
else
{
 // Identify all other essence types
 PDList = MainParser->IdentifyEssence(InFile);
}

// If no entries were returned we couldn't identify the essence
if(PDList.size() == 0)
{
 error("Couldn't identify the essence type\n");
 return false;
}

// Select an appropriate wrapping mode
WrappingConfigPtr WrapConfig = MainParser->SelectWrappingOption(InFile, PDList);
```

It is worth using the above code as an example of the use of smart pointers in MXFLib. If the essence type is MPEG, a new MPEG 2_VES_EssenceSubParser object will be created and an EssenceSubParserPtr called SubParser will reference it. The pointer type is a pointer to an EssenceSubParser, which is the base class of MPEG2_VES_EssenceSubParser. At this point, the sub-parser is owned by a single smart pointer. Now one of two things will happen: If the file is not one that can be parsed by this sub-parser, then no more references will be made and the sub-parser will be deleted when pointer SubParser goes out of scope (at the closing brace of the if statement). Alternatively the sub-parser may identify one or more valid streams to wrap and will build a ParserDescriptor for each. These descriptor objects each include a smart pointer to the sub-parser, so it is now multiply owned and will not be deleted when the SubParser pointer goes out of scope. If the subsequent call to SelectWrappingOption is successful, a new WrappingConfig object will be created that also contains a smart pointer to the selected sub-parser. Now the ownership of the sub-parser is shared between this wrapping configuration object and one or more parser descriptors in PDList. If PDList is deleted or goes out of scope, then the sub-parser will be solely owned by WrapConfig and will be deleted when it goes out of scope. In fact it is good practice to ensure that the ParserDescriptorList is cleared as soon as practical after the call to SelectWrappingOption. This is because more than one sub-parser may have identified the essence and so will still be in memory because PDList contains smart pointers to each sub-parser. Once one of sub-parsers has been chosen, the rest of them should be deleted, which will happen automatically if PDList is cleared. This can be achieved with the following line:

```
// Clear all other parsers
PDList = NULL;
```

Essence Writing—BodyWriter

The MXF File Format allows a great deal of flexibility in the arrangement of essence and index data within the file body. Managing the writing of this data can be complex, especially if there are a number of essence containers. The BodyWriter class simplifies this task while still giving a high degree of flexibility.

The BodyWriter manages not only the writing of essence and index data but also the file header and footer as well as any metadata repetitions within the file body. In fact, the BodyWriter writes the whole file, not just the body!

Key methods of the BodyWriter class are:

```
BodyWriter(MXFFilePtr DestFile);
```
Construct a new BodyWriter object attached to the specified output MXF file

```
bool AddStream(BodyStreamPtr Stream);
```
Add the specified BodyStream to the writer (returns false on error)

```
void SetKAG(UInt32 NewKAG);
```
Set the KLV Alignment Grid value to use for partitions written by this writer

```
void SetPartition(PartitionPtr ThePartition);
```
Set the template partition pack, with attached metadata, to use when writing partitions

```
void WriteHeader(bool IsClosed, bool IsComplete);
```
Write the header partition

```
void WriteBody();
```
Write the file body, including all essence supplied by the attached BodyStream objects

```
void WriteFooter(bool WriteMetadata = false, bool IsComplete = true);
```
Write the file footer, optionally with metadata

The WriteBody() method will write the complete body, returning when all body partitions have been written. If greater control is required, for example to manage the size of body partitions when multiplexing multiple essence containers, the following method can be used:

```
Length WritePartition(Length Duration = 0, Length MaxPartitionSize = 0);
```
Write the next partition of the file body, including essence.

If Duration is greater than 0, the partition will end as soon as possible after writing that many edit units of essence—or when no more essence is available for this partition. If MaxPartitionSize is greater than 0, the partition will end as soon as possible after that many bytes have been written in the partition. When all body partitions have been written, method BodyDone() returns true.

A BodyWriter object manages a number of BodyStream objects, each of which represents an Essence Container within the file. A BodyStream has a master essence stream and zero or more sub-streams. Master and sub-streams are all attached to EssenceSource objects that provide packetized essence ready for wrapping.

Key methods of the BodyStream class are:

```
BodyStream(UInt32 SID, EssenceSourcePtr EssSource);
```
Construct a new BodyStream object with a given stream ID and attached to an EssenceSource

```
void AddSubStream(EssenceSourcePtr &SubSource);
```
Add a sub-stream attached to an EssenceSource

```
void SetWrapType(WrapType NewWrapType);
```
Set the wrapping type for this stream, where WrapType is StreamWrapFrame or StreamWrapClip

BodyWriter Example

The following code shows how to write an MXF file with an interleaved body containing frame-wrapped MPEG picture essence and uncompressed wave sound essence.

```
// Open a new output MXF file
MXFFilePtr OutFile = new MXFFile;
OutFile->OpenNew("Test.mxf");

// Build a new BodyStream using BodySID 1 and an existing picture essence source
BodyStream Stream = new BodyStream(1, MPEGSource);

// Add an existing sound essence source as a sub-stream
Stream->AddSubStream(WaveSource);

// Set frame wrapping
Stream->SetWrapType(StreamWrapFrame);

// Build a new BodyWriter attached to the output file
BodyWriterPtr Writer = new BodyWriter(OutFile);

// Add the interleaved essence stream to the writer
Writer->AddStream(Stream);

// Supply an existing partition pack, with associated metadata
Writer->SetPartition(ThisPartition);
```

```
// Write the closed and complete header
Writer->WriteHeader(true, true);

// Write the body
Writer->WriteBody();

// Write the footer, without metadata
Writer->WriteFooter(false);

// Close the MXF file
OutFile->Close();
```

Advanced Essence Reading and Writing

The BodyReader and BodyWriter classes provide easy access to MXF essence; however, advanced users may find this handholding goes too far and reduces the available options. In these cases, more flexibility can be achieved using classes such as GCReader and GCWriter at the cost of more complex code. Such advanced topics are beyond the scope of this introductory chapter, but readers can be assured that more options are available if required.

Indexing

IndexTable Class

Index tables are represented in MXFLib by objects of the class IndexTable. The most important method of the IndexTable class is:

```
IndexPosPtr Lookup(Position EditUnit, int SubItem = 0, bool Reorder = true);
```
Perform an index table lookup

Lookup returns a smart pointer to an IndexPos structure containing the following properties:

```
Position ThisPos;
```
The position (in file package edit units) of the data of which Location indexes the start

```
Position Location;
```
The byte offset of the start of ThisPos edit unit in the essence container

```
Rational PosOffset;
```
The temporal offset for this edit unit (if Offset = true, otherwise undefined)

```
bool Exact;
```
True, if ThisPos is the requested edit unit and the location is for the requested sub-item
False, if it is a preceeding edit unit or the requested sub-item could not be identified

```
bool OtherPos;
```
True if ThisPos is not the requested edit unit (because that edit unit is not indexed)

```
bool Offset;
```
True if there is a temporal offset (stored in PosOffset, only set if Exact = true)

```
Int8 KeyFrameOffset;
```
The offset in edit units to the previous key frame

```
Int64 KeyLocation;
```
The location of the start of the keyframe edit unit in the essence container

```
UInt8 Flags;
```
The flags for this edit unit (zero if ThisPos is not the requested edit unit)

Several of the properties in the IndexPos structure are related to the fact that index tables do not necessarily index every edit unit in an essence container, or every sub-stream within an interleaved container. If the requested edit unit, or the requested sub-stream, is not indexed, then the result of a Lookup() call will be the nearest indexed item *before* the requested item. The following table shows what is returned depending on whether the requested item is contained in the index table:

Sub-Stream Indexed:	Exact	OtherPos	What Is Indexed by Location
Requested edit unit located in index	true	false	The first KLV of this sub-stream in the requested edit unit.
Requested edit unit not located in index	false	true	The first KLV of the first sub-stream in a preceding edit unit whose position is given by ThisPos.
Sub-Stream Not Indexed:	Exact	OtherPos	What Is Indexed by Location
Requested edit unit located in index	false	false	The first KLV of the first sub-stream in the requested edit unit.
Requested edit unit not located in index	false	true	The first KLV of the first sub-stream in a preceding edit unit whose position is given by ThisPos.

Table 14.1 IndexPos property values for exact or closest-match conditions

Reading Index Table Data

Whenever a partition is read from an MXF file, it may contain one or more index table segments. This can be easily determined by checking the IndexSID property of the partition pack for a non-zero value. If the partition does contain index table data, that data can be read using the ReadIndex() method of the Partition class. The following example shows this:

```
PartitionPtr Header = ReadPartition();

UInt32 IndexSID = Header->GetUInt(IndexSID_UL);
if(IndexSID != 0)
{
  // Read the index segments from this partition and add them to the correct table
  Header->ReadIndex(IndexTableMap[IndexSID]);
}
```

Generating and Writing Index Tables

The BodyWriter class manages the generating and writing of index tables. These tables can be complete or sparse, and can be written in various locations. The indexing is configured using the IndexType enumeration that includes the following options:

VBR[4] Indexing options:

`StreamIndexFullFooter`
A full index table will be written in the footer if possible (or an isolated partition just before the footer if another index is going to use the footer)

`StreamIndexSparseFooter`
A sparse index table will be written in the footer if possible (or an isolated partition just before the footer if another index is going to use the footer)

`StreamIndexSprinkled`
A full index table will be sprinkled through the file; one chunk in each of this essence's body partitions, and one in or just before the footer

`StreamIndexSprinkledIsolated`
A full index table will be sprinkled through the file; one chunk in an isolated partition following each of this essence's body partitions

CBR[5] Indexing options:

`StreamIndexCBRHeader`
A CBR index table will be written in the header (or an isolated partition following the header if another index table exists in the header)

`StreamIndexCBRHeaderIsolated`
A CBR index table will be written in an isolated partition following the header

`StreamIndexCBRFooter`
A CBR index table will be written in the footer if possible (or an isolated partition just before the footer if another index is going to use the footer)

`StreamIndexCBRBody`
A CBR index table will be written in each body partition for this stream

`StreamIndexCBRIsolated`
A CBR index table will be written in an isolated body partition following each partition of this stream

`StreamIndexCBRPreIsolated`
A CBR index table will be written in an isolated body partition before each partition of this stream

These options are set on a per-BodyStream basis using the SetIndexType() method and the index stream ID is set using the SetIndexSID() method. If desired, options can be combined using bit-wise "or," or using the AddIndexType() method. The following example code would write segments of a full VBR index table in each body partition, with a sparse index table in the footer containing one entry for the first edit unit in each partition. The body partitions will be limited to 16 edit units each.

[4] Variable Bit Rate

[5] Constant Bit Rate

```
// Open a new output MXF file
MXFFilePtr OutFile = new MXFFile;
OutFile->OpenNew("Test.mxf");

// Build a new BodyStream using BodySID 1 and an existing picture essence source
BodyStream Stream = new BodyStream(1, MPEGSource);

// Add an existing sound essence source as a sub-stream
Stream->AddSubStream(WaveSource);

// Set frame wrapping
Stream->SetWrapType(StreamWrapFrame);

// Configure a sprinkled full index table, and a sparse version in the footer
Stream->SetIndexType(StreamIndexSprinkled);
Stream->AddIndexType(StreamIndexSparseFooter);
Stream->SetIndexSID(2);

// Build a new BodyWriter attached to the output file
BodyWriterPtr Writer = new BodyWriter(OutFile);

// Add the interleaved essence stream to the writer
Writer->AddStream(Stream);

// Supply an existing partition pack, with associated metadata
Writer->SetPartition(ThisPartition);

// Write the closed and complete header
Writer->WriteHeader(true, true);

// Write the body, starting a new partition every 16 edit units
while(!Writer->BodyDone())
{
  Writer->WritePartition(16);
}

// Write the footer, without metadata
Writer->WriteFooter(false);

// Close the MXF file
OutFile->Close();
```

Summary

The following table gives a summary of the classes introduced in this chapter:

Basic Types:	
DataChunk	A resizable memory block
Identifier<>	An identifier, the base class for the following:
UL	A Universal Label
UUID	A Universally Unique IDentifier
UMID	A Universal Material IDentifier
Smart Pointers:	
SmartPtr<>	A smart pointer to an object, responsible for deleting objects when no longer required

RefCount<>	The base class from which all smart pointer targets must be derived, counts the number of smart pointers referencing each object.
Metadata Items:	
MDObject	A metadata object, this may be a set or pack containing other MDObjects, or a single item with a value.
MDValue	The value of a metadata object
MXF File Components:	
MXFFile	An MXF file
RIP	The Random Index Pack, records the position of every partition pack in an MXF file.
Partition	A single partition pack, optionally with an attached instance of header metadata.
Higher-Level Metadata:	
Metadata	The root of an instance of header metadata, roughly equates to the Preface set.
Package	A package within a Metadata object
Track	A track within a Package object
SourceClip	A SourceClip within an essence Track object
TimecodeComponent	A TimecodeComponent within a timecode Track object
DMSegment	A DMSegment within a descriptive metadata Track object
Essence Processing:	
KLVObject	A single KLV of essence data
KLVEObject	An encrypted KLV of essence data
Encrypt_Base	The base class from which to derive classes to handle encrypting of KLVEObjects.
Decrypt_Base	The base class from which to derive classes to handle decrypting of KLVEObjects.
BodyReader	An object that handles reading of an entire MXF file body.
GCReader	An object that reads and parses the KLVs from a single Generic Container.
GCReadHandler_Base	The base class from which to derive classes to receive essence KLVs read by a GCReader.
BodyWriter	An object that handles writing of an entire MXF file.
BodyStream	A single stream within a BodyWriter.
GCWriter	An object that writes a single Generic Container.
EssenceSource	Supplies data to be written by a GCWriter.
EssenceParser	Parses a non-MXF essence file and provides an EssenceSource object to supply essence to a GCWriter.
EssenceSubParser	Parses a specific type of non-MXF essence file, this is the base class for a number of specialized essence sub-parsers.
Indexing:	
IndexTable	An index table for a single Essence Container
IndexPos	The result of an index table look-up

Table 14.2 MXFLib classes introduced in this chapter

15 Practical Examples and Approaches to Using MXF

At the time of writing this book, MXF is a new file interchange and storage format that is set to play a significant part in professional program production and distribution. MXF will allow interoperability between equipment and systems from different manufacturers and interoperability between systems belonging to different organizations. MXF is already central to major investments of many broadcasters and program makers.

In planning this book, it was thought that it would be informative to give examples of the different approaches taken by end users and by manufacturers when adopting this new format for their production systems and equipment.

As an illustration of architectures being planned and implemented by broadcasters, we have contributions from NOB and the BBC; these are public service broadcasters in the Netherlands and the UK, respectively.

From industry, we have short contributions from Grass Valley, Panasonic, Sony, Pinnacle Systems, and Omneon Video Networks. These contributions show, in their different ways, the issues that each company has faced in implementing and integrating MXF into their product range.

We hope that, through these different perspectives, the reader can get a flavor of the real-world application of MXF.

MXF and Infrastructure Change at NOB
Henk den Bok

Embracing the Digital Workflow

The broadcast processes for the Dutch public television channels went through a fundamental change in 2005. Almost all activities associated with public television broadcasting migrated into the digital world. Four large projects, that had been germinating and cross-fertilizing for some years, came to fruition:

- **PowerStation** provides a completely new broadcast scheduling database. In this database, broadcasters can announce and specify television programs from their own offices, and channel coordinators can compile announced programs into a broadcast schedule.

- The **Digital Facility** (abbreviated as DDV in Dutch) will provide a completely new broadcast platform, entirely file-based and using the MXF standard.

- The **Digital Archive**, the new media library of the Netherlands Institute for Sound and Vision, will provide a future-proof repository for television and radio programs—everything, of course, in digital (file-based) format.

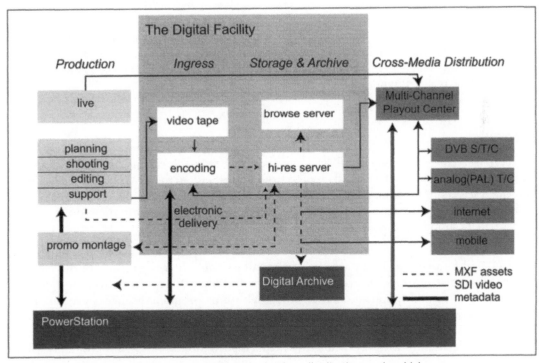

Figure 15.1 Process architecture for television production, distribution, and archiving

- The **Multi-Channel Playout** center (planned for 2006) and interfaced closely to the DDV, will be realized as the last step and will integrate the functionality of control rooms of three television channels into one multi-channel control room.

NOB Cross Media Facilities, primarily responsible for the continuity of the entire public broadcast process, hosts and operates these three platforms and, together with other interested parties, has been heavily involved in the design and implementation of the platform.

Contribution

A broadcast is "born" in PowerStation, sometimes months in advance. In the course of the period prior to broadcasting, more and more information about the program is entered as metadata into the database. Two important steps in this process involve linking the final copy of the broadcast material with the information in the database and placing the program in the final broadcast schedule.

DDV will broadcast all programs from video servers rather than tape. However, when DDV goes online, many Dutch broadcasters will, at first, continue to submit their programs on Digital Betacam tape. To make the transition as smooth as possible, DDV provides two ingest stations to facilitate the conversion from tape to MXF as part of the platform.

Broadcasters who are keen on getting rid of the burden of transferring material to and from video tape will be able to upload their programs directly to the *inbox* of DDV. Using MXF as the interchange format, together with a limited set of permitted encodings within MXF (D10-30 and D10-50 at first), a clear-cut interface is realized, leaving little room for confusion and sources for error. In this way, a high level of fidelity in, and interoperability with, the new digitally submitted material can be realized right away.

Playout

All material is collected in file-base format one week prior to broadcast, on a large and fast storage facility (SAN). Driven by the playlists rooted from PowerStation, the MXF files are uploaded to the video servers in time, waiting to be played out. After broadcast, the material is kept on the SAN for another two weeks to allow interested parties to obtain copies or to transfer the material to permanent storage (archiving).

Having all television programs online in the best possible quality enables unique opportunities to reuse the assets in novel ways. Two areas will particularly benefit from the digital availability of these assets through streamlining their workflows: a) Internet delivery will obtain a higher level of flexibility and automation when publishing programs as media streams via the ability to transcode them directly from MXF and b) new theme channels, launched in DTV and on the Internet, will be able to integrate easily re-runs of recent programs into their automated playlists. In this way, true cross-media distribution of television programs will be facilitated.

Archiving

Since MXF and the contained media encodings are based on international standards, MXF is particularly suitable for archiving essence in a digital way. To make use of this new possibility, the Digital Archive was closely interfaced with the DDV to provide a transparent transfer to permanent storage of MXF files selected by the librarians of the Netherlands Institute for Sound and Vision. The metadata belonging to the program is transferred from PowerStation to the Netherlands Institute for Sound and Vision's own library database.

Metadata

In the new system, the metadata is strictly separated from the essence. In the broadcasting system, the metadata is handled entirely in PowerStation. This situation is partly dictated by the workflow, formal responsibilities, and the way the Dutch broadcasting industry is organized. Since many parties in the Netherlands are involved in this process, the most logical choice was to maintain the metadata database in a central location rather than passing fragments of it, together with the content, through the system. At the same time, the separation between metadata and essence eliminated the need for complex software-handling metadata in MXF so that MXF implementations of various vendors could be used with minimal modification, and the tight deployment schedule of the project could be met.

After broadcast, the metadata from PowerStation is imported into the searchable databases of the Digital Archive, enriched, annotated, and managed by the Netherlands Institute for Sound and Vision.

MXF within a BBC Production Infrastructure
Peter Brightwell

Context

In recent years, the BBC has been addressing many of the issues that will become critical to ensure its long-term future as a provider of high-quality content to the British public and to external customers. Rapid advances in digital technology offer great potential for providing audiences with much more content accessed on a wide range of platforms, provided that material can be produced efficiently and cost effectively.

As part of this work, the BBC is addressing a number of key technical areas:

- There will be a significant move away from the present dependence on physical media, especially tapes. Storage, duplication, transportation, and management of tapes currently form a significant proportion of the BBC's costs. Staff will soon use desktop and handheld tools to replace VHS tapes for viewing, logging, and approval. It is anticipated that all production will be tapeless by 2010.

- A strategy for identifying, tracking, describing, reusing, and delivering content in a systematic way is being developed. This includes defining corporate standards for creation and management of metadata, and development of a distributed asset-management architecture.

- Closer working relationships with external organizations are being fostered, including secure remote viewing and electronic delivery of content.

- The BBC's network, storage, and security infrastructure is being significantly enhanced to support wide-scale working with electronic audiovisual content, including HD.

- The current rapidly changing nature of the business means that the BBC recognizes the crucial and timely need to adopt open standards. This is particularly true for archive content formats, where wrong decisions taken now may have repercussions for years to come. MXF will be a key standard in this area.

"OneVision" Project within the BBC

OneVision was an important project to inform the BBC's strategic deployment of tapeless production services. It reached a successful completion in early 2005. OneVision has included pilots and studies with technical, business, and process elements. Its most high-profile activity was to pilot the use of desktop production tools to support the Natural History Unit's *Planet Earth* production in Bristol. This was complemented by a set of trials and workshops at the BBC's Information and Archive (I&A) department in west London. This included development of a system—Atlas—to test I&A processes supporting the transition to tapeless production. Atlas provided a centrally managed archive with cataloguing, storage, and content management functions. It used products from several vendors, and has implemented an interoperability solution, summarized in Figure 15.2.

A transaction server routed XML messages between the different systems to achieve functions such as requesting new content to be ingested and registering content in the archive. The broadcast quality content took the form of long-GOP MPEG-2 422P@ML video and uncompressed stereo audio. These were wrapped within MXF OP1a files with video and audio interleaved on a frame basis. The files were generated and used by the ingest

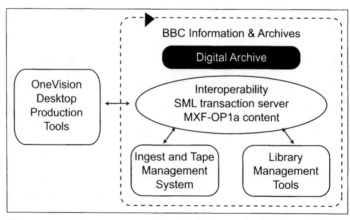

Figure 15.2 Systems associated with the BBC OneVision project

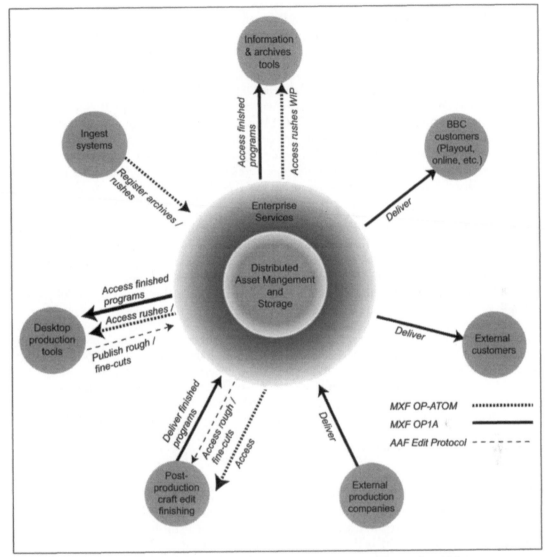

Figure 15.3 Target architecture for interoperability in production, distribution, and archiving

system (TMD Mediaflex and Snell & Wilcox MPEG Mastering Unit) and the OneVision desktop production tool (Siemens Colledia for Production, as used for the Natural History Unit pilot).

Future Architecture

The OneVision project also studied longer-term interoperability requirements of digital production systems. This involved modeling the business and IT context and requirements and deriving a logical architecture to support interoperability, as summarized in Figure 15.3. Although content may be physically held in a wide range of locations and on a variety of types of storage, all content will be registered, located, and accessed by means of a set of services that are common across the enterprise.

The use of standard formats, in particular MXF and AAF, features prominently in this architecture. Rushes and work-in-progress (WIP) material will often be accessed directly by production tools, and so where possible the audio and video will be held as separate MXF OP-Atom files. For example, an OP1a file captured on a Sony XDCAM camera would be "decomposed" into its individual video and audio elements. AAF Edit Protocol files will be used as the basis for edit interchange between desktop production tools and craft/finishing tools, ranging from simple cuts-only compositions, as produced by a basic assembly operation, to a fine-cut including some effects. The AAF files will reference the OP-Atom files using UMIDs. The use of AAF files to carry logging metadata is also being considered.

For delivery of finished programs, use of regular MXF operating patterns is more appropriate. At the time of writing, the BBC envisages the use of OP1a as this is most widely supported by manufacturers. However, as the specifications are refined—e.g., for delivery to playout areas, adoption of higher patterns may be required. Transformation services will be needed to perform any required wrapping and unwrapping of MXF files and conversion between different operating patterns. These services may also perform essence format transcoding; for example a) to support delivery of a finished program in MPEG-2 where rushes are in a mixture of DV and MPEG, and b) manipulation of metadata such as TV Anytime metadata (to support home storage), which may be derived from the production metadata. AAF/MXF will provide a suitable standard interface format for such services. Another service, the Production Gateway, will provide a standard interface for secure delivery of content between the BBC and its external customers and providers. Although this service will support multiple formats, MXF and AAF will be preferred, as the service will be able to make use of the metadata contained within them. Trials of some technical aspects of the Production Gateway are already in progress, as are trials of delivery of MXF OP1a files to playout areas.

Next Steps

At the time of writing, the BBC and its technology services provider (Siemens Business Systems) are defining a reference architecture for the future deployment of digital production services. This will build upon the work of the OneVision project, and the use of MXF and AAF is expected to form an important part of the long-term success of this service. It will be informed by ongoing research and specification of how these formats can best support the BBC's changing requirements for content creation. The future definition of requirements for the generation and management of metadata and unique identifiers will further aid progress, as will user trials and technical assessment of MXF/AAF-capable hardware and software. This needs to be supported by the development of easy-to-use compliance-testing tools.

Implementing MXF for Grass Valley Products
Bob Edge

Implementing MXF (SMPTE 377M) in the Grass Valley product line offered some interesting choices. The Grass Valley product line includes cameras, telecine/datacine machines, baseband video to IP network encoders/decoders, news systems, professional servers, and other related products. We have always planned to offer MXF in our product families while continuing to support our existing professional audio/video network interchange format; GXF (SMPTE 360M). End users have been storing GXF files in IT storage-based archives since around 1995. End users also have a large installed base of our products, and other vendors have offered products that use GXF as a network-transfer format or as an archive file format for IT storage libraries. This section will focus on a few products that provide an overview of the ideas and architectures we employed to add MXF to our product line.

Grass Valley's experience with GXF has served as a foundation for planning our implementations of MXF. Using this experience, and working with some end users, resulted in MXF implementation strategies and plans that protected the installed base and, more importantly, allowed us to offer forward-looking designs.

Grass Valley is developing a new series of IT storage-based cameras and a VTR-like device that utilize the same storage media. Disk and flash memory-based cameras are a relatively new class of products, and we are using MXF as the on-disk file format. These products are the first in the industry to use this specific removable disk so backwards-compatibility is not a constraint.

An MXF Strategy for Existing Server and News Systems

A few key decisions resulted in a sound strategy for supporting MXF in the Grass Valley news and server products. First, we felt a commitment to continue to support our current GXF format in addition to MXF. This provided end users with the opportunity to make a MXF or GXF choice based on what was best for their operation, workflow, and business. Another fundamental decision was the concept of a modular (hardware and software) solution for the installed base of server systems. End users of Grass Valley Servers have purchased thousands of network-capable GXF servers. Many of these use Fibre-Channel IP networks with new installations using Gigabit Ethernet and some looking to 10 Gigabit Ethernet for future installations. Offering a hardware module with appropriate network interfaces and file-format conversion software allowed established facilities to transition to MXF at a nominal cost while protecting a significant capital investment.

Interchange and Interoperation of MXF and GXF Files

One challenge facing the design team was dealing with differences in the basic design of MXF and GXF. At a distance, they both do the same thing and have similar features, even though the formats are very different at the bitstream level. As one gets closer to the details, one discovers that MXF has more features and a richer metadata model. Indeed, MXF has a very broad feature set with many options; so many different types of MXF files can be created.

When we started working on MXF as an interchange format between servers and news systems, we found that a limited set of features were in use. The conversion between the basic audio-video file formats is conceptually simple and to date no serious problems have been found.

Both formats support user-defined metadata transport. In GXF this is known as *user data* and in MXF it is called *dark metadata*. MXF's dark metadata is stored as GXF user-data when MXF files are captured. Likewise, GXF user data is encoded as MXF dark metadata for outbound files. These features allow interoperation of MXF and GXF files in established facilities and applications.

MXF has a rich descriptive metadata set called DMS-1. This metadata scheme covers a very broad set of applications and can become quite large in terms of storage requirements. GXF user data storage space is limited in some older products; therefore, some MXF files with large DMS-1 metadata sets cannot be stored. At the time this was written, this has not been a problem at any end user sites. We are working to expand our new products metadata capabilities.

Solutions for Servers

Offering a modular hardware/software device has some significant benefits. To begin with, this device supports network technology conversions between Fibre Channel and Gigabit Ethernet if needed and it allows an interchange of GXF and MXF files. The types of network technologies supported and file formats conversions offered can be augmented in the future.

The modular file format and network converter also allow a direct connection to the large-scale shared storage system that is part of the Grass Valley product line. When devices are directly attached to the Grass Valley shared storage system, very high file transfer bandwidths have been achieved.

A key advantage of this architecture is having a physically and logically modular component to do these conversions; this allows software upgrades without changing most of an on-air station's devices. With a short-term need to respond to initial misunderstandings in the MXF standards and initial interoperability difficulties between different vendors' implementations, having a modular and easily upgradeable component provides a substantial benefit for Grass Valley and the end user. The basic strategy of offering a modular device to support MXF across existing Grass Valley's server product family has proven to be a sound plan.

One of the next steps for MXF on our servers is an integrated MXF offering; that is, MXF at the network interface, not "on the disk." We will continue to store files on disk as *codec-ready* files. These files are the basic data streams that an encoder generates or a decoder needs. Examples are PCM audio streams or MPEG Elementary Streams. The objective is to minimize processing during real-time operations. We convert MXF files to and from the storage format during the file transfer operation. The MXF-to-internal format-conversion software is based on the proven software developed and deployed in the modular device discussed above.

Storing codec-ready streams on disk has several advantages. First of all, having codec-ready streams improves the performance for a given hardware base. More importantly, we can deal with any anomalies such as large chunks of metadata in the MXF file during the non-real-time file-transfer process instead of during real-time playout operations. This also allows us to continue to support GXF and possibly other formats (e.g., QuickTime) with a single playout and record engine.

There are a few disadvantages. The most important is if an incorrectly formed MXF file is received, the file transfer will fail to complete. In an operational situation this is probably an advantage since a captured file would probably not be playable. The early discovery that the contents of a file are corrupted gives the operations staff time to take appropriate actions.

MXF "On the Disk"

In certain applications, using MXF as the basic storage format has clear advantages. One of these applications is an IT storage-based camera and another is archiving material on IT storage systems. Since an archive is intended to store material for a long time and direct playout of many concurrent channels is not an important feature, MXF is a good candidate archive file format. It has respectable industry acceptance and is well documented.

For an IT storage-based camera and an associated VTR-like device, MXF offers several advantages; the most important is the promise of interoperability with a wide range of other IT products. To facilitate interoperability, Grass Valley is using an interleaved audio-video MXF file. The interleaved audio-video stream behaves like a traditional device so the effort required to use the new technologies in established applications is minimized.

Another situation where MXF is a good choice as a storage format is for store-and-forward servers, encoders, and similar devices. The key is to use MXF in applications where the format of the file can be controlled and the "on the disk" format does not need to be edited beyond simple changes like setting in-points and out-points.

News Systems

A different approach has been taken with the Grass Valley News Systems. We also have a large installed base; however, the goals were different. Our first objective was to offer an integrated MXF (MXF at the network interface) to satisfy our current end users' needs. We also wanted to support a wide range of MXF devices, including cameras that are based on IT storage devices, as well as MXF file I/O on Ethernet.

One of the key characteristics of Grass Valley's news products is simple, fast-editing solutions. Storing MXF on the disk makes certain operations, such as voice-overs and off-speed play of the video with normal play of the audio, difficult. When trying to do voice-overs in an interleaved MXF file, one must replace the audio stream in the MXF file. Since the audio in an interleaved MXF file is mixed with the video and MXF's structural and possibly descriptive metadata, this is a complex solution.

A commercially available MXF tool set was used to build the integrated MXF solution for the news systems. This allowed us to offer a wide range of capabilities with reasonable performance in a timely manner. We also believe that using a commercial MXF SDK (software developers kit) will allow us to respond to technology changes quickly, which is critical in the news environment. For the foreseeable future, we will continue to use the native news systems on-disk format. MXF conversions are done during the file-transfer process. For the news products we believed using an off-the-shelf SDK was the best approach. This approach has proven to be a sound choice.

Additional Grass Valley Products and MXF

As time goes on, more products will offer material exchanges with IP networks and MXF as an interchange format. In some cases, these products may have limited memory, low latency requirements, limited power available, or other constraints. Specific device features and requirements will result in using different strategies for each device family's MXF implementations. For example, a device that is implemented largely in hardware with limited computing resources and low latency requirements will probably not find workable commercial MXF software development kits. Integration with the low-level hardware and meeting the low-latency requirements with generalized designs is difficult at best.

In some circumstances, the industry appears to be uncertain about the use of MXF. This occurs when formats such as DPX (SMPTE 268M) or MPEG Transport Streams are already very deeply established in existing workflows. In some of these cases, the conversion costs are higher than the potential savings from using a single format. In this situation, the established format will continue to be used. In some situations, the conversion costs and payoff are moderate; converting to MXF may be deferred.

For products where no established file format is in use, MXF is a sound choice. The specifics of the design and implementation can be tailored to the end user's requirements without significant investments in compatibility features or compromising the new design to work with established architectures. The new cameras and an associated VTR-like device that are using flash memory cards and removable disk storage devices are good examples.

Conclusions

In certain cases, an optimized MXF implementation offers high performance, low latency, or other advantages. In other situations, a commercially available MXF development kit is the best choice. Grass Valley will continue to use different strategies so we can offer the best products to the end user.

We have found that using MXF on data storage devices is a very good solution for IT storage-based cameras, archives, and store-and-forward servers. Trying to edit MXF files or performing rich playout operations (off speed play...) can be difficult. One solution is the MXF's Op-Atom single track format. However, we have found that, in some situations, using codec-ready streams on disk to be a simpler solution as this has very good performance characteristics. As with many things, one solution does not fit all problems.

Grass Valley has a wide range of products that support many applications in broadcasting. These begin with the cameras, and datacine machines and continue to routers, switchers, servers, and news systems, with many supporting products along the material path. Implementing MXF in these products requires some thoughtful design decisions to maximize the value to the end-user while supporting current workflows and anticipating future needs.

Many vendors are offering MXF products today. The promise of multi-vendor interoperable exchange of material in the file domain will result in substantial changes in production, post-production, and station operations.

Panasonic: Use of MXF in a Solid-State-Memory-Based Video Acquisition System

Hideaki Mita, Haruo Ohta, Hideki Ohtaka, Tatsushi Bannai, Tsutomu Tanaka (Panasonic AVC Networks Company, Matsushita Electric Industrial Co. Ltd. Osaka)

Philip Livingston (Panasonic Broadcast & Television Systems Co., Secaucus, NJ)

Overview

Panasonic P2 was developed as the next-generation acquisition system and, by creating truly "non-linear acquisition," was designed to liberate users from the linear limitations of tape and to overcome the operational limitations of optical disk in the field. Modeled after the well-understood solid-state digital still camera revolution, P2 uses four "off-the-shelf" postage-stamp-sized Consumer SD card semiconductor memory devices housed in a rugged PCMCIA Type II form-factor case with a CardBus interface to form a high speed, random-access recording media.

When Panasonic considered development of a solid-state-memory-based video acquisition system, it rapidly became clear that the equipment would be far more computer-like than VTR-like. In addition, while it also became clear that "non-linear acquisition" meant that the resultant recording could be accessed immediately and played or edited randomly, it was equally clear that users would expect to move the content quickly and seamlessly to platforms and products provided by other manufacturers and to perform those operations without file conversion. This dictated that the content storage method and organization would be a file format (as opposed to a tape format) and it should be both "standardized' and appropriate to the processes that logically follow acquisition. In consultation with several leading non-linear editing system manufacturers, Panasonic decided MXF Operational Pattern Atom was the most appropriate format in which to store the audio and video essence data.

Content File Format

Content File Structure

The structure of the content on a P2 card consists of logical *clips* that each contain a video MXF file, one or more audio MXF files, an XML clip metadata file, as well as implementation dependent optional files; i.e. a Bitmap thumbnail file, a WAVE voice memo file, and an MPEG-4 proxy file. These files are stored under directories within the P2 card as shown in Figure 15.4.

A Unique Material IDentifier (UMID), a globally unique ID for A/V material, is generated and assigned to the content on the P2

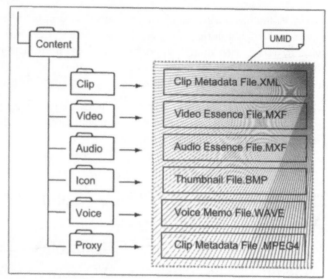

Figure 15.4 Content structure on P2 card

card at the time of the content creation (recording), and is given to the video and audio essence, the clip meta-data, and the proxy. Should the content be moved or copied from the P2 card to another media that has a different directory structure wherein the link between files of a given clip could be lost, it is possible to associate the essence and its related metadata using the UMID.

MXF Essence File

As described earlier, MXF (Material eXchange Format) is a fundamental file exchange format consisting of several operational patterns (OP) or file configurations that have been standardized by the SMPTE. To assure interoperability with other devices and systems, the P2 system adopted MXF, and more specifically uses OP-Atom (Operational Pattern Atom), one of the operational patterns within the MXF standard. Op-Atom was selected as the data structure because the video essence and the audio essence are wrapped independently and stored in separated files, making

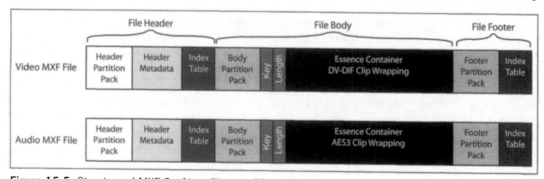

Figure 15.5 Structure of MXF Op-Atom file on a P2 card

them immediately accessible and suitable for the independent (split) audio or video editing after recording. Since direct and immediate editing is one of the key features of the P2 system, Op-Atom is the most suitable structure within the MXF standard.

The structure of the Op-Atom audio and video essence files recorded on the P2 card is based on the structure recommended in the MXF standard, and is shown in Figure 15.5. Each file consists of three parts, a file header, a file body, and a file footer. The file header contains a header partition pack, the header metadata, and an index table. The file body is a single essence container that carries the video or audio data. In the video MXF file, the DV, DVCPRO, DVCPRO50, or DVCPROHD compressed data is embedded in a DV-DIF stream and mapped into the essence container. In the audio MXF file, uncompressed AES-3 audio data for each channel is mapped into the essence container; i.e. in the case of 4-channel audio, four Audio MXF files exist. The file footer contains the index table, which is the same as that in the file header.

In order to give greater flexibility in audio editing, Clip wrapping has been adopted for the P2 system in both video and audio essence files. By using clip wrapping and setting the edit unit to an audio sample, audio editing is possible at any point on an audio sample basis.

Metadata

The P2 system has two types of metadata: *structural metadata* and *descriptive metadata*. Structural metadata is the metadata required for full-featured use of the video and audio essence stored in the MXF file, such as the parameters of the essence. On the other hand, the descriptive metadata represents additional information about the video and audio essence that adds functionality and efficiency.

The structural metadata is recorded in both the header metadata section of the MXF files and the clip metadata XML file. While it is expected that the metadata structure and information carried

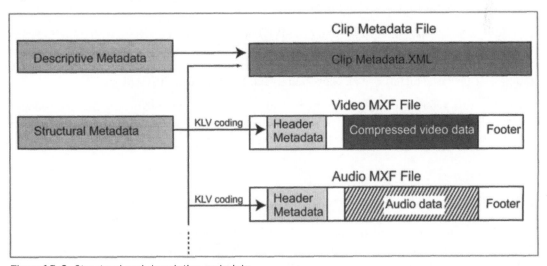

Figure15.6 Structural and descriptive metadata

in the MXF file will be popular and useful in the future, having a separate XML metadata file that also carries the structural metadata enables easy conversion of P2 content to the data structure of an existing system with the same essence structure but a different header structure. This is useful in viewing applications and it also allows editing using the clip metadata and the proxy data without using the essence file, so users who have decided to use the optional proxy and low resolution editing to augment the direct editing features in the P2 system will find their requirements facilitated by this structure.

Sony: Practical Applications for MXF
Paul Cameron

In this section, we take a look at three technologies from Sony that make use of MXF. The first is the e-VTR, a bridge between the traditional tape-based world and contemporary disk-based production environments. The second is XDCAM, a disk-based camcorder. The third is the XPRI non-linear editor which, in its latest version, fully integrates MXF as part of the craft of making programs.

The e-VTR

Introducing the e-VTR

The Sony e-VTR is a machine that bridges the gap between the tape-based world and the disk-based world, between the stream and the file. This transfer has never been an easy one for television and post-production companies to handle.

The Sony e-VTR is a combination of an MSW-2000 series studio machine with a high performance network adaptor. The MSW-2000 series (known as "IMX") is a ½-inch recording format that records MPEG2 422P@ML, I-frame only, at 50 Mbit/s. The addition of a network adaptor allows ½" tape based material to be converted to and interface with MXF files.

There are two versions of this adaptor, the older BKMW-2000 and the recently introduced BKMW-3000. Both are available as a kit that can be fitted to any existing MSW-2000 series machine to turn it into an e-VTR, or pre-built into the VTR.

e-VTR Features

The e-VTR operates in conjunction with a computer, commonly a PC. This computer acts as an e-VTR controller and a destination for the MXF file produced by the e-VTR. The 2000 version of e-VTR supports ftp-based transfer over an Ethernet network, while the 3000 version also allows for http-based transfers, allowing MXF files to be sent through network firewalls, something that is not possible under ftp control with the 2000 version.

e-VTR Manager

e-VTR Manager is a software utility that allows users to specify files from the material on the tape in the e-VTR and download the material as an MXF file into the computer. The beginning and end of each MXF file is specified by its in-point and out-point on tape. The file details are held in the network adaptor's memory as long as the tape is in the e-VTR.

Telefile Operation

Telefile is a special label that can be attached to any ½" tape. It contains a memory chip, a small radio transceiver, and an aerial. Every e-VTR contains a radio transceiver that uses the radio link to transmit power to the Telefile label and then to send and receive data.

The e-VTR uses Telefile to hold file details when the tape is ejected from the e-VTR. Thus, tapes can be prepared, specifying where MXF files will be created, and the tape placed back into archive. Any user can then take the tape from the archive, view its file list, and extract any MXF file from the tape at the time it is needed.

Lo-Res Proxy Generation

The 3000 version of e-VTR can also produce a low resolution—known as lo-res proxy—copy of the original material. This lo-res proxy can be copied over a network far quicker than its hi-res original, it reacts quicker, and looks perfectly good in non-linear editor interfaces.

The e-VTR proxy MXF files contain MPEG4 15 frame long-GOP video at 1.5Mbps and A-law compressed audio. These files comply with SMPTE 381M and 388M.

e-VTR Manager allows users to select if they want to download the tape material as a hi-res MXF file, a lo-res proxy MXF file, or both hi-res and lo-res files.

Building MXF Files from ½"-Tape Material

The simplest method of building MXF files with an e-VTR is to use the e-VTR Manager software to specify the files, and then use ftp to download these files to the computer. The e-VTR Manager shows all the files specified on the e-VTR. This includes the default files, like "&whole.mxf" for the whole tape, and all the files specified by users. Each file can be specified by size and start timecodes, or by start and end timecodes. At this point they do not actually exist. They are virtual files. The actual MXF files are created when they are downloaded to the computer.

Integrating e-VTR with an Asset Management System

In most systems, the e-VTR is not controlled by the e-VTR Manager and simple ftp control, but by a more complex high-level asset management system which also presents a more friendly user interface. This system still uses ftp commands to control the e-VTR and extract material from the tape as a series of MXF files. However, this extra layer of software isolates the user from the low-level ftp commands and presents a simple interface that makes the whole process easier to control and understand. Furthermore, this software is often integrated with other software elements, such as database management or transmission logging software.

Automating MXF File Generation

There are essentially two methods of automating the process of generating MXF files from ½" tapes. The first is to simply turn the various segments of material on each tape into MXF files on disk. The second is to browse through the tape and select segments that will be turned into MXF files on disk.

Automatic MXF File Creation

Traditionally, archived tapes have existed in two basic forms, single segment tapes and multi-segment tapes. A single segment tape contains one piece of material. A multi-segment tape contains many pieces of material. A movie, or a television program, would probably fill one tape, making it a single segment tape. However, many advertisements, which are often no longer than a few seconds long, are often placed on one tape, making it a multi-segment tape.

A popular method of automatically generating MXF files from archive tapes is to place them in a system comprising an e-VTR, a robotics machine like a Flexicart, and controlling software such as Autocat. Autocat controls Flexicart to read each tape's barcode and enter the details into its database. It then controls Flexicart to move the tapes one by one into the e-VTR. The e-VTR plays each tape converting each segment into an MXF file on the hard disk server.

XDCAM

XDCAM records MXF files right from the start onto removable media held within the camcorder. XDCAM also records lo-res proxy files, thumbnails (index pictures), and metadata, at source, in the camcorder or recorder. However, broadcasters can use XDCAM in much the same way as they would conventional tape, and it allows for a similar or cheaper cost structure to conventional broadcast video tape.

Professional Disk

Professional Disk is the medium used to record XDCAM. It has its roots in DVD which, in turn, has its roots in CD. In particular, Professional Disk is based on DVD-RW and CD-RW, the re-recorderable versions of DVD and CD. The most obvious difference between Professional Disk and both CD and DVD variants is that Professional Disk is encased in a cartridge.

The cartridge allows for a record-disable switch, and a set of coding holes to define the type of Professional Disk, an idea that will become important should a different version of Professional Disk be introduced in the future. Inside the cartridge is a disk with the same dimensions as a CD and DVD. However, the disk has a different layer structure to both CD and DVD.

Basic Data Recording on Professional Disk

Data is recorded to XDCAM as a series of Recording Unit Blocks (RUBs). Each RUB is 64kB large. The disk is recorded from the centre outwards, in common with DVD and CD technology.

The recording is made in a series of annuli, each one containing about two seconds of material. Each annulus comprises many rotations of the disk. Each annulus contains information for high-res material, low-res proxy, audio, and metadata.

When recording is finished, header and footer data are written to the last annulus, and non-real time metadata is written to the non-real time data area. Salvage marker data is written between each annulus. Salvage markers allow XDCAM to solve one of the most crucial problems facing any file-based recording system—that is, what happens if the power dies half way through a recording? Conventional tape recorders do not need to worry about this problem. Any recording up to the point the power is lost are retained. If power is lost and re-established, XDCAM will find that the last clip has no footer and will search back for the last good salvage marker. This is then replaced with a good footer, thus rescuing the last clip.

Editing with MXF in the XPRI Non-Linear Editor

The Sony XPRI non-linear editor (NLE) allows for standard definition, or high definition editing and, with version 7, MXF and XDCAM compliance has been fully integrated.

Traditional Approach to Capturing Material

The traditional method of capturing video and audio material into an NLE is to play a conventional video tape into the NLE and digitize the signal to produce a data stream that can be built into a clip in the hard disk. The traditional digitizing process can only be performed in real time, and the material cannot normally be used until the whole clip is digitized and available in the bin.

Improving the Capture Process with MXF

Using MXF in the XPRI workflow allows clips to be captured into XPRI far quicker than real time. The capture process is no longer a matter of digitizing the material, but simply copying the file. This copy process is often as fast as the network will allow.

Using Lo-Res Proxy Files

The idea of using low-resolution copies of the original video material, so called lo-res proxies, has radically improved the way editors put together programs. Lo-res proxies are highly compressed copies of the original video material. These lo-res MXF files can be copied quickly across a computer network, and once in the NLE, react quicker than the original. Once the sequence is completed, the lo-res proxies can be replaced with their hi-res originals.

Sony: Long-GOP MPEG-2 Mapping for MXF File Storage Applications

Jim Wilkinson

The full specification of the Sony MXF mapping for long-GOP MPEG2 has been published by SMPTE as the Registered Document Disclosure, RDD-9. This section provides a summary of that document. Those parties implementing files conforming to this application specification should refer to the published version of RDD-9 that contains far more detail than can be presented in this section of this chapter.

File Structure

The file structure conforms to MXF operational pattern OP1a (SMPTE 378M).

Figure 15.7 below shows the outline of the MXF file structure. The file consists of one header partition, one or more body partition(s), one footer partition, and is completed with a random index pack.

The audio-visual essence is present only in a sequence of one or more body partitions. The system, picture, sound, and optional data items are mapped into the generic container and placed in each body partition using frame wrapping. A body partition consists of a sequence of edit units (frames) that comprise the MPEG2 GOPs as shown in Figure 15.7. The number of GOPs in a partition can be one or more up to a maximum partition duration of ten seconds.

Because of the long-GOP MPEG structure of the picture item, index tables are segmented and each segment indexes the essence of the *previous* partition. Thus, the first index table segment is present at the beginning of the next partition and the last index table segment is present in the footer partition. The partition pack data structure provides a property to define the size of any index table segment in its partition; thus the presence (or not) and the offset to the essence edit unit is easily decoded.

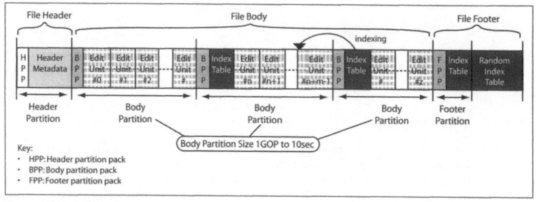

Figure 15.7 Outline of an MXF file

Some aspects of this file structure are indicated below.

- It is only necessary for an encoder to build each index table segment from the previous body partition and body partitions are limited to 10 seconds duration.

- It is easy for a decoder to play out while building indexing information as the file is received.

- It is easy to create a "partial file."

Index Table Usage

The long-GOP essence requires the use of index table segments. Index entry and delta entry arrays are both required. One index table segment is placed at the beginning of each body partition, except for the first body partition, and it indexes the essence of the previous partition. The last index table segment is placed in the footer partition. The relationship between index tables and the essence that it indexes is illustrated in Figure 15.8.

Having each index table segment index the essence of the previous body partition permits real-time creation of MXF files to be performed with minimal buffering and avoids unnecessary delay. In this mapping specification, the picture essence is VBE (Variable Bytes per Element) and the sound essence is CBE (Constant Bytes per Element).

Random Index Pack (RIP)

The random index pack is provided to rapidly locate partitions scattered throughout an MXF file as

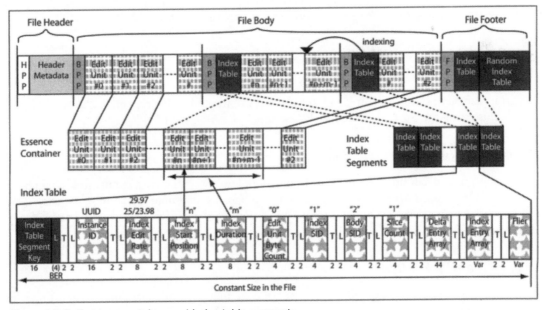

Figure 15.8 Essence container and index table segments

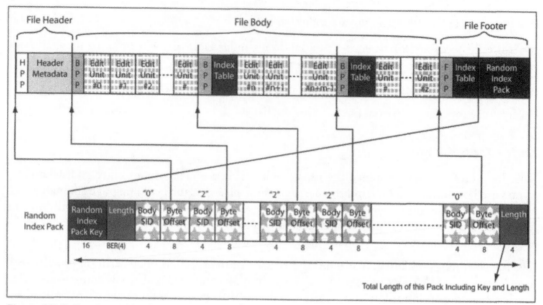

Figure 15.9 Random Index Pack

illustrated in Figure 15.9. This fixed length pack defines the BodySID and Byte Offset to the start of each partition (i.e., the first byte of the partition pack key). This pack can be used by decoders to rapidly access index tables and to find partitions to which an index table points. The random index pack is not required but is highly recommended as a decoder performance enhancement tool. If present in the file, it follows the footer partition and it is always the last KLV item in a file.

Frame-Wrapped Structure

This application specification defines frame-based wrapping only.

An arrangement of system, picture, and sound items in a frame-based wrapping is shown in Figure 15.10 illustrating the use of 4 channels AES3 audio.

Generic Container Specification

This application specification defines each frame to contain a system item; a picture item containing a single KLV wrapped MPEG2 video elementary stream; a sound item containing, typically, 2, 4, or 8 separate AES3 audio channel elements; and an optional data item as illustrated respectively in Figures 15.11, 15.12, 15.13, and 15.14.

Use of the KLV Fill Item

Within any MXF partition containing an essence container with this mapping specification, the KAG value defined in the partition pack has the value of 512 (02.00_h) and the first byte of the key

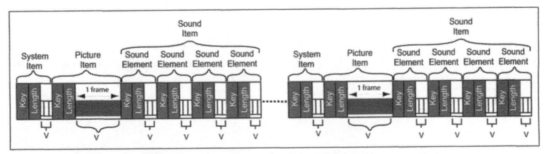

Figure 15.10 Frame wrapping of system, picture, and sound elements

of the first element of each item is aligned to the KLV alignment grid of that partition. For each item in a content package, the length of the KLV fill item should be the minimum required to align to a KAG boundary.

System Item Mapping

The system item in each edit unit consists of a system metadata pack and a package metadata set. The data structure is illustrated in Figure 15.11. The mapping of the system item data complies with that defined in SMPTE 385M. The structure of the package metadata set is defined in SMPTE 385M and items in the set are defined in SMPTE 331M.

Linear timecode (LTC) data is carried in the User Date/Time Stamp, and the UMID and the KLV metadata are carried in Package Metadata set as indicated in Figure 15.11.

UMID (basic or extended)	Tag = 83_h (SMPTE 331M)
KLV metadata	Tag = 88_h (SMPTE 331M)

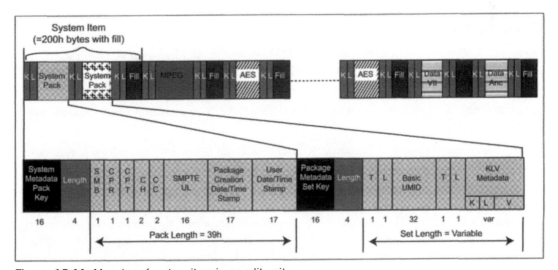

Figure 15.11 Mapping of system item in an edit unit

Picture Item Mapping

The picture item contains a single frame of long-GOP MPEG-2 elementary stream data, thus the data length of each picture element in an edit unit is a variable value. The location of the picture item in each content package is illustrated in Figure 15.12.

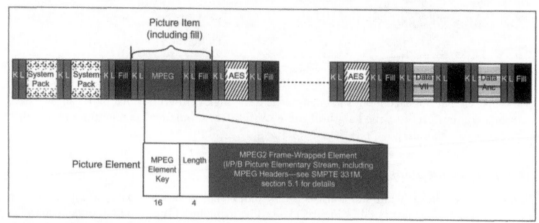

Figure 15.12 Mapping of picture item in edit unit

MPEG2 Temporal Reordering

The compressed video pictures are reordered from their display order according to the MPEG specification. This reordering is applied only to the MPEG elementary stream data. All other items in the content package retain their natural temporal order.

Sound Item Mapping

Each AES3 sound element complies with 382M using the AES3 mapping specification. The mapping of the sound item is as illustrated in Figure 15.13.

The number of audio data channel numbers is limited by the MXF generic container to a theoretical maximum of 128, but current implementations use 2, 4, or 8 channels and a realistic upper limit is 16 channels.

In the case of audio locked to video at 25 content packages per second or multiples, each sound element will contain the same number of samples, for example 1920.

In the case of audio locked to video at 30*1000/1001 content packages per second, the number of samples in each sound element will contain the same number of samples, but the value for each frame will vary to maintain a correct aggregate rate. Typically, the number of samples varies according to a 5-frame sequence, 1602, 1601, 1602, 1601, and 1602. The number of samples in each content package is calculated from the Length field of the surrounding KLV packet, divided by the value of the BlockAlign property of the AES3 Audio Essence Descriptor.

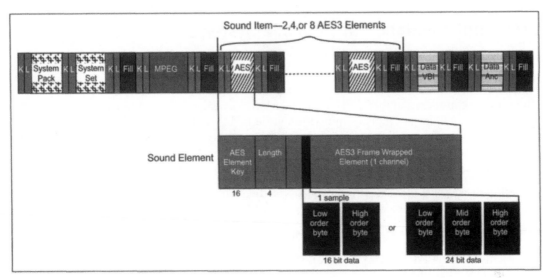

Figure 15.13 Mapping of sound item

In the case of audio locked to video at 24*1000/1001 content packages per second, each element will contain the same number of samples, for example 2002.

Data Item Mapping

Any data item in each edit unit may include two kinds of data element: a VBI line element and an ancillary data packet element. These are both illustrated in Figure 15.14. Both use data elements as specified in SMPTE 331M that are mapped according to SMPTE 385M for use in MXF. Use of either of the data elements in the application specification is optional.

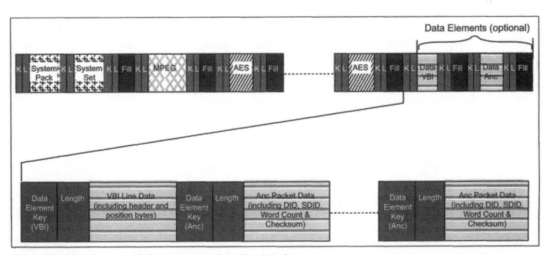

Figure 15.14 Mapping of data elements into the data item

MXF Implementation at Pinnacle Systems
Mike Manlove

The primary consideration that drove Pinnacle's MXF investigation was random file access. The ability to cue and play at any edit unit within a file is required in most of our broadcast server installations and is an absolute necessity for editing products. Due to its importance, and due to the related technical challenges, satisfaction of this requirement was the most time-consuming aspect of the investigation.

The phrase *random access* actually encompasses three different use cases. Listed in order of increasing complexity, these are:

- Play-after-record (play a file after the record has completed).

- Local play-while-record (play during record; record and play devices have direct access to a common storage medium).

- Streaming play-while-record (play during record; file is streamed from the record device's storage medium to the play device's storage medium, or directly to the play device).

There is little difference among these three cases if the only requirement is linear play from the beginning of the file. The need for random access is what makes the problem interesting.

The other considerations were efficient interchange between our server and edit products, ease of implementation (for both capture and playback devices), and compatibility between Pinnacle's products and those of other vendors. The last requirement would seem to be met by virtue of our usage of MXF as the interchange format, but the flexibility of MXF makes it possible to construct legal files that are challenging for some playback devices. Thus, our goal was to develop a straightforward file structure that still offered the necessary random access performance.

The investigation showed that the best fit for our requirements is a partitioned OP1a file with a segmented index table, along with a sparse index table in the footer. A proprietary, external frame table is used to allow random access during recording, as the investigation (summarized below) turned up no other solution that offered the required performance.

The basic file characteristics are:

- Metadata contained in the header and footer.

- Content partitioned by time (new partition every 10 seconds, but each GOP must be contained within a single partition).

- No repeated metadata in body partitions.

- Edit units may be variable size (cannot count on fixed EU size to simplify index table issues).

- Segmented index table. Each body partition contains an index table segment that indexes the preceding partition.

- Sparse index table in the Footer.

- A random index pack is required.

These characteristics were taken from an operational specification that had already been proposed for use among several vendors, so this was a logical starting point. Providing the required random-access performance required an investigation of various index table (IT) implementations. We considered the following possibilities:

1. Complete index table in the header.

2. Complete index table in the footer.

3. Segmented index table.

4. Proprietary external frame table.

Encoder and Decoder Characteristics

There are several Pinnacle Systems devices that transform video and audio essence between MXF and non-MXF formats. Those that accept non-MXF input and produce MXF files are called encoders, and those that accept MXF files and produce non-MXF output are called decoders. The supported non-MXF formats include uncompressed video and audio (either analog or digital), MPEG transport stream, etc. An encoder digitizes and compresses its inputs, if necessary, and generates all the extra data required for wrapping the essence in an MXF file (metadata, index table segments, etc.). A decoder parses the MXF metadata, extracts the essence, decompresses it, if necessary, and presents it in one or more of the supported non-MXF formats.

Encoders and decoders can produce and accept various types of MXF files; they are not restricted to the Pinnacle-standard file type described in this document. The standard file type is used unless some other type is specifically required, as it offers the best random-access performance.

Encoder Implementation Considerations

Putting a complete index table in the header requires the encoder to either pre-allocate room for the index table or rewrite the entire file (with the finished index table) after the file has been completely recorded. Pre-allocation is possible if the file's duration is known in advance, but this is generally not the case in our installations. Rewriting a finished file would be an intolerable waste of I/O bandwidth. Based on these two facts, this option was rejected.

A complete index table in the footer makes no pre-allocation demands on the encoder, but it requires the encoder to keep the growing index table in memory until it can be written out at the end of the encode. The fact that memory is limited places an upper limit on the length of a file, which is a problem. This option was marked as undesirable but it was not immediately rejected.

A segmented index table makes minimal demands on the encoder. No pre-allocation is necessary, and the encoder only needs to keep one partition's worth of index table in memory. This option looked very attractive from the encoder point of view, and it matches the index table disposition described in the basic file characteristics. This was the favored implementation.

We didn't actually consider a proprietary frame table when the investigation was started, but rather after the performance weaknesses of the other options become apparent (as will be discussed below). From an encoder point of view, though, this option presents no serious problems. The encoder must maintain a second open file, but it can update this file at whatever interval is appropriate for the encoder's available memory.

Decoder Performance Considerations

Play-After-Record

The fastest access to a random edit unit will be attained when a complete, contiguous index table is available and the file is not partitioned. The offset of the last edit unit in the file can be computed as quickly as the offset of the first edit unit. As discussed above, however, this happy circumstance did not appear to be compatible with Pinnacle's requirements.

Partitioning slows down random access, because the index table doesn't say which partition contains a given frame (specifically, which partition contains a given essence-relative offset). The decoder must examine the BodyOffset field of some number of partition packs in order to find the enclosing partition. Making a good guess as to the enclosing partition is helpful here, as is the caching of BodyOffset fields as they're examined.

Segmenting the index table causes a similar problem: the decoder has to search index table segments in order to find the one containing the desired entry. However, this search time doesn't necessarily add to the partition search time, as the index table segment and the partition that contains the edit unit will generally be related in some way (this is not required by the MXF spec, but is a reasonable assumption). The decoder has to examine the partition pack before it can locate any index table segment that may be contained within a partition, so it has already seen that partition's BodyOffset and can use it to help find the partition containing the desired edit unit. In most implementations, this will either be the partition that contains the index table segment or the preceding partition.

Thus, a segmented index table in a partitioned file can be expected to offer good play-after-record performance. Assuming that the decoder can make reasonable guesses as to which partition contains the desired index table segment, access time should not degrade badly with increasing file length. A "guess" based on bitrate, edit rate, and edit unit number generally yields good results at any point in a file.

Of course, this analysis assumes the presence of a random index pack. If the RIP is absent, any partitioned file is going to exhibit unsatisfactory random-access performance. In this case, the decoder will generally have to search backward from the footer, so performance will degrade linearly with file length. Caching of discovered partition packs is almost a necessity.

Local Play-While-Record

This use case reveals a serious flaw in the segmented-index table option: The RIP is not present until the file has been fully recorded, so play-while-record random access performance will be hard to predict. While partition-pack caching can be used to optimize multiple accesses to the same file, the first random access to a still-recording file will not benefit from caching. In the worst case, this access requires the examination of every partition pack in the file.

To make matters worse, there is no easy way to even find the last partition pack in the file while it's still being recorded. One solution to this would be the introduction of a dark metadata component that holds a copy of the RIP near the beginning of the file. But this introduces another pre-allocation requirement. Without a RIP (or dark-metadata equivalent), the only solution is a brute-force search backward from the end of the file. This has unacceptable effects on both random-access delay and overall I/O system bandwidth.

These difficulties led us to consider and ultimately decide on the use of a proprietary frame table (FT) that is external to the MXF file. The proprietary FT stores absolute file offsets rather than essence-relative ones, which allows the decoder to locate any edit unit without a RIP being present. The encoder can update the FT at regular intervals, which minimizes encoder memory usage and makes new FT entries available to playback devices soon after the corresponding edit units are recorded. Finally, the proprietary FT does not require any sort of index table pre-allocation within the MXF file.

We briefly considered a scheme whereby each partition was exactly the same length, with the length being a function of the bitrate. This lets the decoder find the partition packs without a RIP. However, there is no good way to explicitly specify the partition size to the decoder without resorting to dark metadata, and the required padding resulted in a great deal of wasted space (particularly in the case of long-GOP material). Also, the fixed-size partitioning conflicted with fixed-duration partitioning, which we wanted to keep for inter-vendor compatibility. So this scheme was rejected as being impractical.

Streaming Play-While-Record

This is the most difficult case of all. In addition to the difficulties it shares with first two cases, the streaming case lacks access to a common storage medium. The best solution here is an "active" receiver; that is, one which observes the KLV headers in the incoming stream. Such a device can maintain a local frame table that maps frame numbers to absolute offsets, and thereby offer immediate access to any item as soon as that item has been fully received (once the next KLV header has been seen). Some Pinnacle products have this functionality, but not all, so we could not use this in the general case.

The solution is the same proprietary frame table that was necessitated by the local play-while-record case. The additional difficulty is that updates to the FT must be "pushed" across the streaming connection to the receiver as they occur. Any delay here will be seen at the receiving end as an additional delay between the time when an edit unit is physically present at the receiver and the time when it can actually be accessed.

Conclusion

Pinnacle's standard MXF file format is a solution to one very specific operational requirement. Although the external frame table is proprietary, the MXF file itself is quite straightforward. This combination offers excellent performance for a particular set of use cases that only include Pinnacle equipment, while also providing easy interchange between Pinnacle products and those of other vendors.

The use of proprietary solutions must always be weighed carefully, due to the narrow applicability of the resulting features. In this case, it has proven to be worthwhile.

Read-While-Write Guidelines
Todd Brunhoff, Omneon Video Networks

In general, reading assumptions and writing constraints are independent of any operational pattern. However, complexity rises when any of the following are true:

1. Containers hold elements that are VBE (variable bytes per element), rather than CBE (constant bytes per element).

2. The number of essence containers is greater than one; that is, use of operational patterns b and c.

3. The number of partitions employed in the MXF file is more than just a header and footer partition.

The guidelines below are intended to minimize complexity for readers and writers while making partly rendered MXF files playable by real-time systems. For consistency, I refer to MXF files with internal or external essence files as "movie files." This is to more clearly distinguish them from external essence files, which may or may not be MXF files.

General Format Guidelines

There are two general guidelines that I recommend on the construction of an MXF file. These should be observed for any system that needs to achieve real-time recording or playout with storage in an MXF file.

1. Any movie adhering to OP{1,2,3}a should use only internal essence. The additional complexity of external essence files in this case is pointless because when multiple essence is interleaved in a single container, it can only be understood by an MXF parser, and there is no performance benefit in having structural metadata in a file separate from the essence. Hence, the essence might as well appear in the movie file. An exception to this would be an OP{1,2,3}a file pointing to a single external essence file, such as DV or WAV or MPEG. In this case, the external essence files can be understood by other software, and thus may have value in that form.

2. Any movie adhering to OP{1,2,3}{b,c} should use only external essence. There is great complexity in interleaving containers, as opposed to interleaving essence elements with Op{1,2,3}a. It is possible to create a movie with two containers, with one container in the header partition and one container in a single body partition. However, a movie of great length would essentially be a file system within a file, much like tar, or zip. This makes for poor reading efficiency for a real-time playout system, since data must be read from two places in the file. It is also possible to improve reading efficiency by interleaving containers, with locality of reference improving as the size of the interleave decreases. However, the complexity of a file constructed this way increases in direct proportion to the number of partitions. I conclude that it is better to use external essence with OP{1,2,3}{b,c}, combined with a small number of partitions.

Readers and Writers

There are two kinds of writers: dumb writers like ftp, and smart writers that understand the MXF file format. Dumb writers may be employed to copy an MXF file from one server to another, while smart writers are more likely to be a full-featured recorder or a partial restore process. The same is true of readers: some smart, some dumb. What follows is a process to handle all four: smart and dumb readers and writers.

If a playout system uses some internal file format other than MXF, then some pre-processing is probably necessary, but can be minimized by following the assumptions and constraints below.

Dumb Readers

A file transfer service like ftp knows nothing about the content or properties of any file, so any intelligence must be provided at some higher level, such as an archive system that uses ftp to transfer movies and essence. The assumptions below view this collection of systems as a dumb reader:

- Movie files cannot be read until they are complete. This means that a dumb reader must know that the movie is complete without looking at the movie file. Generally, this means that if the movie file has been modified recently, say, within the last 10 seconds, then the dumb reader should assume the movie is not yet complete. How the dumb reader knows if a file is a movie, and when it was last modified is unspecified.

- An alternative to the above is: If a movie file is read before it is complete, it should be read again in its entirety when it is complete.

- External essence files can be read at any time. This requires that a dumb reader know whether a file is indeed external essence. And it requires that the dumb reader is able to detect whether a file has been modified recently, and that when it reaches the end of file, the transfer pauses until either a) the file grows in length, or b) the elapsed time between the last modified time and the present exceeds, say, 10 seconds.

The intent of these assumptions is to prevent a dumb reader from attempting to consume any file that might be being written by a smart writer.

Dumb Writers

Like a dumb reader, a dumb writer knows nothing about the content of any file. The source for what a dumb writer writes may also make it a dumb reader; in which case the assumptions above apply to the source. Specifically, a dumb writer should assume that:

- Any file it writes (or copies) is always written from left to right.

Smart Writers

A smart writer understands the details of MXF file construction and the goal is to create files in a left-to-right manner as much as is possible. It must observe the following constraints:

- Once header and body partitions are on disk, their location should not change. It is possible that this must be violated at times, such as if structural or descriptive metadata is added. This should be minimized by allocating some fill items to absorb small changes. If a movie file has only external essence, then it may be reasonable to rewrite the entire movie. However, if the movie contains internal essence, rewriting a (large) movie file should be avoided at all costs. Footer partitions and RIP (random index packs), may move at any time.

- The value of the start position and duration in the material package's Sequences and SourceClips should be updated frequently to reflect all essence that is valid and available on disk.

- Every partition with essence must contain an index table that describes all essence elements in the partition. (Note: MXF allows index tables to describe elements in any partition. While this works, it may prevent smart readers from correctly calculating the size of a partition, or from playing essence as soon as it reaches the disk. Insisting that index tables describe elements only in the same partition allows a smart reader to immediately have access to corresponding essence elements on disk.)

- The KLV for the index table must be created in its final size for the estimated size of the partition; that is, if the intended size of the partition contains 1000 elements, then the size of the index table segment must be precisely large enough to hold 1000 Delta or Index entries. Once written to disk, the location of the index table should not change, although its size and contents may change.

- The index segment's initial start position and duration values must indicate the first and last element in the partition. Especially, the duration should not be marked as -1. It is not necessary to update these values until the partition becomes complete. This allows the writer to write only the index or delta table entries at the end of the table.

- After a partition is laid out, an index table and the essence container must be filled from left to right. This means that, initially, an index table segment will have all set values filled in up to, but not including, the Delta or Index Entry Array, and all values in the array will be zero. This allows the writer to allocate the partition; write out the header metadata, if any; write out initial 74 bytes of the index segment; and nothing more.

- Essence elements must be written before Sequence duration, SourceClips duration, and index table entries are updated and written to disk; that is, an index table entry with non-zero values should not appear on disk before the corresponding essence element.

- A footer and an RIP should be present at the end of the movie file. However, if a movie is growing in length, a footer and RIP may be overwritten with a new body partition, followed by the new footer and RIP.

- The size of a partition may change after it is filled up, either because the movie turned out to be shorter than anticipated, or the estimated size did not exactly match the collection of VBEs in the partition. Before moving on to allocating the next body partition, the following items must be resolved:

- The header must be marked complete.
  - If the header does not contain metadata it should be marked closed.
  - The index table start, duration and set values must be updated, if necessary, to reflect the final number of elements in the partition.
  - Any hole following the index table or following the last essence element must be replaced with a filler KLV. The writer may choose to relocate the next partition back to cover the hole after the last essence element.

Smart Readers

Smart readers must be tolerant of both smart and dumb writers. However, the combination of the layout of the partitions, and whether the file is being created by a smart or dumb writer, may govern whether any of the content can be used before the writing is complete. Generally, if a movie is constructed within the format guidelines and the constraints for smart writers, then a smart reader will be able to process nearly all essence on disk at any instant. Note that an MXF file may have been constructed at some earlier time by a smart writer, and then written by a dumb writer.

Below is a list of assumptions for smart readers, and guidelines to validate the assumptions while a file is being read.

- A reader may need to adopt an observed heuristic about how close it is to the "end" of a movie from which it may try to obtain essence. The caching properties of the underlying file system may mean that some blocks of data reach the disk before others, causing a short-term inconsistency in the state of the file.

- If a partition header is not marked complete, the reader should assume everything in the partition must be reloaded if the files modification time changes.

- If an index table entry contains all zeros, then the reader should assume the essence element is not available. Similarly, if the Sequence or SourceClip's length does not indicate that an index table entry is part of the clip, then the essence beyond the end of the clip should be considered unavailable.

- A reader should first look for an RIP at the end of a movie. If one exists, it should assume that it defines all partitions, and thus the size of every partition. This is important when reading MXF files whose Sequence, SourceClip, and index table have a length of -1. In this case, the only thing that defines the length of the tracks is the size of the partition, which in turn defines the size of the essence containers.

- If a reader cannot locate an RIP, it is likely the file is being written by a dumb writer. Partition sizes may be discovered left-to-right by using the index table in a partition to calculate the location of the last essence element in each partition's container; another partition header may be located immediately following. If the partition's index table contains a duration of -1, or it describes elements in other partitions, it may not be possible to determine the size of the partition. Once that next partition header has been successfully parsed, the reader can calculate the number of CBE essence elements in the partition.

- If a) no RIP is available, b) index tables contain durations of -1, c) essence elements are CBE, and d) all essence is internal, then the reader may conclude that the partition extends to the end of the file, and that the instantaneous length of the movie can be estimated from the length of the file. If the essence elements are VBE, the reader may conclude that the movie cannot be parsed efficiently until it is more complete.

16 JPEG 2000 Essence Container and Its Application

Jim Wilkinson

Introduction

This chapter explains the standards used for encapsulating *JPEG 2000* into MXF. The JPEG 2000 *codestream* is specified by the ISO-IEC15444-1 standard.[1] Essentially, JPEG 2000 is an update to the JPEG standard widely used for still picture compression. The primary difference is that the JPEG 2000 picture transform uses *wavelet filters* rather than the more common *DCT* (discrete cosine transform). JPEG 2000 is a good deal more complex than the original *JPEG* standard, but is also much more capable of rendering superior pictures. The most important development is that the source images can exceed 8-bits resolution—a prerequisite for high-quality imaging. More information on JPEG 2000 can be found at: *http://www.jpeg.org/jpeg2000/*.

JPEG 2000 codestreams represent the coded data of a single picture. Sequences of pictures can be coded easily by simply concatenating the codestreams and this is the approach described in this chapter. There is also a specification for wrapping these codestreams in the ISO file format (based on Apple's QuickTime format) defined specifically for JPEG 2000, and this is

---

[1] The best complete reference for the JPEG 2000 standard is *JPEG 2000: Image Compression Fundamentals, Standards, and Practice* written by David S. Taubman and Michael W. Marcellin, who were both instrumental in developing this standard. The book is published by Kluwer Academic Publishers, dated 2001, and has the ISBN: 079237519X.

likely to be widely used in most software applications. However, the seven major Hollywood studios set up an organization called *Digital Cinema Initiatives* (DCI) whose purpose was to define a specification for digital cinema. This specification was the keystone for the development of SMPTE standards that specified digital cinema. At the time of writing, the many documents involved in specifying digital cinema are mostly still in development, with some closer to publication than others. Part of the DCI specification was the selection of JPEG 2000 as the compression process for delivery of digital movies to theaters. There has been much testing of JPEG 2000 to confirm that it delivers the highest quality content, and all the tests that have been done suggest that viewers are going to see digital movies of excellent quality. Following the selection of JPEG 2000 as the compression tool of choice, the second step was the selection of file format: MXF was chosen, largely for its freedom from patents and the associated royalties.

The requirements for mapping JPEG 2000 codestreams to MXF needed two separate documents; a) a generic mapping for all JPEG 2000 codestreams to MXF for any application and b) a supporting applications document to specify how the generic document is used in digital cinema. This chapter describes both generic and application documents.

It should be noted that there might be a further MXF standard document that describes the mapping of the JPEG 2000 ISO file format to MXF. At the time of writing, this document is still unavailable. But, in any event, any ISO-IEC motion JPEG 2000 file that is converted to an MXF file should transfer appropriate file metadata to the MXF file.

JPEG 2000 and MXF

The MXF JPEG 2000 standard defines the mapping of JPEG 2000 codestreams into a picture essence track of the MXF generic container.

As always in MXF specifications, there is the caveat that the specifications define the data structure at the signal interfaces of networks or storage media. They do not define internal storage formats for MXF-compliant devices. This is to permit devices to divide the MXF file into its native components and rebuild an MXF file "on-the-fly" for playout.

The standard defines the mapping of the JPEG 2000 codestream into either a frame-wrapped or clip-wrapped MXF generic container. In the case of frame wrapping, each JPEG 2000 codestream is individually mapped into a frame, whereas in clip-wrapping a sequence of JPEG 2000 codestreams is mapped into a clip. The keys for KLV coding are defined, as are the universal labels for the essence container and essence compression. To complete the specification the essence descriptor use is also defined.

JPEG 2000 Coding Summary

JPEG 2000 is a picture-by-picture coding scheme, so each picture is independently coded and can be extracted as an independent entity. Sequences of JPEG 2000-coded bitstreams can be easily concatenated to form a sequence of compressed images.

A JPEG 2000 coded bitstream for a single compressed image is known as a codestream. This codestream is defined by a start codeword that identifies the start of the codestreams and an end codeword that identifies the end of the codestream. In between the start and end codewords are other codewords for identification of key parts of the codestream, together with the raw compressed image data. The syntax of the codestream is fully defined in ISO-IEC15444-1.

MXF Generic Container Wrapping

The mapping of JPEG 2000 codestreams can be either by frame wrapping or by clip wrapping. The paragraphs below describe both these wrappings.

Frame-Based Wrapping

The generic container that frame wraps JPEG 2000 compressed image data does so using one KLV triplet for the codestream of each picture as illustrated in Figure 16.1. The key value of the KLV triplet is specified below. The length is typically 4 bytes and the value is the codestream for a single coded picture and starts and ends with the start codewords and end codewords, respectively.

The JPEG 2000 compressed images may be optionally *interleaved* with other essence components in the frame-wrapped generic container as illustrated in Figure 16.1.

Note that, for interoperability, these other essence components need to have been defined by some other MXF-mapping standard with frame-wrapped capability. For simplicity of operation, it is usual that each frame contains essence data that is independent of adjacent frames. Interleaved *essence elements* that are inter-frame coded are not prohibited, but their inclusion might have an impact on the performance of codecs. Another vital consideration is that, in each interleaved frame, all the essence elements should be time coincident within the limits of human recognition.

Clip-Based Wrapping

The clip-wrapped JPEG 2000 essence element may be the sole component in the MXF generic container *content package*.

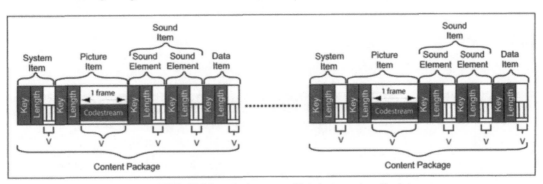

Figure 16.1 Frame-wrapped JPEG 2000 codestreams with interleaved audio data

Solo Clip Wrapping

The clip-wrapped JPEG 2000 essence element may be the sole component in the MXF generic container content package. If so, it has one KLV triplet containing a sequence of JPEG 2000 codestreams as illustrated in Figure 16.2.

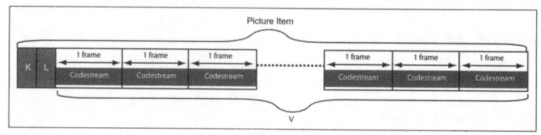

Figure 16.2 Clip-wrapped JPEG 2000 codestream sequence

Clip-Wrapped with Other Essence Components

The clip-wrapped JPEG 2000 essence element may also be used in the MXF generic container content package in sequence with other clip-wrapped essence elements, and this is illustrated in Figure 16.3. Note that each essence element should have the duration of the entire clip.

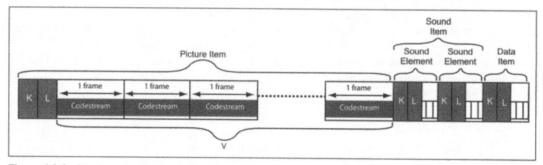

Figure 16.3 Clip-based wrapping with other essence elements

KLV Coding

The key value for a JPEG 2000 picture item is shown in Table 16.1.

Byte No.	Description	Value (hex)	Meaning
1~12	Defined in SMPTE 379M	06.0E.2B.34. 01.02.01.01. 0D.01.03.01	See Chapter 6, Table 2
13	Item type identifier	15	GC picture item (as defined in SMPTE 379M)

Byte No.	Description	Value (hex)	Meaning
14	Essence element count	kk	Count of picture elements in the picture item
15	Essence element type	08 09	Frame-wrapped JPEG 2000 picture element Clip-wrapped JPEG 2000 picture element
16	Essence element number	nn	The number (used as an Index) of this picture element in the picture item

Table 16.1 Key value for KLV coding of JPEG 2000 wrapped codestreams

Notes

- Byte 14 is a count of the number of picture elements in the picture item of the generic container. Typically, it has the value of 1. It might have the value "2" if, for example, the file contained stereoscopic pictures. (Note that, within MXF, the term "element" is used both to refer to a single element within the content package and also as a general description of an element over the duration of the container.)

- Byte 15 identifies whether the KLV packet carries frame-wrapped or clip-wrapped JPEG 2000 codestream data.

- Byte 16 is a unique number for this instance of the element within the picture item. For typical applications, where there is a single element (i.e., byte 14 is 1), this byte is typically 0. For stereoscopic pictures where the value of byte 14 is 2, two values are needed, one for the Key of each Element—and these would have different values, such as 0 and 1 (or 1 and 2).

Header Metadata Usage

File Descriptor Sets

The *file descriptor* sets are those structural metadata sets in the *header metadata* that describe the *essence* and *metadata elements* defined in this document. The structure of these sets is defined in the MXF File Format Specification (SMPTE 377M) and in some generic container mapping specifications.

File descriptor sets should be present in the header metadata for each essence element. The file descriptor sets for essence types not defined in this standard may be found in either SMPTE 377M or the appropriate MXF essence mapping standard.

With the exception of those properties that have been defined in SMPTE 377M, all 2-byte local tag values in descriptors are dynamically allocated (Dyn). The translation from each dynamically allocated local tag value to its full UL value can be found using the primer pack mechanism defined in SMPTE 377M section 8.2 (primer pack). The full 16-byte UL values are defined in SMPTE RP210.

JPEG 2000 Picture Sub-Descriptor

Essence tracks that use the JPEG 2000 essence mapping may use the values of the JPEG 2000 picture *sub-descriptor* described in Table 16.3. The JPEG 2000 picture sub-descriptor is coded as a local set using 2-byte tag values and 2-byte length values consistent with all MXF descriptors.

This sub-descriptor is a supplementary essence descriptor that can be strongly referenced by any file descriptor. It is intended that this JPEG 2000 *sub-descriptor* be referenced either by the CDCI picture essence descriptor or the RGBA picture essence descriptor, both of which are defined by SMPTE 377M. In order that the strong reference can be made, the MXF generic descriptor (as defined in SMPTE 377M) has an additional optional property as defined in Table 16.2.

Element Name	Type	Len	Local Tag	UL Designator	Req?	Description
All elements from the generic descriptor defined in SMPTE 377M table 17						
Sub-descriptors	StrongRefArray (Sub-descriptors)	8+16n	Dyn	06.0E.2B.34. 0101.01.0A. 06.01.01.04. 06.10.00.00	Opt	Ordered array of strong references to sub-descriptor sets

Table 16.2 Additional optional property for the MXF generic descriptor

The new "Sub-descriptors" property thus allows either the CDCI or RGBA picture essence descriptors to reference a JPEG 2000 sub-descriptor described below in Table 16.3.

Element Name	Type	Len	Local Tag	UL Designator	Req?	Description
Set Key	UL	16	N/A	See Table 16.4 below	Req	Key for this local set
Length	Length	16	N/A	N/A	Req	The BER length of all the elements in the set
Instance UID	UUID	16	3C.0A	06.0E.2B.34.0101.01.01. 01.01.15.02.00.00.00.00	Req	Unique ID of this instance [RP210 The ISO/IEC 11578 (Annex A) 16 byte Globally Unique Identifier]
Generation UID	UUID	16	01.02	06.0E.2B.34.0101.01.02. 05.20.07.01.08.00.00.00	Opt	Generation Identifier [RP210 Specifies the reference to an overall modification]

Element Name	Type	Len	Local Tag	UL Designator	Req?	Description
Rsiz	UInt16	2 bytes	Dyn	06.0E.2B.34.0101.01.0A. 04.01.06.03.01.00.00.00	Req	An enumerated value that defines the decoder capabilities. Values are defined in ISO/IEC 15444-1 annex A.5 table A-10. Other values may be defined in amendments to ISO/IEC 15444-1 or in related international standards documents.
Xsiz	UInt32	4 bytes	Dyn	06.0E.2B.34.0101.01.0A. 04.01.06.03.02.00.00.00	Req	Width of the reference grid, as defined in ISO/IEC 15444-1 annex A.5.1.
Ysiz	UInt32	4 bytes	Dyn	06.0E.2B.34.0101.01.0A. 04.01.06.03.03.00.00.00	Req	Height of the reference grid, as defined in ISO/IEC 15444-1 annex A.5.1.
XOsiz	UInt32	4 bytes	Dyn	06.0E.2B.34.0101.01.0A. 04.01.06.03.04.00.00.00	Req	Horizontal offset from the origin of the reference grid to the left side of the image area, as defined in ISO/IEC 15444-1 annex A.5.1.
YOsiz	UInt32	4 bytes	Dyn	06.0E.2B.34.0101.01.0A. 04.01.06.03.05.00.00.00	Req	Vertical offset from the origin of the reference grid to the top side of the image area, as defined in ISO/IEC 15444-1 annex A.5.1.
XTsiz	UInt32	4 bytes	Dyn	06.0E.2B.34.0101.01.0A. 04.01.06.03.06.00.00.00	Req	Width of one reference tile with respect to the reference grid, as defined in ISO/IEC 15444-1 annex A.5.1.
YTsiz	UInt32	4 bytes	Dyn	06.0E.2B.34.0101.01.0A. 04.01.06.03.07.00.00.00	Req	Height of one reference tile with respect to the reference grid, as defined in ISO/IEC 15444-1 annex A.5.1.
XTOsiz	UInt32	4 bytes	Dyn	06.0E.2B.34.0101.01.0A. 04.01.06.03.08.00.00.00	Req	Horizontal offset from the origin of the reference grid to the left side of the first tile, as defined in ISO/IEC 15444-1 annex A.5.1.
YTOsiz	UInt32	4 bytes	Dyn	06.0E.2B.34.0101.01.0A. 04.01.06.03.09.00.00.00	Req	Vertical offset from the origin of the reference grid to the top side of the first tile, as defined in ISO/IEC 15444-1 annex A.5.1.

Element Name	Type	Len	Local Tag	UL Designator	Req?	Description
Csiz	UInt16	2 bytes	Dyn	06.0E.2B.34.0101.01.0A. 04.01.06.03.0A.00.00.00	Req	The number of components in the picture as defined in ISO/IEC 15444-1 annex A.5.1. If this sub-descriptor is referenced by the CDCI descriptor, the order and kind of components is the same as defined by the essence container UL in the MXF file descriptor. If this sub-descriptor is referenced by the RGBA descriptor, the order and kind of components is defined by the pixel layout property of the RGBA descriptor.
Picture Component Sizing	J2K ComponentSizingArray	8+3n bytes	Dyn	06.0E.2B.34.0101.01.0A. 04.01.06.03..0B.00.00 .00	Req	Array of picture components where each component comprises 3 bytes named Ssizi, XRSizi, YRSizi (as defined in ISO/IEC 15444-1 annex A.5.1). The array of 3-byte groups is preceded by the array header comprising a 4-byte value of the number of components followed by a 4-byte value of "'3'.."
Coding Style Default	J2K CodingStyleDefault	var	Dyn	06.0E.2B.34.0101.01.0A. 04.01.06.03.0C.00.00.00	Opt	Default coding style for all components. Use this value only if static for all pictures in the essence container. The data format is as defined in ISO/IEC 15444-1, annex A.6.1 and comprises the sequence of Scod (1 byte per table A-12), SGcod (4 bytes per table A.12) and Spcod (5 bytes plus 0 or more precinct size bytes per table A.12)

Element Name	Type	Len	Local Tag	UL Designator	Req?	Description
Quantization Default	J2K Quantization Default	var	Dyn	06.0E.2B.34.0101.01.0A. 04.01.06.03.0D.00.00.00	Opt	Default quantization style for all components. Use this value only if static for all pictures in the essence container. The data format is as defined in ISO/IEC 15444-1, annex A.6.4 and comprises the sequence of Sqcd (1 byte per table A.27) followed by one or more Sqcdi bytes (for the ith sub-band in the defined order per table A.27).

Table 16.3 The MXF JPEG 2000 sub-descriptor

JPEG 2000 Picture Sub-Descriptor Key Value

The key value for KLV coding the JPEG 2000 picture sub-descriptor is defined in Table 16.4 below.

Byte No.	Description	Value	Meaning
1~13	As defined in SMPTE 377M, table 13	06.0E.2B.34.0 2.53.01.01.0D. 01.01.01.01	Value for all MXF structural metadata sets
14~15	Set kind	01.5A$_h$	Defines the Key key value for the JPEG 2000 picture sub-descriptor
16	Reserved	00$_h$	Reserved value

Table 16.4 Key value for the JPEG 2000 picture sub-descriptor

Using the MXF JPEG 2000 Sub-Descriptor

The JPEG 2000 picture sub-descriptor is a sub-class of the MXF header metadata *abstract super-class* and inherits only the *InstanceUID* and *GenerationUID* properties. It is not a part of the essence descriptor hierarchy and this is an important difference compared to the mainstream essence descriptors. The key feature is that this provision for sub-descriptors allows any descriptor to make a strong reference to the sub-descriptor and allows any MXF file descriptor to add it without consideration of the essence descriptor hierarchy.

Thus the new "Sub-Descriptors" property in the MXF generic descriptor allows either the CDCI or RGBA picture essence descriptors to inherit this property, thus enabling a *strong reference* to be made to the JPEG 2000 picture sub-descriptor (or any other sub-descriptor).

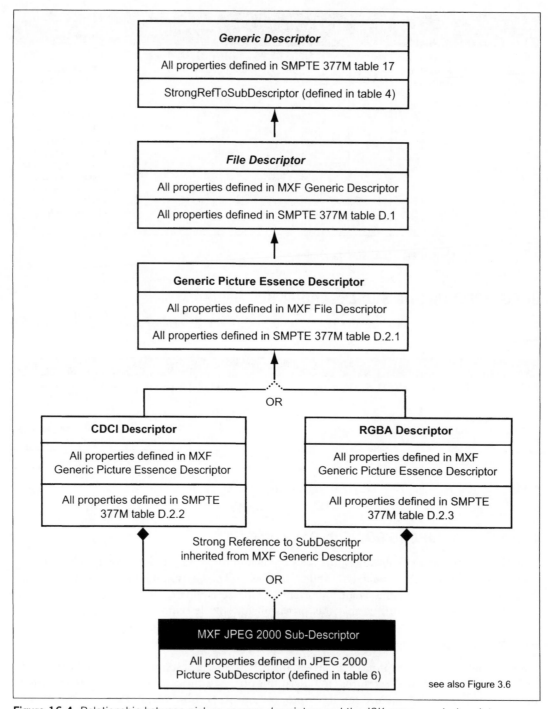

Figure 16.4 Relationship between picture essence descriptors and the J2K essence sub-descriptor

The JPEG 2000 picture sub-descriptor does not include all the properties from the codestream, but only includes those properties from the main header of the codestream that are required in the JPEG 2000 MXF mapping specification.

The values of the metadata defined in the sub-descriptor above are considered to be copies of values used in the syntax of the JPEG 2000 codestream. Thus if there is any discrepancy between values, those in the codestream take precedence and the values in the sub-descriptor should be updated.

Figure 16.4 on the next page illustrates the chain of MXF descriptors and their relationships.

Descriptor Value

File Identification

The content of the file is identified using the essence container UL and the compression UL. The former is used within a batch of ULs in partition packs and the preface set and on its own in the picture essence descriptor. Its use in the partition packs is to provide decoders with identification of the essence kind in order that they may quickly signal whether or not they can decode the essence or, for more sophisticated decoders, that they may make arrangements for a new decoder for the essence kind. The compression UL is present only in the picture essence descriptor.

Essence Container UL

The values for the essence container UL are given in Table 16.5.

Byte No.	Description	Value (hex)	Meaning
1-13	Defined by the generic container	06.0E.2B.34.01.02.01.01. 0D.01.03.01	See Chapter 6, Table 2
14	Mapping kind	0C	JPEG 2000 picture element (as listed in SMPTE RP224)
15	Content kind	01 02	Frame-wrapped picture element Clip-wrapped picture element
16	Reserved	00	

Table 16.5 Specification of the essence container label

Compression UL

The UL values used to identify the JPEG 2000 compression are given in Table 16.6.

Byte No.	Description	Value (hex)	Meaning
1-8	Registry designator	06.0E.2B.34.04.01.01.07	This value is defined in SMPTE RP224 (version 7)
9	Parametric	04	Node used to define parametric data
10	Picture essence	01	Identifies picture essence coding

Byte No.	Description	Value (hex)	Meaning
11	Picture coding characteristics	02	Identifies picture coding characteristics
12	Compressed picture coding	02	Identifies compressed picture coding
13	Individual picture coding	03	Identifies individual picture coding
14	JPEG 2000 picture coding	01	Identifies JPEG 2000 picture coding
15	JPEG 2000 picture coding variant	01	Identifies JPEG 2000 coding according to ISO/IEC 15444-1
16	JPEG 2000 picture coding constraints	xx	Identifies coding constraints for the intended application. A value of "00_h" indicates a generic application that has no coding constraints. Other specifications will define the meaning of non-zero values.

Table 16.6 Specification of the picture essence compression label

File Structure

Frame wrapping maintains each content package of the generic container as a separate editable unit with the contents of the *system*, *picture*, *sound* and *data items* in synchronism. If a frame-wrapped essence container is partitioned, then the partitioning process should not fragment the individual content packages.

If the essence container is clip wrapped it is recommended that each essence element be divided into sub-clips each of identical *duration*, then multiplexed the sub-clips from each essence element with the same timing into a sequence of partitions. The partition sequence is then repeated as needed.

Index Table Usage

Since the coding is frame-based and uses frame wrapping, the *KLV fill* item can provide for a constant edit unit size for all frames in many applications.

Where the application defines a constant *edit unit size* value, an *index table* is required because it is so simple to implement. This includes the cases where the JPEG 2000 essence element is the sole essence component and also where it is interleaved with other essence components.

Where the application has a variable edit unit size value, an index table should be used wherever possible even though it is more complex to implement.

Application of the KAG and the KLV Fill Item

There are no specific KAG requirements for the JPEG 2000 mapping. MXF encoders and decoders must comply with the KAG rules defined in the MXF specification (specifically SMPTE 377M section 5.4.1). The default value of the KAG is "1."

Constraining J2K for Use in Digital Cinema Applications

The initial reason for creating the generic JPEG 2000 codestream mapping document was the request by the Digital Cinema Initiatives (DCI) organization of the seven major Hollywood studios. However, to accommodate the ability for other applications involving JPEG 2000, the primary mapping document, as described so far, is generic—as is the JPEG 2000 coding specification itself. A second document is needed that defines the "profiles" of the JPEG 2000 coding constraints and the constraints on the MXF file structure. This document is a SMPTE standard that provides those constraints for the specific application within digital cinema (also called D-Cinema).

JPEG 2000 Codec Constraints

The JPEG 2000 codec is constrained through ISO-IEC 15444-1:2004 amendment 1 "Profiles for digital cinema applications." This amendment defines two *profiles* for D-Cinema usage referred to as 2K and 4K where the 2K profile defines a maximum image size of 2048*1080 pixels and the 4K profile defines a maximum image size of 4096*2160 pixels. The remaining constraints are parameter definitions that are specific to JPEG 2000 coding so are not relevant to this book.

MXF File Structure Constraints

The generic container is limited to frame wrapping and contains only JPEG 2000 codestreams as the single essence element. There is no clip wrapping.

Interleaving other essence elements such as sound and other essence data (such as subtitles) is not permitted. These are coded as separate MXF files and all the MXF files for distribution to theatres are bound together by external packaging files. This is akin to existing movie distribution where the film media is supplied with a separate audio tape.

JPEG 2000 D-Cinema Identification

The specific values used for identification of the picture essence container and the picture essence compression ULs are as defined next in Tables 16.7 and 16.8 respectively. Note that, at the time of writing, the version byte (byte 8) of the compression UL is not yet defined, but should have the value "09_h."

Essence Container UL

Byte No.	Description	Value (hex)	Meaning
1-14	JPEG 2000 Essence container	See Table 16.4	As defined in Table 16.4
15	Content Kind	01	Frame-wrapped picture element
16	Reserved	00	

Table 16.7 Specification of the essence container label for JPEG 2000 D-Cinema profile

Picture Essence Compression UL

Byte No.	Description	Value (hex)	Meaning
1-15	JPEG 2000 Compression	See Table 16.5	As defined in Table 16.5
16	JPEG 2000 Picture Coding Constraints	03 04	Identifies coding constraints for the 2K D-Cinema profile. Identifies coding constraints for the 4K D-Cinema profile

Table 16.8 Specification of the picture essence compression label for JPEG 2000 D-Cinema profile

Application of the RGBA Picture Essence Descriptor

The standard specifies the use of the RGBA picture essence descriptor together with the JPEG 2000 picture sub-descriptor defined above. Although the D-Cinema components are specified as the CIE "X," "Y," and "Z" device-independent colors, these D-Cinema colors can be identified through definition of the components in the pixel layout property in the RGBA picture essence descriptor.

But there was a complication in using the pixel layout property in that the character choices were already defined. This was solved by using the hexadecimal values, "D8," "D9," and "DA," to represent the characters "X," "Y," and "Z," respectively, with the most significant bit set to "1."

Table 16.9 illustrates the RGBA picture essence descriptor fields that are used in D-Cinema applications. For simplicity and readability, not all columns are shown in the table. The reader should note that the values given here are for guidance only and should not be used without first checking the defining SMPTE document.

The RGBA picture essence descriptor below includes all the properties from the file descriptor, the generic picture essence descriptor and the RGBA picture essence descriptor. Those properties that are for MXF management or are optional in the file descriptor, generic picture essence descriptor, and RGBA picture essence descriptor are not generally shown in Table 16.9 except where useful benefit is gained.

Application of the JPEG 2000 Picture Sub-Descriptor

Values for the JPEG 2000 picture sub-descriptor are provided in Table 16.10. Readers should note that the values given here are for guidance only and should not be used without first checking the relevant standards.

Note that the use of the letters "X" and "Y" in Table 16.10 are not related to the 'X'Y'Z' color space but refer to the horizontal and vertical image size parameters.

Element Name	Type	Len	Default Values - 2K	Default Values - 4K
Rsiz	UInt16	2	03$_h$ (2K D-Cinema Profile)	04$_h$ (4K D-Cinema Profile)
Xsiz	UInt32	4	2048. Other values may be used where the width of the displayed image is less than the width of the image container.	4096. Other values may be used where the width of the displayed image is less than the width of the image container.
Ysiz	UInt32	4	1080. Other values may be used where the height of the displayed image is less than the height of the image container.	2160. Other values may be used where the height of the displayed image is less than the height of the image container.
XOsiz	UInt32	4	0	0
YOsiz	UInt32	4	0	0
XTsiz	UInt32	4	2048 or less	4096 or less
YTsiz	UInt32	4	1080 or less	2160 or less
XTOsiz	UInt32	4	0	0
YTOsiz	UInt32	4	0	0
Csiz	UInt32	4	3	3
Picture component sizing	J2K Component-SizingArray	8+3n	3,3,{11,1,1},{11,1,1},{11,1,1}	3,3,{11,1,1},{11,1,1},{11,1,1}

Table 16.9 Specification of values for the D-Cinema constrained RGBA picture essence descriptor

Item name	Type	Len	Default values - 2K	Default values - 4K
Linked track ID	UInt32	4		
Sample rate	Rational	8	{24,1} {48,1}	{24,1} {48,1}
Essence container	UL	16	See Table 2	See Table 2
Picture essence coding	UL	16	See Table 3	See Table 3
Frame layout	UInt8	1	0	0
Stored width	UInt32	4	2048. Lower values may be used where the width of the displayed image is less than the width of the image container.	4096. Lower values may be used where the width of the displayed image is less than the width of the image container.
Stored height	UInt32	4	1080. Lower values may be used where the height of the displayed image is less than the height of the image container.	2160. Lower values may be used where the height of the displayed image is less than the height of the image container.
Aspect ratio	Rational	8	{256,135}. Other values may be used where the image container is not fully occupied with active image pixels.	{256,135}. Other values may be used where the image container is not fully occupied with active image pixels.
Video line map	Array of Int32	16	2, 4, 0, 0 (each value is Int32)	2, 4, 0, 0 (each value is Int32)
Gamma	UL	16	See SMPTE RP 224 (D-Cinema specific value)	See SMPTE RP 224 (D-Cinema specific value)

Item name	Type	Len	Default values - 2K	Default values - 4K
Component max ref	UInt32	4	4095	4095
Component min ref	UInt32	4	0	0
Pixel layout	8-byte array	8	"D8.0C.D9.0C.DA.0C.00.00" in hexadecimal code (see note)	"D8.0C.D9.0C.DA.0C.00.00" in hexadecimal code (see note)
Sub-descriptors	8+16n	24	1, 16, UID (JPEG 2000 picture sub-descriptor instance UID value).	1, 16, UID (JPEG 2000 picture sub-descriptor instance UID value).

Table 16.10 Specification of values for the D-Cinema constrained JPEG 2000 picture essence sub-descriptor

Index

<bext> 156, 157, 158, 159
<fmt> 156
<lvl> 158
<qlty> 158, 159

A

AAF 1, 2, 3, 4, 5, 44, 45, 49, 64, 80, 88, 98, 100, 103, 125, 126, 128, 133, 136, 235, 240, 241, 242, 252, 281, 282, 283, 284, 285, 286, 293, 294, 298, 299, 300

AAF data model 3, 5, 31, 41, 50, 77, 241, 242, 280, 281, 282, 283

abstract 42, 51, 242, 252, 262

abstract superclass 383

access unit 118, 123, 203, 204, 227, 228, 230, 277, 278

active format descriptor 188, 199, 218, 256

active picture 256

addition of a new class 48

address set 73, 256, 260

ADF 192, 193

Advanced Authoring Format (see AAF)

AES3 53, 123, 129, 137, 157, 160, 161, 163, 164, 173, 174, 175, 176, 177, 178, 181, 184, 189, 190, 192, 197, 284, 293, 362, 364

AES audio 32, 53, 105, 148, 160, 161, 164, 172, 206, 207

aggregation 42, 72

ANC 105, 236, 237

anchor frame 274, 276

ancillary data 160, 191, 192, 206, 220

ancillary data packet (see ANC)

ancillary packet data (see ANC)

ANC packets 186, 192, 237, 238, 365

annotation 31, 110, 111, 153, 154, 243, 254, 261, 262, 280, 296, 298

Annotation::AnnotationDescription 154, 158

Annotation::AnnotationKind 153, 255

Annotation::AnnotationSynopsis 153, 154

ANSI fiber channel 130

application specification 67, 104, 106, 109, 125, 134, 360, 362, 365

archive 81, 103, 105, 106, 259, 346, 349, 351, 352, 357, 358, 371

array 40, 41, 53, 62, 89, 139, 140, 143, 145, 146, 159, 163, 164, 199, 236, 382, 389, 390

aspect ratio 90, 188, 199, 218

aspect ratio property 256

assemble editing 14, 15

asset management 55, 93, 95, 101, 103, 357

ATM 130

atomic 98, 99, 100, 108, 121, 149, 150, 151, 170, 172

atomic essence 94, 101, 103, 106, 107, 108, 110, 149, 150, 153, 154,160, 172

audio 114, 148, 154

Audio Essence 170, 284, 364

audio essence 30, 63, 68, 86, 94, 105, 170, 172, 173, 220, 284, 296, 354, 355, 364, 367

auxiliary item 126, 181

B

"best effort" 72

batch 40, 41, 70, 90, 146, 209, 225

BER 17, 18, 19, 20, 45, 60, 62, 76, 88, 126, 127, 133, 136, 138, 143, 159, 161, 182, 184, 186, 194, 195, 197, 198, 216, 380

big-endian 17, 90, 115, 129, 230, 231, 232

BodyOffset 70, 75, 268, 368

BodySID 45, 70, 75, 82, 179, 221, 232, 233, 234, 235, 267, 362

body partition 70, 74, 107, 178, 181, 222, 360, 361, 366, 371, 372, 373

boolean 88, 139, 188, 199, 200, 218, 219

branding set 254

Broadcast Extension chunk 156

broadcast wave 24, 32, 53, 53, 56, 57, 148, 156, 157, 158, 177

butt edit 14, 88

BWF audio 24, 32, 36, 46, 47, 53, 105, 156, 170, 206, 207, 208, 211, 293, 294

ByteOffset 75, 170, 232, 235, 265, 268, 362

C

CBE (Constant Bytes per Element) 213, 214, 231, 265, 266, 267, 269, 270, 272, 339, 361

CDCI descriptor 53, 188, 200, 205, 284, 293

channel status bits 160, 176, 178

channel status data 123, 178

cheese 166, 169, 170, 171, 172

chroma sampling 167, 218

classification set 253, 255, 257

class 14, 78, 91, 92

clip-wrapped file 36, 172, 376

clip framework 30, 242, 245, 250, 255, 256, 259

clip set 239

clip wrapping 58, 66, 116, 121, 130, 140, 142, 143, 144, 148, 149, 170, 175, 206, 227, 228, 355, 377, 378, 386, 387

closed GOP 46, 155, 214, 273, 276

closed partition 70

codestream 375, 376, 377, 378, 379, 385, 387

communications set 256

Complete Partition 71

compliance 105, 189

component set 84

compound element 58, 126, 169, 170

compound item 36, 113, 114, 117, 121, 122, 123, 125, 128, 141, 169, 170

concatenation 99, 100, 115, 145, 191, 196, 375, 376

contacts list set 252, 255

content element 112

content model 112, 113, 114, 117

content package 6, 9, 21, 36, 37, 57, 58, 112, 113, 114, 116, 117, 118, 119, 120, 121, 122, 123, 126, 129, 130, 131, 132, 134, 133, 135, 140, 146, 155, 170, 174, 176, 177, 179, 180, 181, 184, 198, 204, 205, 206, 210, 214, 265, 266, 267, 270, 271, 272, 273, 278, 363, 364, 365, 377, 378, 379, 386

continuous decoding of contiguous essence containers 44, 45

contract set 256

control data set 131, 132, 135, 136

CRC 192, 193, 195

creation date/time stamp 133, 134, 135, 138

cue-words set 257

custom wrapping 116

cut edits 3, 98, 147

D

"Dangling Set" 49

"due process" 91, 258

dark 47, 48, 49, 144, 156, 221, 232, 250, 258, 283

dark metadata 350, 369

DataChunk 309

DataDefinition 74, 297, 298

DataStream 90

data element 20, 21, 58, 90, 117, 118, 120, 129, 141, 174, 180, 181, 184, 189, 221, 230, 232, 235, 237, 279, 365

data item 36, 113, 114, 117, 120, 121, 125, 132, 134, 135, 137, 140, 141, 144, 145, 146, 174, 180, 181, 184, 189, 192, 193, 194, 197, 198, 360, 362, 365, 386

data items 116

data model 1, 3, 5, 13, 31, 40, 41, 45, 48, 49, 50, 51, 77, 82, 109, 243, 249, 260

Data Types Registry 20, 21

DCI (Digital Cinema Initiatives) 376, 387

DCT (discrete cosine transform) 166, 375

DeltaEntry 153, 213, 266, 269, 270, 271, 272, 273, 274

delta entry array 170, 179, 180, 267, 269, 270, 271, 361

derivation 31

describing different audio tracks 153

descriptive metadata 13, 22, 23, 29, 30, 64, 65, 66, 74, 81, 83, 86, 88, 94, 106, 109, 110, 113, 239, 241, 242, 248, 249, 250, 251, 256, 259, 281, 298, 299, 322, 355

descriptive metadata track 30, 64, 88, 153

descriptor 44, 50, 51, 116

device parameters set 256

digital cinema 376, 387

display format code 256

display order 203, 204, 205, 214, 274, 277, 278, 364

distinguished value 72, 78, 89, 314

DM framework 239, 284

DM segment 243, 284

DM SourceClip 247, 284

Dolby E 164, 165

drop frame 29, 84, 139

dublin core metadata 261, 262

duration 25, 26, 27, 28, 30, 36, 57, 58, 59, 68, 69, 72, 80, 83, 84, 86, 88, 89, 108, 109, 115, 116, 118, 119, 120, 121, 138, 149, 151, 152, 172, 174, 179, 187, 188, 189, 200, 206, 207, 216, 234, 235, 236, 243, 246, 247, 248, 255, 360, 367, 372, 373, 378, 379, 386

DV 32, 36, 46, 67, 99, 105, 166, 167, 168, 169, 170, 171, 172, 221, 344, 348, 355, 370

DV-DIF 113, 117, 129, 167, 168, 169, 170, 355

DV container 116

dynamic document 257, 258

E

e-VTR 179, 356, 357, 358

EBU/SMPTE Task Force 112, 281

ECC 195, 196

EditRate 26, 69, 80, 83, 84, 109, 151, 152

EditUnitByteCount 153, 170, 265, 266, 269

Edit Decision List 153

edit rate 69, 80, 83, 368

EDL 153

ElementDelta 265

Elements Registry 20, 21

encrypted essence 324

end-swapped UL 310

end-swapped UUID 310

endianness 234

engineering guideline document SMPTE EG42 239

entity-relationship (E-R) 260

Enumeration Registry 21

errored 72, 238

essence 86, 105, 147

essence—external 55, 56, 57, 63, 66, 99

essence—internal 53, 66

EssenceContainerData 53, 74, 82, 267

essence container 13, 15, 21, 22, 23, 35, 44, 45, 46, 53, 54, 55, 57, 59, 67, 70, 99, 103, 112, 114, 115, 116, 119, 120, 121, 123, 124, 125, 127, 134, 138, 139, 140, 142, 146, 147, 150, 153, 160, 164, 170, 174, 179, 181, 182, 187, 188, 189, 193, 197, 200, 209, 210, 211, 212, 213, 215, 216, 232, 233, 243, 246, 247, 266, 267, 268, 284, 355, 361, 362, 370, 372, 374, 376, 382, 383, 385, 386, 387, 389

essence container label 208, 385, 387

essence descriptor 31, 32, 42, 51, 53, 56, 156, 160, 161, 164, 170, 182, 188, 189, 200, 205, 209, 216, 262, 284, 376, 380, 383

Essence Descriptor (AES3) Audio 364

essence element 36, 37, 46, 53, 54, 59, 65, 69, 70, 113, 115, 116, 117, 118, 120, 121, 122, 123, 125, 126, 127, 129, 130, 131, 132, 135, 137, 140, 141, 143, 173, 175, 177, 179, 180, 181, 182, 183, 184, 185, 186, 194, 195, 197, 198, 267, 371, 372, 373, 374, 377, 378, 379, 386, 387

event indicator 254

event set 254

event track 30, 86, 88, 235, 236, 248, 284

eVTR 130, 174, 179

extended UMID 123, 124, 137,145

external audio file 98, 149

external reference 72, 81

F

file descriptor 32, 56, 65, 71, 72, 79, 125,138, 158, 180, 187, 198, 216, 379, 380, 382, 383, 388

file package 25, 26, 27, 28, 31, 33, 34, 37, 40, 51, 53, 54, 55, 56, 64, 67, 70, 78, 79, 80, 93, 97, 98, 99, 100, 101, 108, 110, 147, 150, 151, 152, 153, 158, 164, 169, 170, 210, 212, 216, 243, 247, 262, 266 fill 40, 70, 71, 72, 180, 205, 207, 215, 216, 362, 372

fixed-length pack 18, 19, 20, 61, 122, 128, 129, 131

footer 14, 25, 70, 72, 104, 355, 359, 366, 367, 368

footer partition 69, 70, 72, 107, 178, 179, 360, 361, 362, 370, 372

Format chunk 156

Frame-wrap 379

frame-wrapped 25 Mbps DV-DIF sequence 168

frame-wrapped file 36

frame-wrapped MXF file 169

frame-wrapped MXF generic container 376

FrameworkExtendedLanguageCode 153

FrameworkExtendedTextLanguageCode 110, 111

frame wrapping 58, 66, 98, 107, 116, 120, 140, 142, 143, 144, 148, 149, 165, 169, 174, 177, 192, 206, 207, 211, 214, 227, 231, 237, 360, 362, 363, 377, 379, 385, 386, 387

G

genealogy 28, 31

generalized operational pattern 34, 66, 79, 96, 98

generation UID 42, 138, 187, 198, 216, 248, 249, 380, 383

generic container 10, 22, 23, 35, 36, 37, 38, 40, 44, 57, 58, 59, 69, 70, 71, 82, 112, 113, 116, 117, 118, 119, 120, 121, 122, 124, 125, 126, 127, 128, 130, 133, 134, 136, 139, 140, 143, 144, 148, 169, 177, 179, 181, 189, 190, 191, 196, 197, 201, 204, 205, 210, 221, 222, 227, 231, 233, 237, 267, 268, 269, 271, 360, 362, 364, 376, 377, 378, 379, 385, 386, 387

Generic Container Partition 231

generic container picture item 191

generic stream 38, 39, 221, 222, 223, 224, 230, 231, 232, 233, 234, 235, 236

global set 18

GOP 58, 109, 116, 137, 155, 183, 184, 203, 204, 214, 215, 219, 273, 276, 360, 366

GPS (Global Positioning System) 124, 220

Groups Registry 20

group of files 94, 97

group relationship set 253

H

H-ANC 189, 190, 191, 192, 193, 194, 197, 198

H-ANC packets 192

HD-SDI 130

HDCAM 174

HeaderByteCount 70

header metadata 13, 14, 15, 21, 25, 37, 38, 39, 40, 53, 70, 71, 72, 75, 78, 87, 104, 105, 106, 109, 116, 119, 123, 124, 127, 128, 129, 134, 135, 138, 140, 142, 143, 160, 174, 178, 180, 181, 182, 210, 211, 221, 222, 232, 235, 237, 239, 248, 249, 267, 355, 372, 379, 383

higher operational pattern (OP) 59, 93, 99, 153, 178, 210, 212

house number 94, 106

I

I-frame 155, 202, 203, 205, 206, 207, 213, 214, 219, 265, 276

identification locator 254

Identification set 48, 49, 92, 94, 233, 234

identification set 42

identifier 82, 89, 94, 104, 141, 142, 179, 182, 184, 185, 193, 194, 195, 197, 198, 201, 216, 221, 232, 234, 242, 249, 254, 261, 348, 378, 380

identifier kind 254

IEEE-1394 130

IEEE802 130

image format set 256

Incomplete Partition 72

IndexByteCount 70

IndexEntries 170, 269, 274

IndexEntry 213, 269, 270, 271, 272, 273, 274, 276, 278, 372

IndexEntry Array 179, 180, 267, 269, 361

IndexSID 40, 45, 54, 55, 70, 82, 179, 221, 232, 233, 267

index table 13, 26, 37, 38, 39, 40, 53, 54, 55, 57, 67, 69, 70, 74, 75, 78, 82, 86, 104, 105, 107, 114, 115, 116, 152, 153, 170, 174, 179, 180, 184, 198, 204, 206, 207, 211, 212, 213, 214, 215, 221, 223, 224, 226, 228, 229, 231, 232, 235, 249, 264, 265, 266, 267, 268, 269, 272, 273, 274, 276, 279, 300, 337, 355, 360, 361, 362, 366, 367, 368, 369, 372, 373, 374, 386

index table segment 37, 54, 55, 70, 179, 180, 213, 225, 232, 267, 268, 269, 360, 361, 366, 367, 368, 372

inside the MXF file, essence 99

instance UID 42, 49, 53, 74, 92, 138, 160, 187, 198, 216, 242, 248, 249, 380, 383

Int32 88, 90, 187, 188, 199, 217, 218, 231, 279, 389

Int8 200

interlaced scanned system 186

interleaved 13, 14, 15, 36, 37, 38, 46, 47

interleaving 36, 53, 66, 113, 114, 115, 116, 117, 118, 119, 147, 154, 160, 174, 175, 195, 196, 206, 207, 210, 211, 214, 228, 265, 276, 271, 277, 278, 346, 370, 371, 377, 386, 387

interoperability 8, 11, 23, 34, 49, 66, 104, 109, 110, 115, 119, 130, 168, 216, 222, 227, 237, 239, 241, 342, 344, 346, 347, 350, 351, 354, 377

ISO-7 characters 231

ISO/IEC 11578 380

ISO/IEC 11578-1 282

ISO 11578 89, 92

ISO 639 153

ISO 7-bit character 90

item 16, 17, 18, 19, 20, 36, 37, 45, 58, 59, 77, 117, 159, 161

J

JPEG 2000 375

K

KAG 44, 59, 60, 105, 115, 116, 174, 215, 362, 363, 386

key 16, 17, 18, 19, 20, 23, 34, 36, 49, 51, 54, 58, 59, 60, 61, 65, 70, 72, 74, 76, 77, 78, 87, 91, 122, 123, 125, 126, 128, 129, 132, 133, 135, 136, 142, 169, 182, 184, 185, 193, 194, 197, 198, 216, 222, 224, 225, 229, 230, 234, 235, 237, 250, 251, 252, 258, 376, 377, 378, 379, 380, 383

KeyFrameOffset 276

key frames 215, 255, 274, 276

key point kind 255

key point set 255

KLV 15, 17, 18, 23, 38, 40, 45, 48, 49, 51, 53, 54, 57, 59, 60, 61, 65, 70, 72, 73, 74, 75, 77, 78, 87, 91, 114, 115, 119, 121, 122, 130, 131, 132, 135, 137, 142, 143, 145, 147, 155, 165, 169, 204, 206, 216, 223, 224, 225, 231, 249, 267, 278, 279, 283, 284, 362, 363, 364, 369, 372

KLVEObject 324

KLVObject 324

KLV (Key Length Value) coding 34, 35

KLV alignment grid 116, 363

KLV coding 4, 9, 16, 20, 34, 49, 60, 90, 115, 116, 122, 124, 125, 126, 128, 129,137, 142, 182, 184, 186, 194, 195, 197, 222, 248, 255, 280, 284, 376, 378, 379, 383

KLV fill 179, 184,198, 268, 269, 362, 363, 373, 386

KLV triplet 16, 34, 49, 58, 60, 61, 62, 65, 76, 88, 204, 207, 215, 224, 227, 228, 229, 231, 234, 235, 237, 267, 377, 378

L

label 124

length 18, 34, 40, 61, 62, 72, 73, 74, 76, 77, 83, 88, 89, 90, 308

length field 17, 19, 115, 122, 129, 131, 133, 136, 138, 142, 182, 184, 186, 194, 195, 196, 197, 198

length pack 18

length value 17, 18, 129

Level Chunk 158

little-endian 230, 231, 232

local set 18, 19, 20, 35, 61, 77, 78, 122, 128, 129, 131, 135, 141, 142, 233, 234, 248, 250, 251, 267, 284, 380

local tag 138, 142, 143, 161, 194, 248, 249

local tag value 135, 143, 144, 248, 379

location set 255, 256

locator 45, 62, 63, 94, 139, 151, 216, 257, 293, 295, 300

locators 51, 56, 57, 62, 101, 150, 188, 189, 200

long-GOP 24, 25, 32, 36, 37, 45, 46, 53, 99, 105, 109, 115, 116, 119, 148, 153, 154, 155, 201, 203, 206, 207, 208, 212, 213, 214, 216, 346, 357, 360, 361, 364, 369

lookup 35, 70, 72, 74, 152, 274

lower-level file package 28, 80

lower-level source package 31, 32, 69, 79, 158, 178, 246, 262

lumpy data 86, 220, 221

lumpy essence 234

M

mapping document 37

MasterMob 64, 284, 289, 297, 298

master MXF file 103, 105, 106

master partition 319

material package 25, 26, 27, 28, 29, 31, 33, 34, 40, 45, 53, 55, 56, 64, 65, 66, 68, 69, 79, 80, 81, 84, 86, 93, 97, 99, 101, 102, 103, 104, 105, 111, 147, 150, 151, 152, 153, 169, 243, 246, 247, 262, 284, 372

MDObject 311

metadata dictionary 50, 92, 158, 248

metadata element 90, 114, 116, 122, 129, 131, 137, 140, 174, 180, 191, 192, 193, 194, 197, 379

metadata framework 240, 260

metadata item 129, 130, 131, 135, 136, 137, 138, 140, 143, 144, 194, 237, 239

metadata track 64, 88, 143, 153,181

mono essence 67, 98, 103, 107, 108, 150

MPEG 1, 2, 3, 4, 5, 51, 53, 58, 65, 71, 99, 105, 109, 118, 148, 155

MPEG-2 422P@ML video compression 173

MPEG-2 GOP 183

MPEG2 182, 209, 273, 276, 356, 360, 362, 364

MPEG audio 206, 207

MPEG basics 201

MPEG stream 205

MPEG streams 99, 116, 201, 202, 208

multi-language audio 150, 151

multi-launguage audio 154

multilingual atoms 110

multilingual environment 101, 102, 110

multiplex 13, 15, 37, 38, 46, 47, 115, 119, 202, 211, 220, 265

multiplexing 36, 70, 114, 115, 118, 119, 174, 202, 210, 211, 212, 225, 232, 386

multiple descriptor 51, 53, 170

MXFLib Open Source library 301

MXF data model 44, 45, 50, 77, 83, 109, 240, 241, 280, 281, 283, 286, 294, 297

MXF decoder 33, 34, 45, 48, 49, 56, 60, 62, 65, 66, 70, 72, 76, 89, 92, 93, 97, 99, 237

MXF encoder 33, 34, 45, 47, 48, 65, 66, 69, 72, 88, 90, 97, 99, 118, 119, 160, 231, 386

MXF Master File 110

MXF track 25, 274

N

name-value set 252, 253, 255, 256, 257

network byte order 17, 115, 129

Network Locator 62, 63, 64, 295

non-streaming data 220

Numerical Range Overload 276

O

OP-Atom 64, 66, 67, 103, 104, 108, 172, 348, 352, 354, 355

OP{1,2,3}{b,c} 371

OP{1,2,3}a 370

OP1a 3, 26, 27, 40, 66, 70, 76, 98, 99, 104, 106, 108, 147, 153, 154, 170, 178, 210, 346, 348, 360, 366

OP1b 70, 99, 100, 106, 149, 150, 151, 212

OP1c 101, 106, 150, 151, 153, 211

OP2a 99, 100, 211, 212

OP2b 100, 104, 211, 212

OP2c 100, 101, 102, 103, 106, 111, 211

OP3a 27, 99

OP3b 100

OP3c 76, 103

opaque 156, 221, 223, 236, 237, 238

opaque lump 221

open partition 70

operational pattern 3, 22, 26, 27, 33, 34, 45, 46, 64, 66, 67, 69, 70, 76, 79, 82, 96, 98, 99, 100, 103, 104, 105, 114, 178, 211, 212, 232, 246, 293, 353, 354, 360, 370

optional property 57, 69, 77, 380

organization set 74, 255, 256

origin 26, 28, 45, 68, 69, 83, 84, 151, 265, 296, 381

output timeline 14, 25, 26, 27, 28, 31, 34, 64, 86, 147, 246

ownership 72, 74, 285

P

"person" 242

P/Meta 240, 260, 261

package 69

Package ID 26, 89, 235, 236

partial restore 12, 38, 79, 81, 86, 88, 371

participant set 74, 255, 262

partition 13, 15, 36, 37, 45, 48, 53, 54, 55, 59, 60, 61, 66, 69, 70, 71, 72, 74, 75, 82, 91, 104, 106, 107, 108, 109, 119, 209, 210, 211, 212, 215, 222, 224, 225, 228, 229, 230, 231, 232, 248, 267, 268, 360, 361, 362, 363, 366, 368, 369, 370, 371, 372, 373, 374, 386

partition mechanism 115

partition pack 59, 69, 70, 74, 75, 76, 267, 268, 355, 362, 368, 369, 385

PCM 156, 157, 160, 164, 175, 237, 284, 293, 294, 350

PCMCIA 353

physical descriptor 32, 79, 158, 159, 284

picture element 53, 57, 141, 147, 169, 182, 183, 189, 191, 194, 196, 207, 221, 270, 271, 272, 273, 274, 363, 364, 379, 385, 387

picture essence descriptor 170, 200, 256, 284, 380, 383, 385, 388, 389

picture item 36, 113, 117, 120, 125, 126, 131, 134, 141,180, 182, 191, 193, 194, 195, 196, 360, 362, 364, 378, 379

playlist 34, 45, 98, 211, 212, 344

plugin 65, 221

position 10, 26, 28, 29, 68, 83, 84, 85, 89, 118, 151, 152, 153, 163, 170, 179, 229, 235, 265, 270, 274, 278, 308, 372

PosTable 180, 207, 274, 279

PosTableOffset 206, 264, 277

pre-splicing 99

preface 17, 67, 69, 74, 125, 182, 216, 249, 284, 385

PreviousPartition 74, 75

PrimaryExtendedSpokenLanguageCode 111, 153

PrimaryPackage 64, 65, 69, 104, 108

primer pack 35, 48, 70, 78, 142, 159, 248, 249, 379

production framework 30, 153, 242, 243, 246, 247, 250, 251, 256, 257, 259

production set 239

ProductVersion 90

programming group kind 253

program streams 202, 204

progressive scanned system 186

properties 77, 129

publication set 254

Q

Quality Chunk 158

QuickTime 294, 351, 375

R

random file access 366

random index pack 45, 74, 75, 222, 233, 317, 360, 361, 362, 367, 368, 372

rational 90, 309

register 51, 91, 92

Registered Document Disclosure, RDD-9 360

Registration Descriptor 209

registry 20, 91, 125, 126, 128, 132, 133, 136, 234, 254, 257

reordering 213, 214, 215, 269, 273, 274, 275, 278, 364

reordering of video frames 155

RIFF 156, 159

rights set 256, 262

RIP 75, 361, 368, 369, 372, 373, 374

run-in 9, 69, 45, 75, 76, 104

S

scene framework 30, 242, 247, 248, 250, 251, 255, 260

scene set 239

scripting set 255

SCSI 174

SDI 119, 124, 129

SDTI 130

SDTI-CP 112, 113, 119, 122, 130, 131, 133, 134, 136, 139, 140, 141, 144, 173, 174, 175, 178, 181, 182, 184, 185, 194, 197, 198, 221

sequence 13, 14, 15, 17, 19, 20, 84

sequencing 45, 53, 93

set 77

setting period set 255

shot set 248, 255

SID 40, 45, 53, 82, 232, 233, 234

slice 119, 180, 213, 214, 264, 272, 273

smart pointers 305

SMPTE 12M 29, 84, 137, 298

SMPTE 272M 189

SMPTE 291M 193

SMPTE 298M 8, 16, 89, 91, 282

SMPTE 305M 196

SMPTE 326M 112, 126, 128, 130, 133, 134, 135, 136, 140, 144, 174, 181

SMPTE 328M 183

SMPTE 330M 21, 31, 40, 89, 93, 124, 145, 288

SMPTE 331M 127, 134, 137, 144, 145, 174, 175, 177, 178, 182, 183, 184, 185, 186, 192, 221, 363, 365

SMPTE 356M 173, 181, 182, 183

SMPTE 365M 173

SMPTE 367M 174, 189, 190, 191, 193, 194, 195, 196

SMPTE 368M 174

SMPTE 369M 174, 189, 190, 191, 192, 193

SMPTE 382M 37, 51, 53, 148, 158, 164, 170, 172, 177, 178, 364

SMPTE label 114, 124, 125, 187

SMPTE labels registry, SMPTE RP 224 51, 165, 187, 199, 216, 218, 385, 389

SMPTE RP 204 173, 174, 181, 182

sound 147

SoundEssenceCompression 156, 164, 165

sound element 58, 117, 118, 141, 170, 184, 192, 197, 207, 221, 266, 270, 271, 272, 273, 363, 364

sound item 36, 113, 114, 117, 120, 125, 131, 134, 141, 142, 180, 181, 184, 193, 197, 362, 364, 365

SourceClip 26, 46, 74, 80, 81, 84, 86, 99, 151, 152, 153, 158, 235, 284, 296, 297, 298, 372, 373, 374

SourcePackageID 80, 81, 152, 236

SourceTrackID 80, 152, 236

source package 45, 53, 78, 81, 243, 247

source reference chain 31, 32, 33, 34, 45, 65, 69, 79, 80, 81, 84, 86, 88, 101, 103, 150, 151, 152, 158

specialized MXF operational patterns 76

splice processor 46

StartPosition 26, 80, 152

static track 30, 86, 88, 284

stream 91, 221, 298, 300

streamable 34, 66, 98, 108, 117, 118, 179, 204, 210, 211, 221

StreamID 40, 53, 82, 91, 202, 208, 209, 210, 221, 232, 233

streaming 35, 106, 112, 117, 118, 130, 204, 212, 220, 365, 369

StreamOffset 269, 271, 272

stream partition 221, 222, 223, 231, 232, 233, 235, 236

strings 40, 41, 90, 109, 110, 157, 254, 255

Strongref 74, 89, 159

StrongRefArray 188, 189, 200, 216, 380

strong reference 42, 72, 73, 74, 84, 89, 139, 216, 248, 252, 285, 380, 383

structural metadata 13, 22, 24, 25, 26, 28, 29, 40, 66, 82, 83, 84, 110, 180, 231, 239, 240, 242, 248, 249, 256, 260, 261, 355, 356, 370, 379, 383

sub-descriptor 380, 382, 383, 385, 388, 390

subframe 176

subframes 157, 160

subtitle 14, 69, 104, 105, 114, 222, 387

superclass 42, 51, 242, 252, 299

synchronization 13, 25, 26, 28, 29, 34, 53, 64, 65, 68, 69, 83, 84, 98, 100, 103, 118, 120, 121, 124, 149, 151, 152, 154, 155, 181, 190, 192, 202, 204, 206, 211, 212, 220, 222, 231, 234, 247, 264, 277, 289, 297, 386

system element 36, 57, 122, 128, 129, 132, 140, 141, 142, 143, 206, 266, 363

system item 36, 113, 114, 117, 120, 121, 122, 123, 124, 125, 128, 129, 130, 131, 180, 181, 182, 189, 192, 193, 194, 197, 206, 221, 362, 363

T

tag 18, 19, 21, 35, 48, 61, 70, 77, 78, 83, 91, 137, 138, 142, 248, 249,363

temporal offset 215, 231, 235, 273, 274, 276

Text Locator 62, 63, 295

thesaurus 241, 252, 253, 254, 258, 259

ThisPartition 75

time 83, 86, 151

timebase 83, 121

timecode 8, 25, 28, 29, 45, 83, 84, 85, 105, 123, 124, 134, 145, 284, 297, 298, 357, 363

timecode track 25, 28, 29, 64, 84, 85, 151

timeline 3, 13, 15, 26, 28, 30, 34, 45, 65, 68, 84, 86, 87, 88, 93, 94, 98, 103, 118, 134, 147, 152, 212, 222, 224, 230, 231, 235, 236, 237, 243, 247, 248, 284

timeline track 30, 85, 86, 88, 236

timestamp 90, 163, 202, 224, 235

timing 14, 25, 69, 98, 115, 134, 181, 202, 207, 212, 248, 264

title kind 253

title value 253

top-level file package 28, 31, 32, 35, 36, 37, 40, 51, 54, 56, 64, 65, 66, 67, 69, 79, 80, 81, 82, 84, 86, 87, 103, 104, 216, 246, 247, 262

top-level source package 79

track 13, 14, 15, 21, 25, 26, 27, 28, 29, 30, 36, 40, 54, 55, 56, 57, 58, 59, 64, 65, 66, 67, 68, 69, 79, 80, 81, 83, 84, 86, 88, 89, 110

TrackID 21, 26, 40, 51, 55, 56, 80, 152, 216

TrackNumber 54, 64, 86, 146, 147, 169, 170

track mutation 87, 88

track number 64, 115, 116, 127, 128, 129, 143, 146, 181, 288

transmission order 203, 214

Transport Stream 71, 202, 352

TV Anytime 240, 348

types of data 45, 88, 89, 90, 91, 92, 185, 209, 220

type D-10 format 130, 139, 173, 174

type D-11 format 174, 190

U

UID 42, 158, 248, 249, 287, 390

UInt32 59, 89, 127, 138, 144, 146, 156, 157, 159, 162, 187, 188, 189, 198, 199, 200, 214, 216, 217, 218, 219, 269, 273, 381, 389, 390

UL 15, 16, 17, 19, 20, 21, 35, 41, 48, 78, 89, 91, 92, 93, 94, 98, 99, 124, 126, 134, 138, 139, 144, 159, 161, 162, 165, 170, 179, 182, 187, 188, 189, 193, 199, 200, 209, 216, 218, 248, 249, 250, 254, 257, 258, 282, 379, 380, 382, 385, 387, 388, 389

UMID 6, 9, 21, 31, 40, 41, 45, 47, 53, 55, 56, 69, 79, 80, 81, 82, 88, 89, 93, 94, 103, 106, 123, 124, 137, 145, 152, 157, 158, 236, 288, 348, 354, 363

UML (Unified Modeling Language) 41, 42, 44, 51, 72, 73, 285, 286

unicode 40, 90, 259

Unique Material Identifier 93

Universally Unique Identifier 282

universal label 8, 9, 15, 16, 17, 18, 21, 45, 51, 91, 104, 115, 133, 134, 158, 193, 282, 376

Universal Modeling Language 41, 72, 286

universal set 18, 20, 250, 284

unknown-endian 231

UnknownBWFChunks 159, 160

UnknownChunk 160

URI 57, 62, 63, 64

URN 62

user bits 160, 220

user defined date/time stamp value 135

UTF-16 40, 41, 90, 153, 157, 159

UUID 21, 41, 89, 92, 93, 138, 216, 248, 282, 380

V

value 42, 104, 106, 109

value field 17, 34, 62, 142, 143

variable-length pack 18, 19, 122, 129, 141

VBE (Variable Bytes per Element) 267, 339

VBI 105, 185, 186, 236, 237

VBI/ANC 222

VBI line   236, 237, 238, 365

VBI line data 186

versioning 14, 34, 98, 105

Version Type 89

vertical blanking 236

video essence 14, 63, 68, 86, 94, 105, 114, 116, 149, 172, 353, 354, 355

viewport aspect ratio 256

VITC 29, 105, 123, 124, 190, 194

vocabularies 105, 106, 109, 299

W

WAV 76, 156, 158, 161, 370

wavelet filter 375

WeakRef 89

weak reference 42, 72, 74, 89, 248, 285

X

XML 16, 40, 49, 65, 66, 73, 74, 105, 109, 170, 172, 221, 224, 229, 233, 234, 259, 260, 346, 354, 355, 356

XML dictionary 315

Z

ZDD issue 64

Zero Divergence Doctrine 281